Contents

CU01507600

Foreword

It seems as though mistakes often dominate the outcome of history. Whether it be errors of judgment, either on campaign or on the battlefield, or the misreading of diplomatic intentions involving heads of state, so much of history has turned and does turn on the mistakes of the participants, and many of these errors are all too often rooted in money.

Thus, it was that Napoleon Bonaparte, as Emperor of the French, in his ceaseless obsession to enforce the Continental System (or Continental Blockade) as an economic method to dominate his principal opponent, through shackling the monied interests driving Britain's economic engine, instead helped create the conditions for his own demise. Obviously, this strategy was supposed to deliver a far different result that at the same time would help ensure the stability and longevity of the French Imperial throne. But most importantly, Napoleon did all this in a way that would provide him with an avenue to impose his will. This all-consuming desire to bend events to a certain vision of the world led to the Emperor's legendary mistakes, first involving the invasions of Spain and Portugal on the Iberian Peninsula, and then to his utterly disastrous gambit in 1812 when trying to bring the Russian Tsar to heel.

We are indeed fortunate that Dr Kenton White has brought us this important contribution to Napoleonic literature by providing an absorbing study that provides a new understanding of the conflict in Spain and Portugal. For it was in this theatre of war that Dr White has already provided a lucid and explanatory narrative, *The Key to Lisbon: The Third French Invasions of Portugal, 1810-11,* that thoroughly sets the stage for this wonderful study. Complete with ample context and supported by a wide array of archival material and other impressive sources, White brings to life the many facets of this pivotal 1811 campaign and battle that helped spell doom for Napoleon's financial strategy and impractical command structure with which *maréchal* Massena had to contend. And the author does this while at the same time showcasing the many challenges that the Duke of Wellington impressively overcame.

Command decisions at many levels, the forces involved, along with the all-important logistical challenges and ramifications, are all captured and thoroughly explained. In the end, the reader will clearly understand why mistakes determined the outcome of Massena's last battle, and why one side could not overcome a Holy mess created by flawed strategy, logistical shortages and conflicting personalities, while the other side had an army commander whose operations were not compromised by mistakes at various levels, and who could deliver results despite difficulties

Fuentes de Oñoro

Massena's Last Battle and the Campaign of 1811

Kenton White

Helion & Company

For Jim

Helion & Company Limited
Unit 8 Amherst Business Centre#Budbrooke Road
Warwick
CV34 5WE
England
Tel. 01926 499619
Email: info@helion.co.uk
Website: www.helion.co.uk
X (formerly Twitter): @Helionbooks
Facebook: @HelionBooks
Visit our blog at http://blog.helion.co.uk/

Published by Helion & Company 2025
Designed and typeset by Mach 3 Solutions (www.mach3solutions.co.uk)
Cover designed by Paul Hewitt, Battlefield Design (www.battlefield-design.co.uk)

Every reasonable effort has been made to trace copyright holders and to obtain their permission for the use of copyright material. The author and publisher apologise for any errors or omissions in this work, and would be grateful if notified of any corrections that should be incorporated in future reprints or editions of this book.

ISBN 978-1-804518-24-3

British Library Cataloguing-in-Publication Data.
A catalogue record for this book is available from the British Library.

For details of other military history titles published by Helion & Company Limited, contact the above address, or visit our website: http://www.helion.co.uk

We always welcome receiving book proposals from prospective authors.

that would have otherwise robbed a less capable officer of seizing the fleeting opportunities that led to meaningful victory.

Scott Bowden
Arlington, Texas

Acknowledgements

I stand on the shoulders of giants.

Thank you to Andrew Bamford, previously the series editor at Helion, who had enough faith in me to ask for a follow-on book to my first publication, *The Key to Lisbon*. He was also generous in sharing his research into the British Army of the period, demonstrated in fine style in his book *Sickness, Suffering, and the Sword: The British Regiment on Campaign, 1808-1815*. I thoroughly recommend it to you. Thanks also go to my current editor and fellow Napoleonic enthusiast, Rob Griffith.

I would like to thank the staff at the various archives and museums I have visited or contacted while writing this book, most notably the National Archives at Kew in London, the Arquivo Histórico Militar in Lisbon and the Service Historique de la Défense at Vincennes. They have dealt with my enquiries with patience and forbearance.

I am indebted to Scott Bowden for his assistance in establishing the French *ordre de bataille*. He provided documents that had not been available to me previously, enabling an understanding of what I consider to be the closest thing to a definitive army structure for the battle.

My deepest gratitude goes to *Major-general* Rui Moura of the Exército Português, who has dealt good-naturedly with my questions and provided me with much information on that army and nation, especially understanding Soriano's *Historia da Guerra Civil*. Thanks also go to Pierre Lefebvre for his work in finding more documents in the archives at Vincennes when I was unable to. I would also like to thank Louise Pellier and Diogo Correia for patiently checking some of my translations.

The strongest shoulders have been formed from the love and support of my family. They have provided me with psychological and physical support when it has been most needed. They have been a constant source of inspiration for my endeavours in what has been the worst of times, and I would like to thank each one. For my children, you will always have my love. Thank you, Joel, Nathan, Christian, James, Elizabeth, and William.

To my wife, Rhona, without whom none of this would have been possible, thank you for your love and support. Despite the pressures of work and 'normal' life, she has encouraged me and allowed me the time and space to work. However, as the old saying goes, no good deed goes unpunished. She has accompanied me on walks across what felt, at times, like all of Portugal and some of Spain. She has visited bridges, valleys and ridges whilst displaying tolerance and fortitude. She has endured me standing in the middle of nowhere, excitedly pointing in random directions, explaining how, 200 years ago, men fought for a cause we hardly remember.

Rhona now knows more about the Peninsular War and the campaigns of 1810 and 1811 than she ever realised she wanted to.

Thank you all.

If there are errors in this book, they are entirely mine.

Kenton White
2025

Preface

For a full description of the campaign preceding that described in this book, I would direct you to my earlier publication, *The Key to Lisbon: The Third French Invasion of Portugal, 1810-11.*

The main armies will be referred to as the Portuguese, French and British. In the case where the discussion is about the general operations of the British and Portuguese armies, this will be referred to as the Allied army. Although other nationalities, most notably German, served in the British Army, it was under British service. The same is true for the French army, which incorporated other nationalities into its ranks.

I have converted some of the dimensions used at the time into modern measurements. Therefore, a league is converted into three miles, or five kilometres. I have also tried to use, wherever possible, the native titles and descriptions for troops involved in the campaign. French infantry is described as légère or ligne (light or line). French words may appear incongruous to English speakers as proper nouns are not capitalised. Thus, a French battalion commander is referred to, for example, as *chef de bataillon* Forgeron, not Lieutenant Colonel Smith. In Portuguese, this rank is *Tenente-coronel*. Where the commander of a Portuguese unit has transferred in from the British Army, the Portuguese rank is used.

Throughout the book, army units are referred to by their regimental number where appropriate, and these ordinal numbers also indicate the nationality: British and King's German Legion units, for example, are shown as Xth (or Xst or Xnd) where X is the unit number; Portuguese units are shown as X°; French as Xe. This way, throughout the text, it is possible to discern the nationality of the unit under discussion. The deployment of units, where it cannot be clearly established from contemporary accounts, is based on the practice of placing the senior units on the right of a formation, and the next most senior to its left.

The numbers of troops in each French unit, where mentioned, are taken from the documents in the Service Historique de la Défense, Paris, as well as the works of Fririon and Koch. Fririon's *Journal historique* may not be as reliable as we might expect. He was Massena's chief of staff and would have had access to all the relevant material during the campaign itself. However, there are discrepancies between his *Journal* and the *situations* (returns) from the Service Historique. His history was not published until after his death, so we may not be able to lay blame at his feet. Where there are discrepancies, I have tried to highlight them and the source of any contradictory information.

Those of British and Portuguese units are compiled from several sources, including the National Archives at Kew, Oman's *A History of the Peninsular War*, and Arquivo Histórico Militar, Lisbon, as well as the battle returns for the Portuguese troops from Soriano's *Historia da Guerra Civil*. Both armies appear to have attached brigades to different divisions as deemed necessary during the campaign, and the orders of battle in the Appendix have tried to reflect this as closely as possible. Readers are reminded that Portuguese returns include officers, whereas other Allied units have officers, sergeants and drummers counted separately.

For the more pedantic amongst us, Massena's name, throughout the book, is used without the accented e. I have confirmed this spelling from existing documents in various archives, most notably the situations of the *armée de Portugal*. That spelling is used in both Pelet's and Koch's works (amongst many). This is also confirmed in Marshall-Cornwall's book. He wrote that papers from the then *Prince d'Essling* supported its absence, '… and every signature of Massena which I have seen omits the accent.'[1]

---

1   James Marshall-Cornwall, *Marshal Massena* (London: Oxford University Press, 1965), p.290.

Introduction

Lieutenant General Sir Brent Spencer speaking to Wellington:

> We are about, my Lord, to engage in a very hazardous campaign, and no one can tell what may befall any one of us. I am sure I trust most sincerely that nothing will happen to your Lordship. It would be a great misfortune to the army if it were to lose you; but still you might be killed, and I think it necessary that I should ask you what are your plans, in order that I may be able to carry them out in case I should unfortunately succeed to the command of the army.

Lord Wellington's reply:

> Plans? — ah, plans. I haven't got any plans, except that I mean to beat the French. If I can't do it in one way, I will in another.[1]

Of History

Andrew Halliday, the Assistant Inspector of Hospitals who had served in the Peninsula, asked Wellington whether he would cooperate in writing a history of the war currently underway. Wellington replied:

> The events in this country of the last three years are fit subjects for the historian, and if well and truly related, may be deemed deserving the consideration of political and military men. But I am apprehensive that the time is not yet arrived in which either the facts themselves can be stated with accuracy or truth, or the motives for the different occurrences stated.[2]

Wellington was to maintain this scepticism about the history of battles. When John Croker suggested writing a history of Waterloo, Wellington is reputed to have said:

---

1   Mary Viscountess Combermere and Captain W. W. Knollys, *Memoirs and Correspondence of Field-Marshal Viscount Combermere* (London: Hurst and Blackett, 1866), vol.1, pp.191–192.
2   To Dr Andrew Halliday, Cartaxo, 15 January 1811, in Antony Brett-James (ed.), *Wellington at War 1794-1815: A Selection of His Wartime Letters* (London: Macmillan, 1961), p.209.

The object which you propose to yourself is very difficult of attainment, and, if really attained, is not a little invidious. The history of a battle is not unlike the history of a ball. Some individuals may recollect all the little events of which the great result is the battle won or lost; but no individual can recollect the order in which, or the exact moment at which, they occurred, which makes all the difference as to their value or import – Then the faults or the misbehavior [sic] of some gave occasion for the distinction of others, and perhaps were the cause of material losses; and you cannot write a true history of a battle without including the faults and misbehavior of part at least of those engaged.[3]

Croker recorded the Duke as mentioning at another time, '… besides almost inevitable inaccuracy, there was the risk – indeed, the certainty – that you could not tell the whole truth without offence to some, and perhaps satisfying nobody.'[4] Croker also mentions the recollections of the Duke and Lord Anglesey (Sir Henry Paget, titled the Earl of Uxbridge during the Waterloo campaign) of Quatre Bras being at odds with each other. The aides-de-camp of both also differed in their recollections, but at odds with their commanders. If senior officers on-the-spot, and their aides, could not agree on the generalities of a battle, Croker commented that, 'Such differences invalidate all history.'[5]

One might then ask why attempt to write the history of a battle at all? Most military historians strive for understanding. For some, it is to explain events to serving military officers to better illuminate their role. For others, it is the fascination of military manoeuvres and the panoply of battle. There are as many reasons as there are historians, possibly more. This volume has been written with two goals in mind. Firstly, to complete my history of the third French invasion of Portugal, as told in the volume *The Key to Lisbon*. Secondly, to attempt a description of the Battle of Fuentes de Oñoro, which has received little in the way of comprehensive description. The overarching aim is to use the enormous range of material available to provide an account of the campaigns of 1810 and 1811.

The Battle of Fuentes de Oñoro has a status based largely on the *History of the War in the Peninsula* by William Napier. His *History* received widespread praise for its compelling prose and intense depictions of combat, yet it faced criticism for its lack of precision and partiality. From the results of my research on the 1810 and 1811 campaigns, I am obliged to say that I agree with the criticism. Some of Napier's descriptions of the battle display only a passing resemblance to those described by many other first-hand witnesses. I have deliberately chosen to avoid his 'compelling prose' and used Napier sparingly and only where the information contained within

3   Paris, 8th August. 1815, John Gurwood (ed.), *The Dispatches of the Field Marshal The Duke of Wellington. An Enlarged Edition in Eight Volume* (London: Parker, Furnivall, and Parker, 1847), vol.8, p.231.

4   John Wilson Croker, Louis J Jennings (ed.), *The Croker Papers: The Correspondence and Diaries of the Late Right Honourable John Wilson Croker …* (London: Murray, 1885), vol.1, p.352.

5   Croker, *The Croker Papers*, vol.1, p.347.

can be corroborated by others. This also applies to the works of other authors known for their hyperbole, notably *sous-lieutenant* Parquin and *capitaine* Marbot.

In addition to Napier, Oman and Fortescue have provided narratives of varying detail and accuracy. Additional authors have briefly touched on the battle. In many subsequent publications, the three versions mentioned above have been used as foundations, adding nothing to our understanding, and in some cases propagating myths and falsehoods.

History books should present the information available at the time of writing. The aim of this book is to give you the information I could gather and to present a narrative from the perspective of those present. In my research, I have attempted to let those taking part speak for themselves and to use information from the participants of the time, rather than interpretations of that information. I have sought to return to the original sources and to present the events based on them. This does lead to some conclusions that are at odds with the accepted history. Where information is available both in the archives and published sources, I have endeavoured to cite both, so that you may avail yourself of the same material. Where information is unattributed in other sources, I have attempted to locate its origin. If I cannot, I have been reluctant to use that information, and if I have, then I have felt the need to make the point clearly.

My intention has been, as with my previous works, to return to original sources and accounts to attempt to reconstruct as much of a narrative of the battle and wider campaign as possible. In some places, such as the French attack on the right flank of the Allied army on 5 May, it is impossible to provide a detailed chronology of the events. The exact order in which the events of the 5th unfolded is uncertain. Witnesses give a different sequence depending on which unit they belonged to and where they were placed on the field. A soldier standing at one end of a battalion formed in line, shrouded in smoke and dust, will have a different perspective on events to a comrade at the other end, or a trooper in a cavalry squadron hundreds of yards away. In presenting the events, a loose chronology has been indicated, but this may not be completely reliable. A certain flexibility is needed to interpret the general flow of the battle.

I anticipate that this history is not invalidated by any of the limitations noted above. With Wellington's words in mind, I trust that this work will offend no-one, and will hopefully avoid satisfying nobody.

As the clouds of war gather on the edge of Europe once more, a clearer understanding of what causes war and how we can achieve peace is needed more than ever.

Dramatis Personæ

Portuguese

Bacelar, *Tenente-General* **Manuel Pinto de Morais**, 1º Visconde de Monte Alegre, was instrumental in organising and commanding Portuguese regular and militia forces, particularly in the northern provinces of Portugal.

Barbacena, *Tenente-coronel* **Francisco Furtado de Castro do Rio e Mendoça,** 7º Visconde de Barbacena, commanded a brigade of Portuguese cavalry.

Correia, *Sargento da Milícias* **José Augusto**, served in the Militia under Colonel Trant. He became involved in politics following the end of the war. He was often referred to with the epithet 'Leal' (loyal in Portuguese).

da Silveira Pinto da Fonseca, *General* **Francisco,** 1º Visconde de Amarante, fought against the French and Spaniards in 1801 in the War of the Oranges. He supported the government of the regent in 1808 and was appointed governor of Tras-os-Montes.

Forjaz, Miguel Pereira, Conde da Feira, was the Secretary of the Regency responsible for the affairs of War and the Navy, and Foreign Affairs. He worked well with Wellington and Beresford and was respected by them both.

Spanish

Sánchez García, **Don Julián,** was the commander of a Spanish guerilla force. His guerillas had been responsible for taking several convoys from the French, and he was especially active in the region between Salamanca, Ciudad Rodrigo and Almeida.

de la Cuesta, *Capitán General* **Gregorio García**, commanded the Spanish armies in the Peninsula. entered military service in 1758. His relationship with Wellington was strained. He was known for his stubbornness, deep distrust of foreigners, and rigid adherence to outdated tactics.

German

Dursbach, *Major,* commanded the outposts of the 1º Infantaria blockading Almeida.

Krauchenburg, **Captain Georg**, was an officer in the 1st King's German Legion Hussars.

Krauchenberg, Captain Ludwig, was an officer in the 1st King's German Legion Hussars and he was wounded at the Battle of Fuentes de Oñoro.

Schaumann, August, served in the Commissariat Department as a civilian officer attached to the 1st Hussars of the King's German Legion (KGL).

von Arentschildt, *Major* **Karl Ernst Viktor Anton**, was an officer in the King's German Legion who transferred into service in the Portuguese Artillery. Not to be confused with his namesake below.

von Arentschildt, Lieutenant Colonel Friedrich, commanded the 1st King's German Legion Hussars, and temporarily commanded a cavalry Brigade in 1811 in place of Anson.

French

de Baudus, *chef de bataillon* **Marie Elie Guillaume**, was aide-de-camp to *maréchal* Bessières.

Béchet, *adjudant-commandant* **Louis Samuel**, Baron de Léocour, was aide-de-camp to *maréchal* Ney, and was appointed *chef d'état-major* of VI corps in 1809.

Belmas, *chef de bataillon du Génie* **Jacques Vital**, was an officer in the engineers.

Berthier, *maréchal* **Louis Alexandre**, Prince de Neufchâtel et Wagram, was Napoleon's Chief-of-Staff.

Bessières, *maréchal* **Jean-Baptiste**, Duc d'Istrie, was a fine cavalry commander, but out of his depth as a commander of large formations. He was known to be somewhat prickly and stubborn. Bessières would be killed by a cannon ball on the eve of the Battle of Lützen in 1813.

Bonaparte, Napoléon, *Empereur des Français*.

Brenier de Montmorand, *général de brigade* **Antoine-François**, had served in Junot's invasion of Portugal in 1807 and had fought at Vimiero. He was captured by the British and repatriated in 1809. He was appointed governor of Almeida by Massena in 1810.

Charbonnel, *colonel* **Joseph-Claude-Marie**, Count de Salès, a general of artillery, he commanded the artillery of the 5e Corps in Spain, then the 6e Corps in Portugal.

Claparède, *général de division* **Michel**, served with distinction during the French Revolutionary. He rose through the ranks and became one of Napoleon's most reliable divisional commanders.

Clarke, *général de division* **Henri**, Duke de Feltre, was *Ministre de la Guerre* from 1807.

Clausel, *général de division* **Bertrand**, served in the Revolutionary Wars. He served in various campaigns, including those in the Low Countries, Italy, Haiti, and Spain, and held independent commands during the Peninsular War. His surname is sometimes spelled Clauzel.

Conroux, *général de division* **Nicolas François**, had fought as a *général de brigade* at Austerlitz. He was mortally wounded at the Battle of Nivelle.

Delagrave, *colonel* **André**, was a staff officer in the *armée de Portugal*. He was an aide-de-camp to Junot. His surname is also written as De La Grave.

Doisy De Villargennes, *sous-lieutenant* **Adelbert J.,** was commissioned into the 26e Ligne in 1809.

Drouet, *général de division* **Jean-Baptiste,** Comte d'Erlon, commanded IX corps. He was known as a capable, if somewhat literal-minded, general.

Fain, *baron* **Agathon-Jean-François,** was a key French official and historian who served as a private secretary and archivist to Napoleon Bonaparte. His role gave him privileged access to the inner workings of Napoleon's court, particularly during campaigns.

Ferey, *général de division* **Claude,** Baron de Rosengath, commanded the 3e division of VI corps, and had been prominent in commanding the rearguard under Ney during the retreat from Santarém. He was killed at Salamanca in 1812.

Foy, *général de division* **Maximilien Sébastien,** Baron de l'Empire, had begun his military career in the artillery. He opposed Napoleon's usurpation of power in 1802. He was promoted to command a brigade in Heudelet's division of VIII corps in 1808. Wounded at Buçaco, he was promoted to *général de division* after carrying Masséna's dispatches to Napoleon.

Fririon, *général de brigade* **François Nicolas Mathus,** was Massena's chief of staff. He had volunteered in 1782 as a private in the Royal Army.

Fromentin, *lieutenant* **Jean-Rodolphe,** was an officer in the 25e dragoons. He served on Montbrun's staff.

Fournier, *général de brigade* **François,** was an outstanding cavalry officer with a typical Hussar's reputation for womanising, daring, and duelling with anyone he felt had offended him. He earned the nicknames 'the Demon of the Grande Armée' and 'the worst of the Emperor's subjects'.[1] His life would form the basis of Joseph Conrad's story *The Duel*, later made into the film *The Duellists* by Ridley Scott.

Gourlez, *général de brigade* **Auguste-Etienne-Marie,** Baron de Lamotte, was a cavalry general and commanded a light cavalry brigade under Ney. Blamed partially for the debacle at Foz de Arouce and accused of negligence, he was arrested and sent back to France. However, there is some contradiction about when he was sent back, as a de Lamotte appears as being captured at Funetes de Oñoro.

Guingret, *capitaine* **Pierre-François,** was an officer of the 6e Légère in Marchand's division of Ney's VI corps. He had served with the regiment since the Battle of Jena in 1806.

Junot, *général de division* **Jean Andoche,** Duc d'Abrantès, commanded VIII corps. He was known as a rash and temperamental general. He had led the invasion of Portugal in 1807 when his army occupied Lisbon. He was wounded in the face in 1810. In January 1813, Junot made his way back to France, but his mental state deteriorated rapidly. On the 29th of July 1813 he defenestrated himself and died.

Lambert, *intendant général* **François,** Baron de l'Empire, was a military administrator appointed *intendant général* of the *armée de Portugal* in April 1810.

Levesque, *colonel* **Louis Marie,** comte de la Ferrière, commanded the 3e hussards.

---

1   Gene Moore, 'History and Legend in "The Duel"', *The Conradian*, 41.2 (2016), p.36.

Lemonnier-Delafosse, *capitaine* **Marie Jean Baptiste**, was an officer in the 31e légère, part of Heudelet's division of II corps.

Loison, *général de division* **Louis-Henri,** Comte de l'Empire, joined the Royal Army in 1787, and swiftly ascended the ranks during the French Revolutionary Wars due to his exceptional bravery. Within four years, he advanced from a junior officer to the position of *général de brigade*. He served under Junot in the 1807 invasion of Portugal.

Marbot, *capitaine* **Jean-Baptiste Antoine Marcelin,** was an aide-de-camp to Massena. His autobiography, the Memoirs of General Baron de Marbot, contains many risqué stories concerning Massena's sex life, and some dramatic incidents. It is to be read with some circumspection. Arthur Conan Doyle's character Brigadier Gerard is to some extent based on Marbot.

Marcel, *capitaine* **Nicolas**, was an officer in the 69e ligne.

de Marmont, *maréchal* **Auguste Frédéric Louis Viesse**, duc de Raguse, was an acquaintance of Napoleon's and served as his *aide-de-camp*. He had only recently been made a *maréchal* but would succeed Massena as commander of the *armée de Portugal*. He would be severely wounded at the Battle of Salamanca in 1812.

Massena, *maréchal* **André**, Prince d'Essling, was one of Napoleon's most capable Marshals, having risen from the ranks of the pre-Revolutionary army. He suffered from a lung ailment contracted during earlier campaigning and had lost an eye to Napoleon during a hunt at Fontainebleau in 1808. He had been reluctant to take up command of the *armée de Portugal* in 1810, claiming that advanced age and infirmity made it impossible for him to campaign again. He died in 1817.

Merle, *général de division* **Pierre Hugues Victoire**, commanded the 1e division of II corps. He had been wounded at Buçaco the previous year.

Montbrun, *général de division* **Louis Pierre,** Comte de l'Empire, commanded the cavalry reserve of the *armée de Portugal.* A talented cavalry commander, he was brave on the battlefield but not reckless. *Maréchal* Marmont considered him to be one of only three generals capable of commanding large formations. He was killed at Borodino in 1812.

Ney, *maréchal* **Michel**, Duke d'Elchingen, was the commander of VI corps, and had commanded this formation since 1804. He had risen from the ranks of a cavalry regiment to NCO, achieving a commission following the Revolution. Made a *maréchal* in 1804, he was renowned for his bravery, and hot-headedness, in battle. He may have suffered from what we now describe as PTSD.

Oudinot, *lieutenant* **Victor**, Duc de Reggio, was the eldest son of *maréchal* Nicolas Oudinot. He was ADC to Massena.

Noël, *chef de bataillon* **Jean Nicolas Auguste**, was the commander of artillery for Clausel's division of VIII corps.

Parquin, *sous-lieutenant* **Denis-Charles**, was in the 20e Regiment of *Chasseurs a Cheval*.

Pelet, *chef de bataillon* **Jean-Jacques,** had joined the army as an infantryman, but transferred to become a topographical engineer. He served as Massena's chief aide-de-camp from 1805.

Reynier, *général de division* Jean Louis, Comte de l'Empire, was the commander of II corps. He had joined the artillery in 1792 and had fought alongside Massena in Italy in 1805.

Solignac, *général de division* Jean-Baptiste, had served as Masséna's chief of staff in 1796 in the Army of Italy. Actively involved in the coup of 18 Brumaire, he led the grenadiers who chased the deputies from the chamber. He was dismissed twice from the army for embezzlement.

Soult, *maréchal* Jean-de-Dieu, Duke of Trévise, commanded the V Corps of the *Armée d'Espagne*.

Soult, *général de brigade* Pierre Benoît, was the younger brother of Marshal Soult and commanded the cavalry of II corps.

Sprünglin, *capitaine* Emmanuel-Frédéric, was a Swiss officer on the staff of VI corps.

Thiébault, *général de division* Paul Charles, had served on Massena's staff at the siege of Genoa in 1800. He became governor of Old Castile in 1811.

Trelliard, *général de division* Anne François Charles, had commanded the reserve cavalry during 1810. He was replaced by Montbrun and then seems to have been used to command a unit of *dragons* in the rearguard. He does not appear in the *situation* of 1 May 1811.

Watier, *général de brigade* Pierre, commanded a Brigade of cavalry as part of Bessières' reinforcements to the *armée de Portugal*.

British

Beresford, *Marechal* William, was a British Lieutenant General appointed to the post of *Marechal Commandante em Chef* of the Portuguese Army, in 1809. He reformed the Portuguese Army, enabling it to take the field in 1810 as an equal with its British counterpart.

Bevan, Lieutenant Colonel Charles, commanded the first battalion of the 4th, or King's Own, Regiment. He was held responsible for the escape of the Almeida garrison. He took his own life, thinking his reputation had been tainted beyond repair.

Brotherton, Captain Thomas, served in the 14th Light Dragoons.

Brunton, *Capitão* Richard, originally joined the 43rd Light Infantry, and transferred into Portuguese service on 1 March 1811, joining the 6° Caçadores.

Bull, Captain Robert Alexander, was an officer in the Royal Horse Artillery. He served during the Peninsular War and at Waterloo.

Cameron, Lieutenant Colonel Philips, commanded the 79th Cameron Highlanders and was mortally wounded on 5 May.

Campbell, Major General Alexander, commanded the 6th Division. He had been wounded at Talavera and had been in England recuperating, returning in January 1810. He returned to England later in 1811 after his health deteriorated.

Cole, Major General Sir Lowry, commanded the 4th Division. He would be wounded at Albuera and Salamanca.

Costello, Sergeant Edward, served in the 95th Rifles.

Cotton, Lieutenant General Sir Stapleton, was overall commander of Wellington's cavalry, and known for his magnificent uniforms. Although criticised during the campaign for errors of command, he was well liked by his men, and respected by Wellington.

Cowell-Stepney, Ensign John, was an officer in the Coldstream Guards.

Cocks, Major Edward, served with the 16th Light Dragoons, and was at times employed in intelligence gathering. He was killed at Burgos in 1812.

Cochrane, Lieutenant Colonel Basil, commanded the 1/36th Foot.

Craufurd, Brigadier General Robert, known as 'Black Bob' to his men. He commanded the Light Division. He was temperamental as well as being a strict disciplinarian, but also known for his courage under fire. He was prone to rash – or daring depending on one's viewpoint – action, and was trusted by Wellington to perform the demanding outpost duties for the army. He was loved and feared by his men in equal parts. He was mortally wounded whilst directing the attack in the breach at Ciudad Rodrigo in January 1812.

Donaldson, Sergeant Joseph, served in the 94th Foot.

Eadie, Private Robert, served in the 79th Foot.

Erskine, Major-General Sir William, 2nd Baronet. He was known as a rash, and sometimes incompetent, commander. Highly strung, he was also a user of 'stimulants' according to S.G.P. Ward.[2] Despite some prominent failures of command, he continued to have Wellington's confidence. He may have suffered from what we now describe as PTSD. On 13 February 1813 he defenestrated himself 'in a fit of delirium'. His last words were, allegedly, 'Now why did I do that?'

Freer, Lieutenant William, was an officer in the 43rd Light Infantry, part of the Light Division

Grattan, Lieutenant William, was an officer in the 88th Foot.

Hall, Cornet Francis, Served in the same squadron of the 14th Light Dragoons as Thomas Brotherton.

Harris, Private John, served in the 95th Rifles.

Head, George, was a clerk in the commissariat attached to the Royal Artillery.

Houston, Major General Sir William, commanded the newly formed 7th Division of the British Army. He had previously commanded a brigade in the 4th Division.

Jenkinson, Robert, Second Earl of Liverpool, was the Secretary of State for War between 1809 and 1812.

Kincaid, Captain John, served in the 95th Rifles.

Leach, Captain Jonathan, served in the 95th Rifles.

Leith Hay, Captain Andrew, was the eldest son of General Alexander Leith Hay and served as aide-de-camp to his uncle, Major General James Leith, who commanded the 5th Division.

Mackinnon, Major General Henry, commanded a brigade in Picton's 3rd Division. He was killed at Ciudad Rodrigo in 1812.

Mills, Ensign John, served in the Coldstream Guards.

---

2   Ward, 'Brenier's Escape from Almeida, 1811', p.34.

Murray, Lieutenant Colonel Sir George, served as Quartermaster General and played a vital role in the planning and execution of Wellington's operations.

Napier, Major Charles, commanded the 50th Foot

Napier, Major George, served in the 1/52nd Foot.

Napier, Captain William, served with the 1/43rd Foot.

Pack, *Brigadiero* Denis, commanded a Portuguese brigade that was very often attached to the Light Division.

Picton, Major General Sir Thomas, was the hot-tempered, often foul-mouthed commander of the 3rd Division. He was renowned for his courage but disliked by many of his fellow officers and men for his irritability and strict application of discipline. He would be killed at Waterloo.

Scovell, Major George, served as Deputy Assistant Quarter Master General and played a crucial role in British military intelligence. A skilled linguist and cryptographer, he was instrumental in deciphering French messages.

Simmons, Second Lieutenant George, served in the 95th Rifles.

Smith, Lieutenant Harry, served in the 95th Rifles.

Sontag, Major General John, commanded a brigade in the 7th Division. He was born in the Hague, and was a naturalised British citizen.

Spencer, Lieutenant General Sir Brent, was given command of the army when Wellington travelled South to Badajoz. He sent pessimistic letters home which implied imminent defeat of the army. He returned home in July 1811, replaced by Graham, and never returned to the Peninsula.

Stewart, Brigadier General Charles William, 3rd Marquess of Londonderry, half-brother of Castlereagh, he commanded a brigade of cavalry during the retreat to La Coruña in 1808-1809. He was the Adjutant-General in 1811, but despite this being an administrative job he often found ways to get into action. He would change his surname to Vane after marrying Lady Frances Anne Vane in 1819.

Stewart, Major General Sir William, had been Lieutenant Colonel of the Experimental Corps of Riflemen, and became Colonel of the 95th. He was appointed to command the 2nd Division in 1810.

Stewart, Sir Robert, Viscount Castlereagh, from 1805 served as Secretary of State for War. In 1809 he resigned after fighting a duel with George Canning, then Foreign Secretary. He returned to Government in 1812 as Foreign Secretary.

Stuart, Charles, Baron de Rothesay, was a British diplomat who became joint *chargé d'affaires* in Madrid in 1808. As envoy in Lisbon (1810–1814) he was made a member of the Portuguese regency council. His presence in Lisbon was crucial for Wellington.

Stothert, Captain William, was an officer in the 3rd Foot Guards.

Tomkinson, Lieutenant William, served in the 16th Light Dragoons.

Torrens, Lieutenant Colonel Sir Henry, was the military secretary to the Duke of York. He had served under Wellesley during the early campaign in Portugal and was present at the battles of Roliça and Vimiero.

Trant, *Coronel* Nicholas, commanded Portuguese militia which operated in the rear of the *armée de Portugal* during the campaigns of 1810 and 1811.

Waters, Major John, was attached to the Portuguese army and performed intelligence duties.

Wallace, Lieutenant Colonel John Alexander, commanded the 1/88th Foot.

Wellesley, Lieutenant General Arthur, Viscount Wellington, had been a successful general in India, and had been placed in command of the British Army in Portugal following the evacuation from La Coruña and death of Sir John Moore in January 1809. He had successfully fought the French army on several occasions previously.

Wheeler, Private William, served in the 51st Light Infantry. Brigaded under General Sontag with the 85th, Chasseurs Britanniques and Brunswick Oëls, it was part of Houston's newly formed 7th Division.

1

The Background to the Campaign

Between 1792 and 1810, five coalitions were formed to reverse the effects of the French Revolution and subsequent empire. Most of the campaigns fought as part of these coalitions had taken place in central or eastern Europe. In 1801, the War of the Oranges was fought between a Franco-Spanish coalition and Portugal. Portugal was invaded by French and Spanish troops, and although the Portuguese put up a fierce but short-lived defence, a peace treaty was signed at Badajoz, resulting in the ceding to Spain of the region around Olivença.

A short period between 1801 and 1803 had seen peace involving the French and the main paymaster of the coalitions, Great Britain. The Treaty of London, signed in October 1801, laid the foundation for the broader Treaty of Amiens. Islands and territories were ceded and returned to their former owners, and trade was renewed between former enemies. However, as Napoleon continued to interfere in the affairs of other nations in Europe, and the British government refused to honour some of the clauses of the Treaty, such as removing its troops from Malta, Britain ended the Treaty by declaring war on France in May 1803.

Napoleon established himself as Consul-for-life by plebiscite in August 1802, gaining more than 99 percent of the vote. In practice, this peace marked the transition from the Revolutionary Wars to the Napoleonic Wars. Napoleon proclaimed himself as Emperor of the French in 1804, and in December of that year an Anglo-Swedish agreement marked the beginning of the Third Coalition against Napoleon. Subsequently, by April 1805, Britain formed an alliance with Russia, and Austria, motivated by a desire for revenge against France, joined the coalition a few months later.

Intended for an invasion of Britain, Napoleon formed the *grande armée* around the Boulogne camp and placed his newly appointed *maréchaux* to command the Corps armée. Michel Ney was appointed to the command of VI corps, Bessières commanded the Imperial Guard, Soult the IV corps. Others, such as Drouet, Ferey, Merle, Claparède, Trelliard and Walthier were commanding divisions and brigades in the army, and all will become familiar in the account of the campaign of 1811.

Reassessing the strategic situation in 1805, Napoleon launched the *grande armée* against Russia and Austria, culminating in the Battle of Austerlitz, possibly Napoleon's greatest victory. The following few years saw further attempts by Russia, Austria and Prussia to defeat Napoleon in battle, which were all doomed to failure, although in some cases, such as at Eylau, the outcome was less than positive for the Emperor.

War, as described by Clausewitz, is '... not merely an act of policy but a true political instrument, a continuation of political intercourse, carried on with other means.'[1] The Emperor of the French, Napoleon Bonaparte, understood this. In pursuit of his political goals, he instituted the Continental System, also known as the Continental Blockade. This was a comprehensive economic and trade policy imposed between 1806 and 1814. Napoleon instigated this system with the Berlin Decree on 21 November 1806 in response to the naval blockade of the French coast enacted by the British government in May of that year. Napoleon wanted to bring down the Tory government, expecting it to be replaced by the Whigs, who would be likely to agree a peace deal.

The main objective of this system was to weaken the British economy and disrupt British trade, which was seen as a significant threat to French dominance in Europe. Napoleon attempted to enforce a strict embargo on European countries under his influence, prohibiting them from trading with the British. This meant that these countries were not allowed to import British goods or engage in commercial activities with Britain. The embargo and trade restrictions placed a heavy economic burden on the countries subjected to the system. Many European nations experienced shortages of goods, leading to economic difficulties and public discontent. This inevitably led to strained relations between France and its allies, as many were reluctant to comply fully with the economic restrictions. To bypass the Continental System, smuggling of British goods into Europe became widespread. This created deep political disagreements within the Empire, which were to manifest themselves as nationalist uprisings in the coming years as Napoleon sought to strengthen his hold on Europe. While the Continental System did impact the British economy to some extent, it did not achieve its primary goal of weakening Britain significantly. Instead, it proved to be a major disruption to European economies.

One country stood in the way of closing the continent. Napoleon had demanded, through the Spanish Prime Minister de Godoy, that Portuguese ports be closed to trade from Great Britain. The Portuguese government refused. There had been a long-standing alliance between Portugal and Britain, and the two trading nations would be seriously hit economically if trade were to be blocked. The French invaded with the army under the command of *général de division* Jean-Andoche Junot, and this resulted in the French occupation of Portugal, with Lisbon under their control, and an enforced ending of trade with Britain. Junot was granted the title of *duc d'Abrantès* for his success. The Portuguese Royal family and government escaped aboard British vessels and sought refuge in Brazil. Portugal was brought into the Continental System, and its army was disbanded.

The response of the British government was swift, if a little uncoordinated. A force assembled in Cork under Lieutenant General Sir Arthur Wellesley for a potential invasion of Venezuela was redirected to Portugal and sailed in July 1808. However, concerns soon arose that the French presence in Portugal was stronger than initially estimated, prompting the decision to send additional forces. In response, a more senior commander, Lieutenant General Sir Hew Dalrymple, was

---

1   Carl von Clausewitz, Michael Howard and Peter Paret (trans), *On War* (London: David Campbell, 1993), p.99.

appointed, despite having no prior experience commanding an army in the field. The first troops landed at Mondego Bay on 1 August 1808. Once assembled, the army advanced towards Lisbon. Temporarily in command, Wellesley successfully confronted and pushed back the French at Roliça, achieving a victory at Vimiero on 21 August. However, at the moment of victory, he was displaced by the arrival of Lieutenant General Sir Harry Burrard, closely followed by the commander-in-chief, Sir Hew Dalrymple.[2] Soon after, Lieutenant General Sir John Moore also arrived. He wrote, 'Sir Hew Dalrymple was confused and incapable beyond any man I ever saw head an army.'[3] Despite Junot being in a difficult position, Dalrymple was reluctant to fight any more battles, and negotiations, which would result in the Convention of Cintra, followed. This was an agreement under which the occupying French forces withdrew from Portugal and were transported back to France aboard Royal Navy ships.[4] An enquiry was conducted regarding the Convention, leading to Burrard, Dalrymple, and Wellesley being recalled to London to appear before an official enquiry to account for their actions.[5] All were cleared, but only Wellesley returned to active duty. Junot would return to the Peninsula as commander of VIII corps in 1810.

The French defeat at Bailén in July 1808 gave heart to Spanish resistance, but it also provoked Napoleon to come to Spain personally to lead the French armies there. Moore assumed command of the British Army and advanced into Spain. In a fast-moving campaign beginning in October 1808, Napoleon defeated the Spanish and almost caught the British forces dispersed. A bold initiative by Moore soon turned to near disaster as the British Army was almost surrounded by Napoleon's forces. Through mountainous terrain and in dreadful weather, Moore withdrew the army, reaching La Coruña in January 1809 for evacuation by the Royal Navy. The two flank brigades commanded by Alten and Craufurd were directed to evacuate at Vigo. Moore accepted battle outside La Coruña to cover the evacuation of his army. Napoleon had already left, giving *maréchal* Soult the satisfaction of fighting the battle and witnessing the British embark. Sir John Moore lost his life but the evacuation was carried out successfully.

In April, Wellesley returned to Portugal as commander of the British forces. Viscount Castlereagh, then Minister for War, wrote to Wellesley that, 'The defence of Portugal you will consider as the first and immediate object of your attention. But ... His Majesty ... leaves it to your judgement ... how your efforts can best be combined with the Spanish as well as the Portuguese troops in support of the common cause.'[6]

---

2   Wellesley to the Duke of Richmond, Camp at Vimeiro, 22 August 1808, Gurwood, *Dispatches,* vol.3, p.95.
3   Quelus Camp, 2 October 1808, J.F. Maurice (ed.), *The Diary of Sir John Moore* (London: Arnold, 1904), vol.2, p.270.
4   Definitive Convention for the evacuation of Portugal by the French Army, 30th August 1808, Gurwood, *Dispatches,* vol.3, pp.104–106.
5   Court of Inquiry, 14th November to the 27th December 1808, Gurwood, *Dispatches,* vol.3, pp.135–178.
6   Castlereagh to Wellesley, Downing Street, 2 April 1809. The 2nd Duke of Wellington (ed.), *Supplementary Despatches, Correspondence, and Memoranda Of Field Marshal Arthur Duke of Wellington, K.G* (London: Murray, 1860), vol.6, pp.210–211.

After the evacuation of the French from Portugal in 1808, there was no functioning Portuguese regular army.[7] To assist in rebuilding a credible force, Major General William Carr Beresford was appointed to command and named *Marechal* of the Portuguese Army in February 1809. While some speculate that Sir Arthur Wellesley recommended him, others propose that his appointment was possibly influenced by his knowledge of the Portuguese language, having previously been the governor of Madeira.[8] Napier was later to assert that the appointment was a result of favouritism and political manoeuvring in London, which Beresford robustly countered.[9] Beresford, recognised for his administrative skills, was entrusted with the responsibility of recruiting, reorganising and reequipping the army. In the same way that many British soldiers would accept service in the Portuguese army in return for an increase in rank, Beresford was promoted from major general to a local lieutenant general. As part of the reorganisation, he had British drill manuals translated into Portuguese to standardise the training across all formations. British NCOs and Officers were brought into Portuguese service to train the new recruits. Transfers into Portuguese service offered an increment in rank, for example from captain to major. On the 21st of March 1809, Beresford issued his inaugural *Ordem do dia* (order of the day), emphasising the importance of discipline and the fulfilment of soldierly duties.[10]

In March 1809, Soult launched an invasion of northern Portugal, capturing Porto. Wellesley successfully ousted Soult's forces on 12 May 1809, compelling him to abandon Portugal, leaving much of his artillery and baggage behind during the rushed withdrawal. Wellesley then proceeded southward, in collaboration with the Spanish army of *Capitán General* de la Cuesta, to confront *maréchal* Victor's forces. In the initial phase of the campaign, the slow manoeuvring of the Spanish forces meant Victor succeeded in evading a precarious situation which threatened him with destruction. Victor regrouped with Sebastiani's and King Joseph's forces, leading the French westwards again. A significant battle unfolded at Talavera de la Reina, where the Allies successfully repelled several French attacks but suffered heavy casualties in the process. Despite this victory, the French threatened Wellesley's lines of communication, and he retreated to the Portuguese frontier. Following Talavera, Wellesley was elevated to Viscount Wellington, and henceforth, he will be referred to by this title.

Facing some complex challenges, Wellington needed to devise a comprehensive plan for the upcoming campaign. The unreliability of the Spanish forces as experienced during the Talavera campaign and subsequently, coupled with the limited financial support from the Portuguese, added to his difficulty. Moreover, the existing distrust among some of his officers, and within the British government, posed

---

7   Monteiro Miguel Corrêa and others, *The Lines of Torres Vedras: A Defence System to the North of Lisbon* (Torres Vedras: PILT, 2011), pp.93–95.

8   Marcus de la Poer Beresford, *Marshal William Carr Beresford: The Ablest Man I Have yet Seen with the Army* (Dublin: Irish Academic Press, 2019), pp.60–61.

9   William Carr Beresford, *Strictures on Certain Passages of Lieut.- Col. Napier's History of the Peninsular War* (London: Longman, Rees, Orme, Brown and Green, 1831).

10   *Colecção Das Ordens Do Dia Do Illustrissimo e Excellentissimo Senhor Guilherme Carr Beresford, Anno 1809* (Lisboa: António Nunes dos Santos).

additional hurdles. Reports indicating the perceived indefensibility of Portugal created a backdrop of uncertainty. Wellington was acutely aware of the restricted supply of manpower from Britain, recognising that the forces at his disposal alone would be insufficient to confront the numerically superior French. A view prevailing among the French and certain segments of the Portuguese population suggested that the British would retreat hastily to their ships in the face of an enemy invasion.

The success of the upcoming campaign would rely on safeguarding Lisbon and ensuring the autonomy of Portugal. Wellington articulated his plans clearly, outlining both his intentions and his understanding of the enemy's likely actions. The outline of the plan comes out in a few short sentences in a letter to Castlereagh:

> My opinion is, that we ought to be able to hold Portugal, if the Portuguese army and militia are complete. The difficulty upon this sole question lies in the embarkation of the British army. There are so many entrances into Portugal, the whole country being frontier, that it would be very difficult to prevent the enemy from penetrating; and it is probable that we should be obliged to confine ourselves, to the preservation of that which is most important, the capital.[11]

Wellington's strategy could be characterised as 'indirect' or, in his own words, his 'cautious system.'[12] These considerations fulfilled the British government's broader policy of active resistance against Napoleon's rule in France and the pursuit of military success against him in Europe. He aimed to avoid a direct engagement whenever feasible, opting to pull his forces back in response to the enemy's advance, with the aim of drawing the French forces toward the fortified positions encircling Lisbon. In cases where a battle became inevitable or presented itself as a practical option, Wellington was confident that he could fight without jeopardising the army.

At the heart of his defensive strategy, focussing on, 'that which is most important', were the fortifications built across the approaches to Lisbon. The Lines of Torres Vedras, constructed between 1809 and 1810, were a network of earthworks aimed at safeguarding Lisbon from potential French occupation. Comprising three lines, each equipped with numerous redoubts and artillery batteries, they were positioned on elevated terrain, surrounded by trenches, and reinforced with various obstacles such as water inundations and *chevaux de frise*.[13] The defence of these lines was entrusted to Portuguese *milícia* and *Ordenança*, supported by artillery and some regular troops, while the field army remained in reserve to counterattack any breakthrough.

What had happened in the previous months?[14] By 1809, Napoleon had effectively gained dominion over almost the entire continent of Europe. In the preceding four

---

11   Wellington to Castlereagh, Merida, 25th August 1809, Gurwood, *Dispatches*, vol.3, p.453.

12   Wellington to t Liverpool, Celorico, 19 August 1810, Gurwood, *Dispatches*, vol.4, p.234.

13   This is a defensive obstacle, here made generally from tree branches positioned with the branches facing the enemy. They restrict movement and are difficult to penetrate.

14   For a detailed analysis of the campaign through to the withdrawal from Santarém, please see Kenton White, *The Key to Lisbon: The Third French Invasion of Portugal, 1810-11* (Warwick: Helion & Company, 2019).

years, he had engaged in and emerged victorious from a series of campaigns against the Russians, Prussians, Austrians, and Spanish. However, a Fifth Coalition was raised against Napoleon in 1809, consisting of Austria, Spain, Portugal and Great Britain. Wellington was aware that if Napoleon were successful against Austria, it would free up large numbers of reinforcements which the French would send to Spain.[15] Nevertheless, this would take time to arrange, and it would give Wellington the opportunity to prepare.[16] In 1809, Wellington had written, 'My opinion was, that even if Spain should have been conquered, the French would not have been able to overrun Portugal with a smaller force than 100,000 men'.[17] Wellington had to address when the invasion would occur and where it would originate.

At the decisive Battle of Wagram in July 1809, Napoleon sealed his triumph against Austria. His endeavours in creating the Confederation of the Rhine and asserting authority over various client states had yielded temporary stability in central Europe, yet he was acutely aware of the fragility of his position. The Continental System was beginning to break down by 1811. Sweden and Russia were openly importing goods from Britain and selling them throughout Europe. Despite this, Napoleon's secretary *baron* Fain wrote, 'The Continental System is uppermost in his mind, he is more taken up with it than ever, too much so perhaps!'[18] Discontent smouldered among the vanquished Emperors, eagerly awaiting an opportunity for retribution against Napoleon. For the time being, however, the primary opposition to the French consisted of Great Britain, Spain, and Portugal.

Napoleon planned to lead an army of 100,000 soldiers, including the *garde impériale*, into Portugal. However, he was swept up in his new marriage to the *Erzherzogin* Marie-Louise of Austria and needed to appoint a commander. A limited number of Napoleon's *maréchaux* exhibited competence in independent command, and those deemed by Napoleon as having potential, notably Soult and Victor, had previously been defeated by Wellington. One of his truly capable independent commanders, Jean Lannes, had been mortally wounded at the Battle of Aspern-Essling, prior to Wagram, in 1809. André Massena, recognised as one of Napoleon's most seasoned *maréchaux*, was eventually appointed to command. He had been made *prince d'Essling* by Napoleon after Aspern-Essling and Wagram. Napoleon had written of him, to Eugène de Beauharnais, Viceroy of Italy, in 1809: 'Massena has military talents before which one must bow; one must forget his faults, as all men have them. In giving you command of the army, I made a mistake; I should have sent you Massena and given you command of the cavalry under his orders.'[19]

---

15   Wellington to Viscount Castlereagh, Merida, 25th August 1809, Gurwood, *Dispatches,* vol.3, p.453.

16   Wellington to the Right Honourable J Villiers, Badajoz, 20th November 1809, Gurwood, *Dispatches,* vol.3, p.601.

17   Memorandum on the defence of Portugal, London, 7th March 1809, Gurwood, *Dispatches,* vol.3, pp.181–182.

18   Fain, quoted in Adam Zamoyski, *1812: Napoleon's Fatal March on Moscow* (London: HarperCollins, 2004), p.70.

19   15144, A Eugène Napoléon, vice-roi d'italie, a caldiero. Burghauseu, 30 avril 1809. H. Plon and J. Dumaine (ed.), *Correspondence de Napoléon I* (Paris: Imprimerie Impériale, 1865), vol.18, p.525.

Although initially reluctant to accept, Massena was, on 17 April 1810, through an Imperial Decree, designated as the *commandant en chef* of the *armée de Portugal*.[20] Napoleon was relying on Massena's experience and determination. However, Massena was still suffering from injuries received during the 1809 campaign. Several aspects of Massena's character have been mentioned in other histories, most notably that he took his mistress on campaign with him.[21] He was somewhat negligent in his appearance, and this was at odds with some of the other commanders such as *général de division* Junot and *maréchal* Bessières. According to one of his junior aides-de-camp, 'Massena combined an excellent heart with a sharp and penetrating mind', but was perhaps a little too distant from his soldiers to be loved in the same way as Ney.[22]

Napoleon had assured Massena of a force of 70,000 soldiers, a further 20,000 stationed in Valladolid under *général de division* Drouet, *comte* d'Erlon, with an additional 13,000 under *général de division* Kellerman. For this campaign, he took care not to send too many of his experienced troops from the *grande armée* in Germany. Additionally, Drouet's Corps was not placed under Massena's command until 1811. Massena thus fielded only 65,000 men for the invasion: a significant reduction in manpower from that promised, and wholly inadequate to fulfil his mission.[23] The lack of control over other army formations and the general reluctance of French commanders to cooperate with each other would prove difficult for Massena.

Massena prepared for the invasion by taking the Spanish fortress of Ciudad Rodrigo on 10 July 1810. This was soon followed by the beginning of the siege of the Portuguese fortress of Almeida. Soon after this town was invested, the main powder magazine exploded, effectively ending the siege. By the middle of September, Massena had organised his forces as best as he could, and, on the 15th, the invasion proper began. 'In Spain large armies will starve and small armies will be beaten' was a saying attributed to Henry IV of France, and something that would be adapted by Wellington into his 'cautious system'. It would prove equally applicable to Portugal and was to prove prophetic in the coming months and years. Wellington's planned use of scorched earth and steady withdrawal to prepared defences was put into practice, waiting for Massena to make a mistake. Thanks to the French advance occurring on the northern, or right, bank of the Mondego, Wellington was able to make use of the excellent defensive position on the Serra do Buçaco, previously identified by him, to offer battle. The Allied army was able to repel two attacks along the Serra,

---

20   606, Imperial Decree, Compiègne, 17th April 1810, *The Confidential Correspondence of Napoleon Bonaparte with His Brother Joseph, Sometime King of Spain. Selected and Translated, with Explanatory Notes, from the 'Memoires du Roi Joseph.'* (New York: D Appleton and Company, 1856), vol.2, p.116.

21   Jean-Baptiste-Antoine-Marcelin Marbot, *The Memoirs of the Baron de Marbot* (London: Greenhill Books, 1990), ii; Marc Oudinot, 'Souvenirs intimes et militaires du général Victor Oudinot, duc de Reggio Campagnes de Portugal : 1810 et 1811', *Napoleonica La Revue*, 5.2 (2009), p.170.

22   Oudinot, 'Souvenirs', p.21.

23   16519, Au prince de Neuchatel et de Wagram, Major Général de l'Armée d'Espagne, Le Havre, 29 May 1810, Plon and Dumaine, *Correspondence de Napoléon I*, vol.20, pp.385–387.

but was forced to retreat once Massena turned the right of the position. Wellington brought the army quickly south to the Lines of Torres Vedras and awaited the French assault. The French invasion had been much delayed by the sieges of Ciudad Rodrigo and Almeida, along with the stops at Viseu and Coimbra and the Battle of Buçaco. This gave sufficient time for the defences around Lisbon to be completed and fully manned before the French forces reached them.

The French pursued Wellington's army closely, but were brought to a halt short of their objective of Lisbon. Massena was furious that no information had been given to him about the extensive defences or the mountainous nature of the terrain north of the capital. With the advancing French were the *afrancesados* the *Marquês* d'Alorna and Manuel Pamplona.[24] They had assured Massena that the country between the Mondego and Lisbon was open and easy to traverse. When the *armée de Portugal* approached the lines, it was clear that the topography was anything but open, and the defences were extensive. Massena raged at the advisors that they had misled him. 'They responded that it was the Marshal's business and not theirs to have received information of the works which Lord Wellington had lately constructed. What the devil! answered Massena, Wellington didn't make the mountains!'[25] The French reconnoitred the defences around Sobral, eventually launching an attack to break through, but this was repulsed. Wellington wrote to Charles Arbuthnot, Secretary to the Treasury, stating, '… they won't draw me from my cautious system. I'll fight them only where I am pretty sure of success; and if I should succeed, they must be destroyed.'[26]

Over the subsequent days, Massena and his staff engaged in reconnaissance to assess the strength of the defensive positions. He narrowly avoided being hit whilst on one of these observations, coming under fire from the cannon in redoubt No. 120. Owing to the strength of the defences and the diminished state of the army, it was thought incapable of launching another assault. Consequently, Massena issued orders to consolidate the army's positions and gather provisions. Despite Wellington's orders to denude the countryside of food, the *armée de Portugal* was able to find enough provisions to survive. According to *chef de bataillon* Pelet, Massena's chief aide-de-camp, there were supplies to be had, and the scorched earth policy demanded by Wellington had not been carried out.[27]

Massena's intention was now to try to besiege Lisbon. Nevertheless, the eventual exhaustion of resources immediately in front of the defences compelled the French forces to withdraw. *Intendant général* Lambert listed the problems the *armée de Portugal* had faced and was still facing:

---

24   Afrancesados: French sympathisers in Spain and Portugal.
25   Charles Stanhope, *Notes of Conversations with the Duke of Wellington, 1831-1851* (New York: Longmans, Green and Co, 1888), p.162.
26   Wellington to the Right Honourable C. Arbuthnot, Alcobaça, 5th October 1810, *Supplementary Despatches*, vol.6, p.612.
27   Jean Jacques Pelet, Donald D. Horward (ed.), *The French Campaign in Portugal, 1810-1811* (Minneapolis: University of Minnesota Press, 1973), pp.375–376.

The campaign of the Portuguese Army; The singularity it presents, by crossing a kingdom without seeing an inhabitant; The painful marches it has had to make in a country intersected by mountains, and deprived of guides who supplement the imperfection of maps; The total exhaustion of the means of clothing, equipment and transport … the inadequacy of resources …[28]

Unwilling to admit complete defeat, Massena planned to withdraw to a more defensible position around Santarém, where he also hoped they would find more supplies to feed the army. Orders were distributed to the respective corps on the 10th for the retreat.[29] The movement of the *armée de Portugal* began on the night of 14 November, helped by a fog which obscured the movement from the eyes of the Allied outposts.[30] The position at Santarém had been chosen well, with much of the front covered by the Rio Maior and the marshy ground along it. By the 18th, the *armée de Portugal* was firmly established in its position. Wellington wrote to his brother on 21 November commenting, 'The French have a position at Santarém, compared with which Busaco [sic] is nothing. However, when it shall be fair weather, and the roads passable, I hope to dislodge them by moving on their flanks.'[31] Wellington, enjoying secure communications and nearly unlimited supplies, was in no hurry. He could afford to wait, allowing starvation to weaken the *armée de Portugal* to the point where they could no longer maintain their new position.

The relocation to Santarém in November 1810 had indeed marked an acknowledgement that the *armée de Portugal* could not sustain its presence in Portugal without significant reinforcement and the reestablishment of supply routes to depots in Almeida and Spain. Despite the withdrawal to Santarém, the two armies sat opposite one another over the winter without meaningful combat. There was occasional skirmishing between picquet, but generally both sides left the other alone. Some sentries were positioned just yards from their enemies; occasionally, they exchanged food, tobacco, and drinks, or even played games together.[32] Wellington was able to report that there was no significant change in French activity in their new position.[33] The Allied troops remained in their quarters until the early spring of 1811.

---

28   Rapport de l'intendant General Lambert au Prince Berthier, Major-General, sur la situation de l'armee de Portugal, Alenquer, 20 October 1810. John T. Jones and Harry Jones, *Journals of Sieges Carried on by the Army Under the Duke of Wellington, in Spain, During the Years 1811 to 1814* … (London: John Weale, 1846), vol.3, p.187.

29   Service historique de la Défense (SHD): Dispositions générals pour un changement de position de l'armée, 10 novembre 1810. *Armée de Portugal. Correspondance du Même Au Même (Octobre-Décembre 1810)* 1810, 7C10; François Nicolas Fririon, *Journal Historique de la Campagne de Portugal, Entreprise Par Les Français, Sous Les Ordres du Maréchal Masséna, Prince d'Essling, (Du 15. Sept. 1810 Au 12. Mai 1811)* (Paris: Leneuve, 1841), pp.109–111.

30   Fririon, *Journal Historique*, p.112.

31   Wellington to Henry Wellesley, Cartaxo, 21st November 1810, Gurwood, *Dispatches*, vol.4, p.425.

32   Edward Costello, *The Adventures of a Soldier; or, Memoirs of Edward Costello* (London: Henry Coulburn, 1841), p.83.

33   See for example, Wellington to Liverpool, Cartaxo, 2nd March 1811, Gurwood, *Dispatches*, vol.4, p.646.

Not wishing to be seen to concede defeat, Massena held the army outside Lisbon until March 1811. After a miserable winter, he was finally forced to accept that the army could not remain at Santarém. Starvation had reduced the army's numbers and condition, and, eventually, the outcome was beyond even Massena's experienced grasp. He ordered the army to withdraw north with the intention of crossing the Mondego at Coimbra and then consolidating its position whilst gathering supplies and resting the army.

The *armée de Portugal*, under one of its most distinguished *maréchaux* had been defeated in battle at Buçaco and denied victory outside Lisbon. He would now undertake a gruelling withdrawal across land already devastated by two armies and the local population.

2

The Army Remained Calm

Santarém

The *armée de Portugal* had been in its cantonments around Santarém since withdrawing to the strong defensive position in November 1810. Wellington's scorched earth plans were beginning to bite, but the French troops had been successful in finding supplies that should have been either destroyed or moved to within the Lines around Lisbon. *Général de division* Marchand wrote to his wife on 5 January 1811:

> We had to send detachments far away to find the hiding places of the inhabitants and bring the supplies back to the camp. You can imagine that soldiers forced to loot 5 or 6 leagues away to survive naturally act on their own and commit the most dreadful excesses. The atrocities they commit upon returning from these expeditions are unimaginable; they bring back chickens, wheat, and wine, and we ourselves are forced to live off the results of this plundering.[1]

With most of the food hoards discovered, and no supplies arriving from Spain, the French eventually ran out of adequate provisions to remain. Wellington had written of the French situation:

> It is certainly astonishing that the enemy have been able to remain in this country so long; and it is an extraordinary instance of what a French army can do … With all our money, and having in our favor [sic] the good inclinations of the country, I assure you that I could not maintain one division in the district in which they have maintained not less than 60,000 men and 20,000 animals for more than two months.[2]

But by February 1811, the *armée de Portugal* was in a desperate situation: 'Their clothing was in a deplorable state; soldiers were without shoes. Eight to nine months' pay was owed to the army. In the midst of these sufferings and privations, far from the homeland, and in the face of an enemy who refused to fight, the army remained

1   Louis Samuel Béchet, *Souvenirs (Écrits En 1838-1839) : Publiés et Annotés Par Christian Schneider* (Paris: Editions Historiques Teissèdre, 2000), p.358.
2   Wellington to Liverpool, Cartaxo, 21st December 1810, Gurwood, *Dispatches,* vol.4, p.469.

calm and patient.'[3] Béchet described the situation at Santarém as no longer tenable; '… we had exhausted the country far behind us, the reinforcements we awaited did not arrive, and the expected diversion never materialised.'[4]

Massena received news of some reorganisation of the northern provinces of Spain and the appointment of Bessières as the commander of the new *armée du Nord*. A responsibility of the army was to maintain communications between Valladolid, Salamanca and Almeida. Additionally, Napoleon ordered Bessières that, '… in unforeseen circumstances, he must support the Army of Portugal and provide it with assistance; I also inform him that the 9th corps would be under his command in the event that this corps re-enters Spain.'[5]

Général de brigade Foy had been sent to Paris on 31 October 1810 escorted by 50 *dragons* from the 3e régiment provisoire and a detachment of infantry. He was to give Napoleon reports on the situation in Portugal. He returned to the *armée de Portugal* on 5 February carrying new instructions from the Emperor. Foy brought with him a motley collection of reinforcements. These included the 4e batallions of the 4e légère and the 47e and 70e ligne, along with nearly 140 men from the 3e, 10e and 11e dragons. There were also some 470 assorted infantry, cavalry and artillery troops along with more than 100 horses.[6] He was accompanied by 30 medical officers. Although a welcome addition to the strength of the army, these few troops would be an additional strain on the already depleted food supply.

The Meeting at Golegã

On 18 February, Massena invited his commanders for lunch at *général de division* Loison's headquarters at Golegã. The intention was to discuss the new instructions which had been received from Napoleon, and to decide on the next moves for the army. Ney, Junot, Reynier, Fririon, Éblé, Lazowski, Solignac and Foy were to attend. One commander who was not invited was Drouet, commander of IX corps, who, although supporting the *armée de Portugal*, was not under Massena's command. Massena began by recounting,

> … the state of misery of the army. All the resources of the territory it occupies are exhausted. The foraging that extends to the sea, the Mondego, the Ceira and the Haut-Zezere, brings in almost nothing. The cavalry and artillery horses, finding no more fodder and reduced to grazing a little weed, are exhausted … The Allies, immobile in their positions, seem to be waiting for

---

3   Fririon, *Journal Historique*, p.134.
4   Béchet, *Souvenirs*, p.360.
5   A Monsieur le maréchal d'Essling, Commandant-en-chef, l'armée de Portugal, Paris, le 16 Janvier, 1811. Quoted in William Napier, *History of the War in the Peninsula and in the South of France, from the Year 1807 to the Year 1814* (London: Frederick Warne and Co, n.d.), vol.3, pp.356–357.
6   Fririon, *Journal Historique*, pp.131–132.

hunger to chase us away, and everything leads us to believe that they will leave us to move first.[7]

If the troops could maintain it, Massena was willing to establish a bridge across the Tagus. The risk was that moving the army across would take several days, and with the proximity of the Allied forces, the bridge could be broken and the army divided and destroyed. Foy recorded, 'The enemy appears willing to defend the passage of the Tagus. Is it necessary for an interest so modest as that of eating for a month in the Alentejo, to risk such an operation?'[8]

Foy related his interview with Napoleon and what the Emperor asked of his army. His instructions were that Massena should stay in Santarém as long as possible, inflicting losses on the Allied army. If Massena felt able, he could move to the left bank of the Tagus once the river level fell sufficiently. However, if he was obliged to withdraw for lack of food, he should retire to the line of the Mondego. Napoleon indicated that maintaining pressure on Britain's only field army, and exacting casualties upon it, might bring a change of government in London and subsequently a withdrawal of the British Army from Portugal. The opposition in London looked for a reason to bring the army home, and a failed campaign or defeat in battle would provide the justification. Foy claimed Napoleon's view could be summed up thus, 'It is less strength than patience that will decide the victory.'[9] This view closely resembled Wellington's thinking; his 'cautious system'.[10] However, 'patiently waiting' indicated a significant change in Napoleon's strategy. From driving the British into the sea through outright military victory, the emphasis had moved to draining the British Army of strength and the British government of money.[11] However, it was Massena's *armée de Portugal* that was shrinking daily and without pay. The Allies, on the other hand, increased in strength, with fresh British troops regularly arriving in Lisbon and Cadiz, and new recruits being absorbed into the Portuguese army. Napoleon's new approach to the situation may explain, to some extent at least, Massena's later behaviour, which led to the battle at Fuentes de Oñoro.

In the meeting, Massena posed three questions, based on the dispatch from Napoleon: should the army cross the Tagus? If so, where, and how was it to be done? Or should the army withdraw behind the Mondego, where there was food, to await reinforcements? It was clear from the discussion that staying at Santarém was not a realistic possibility. Ney, ever loyal to his Emperor, expressed the opinion that he had to conform to the Emperor's intentions as reported by Foy. He firmly supported the army remaining where it was and waiting for support from Soult. Consequently, he proposed, the plan to retire to the Mondego had to be ruled out. *Général de division* Éblé proposed crossing the Tagus by bridge to occupy the

---

7   Jean Baptiste Koch, *Mémoires de Massena Rédiges d'apres Les Documents Qu'il a Laissés et Sur Ceux du Dépôt de la Guerre et du Dépôt de Fortifications* (Paris: Paulin and Lechavelier, 1850), vol.7, p.314.

8   Maurice Girod de l'Ain, *Vie Militaire du Général Foy* (Paris: E Plon, 1900), pp.130–131.

9   Koch, *Mémoires de Massena*, vol.7, p.315.

10   White, *The Key to Lisbon* , ch.5.

11   Girod de l'Ain, *Vie Militaire du Général Foy*, pp.354–356 Pièces Justificatives.

Alentejo, then establish communications with Soult and keep pressure on Lisbon. The plan to cross the Tagus at Santarém was rejected because of the risk from the Allied artillery batteries nearby. Foy, of those at the meeting who knew Napoleon's mind most closely, suggested waiting at Santarém for Soult to link up with the *armée de Portugal*.

Massena had hoped for material support from Soult, but this had not materialised. Soult and *maréchal* Mortier were involved in the investment of Badajoz, and whilst this might distract Wellington a little, it did not provide Massena with the direct support he needed. The sound of guns had been heard from the direction of Badajoz, but had ceased on the 15th, indicating the fortress had fallen. Foy suggested taking a column of 3,000 men to link up with Soult and bring the two armies together.[12] The army, he insisted, should stay and await the next orders from Paris. *Général de division* Reynier, commander of II corps, disagreed: 'I do not counsel inactivity for an extended period because my troops' suffering needs an end.'[13] The discussion failed to find a clear solution, and so Massena dismissed everyone.

The Allies had not been idle, and artillery emplacements had been built at points on the left bank of the Tagus considered to be likely crossing points for the French. The troops of the 2nd Division under the command of Lieutenant General Rowland Hill occupied the left bank between Chamusca and Rossio. When Hill fell ill, he was replaced by Major General Sir William Stewart, commander of the Division's 1st Brigade.[14] Stewart, a brilliant battalion commander and tactician, was considered a risk when commanding larger formations if he did not have a strong commander instructing him, but the 2nd Division's role was an independent command remote from the main army. Later, Wellington was to write that it was, '... necessary that General Stewart should be under the particular charge of somebody ...'[15] He was apt to show poor judgment in his orders to subordinates and to disobey those of his superiors. Replaced in command of the 2nd Division after two weeks by Beresford, the Division would constitute a significant proportion of the Anglo-Portuguese forces which fought at the Battle of Albuera.

To many in the *armée de Portugal*, the decision to retreat from Santarém seemed to have already been taken. On the 16th, Fririon was ordered to assemble the army's baggage at Tomar, and the following day, much of the artillery was withdrawn, leaving each division with only three guns.[16] On the 19th, Massena sent a message to Ney, which indicated a determination had been made and information on the routes to be taken was needed: 'Monsieur le Maréchal, I beg you to send me the information which you were able to collect on the road from Tomar to Pombal, by Chaos de Maçans, on that from Tomar to Coimbra, by Anciano, finally on the

---

12   Girod de l'Ain, *Vie Militaire du Général Foy*, p.132.
13   SHD: Résumé de la Conference de Gallego, 21 februar 1811. *Armée de Portugal: Correspondance* (1811), 7C12.
14   Wellington to Major General the Hon. W. Stewart. Cartaxo, 2d Dec. 1810, 10 A.M., Gurwood, *Dispatches,* vol.4, p.447.
15   Wellington to Colonel Torrens, Freineda, 6th Dec., 1812, *Supplementary Despatches,* vol.7, p.494.
16   Jean-Nicolas-Auguste Noël, Rosemary Brindle (trans), *With Napoleon's Guns: The Military Memoirs of an Officer of the First Empire* (London: Greenhill, 2005), p.111.

communication between Anciano and Chaos de Maçans and that between Arneiro and Leiria.'[17]

Further confirmation came with instructions for the commanders to ensure transport for all seriously ill men was available, and to make sure that as much of the baggage as possible was ready to move. Because of the wastage of horses, the commanders were instructed to reduce the number used to pull their guns and wagons, possibly even reducing the number to four horses per gun.[18] If there were insufficient horses, they were authorised to seize the horses drawing the wagons of the *cantinières* if necessary, a move that would be unpopular with both the *cantinières* and the soldiers who relied upon them for additions to their meagre provisions.[19] Noël recorded destroying the wagons of the artillery park of VIII corps, throwing the ammunition into a nearby river.[20]

On 25 February, Massena informed Reynier and Junot that he was awaiting news from the Emperor, which was expected by 10 March. He asked them if, by consuming part of their reserve supplies, they could remain in their positions until then. Reynier stated that the only way his troops could hold out was to consume their entire reserves. Junot replied that he would exhaust his bread reserves, in addition to which there was no meat for his cavalry troopers and infantrymen, and the foreign regiments, Irlandaise and de Prusse, were suffering dreadful hardships.[21]

Further dispatches from Paris caused Massena additional problems. Drouet, believed by Napoleon still to be in Ciudad Rodrigo, was ordered to contain the freedom of movement of Silveira, Trant and Wilson's militia units, and keep open communications between Coimbra, Ponte de Mucela and Guarda. This would be a significant task in normal circumstances, but Drouet was near Leiria, not at Ciudad Rodrigo, and now threatened to take his forces northwards to fulfil his Imperial orders. Massena persuaded him to delay his departure, but was now left with little choice but to withdraw the army to recover, reorganise and re-equip.[22]

Retreat

Orders were issued on 1 March for the retreat northwards to take up a position north of the Mondego and to re-establish communications with Almeida. The plan was to move the army in two columns, crossing the Mondego at Coimbra and Penacova or São João de Rei. *Général de division* Montbrun would lead the advanced guard, aiming to thrust to the river and cross before any opposition could be established. However, as Pelet remarked, '... the Mondego, which was almost dry when we saw

---

17   19 février, au duc d'Elchingen. Henri Bonnal, *La Vie Militaire du Maréchal Ney, Duc d'Elchingen, Prince de la Moskowa* (Paris: Chapelot, 1914), vol.3, p.475.
18   Bonnal, *La Vie Militaire du Maréchal Ney*, vol.3, pp.475–476.
19   Cantinières were sutlers or merchants who followed the army and sold wine, food and other supplies. Often women attached to particular regiments, they also nursed sick and wounded soldiers.
20   Noël, *With Napoleon's Guns*, p.111.
21   Oudinot, 'Souvenirs', p.26.
22   Koch, *Mémoires de Massena*, vol.7, p.306.

it in September, would now be a violent river.'[23] Whilst the crossing of the Mondego was established, the rearguard under Ney would aim to delay the Allied army for as long as possible. Thus, the coming campaign would rely on two veteran commanders in the *armée de Portugal*: Ney to hold back the Allied army and Montbrun to establish a crossing of the Mondego near Coimbra. Neither task would be easy, but these commanders had years of experience to draw upon for the coming actions. Despite the need to secure a crossing of the Mondego, Montbrun was not given his final orders until the 11th.

The movement was to begin on the night of 5/6 March. Massena composed an extensive letter to *maréchal* Berthier, Napoleon's chief of staff, in which he expressed his dissatisfaction with the lack of assistance from Mortier's V corps and Soult's forces in Andalusia. He dispatched Foy to Paris, again, to inform the Emperor of his decision. By retiring to the Mondego, Massena believed he could sustain the army for long enough to establish new lines of communication to Spain, but the retreat would be hindered by the accompanying baggage, wounded, and sick.[24] Massena positioned the corps so that VI corps, reinforced during the forthcoming retreat by *général de division* Conroux's 1e division of IX corps and the cavalry of the army, was to concentrate via Tomar at Leiria. On 5 March *général de division* Solignac's division of VIII corps took position at Pernes and awaited Clausel's division. After destroying the bridge there, these two divisions headed for Torres-Novas, arriving at midday on the 6th. VIII corps then overtook VI corps, and once VIII corps had passed, VI corps was to take up the role of rearguard.

Meanwhile, II corps would march via Tomar to Espinhal, and VIII corps would move to Pombal via Chaõ de Maças.[25] On 6 February Napoleon had issued an order placing Drouet directly under Massena's command, but the order would not reach Massena's headquarters in time to be of use in the early part of the retreat.[26] Massena's authority over Drouet, or a lack of official authorisation of it, was to prove problematic in the coming retreat and right up to his eventual replacement by *maréchal* Marmont.

Unaware of Massena's decision to retreat, Wellington visited his forward positions early on 4 March and observed a change in the French defences, but little else. In a letter to Beresford sent at 5:00 a.m. on 6 March, Wellington confirmed the French were retreating.[27] They had used dummies made of straw and dressed in uniforms placed as sentries to confuse Allied observers, allowing the French to gain several hours' march on their pursuers.[28] Although orders to locate and identify the route the French were taking were issued between 5:00 and 6:00 a.m. on the 6th, and troops were sent out, Wellington's forces did not properly catch up with

23   Pelet, *The French Campaign in Portugal*, p.393.
24   Béchet, *Souvenirs*, p.361.
25   SHD: Le Marechal Massena, Prince d'Essling, a S. A. le Prince de Wagram et de Neufchatel, Torres Novas, 6 mars, 1811, *Correspondance*, 7C12.
26   17335, Au Prince de Neuchatel et de Wagram, Major Général de l'armée d'Espagne, a Paris, 6 fevrier 1811, Plon and J Dumaine, *Correspondence de Napoléon I*, vol.21, p.387.
27   Wellington to Beresford, Cartaxo, 6th March 1811, 5am, Gurwood, *Dispatches*, vol.4, p.655.
28   Marie Jean Baptiste Lemonnier-Delafosse, *Campagnes de 1810 à 1815. Souvenirs militaires* (Havre: Alph. Lemale, 1850), p.118.

the French rearguard until they neared Pombal. Extreme measures were taken to ensure the retreat could be affected as quickly as possible. *Général de division* Hulot remarked, '… we were already, for lack of horses, obliged to burn some carriages; I proposed to destroy more, to keep only those necessary and to harness them thoroughly, to be sure of keeping everything without delaying the march or tiring the horses too much … We crossed moors and heights, passing Chao-de-Marsans [sic], Santa-Maria, Pombal and Venda-Cruz.'[29]

The French moved quickly. By 8–9 March, Ney's rearguard was disposed between Leiria and Pombal. The 15e and 25e dragons and light artillery were in front of Leiria with Marchand's division of the 6e légère, 69e, 76e ligne, artillery, 6e and 11e dragons, behind Leiria. Mermet's division, comprising the 25e légère, 27e, 50e and 59e ligne and artillery, was in Leiria. Conroux's division was echeloned in such a way as to cover the artillery park. This was intended to extend, on the left, Marchand's division in the event Wellington tried to turn the flank. Marcognet was posted in Pombal with the 39e ligne, its artillery and the 3e dragons.[30] Ney reported to Massena that, 'I am, therefore, in a position to face the enemy in whatever number he presents himself. I have, counting Drouet's three artillery pieces, 28 guns and four divisions, including one of *dragons*, deployed in such a way as to be equally strong on all points.'[31] However, the French were short of ammunition, and most of their artillery had been sent ahead to avoid being captured by the Allies. This, according to *sous-lieutenant* Villargennes of the 26e ligne, is the reason the French rearguard burned the towns and villages as they passed through. He wrote about the retreat through Leiria:

> The scarcity of ammunition was also a source of uneasiness at head-quarters … The enemy pressed closely on our rear with a powerful artillery, while ours was already far beyond Liria [sic]. There was but one resource left to us. Orders were given to the last column, and as they left the … street, they set fire to both sides of it, and the enemy had the mortification of seeing us quietly reach the position previously appointed.[32]

Ney reported the situation of the artillery of the VI corps to Massena on 2 March. Caissons that could not be taken were burned, except for one for transporting bags of gunpowder extracted from 300 shells abandoned by the artillery of the VIII corps.[33]

Wellington's intelligence network reported this information almost immediately. He wrote to Beresford:

29   Jacques-Louis Hulot, *Souvenirs Militaires du Baron Hulot (Jacques-Louis), Général d'artillerie, 1773-1843* (Paris: Spectateur militaire, 1886), p.340.

30   Bonnal, *La Vie Militaire du Maréchal Ney*, vol.3, p.480.

31   Koch, *Mémoires de Massena*, vol.7, p.345.

32   Adelbert Doisy de Villargennes, *Reminiscences of Army Life Under Napoleon Bonaparte* (Cincinnati: Robert Clarke & Co, 1884), pp.60–61.

33   Bonnal, *La Vie Militaire du Maréchal Ney*, vol.3, p.481.

I think it almost certain, from the enemy's movements, of which I have obtained a knowledge since I saw you, that they are going for Coimbra; but I learn here that they have destroyed many carriages, and much ammunition, and it is said even some guns; and I should therefore conclude that whatever their first step may be, their second will be towards the Spanish frontier.[34]

The advanced guard of the Allied Army, now commanded by Major General Erskine, comprised the infantry of the Light Division and *Brigadeiro* Pack's Portuguese Brigade. The attached cavalry under Lieutenant Colonel Friedrich Arentschildt was composed of the 1st King's German Legion (KGL) Hussars and 1st Royal Dragoons, and Captain Ross's troop of the Royal Horse Artillery (RHA) was in support. Other cavalry units were regularly used in the advanced guard. The 14th and 16th Light Dragoons were temporarily brigaded under Colonel Samuel Hawker of the 14th. Anson was absent in England, and so his brigade's command then devolved temporarily upon Lieutenant Colonel von Arentschildt of the 1st KGL Hussars.[35] Despite this formal, though provisional, organisation, when necessary units were fielded without reference to their brigading.

The Light Division pursued VI corps and established contact with Ney's rear-guard troops as they approached Pombal. Some of the Allied advanced guard kept up with the retreating French only by an unusual expedient. The riflemen rode with the Light Dragoons, mounted behind the troopers. According to Sergeant Costello of the 95th, 'From the friction alone produced on the legs and seat by the dragoon's saddle-bags, it was sometime before the foot-soldier, when placed upon his legs, could move with anything like despatch.'[36] The infantry suffered more than just discomfort. Pieces of kit not normally thoroughly secured were lost through the jolting on horseback.

The main strength of the Allied Army was several marches behind the advanced guard. Major General Nightingall was detached from the main pursuit and ordered to follow Reynier's II corps along its route towards Espinhal. *Capitaine* Lemonnier-Delafosse of the 31e légère, part of Heudelet's division of II corps, recalled the Corps, '… was separated from the army, and received orders to continue its retreat through mountains where only goats could climb; it was, it was said, to flank the army: but it had no enemies on its flanks'[37] Nightingall wrote, 'I had command of the right column consisting at first of my brigade and a regiment of cavalry, and afterwards increased by Campbell's division and the 16th [Light] Dragoons, which placed me on the 8th of March in a very conspicuous place and enabled me to follow Reynier's corps very close.'[38]

---

34   Wellington to Beresford, Thomar, 8th March, 1811, 2 P.M, Gurwood, *Dispatches*, vol.4, p.658.
35   William Tomkinson, *The Diary of a Cavalry Officer*, 2nd edn (London: Swan Sonnenschein & Co Ltd, 1895), p.81.
36   Costello, *Memoirs*, p.90.
37   Lemonnier-Delafosse, *Souvenirs militaires*, p.122.
38   Sarcedo, on the banks of the river Alva. 22nd March, 1811. Michael Glover, 'The Nightingall Letters: Letters from Major General Miles Nightingall in Portugal February to June 1811', *Journal of the Society for Army Historical Research*, 51.207 (1973), p.139.

However, Campbell and the 16th were rerouted to Perucha, leaving Nightingall with only one brigade and one squadron of the 14th Light Dragoons.[39] The 14th were engaged in a small skirmish with some French *dragons* during a hailstorm around the village of Ceras on the Tomar-Espinhal road, but the French were able to draw off unopposed.[40] The majority of the 14th Light Dragoons were redirected to the main body of the army on the 9th. Nightingall complained:

> ... I was left with only my own brigade and only one squadron of the 14th L. Dragoons to follow the whole of Reynier's corps on the Espinal road. I, however, kept close to him, hiding as much as possible my numbers to prevent their finding out the diminution of my force, but Reynier halted at Espinal in a strong position until the 14th when he was obliged to retire by the advance of Lord Wellington and I was, for several days, placed in a very uncomfortable situation without any communication with headquarters and quite close to a large proportion of Reynier's corps ...[41]

Whilst Nightingall pursued Reynier, between Leiria and Pombal the cavalry of the main bodies of the respective armies skirmished continually. The French cavalry piquet, established at Machados to observe the Allied advance, was attacked on the morning of 9 March, but was eventually able to withdraw to the vicinity of Pombal.[42] Pelet wrote, 'VI corps had Mermet's division ahead of the crossroads ... with the cavalry at its head, Marchand's division in reserve, and Marcognet's brigade at Pombal; its artillery and baggage were all perfectly placed and well echeloned.'[43]

August Schaumann, a commissary with the 1st KGL Hussars, wrote, '... we reached a height from which we could see Pombal before us, and on the road thither a column of French infantry and artillery that stretched further than the eye could see.'[44]

11 March – Pombal

Pombal was a small town built around a castle overlooking a bridge over the Rio Arunca.[45] Unlike today, the village was only on the east, or right, bank of the river, clustered around the steep hill upon which the castle stands. The advanced guard of the Allied army approached Pombal along the road from Leiria. Schaumann's regiment, '... together with the heavy cavalry and the horse artillery, marched

---

39 Extracts from the instructions communicated by the Q. M. G. Peraeka, 9th March, 1811, Gurwood, *Dispatches,* vol.4, p.660.

40 Francis Hall, 'Peninsular Recollections, 1811–12', *Royal United Services Institution Journal,* 56.416 (1912), p.1403

41 Sarcedo, on the banks of the river Alva. 22nd March, 1811. Glover, 'The Nightingall Letters', p.139.

42 Bonnal, *La Vie Militaire du Maréchal Ney,* vol.3, p.483.

43 Pelet, *The French Campaign in Portugal,* pp.433–434.

44 August Schaumann, *On the Road with Wellington* (London: William Heinemann, 1924), p.285.

45 What was the Rio Soure is now known as the Arunca.

Pombal Castle from the river. (Author's photo)

as advanced guard at the head of the light division, and in order to expedite our progress, the cavalry carried the knapsacks of the infantry on their saddles.[46]

Although there had been little contact between the rear guard of the *armée de Portugal* and the Light Division, it was not through want of effort, despite *capitaine* Marcel's comment that the *armée* had reached Pombal, '… without the enemy appearing to want to worry us …'.[47] Ney's Corps was initially positioned with Marchand's and Mermet's divisions in front of Pombal, and Leach, with the 95th Rifles and advancing as part of the Light Division, recorded that the French were deployed in the plain before Pombal, '… in considerable force …'.[48] Conroux's division of IX corps was attached to Ney's corps to bolster the numbers of the rearguard.

A skirmish between the cavalry of the Allied advanced guard and that of the French rear guard took place at Pombal. The cavalry, the 1st KGL Hussars to the front with the 16th Light Dragoons in reserve, faced some eight squadrons of *dragons* and *chasseurs à cheval*. Captain (Schaumann wrote he was a major) von Müller's squadron of the Hussars, containing the irrepressible Krauchenburg,[49] charged the French leading squadron and pushed it back onto its supporting squadrons.[50] A

---

46   Schaumann, *On the Road with Wellington*, p.286.
47   Marcel, *Campagnes du Capitaine Marcel, du 69e de Ligne, En Espagne et En Portugal (1808-1814)* … (Paris: Libraire Plon, 1913), pp.125–126.
48   Jonathan Leach, *Rough Sketches of the Life of an Old Soldier* … (London: Longman, Rees, Orme, Brown and Green, 1831), p.197.
49   White, *The Key to Lisbon*, p.178 His name is spelled in two different ways – Krauchenberg and Krauchenburg.
50   Schaumann, *On the Road with Wellington*, p.286.

detachment of the 16th Light Dragoons under Lieutenant Weyland, approaching the French position along the road from Leiria, had taken 30 *dragons* prisoner.[51] Lieutenant William Tomkinson of the 16th Light Dragoons wrote, 'We wounded several, and took a few prisoners, and should have made more, only they were so thick that we could not get into them.'[52] The French perception of this action paints a somewhat different picture, describing the KGL Hussars being thrown back with heavy casualties.[53]

The discordant command structure in the *armée de Portugal* began to cause problems for Ney.[54] Despite appeals from Massena, in writing and in person, Drouet refused to allow Conroux's division to be used by Ney and withdrew IX corps ostensibly to re-establish communications with Spain. Drouet's defence to Massena's accusation of desertion at a critical moment was that he was executing Berthier's orders.[55] As Drouet withdrew towards Miranda do Corvo, Massena wrote to him, 'You have made the decision to leave despite all my appeals to cooperate with the withdrawal. In abandoning us at such a difficult time you will, no doubt, be subject to some self-reproach.'[56] Massena then supposedly addressed Ney with the words: 'Well, Marshal, we will have to make up for an inexcusable abandonment; tomorrow, we will reconnoitre the enemy positions in front of Pombal together and defeat them.'[57] Massena implored Drouet to repair the bridge at Ponte de Mucela. Drouet's reply seems calculated to anger him: 'I cannot at this moment respond to Your Highness positively on this subject, given that his letter requires mature reflection on my part. In any case, I propose to stay tomorrow at Miranda de Corvo, from where I will send you my answer.'[58]

Drouet's intransigence had put Ney in a difficult position: he had been ordered to hold the Allies at Pombal, but now felt he had insufficient forces to do so. He warned that Pombal would have to be evacuated, even though Massena was keen that the rearguard keep the Allied army as far from the main body of the *armée* as possible as it retreated towards Coimbra. Ney wrote to Massena on the 10th, indicating the difficult situation he found himself in.[59] He was aware of the increasing strength of the Allies as their main force closed up with the Light Division. Disagreement escalated between Ney and Massena about the best way to delay the Allies, but being in direct contact with them, Ney was better informed about what was going on. He wrote to Massena, 'Is it with the three brigades that remain to me and not with the entire VI corps that I must hold the position in front or behind Pombal? Yet Count

---

51   Wellington to Liverpool. Villa Secca, 14th March, 1811, Gurwood, *Dispatches,* vol.4, p.664.
52   Tomkinson, *Diary,* p.79.
53   Andre Delagrave, *Campagne de l'Armée Française En Portugal, Dans Les Années 1810 et 1811, Avec Un Précis de Celles Qui l'ont Précédée.* (Paris: Dentu, 1815), pp.167–168.
54   Girod de l'Ain, *Vie Militaire du Général Foy,* p.101.
55   Oudinot, 'Souvenirs', p.27.
56   SHD: Massena à Drouet, le 12 mars 1811. *Armée de Portugal. Correspondance du Maréchal Prince d'Essling, Adressée Aux Généraux Éblé et Reynier Ainsi Qu'au Duc d'Elchingen (1er Janvier-15 Mars 1811),* 1811, 7C11.
57   Oudinot, 'Souvenirs', p.27.
58   Koch, *Mémoires de Massena,* vol.7, p.359.
59   Bonnal, *La Vie Militaire du Maréchal Ney,* vol.3, p.484; SHD: *Correspondance,* 7C12.

d'Erlon leaves at midnight, and therefore I cannot stay any longer in the presence of the enemy.'[60]

Accordingly, he withdrew most of his forces beyond Pombal on the road to Redinha. Mermet's division retired, leaving Maucune's brigade of Marchand's division, comprising three *bataillons* of the 6e légère and three of the 69e ligne, holding Pombal. The 69e ligne, commanded *ad interim* by *colonel* Fririon, and the 6e légère, thus acted as the rear-guard.[61] The 69e was in the town, occupying, '… the avenues, the bridge, and the castle, which, situated on a mountain, served as a remarkable defensive point.'[62] The 6e légère, accompanied by a small unit of artillery and some of the 6e dragons.[63] was posted on the left bank of the river in some woods and walled enclosures.[64]

On the 10th, Wellington wrote:

> The enemy still continue on their ground in front of Pombal, but not, I think, in the strength in which they were yesterday. They are still, however, very strong; and my own opinion is, that they will draw off the corps which they have there in the course of this night. If they do not, I propose to attack them there to-morrow. I think it most likely that they will go back as far as Condeixa, where they will collect their force with more ease than they can at Pombal.[65]

Comprehensive instructions were issued for the attack on Pombal for the afternoon of 11 March. Colonel George Murray, Wellington's Quartermaster General, issued the orders, directing the Light Division to turn the left of the enemy's position, supported by Pack's Brigade, but Pack was not to execute his attack until the turning action by the Light Division began to make progress. The 4th Division was to attack, '… that part of the Enemy's Position which extends along the Coimbra road …'[66] Major General Sir Thomas Picton's 3rd Division was to outflank the town further to the Allied left, supported by Captain Bull's troop of the Royal

60   Koch, *Mémoires de Massena*, vol.7, pp.353–354.
61   Alternatively, Fririon is recorded as being in temporary command of Maucune's brigade. Jules Vassais, *Historique du 69e Régiment d'infanterie (1672-1912)* (Paris: Imhaus, 1913), p.151.
62   Vassais, *Historique du 69e (1672-1912)*, p.151.
63   Pelet records four guns and the 11e Dragons. Ney wrote to Massena that it was one piece of artillery and the 6e Dragons. Pelet, *The French Campaign in Portugal*, p.438; Bonnal, *La Vie Militaire du Maréchal Ney*, vol.3, p.486.
64   Fririon, *Journal Historique*, pp.145–147; Gareth Glover and Robert Burnham, *Riflemen of Wellington's Light Division in the Peninsular War; Unpublished and Rare Memoirs of the 95th Rifles 1808-14* (Barnsley: Frontline Books, 2023), p.105.
65   Wellington to Lieutenant General Spencer, Perucha, 10th March 1810, Gurwood, *Dispatches*, vol.4, p.661.
66   The National Archives (TNA): WO 37/11/24: 'Arrangements for the Attack on the Enemy near Pombal', 11 March 1811, TNA, WO 37/11/24; Arrangements for the attack of the enemy's position beyond Pombal, on the afternoon of the 11th of March, General Sir George Murray, *Memoir Annexed to an Atlas Containing Plans of the Principal Battles, Sieges and Affairs in Which the British Troops Were Engaged During the War in the Spanish Peninsula and the South of France from 1808 to 1814* (London: J Wyld, 1841), pp.43–44.

Horse Artillery. Cavalry patrols from the 14th and 16th Light Dragoons were to be sent out in front of the attacking columns to identify, '… and point out the best fords, in addition to the information which has been already furnished by the people of the country.'[67] The 14th and 16th Light Dragoons would also support the attack. The infantry divisions were to form in two main lines, with a single battalion in a third line as a reserve. 'The Hussars, Royals, and Captain Ross's troop of artillery, will be near the bridge of Pombal, prepared to move forward, when ordered to do so by Sir William Erskine; and the artillery will place itself, as soon as possible, in a situation to cannonade the angle of the enemy's position, and to enfilade the Coimbra road.'[68]

Despite its isolation from the main body of the Allied army, the Light Division pressed the French as they began their withdrawal. The 6e légère, posted in the olive groves outside the town, skirmished with the advancing Allied forces and slowly retreated into the town. The retreat of the 6e légère was accelerated, '… by the arrival of Brigade-Major Mellish, who came up, at the time, with a couple of Ross's guns, and commenced playing upon them.'[69] The French pressed over the bridge, while the, '… batteries greatly inconvenienced [the 6e légère] when crossing the bridge … which is long and narrow.'[70] The 95th Rifles and the 3° Caçadores rushed across the bridge and began to clear the houses.[71] The 6e légère carried out a fighting withdrawal through the town. Captain Kincaid of the 95th wrote, 'Two of our companies, with some Caçadores and a squadron of the royal dragoons, made a dash into it, driving the enemy out, and along with a number of prisoners captured the baggage of young Soult.'[72] Costello recorded that:

> … we had to Sustain at a great disadvantage, a smart fire from the different houses, occupied by the rear guard of the enemy. As soon as we crossed the bridge we took possession of the houses opposite those held by the French, from which we kept up a brisk fire out of the windows. Tired however, with this cross work, several of our men, headed by Lieut. Hopwood, dashed into one of the French holds and found it crowded with the enemy …[73]

Lieutenant Hopwood was seriously injured in the ensuing melee, but some French were taken prisoner whilst the others retreated in the face of the Allied attack. Defending the town, *capitaine* Guingret's unit came under fire:

---

67   Arrangements for the attack, *Memoir Annexed to an Atlas*, pp.43–44.
68   Arrangements for the attack, *Memoir Annexed to un Atlas*, pp.43–44.
69   Costello, *Memoirs*, p.91.
70   Fririon, *Journal Historique*, p.145.
71   Willoughby Verner, *History & Campaigns of the Rifle Brigade* (London: John Bale, 1919), vol.2, p.222.
72   The baggage of *général de brigade* Pierre Benoît Soult is described as being captured at several different skirmishes. John Kincaid, *Random Shots from a Rifleman* (London: Boone, 1847), p.133; Schaumann records the baggage being taken at Sabugal. Schaumann, *On the Road with Wellington*, p.293.
73   Costello, *Memoirs*, p.92.

The 6eme légère, of which I was a part, formed the extreme rearguard: the enemy pushed us vigorously because we had been left a little too far behind the main body: we were caught in the rear and in the flank, for nearly a league, by the fire of their light artillery. I remember that a [shrapnel] shell removed a whole section of my company.[74]

He complained that the French had lost an advantage in their artillery projectiles as they had nothing equivalent to Henry Shrapnel's 'spherical case'. Its effect was also recorded by George Jenkinson of the Royal Artillery, '… annoying their columns of infantry and cavalry with Spherical case …',[75] sending them fleeing in alarm. The casualties were not all one-sided, however. Schaumann recalls Lieutenant Cordemann's detachment of the 1st Hussars, positioned in support of the Light Division, taking casualties from French fire.[76]

As the 6e légère withdrew from Pombal, Ney, mounted on a white horse, rode up and called for them to rally and drive the enemy from the town. 'Chasseurs! You are losing your fine reputation and forever dishonouring yourself if you do not drive the enemy out of Pombal immediately. Come on, let the brave ones follow me!'[77] Fririon instructed the 1e bataillon of the 69e ligne to recapture the castle. The remainder of the 6e légère and another battalion of the 69e penetrated into Pombal, causing some riflemen of the 95th to become separated from their comrades. Costello narrowly avoided capture:

> … when perceiving how few our numbers were, being supported by a single troop only of our German Hussars, they turned round and made it a hard matter for us to escape the consequences of our temerity. Several of the men were out-flanked, and taken prisoners, and for myself, I had to run a great risk, and should certainly have been killed or captured, but for the gallantry of a German dragoon, who riding up, dragged me behind him, and galloped away amidst a volley of shots, unhurt.[78]

The 69e retook the town in a decisive counterattack, pushing the Allied troops out of the town and allowing the remaining troops of Maucune's brigade to break free of contact with the enemy.[79] The French counterattack was corroborated by Tomkinson, who recalled, 'The enemy, seeing we had only one regiment of infantry and the four companies from the 95th up in the town, pushed them back from the furthest part, obliging our troops to shelter themselves in the walls, etc., on this side.'[80]

---

74   Pierre François Guingret, *Relation Historique et Militaire de la Campagne de Portugal, Sous Le Maréchal Massena, Prince d'Essling* (Limoges: Chez Bargeas, 1817), p.139.

75   Major George Jenkinson, RA, quoted in Nick Lipscombe, *Wellington's Guns: The Untold Story of Wellington and His Artillery in the Peninsula and at Waterloo* (Oxford: Osprey, 2013), p.162.

76   Schaumann, *On the Road with Wellington*, p.287.

77   Guingret, *Relation Historique*, pp.140–141.

78   Costello, *Memoirs*, p.93.

79   Henri Charles-Lavauzelle (ed.), *Historique du 69e Régiment d'infanterie*, (Paris: Imprimerie Librairie Militaire, 1887), p.48.

80   Tomkinson, *Diary*, p.80.

The 1st, 3rd, 4th, 5th, and 6th Divisions arrived near Pombal over the course of the evening. Picton wrote:

> ... after a march of above twenty miles, we came up with the rear-guard of the enemy, strongly posted near the town of Pombal; and the third division was ordered to make a movement to the left, to co-operate in a general attack upon the rear-guard : but the fourth division being delayed longer than was calculated, by the badness and narrowness of the roads, it was not carried into execution ...[81]

According to staff officer Captain George Scovell, it was the 3rd Division which was, 'too late on its ground.'[82] A rainstorm overnight served to keep the soldiers of both armies alert to the proximity of the enemy, but without the opportunity to get much rest. Ney finally withdrew his forces overnight, setting fire to the town. The bridge at Pombal was thus intact, allowing an uninterrupted pursuit now that the remaining Allied divisions had caught up with the Light Division.

Following the action at Pombal in which the Portuguese had lost 11 killed, 20 wounded, and one missing,[83] Wellington wrote, 'Upon this occasion Lieut. Col. Elder's battalion of Portuguese Caçadores distinguished themselves.'[84] Oman puts the British losses at six killed and wounded from the 95th.[85] The French losses are more difficult to estimate. Ney reported that the losses were, '... not considerable ...'[86], but there were approximately 50 killed or wounded, mostly from the 6e légère.[87] However, Martinien lists only two officers wounded, neither from the 6e légère or 69e ligne.[88] Writing to Massena late on the 11th, Ney summed up the battle:

> As the enemy continually increased their forces, I had the town set on fire, which forced them to retreat behind the castle and onto the heights to the right of Pombal. I ordered the 1st brigade of the 2nd division to advance and relieve the one that had been engaged in battle all morning, which I am now sending back to Venda do Cruz. [sic][89]

---

81   Philadoze, fifty miles in advance of Coimbra, 24th March 1811 ; and Guarda, 29th. Heaton Bowstead Robinson, *Memoirs of Lieutenant-General Sir Thomas Picton, Including His Correspondence, from Originals in Possession of His Family*, 2nd edn (London: R. Bentley, 1836), vol.2, p.381.

82   TNA: WO 37/7a, George Scovell, *Diary of the Campaigns of 1810-1812. War Office Papers, General Sir George Scovell, Intelligence Branch of Quartermaster General in Spain.* (1812), p.22.

83   Simão José Da Luz Soriano, *Historia Da Guerra Civil E Do Estabelecimento Do Governo Parlamentar Em Portugal*, Segunda Epocha (Lisboa: Imprensa Nacional, 1874), vol.3, pp.355–356.

84   Wellington to Liverpool, Villa Secca, 14th March, 1811, Gurwood, *Dispatches,* vol.4, p.661.

85   Charles Oman, *A History of the Peninsular War: December 1810 to December 1811: Massena's Retreat, Fuentes de Oñoro, Albuera, Tarragona* (London: Greenhill Books, 2004), vol.4, appendix. 6.

86   Bonnal, *La Vie Militaire du Maréchal Ney*, vol.3, p.486.

87   Fririon, *Journal Historique*, p.146.

88   Aristide Martinien, *Tableaux, Par Corps et Par Batailles, Des Officiers Tués et Blessés Pendant Les Guerres de l'Empire (1805-1815)* (Paris, 1899), p.28. Martinien's list only includes officers killed and wounded. .

89   Bonnal, *La Vie Militaire du Maréchal Ney*, vol.3, p.486.

VI corps withdrew a few miles along the Coimbra road in good order, with the rear guard forming up at Venda da Cruz, a little in front of Redinha, to observe the Allied army. Ney, after reporting the events of the day, concluded that he would try to hold the position at Venda da Cruz for as long as possible, '... but I believe that tomorrow the enemy will receive new reinforcements and will force me to retreat to Redinha; However, we will go very slowly and we will fight for every inch of ground.'[90] Massena replied to Ney:

> Redinha is an essential point, and, as we can only abandon it if we know we are unable to put ourselves astride the Mondego, it is important to defend it well : it is not backward that we must place ourselves, but forward; without this, you would be immediately forced back on Condeixa. With the 8th Corps in reserve, it would be necessary for a much superior force to present itself to force us to withdraw to Condeixa.[91]

Orders were issued for the Allied army to advance along the Coimbra road on the 12th with the Light Division as the advanced guard as before. One column, on the left, comprised the 3rd Division with cavalry and Bull's troop RHA in support. The column on the right, comprising the 1st, 4th, and 6th Divisions, would precede the baggage, with the 5th Division bringing up the rear.[92] As the advanced guard moved forward, Venda da Cruz was abandoned by the French rearguard without any significant opposition. Ney wrote to Massena that the Allies' slow pace:

> ... and caution made me believe he feared an ambush; indeed, each time my echelons halted and my artillery fired, the centre column took position while the columns on the flanks continued advancing in an attempt to outflank me. The terrain, being rough and easy to defend, allowed me to hold the enemy from six in the morning until noon, when he began to deploy within cannon range of Redinha.[93]

The Light Dragoons of the 14th and 16th moved with the left column, and Tomkinson noted the arrival of remounts from England. He described the regiments as now being, '... very strong and in good order.'[94] Nightingall's Brigade was keeping II corps under observation at Espinhal, and a troop of the 16th was dispatched to establish communications with him at Venda dos Moinhos via Perucha and Ansião.[95]

---

90   Bonnal, *La Vie Militaire du Maréchal Ney*, vol.3, p.486.
91   Koch, *Mémoires de Massena*, vol.7, p.361.
92   Extracts from the instructions communicated by the Q. M. G., Arrangements for the movement of the army on the 12th March, 1811, Gurwood, *Dispatches*, vol.4, p.663.
93   Bonnal, *La Vie Militaire du Maréchal Ney*, vol.3, p.488.
94   Tomkinson, *Diary*, p.81.
95   The Q.M.G. to Major Gen. Nightingall. Pombal. 12th March, 1811, Gurwood, *Dispatches*, vol.4, p.663.

12 March – Redinha

Having spent a wet night bivouacked on the road between Pombal and Redinha, the Hussars of the KGL pursued the French rearguard, catching up with them in front of Redinha.[96] This was described by Pelet as, '... large village on the left bank of a stream surrounded by ravines.'[97] He judged it very good for defence: the banks of the Anços were steep, and the river over 15 metres wide, making fording it extremely problematic. VI corps took up a position on the high ground on either side of the river, covering the narrow Roman bridge through Redinha. The single bridge across the river was at the end of a defile, and Massena had emphasised to Ney the significance of maintaining control over this position during the ongoing withdrawal of the remaining forces to Coimbra.[98] VI corps remained at Redinha, but according to one of Ney's staff officers, *capitaine* Sprünglin:

> The position was not good, but the Duke of Elchingen had been obliged to occupy it in order to allow the other corps, the artillery, the baggage, and above all the many sick people who were impeding the march of the army, to move away. It was necessary at all costs to delay the march of the English army for a day.[99]

The defile and bridge narrowed to such an extent that the French baggage, artillery and troops could only cross slowly, such that the whole morning was spent moving the long file of sick and baggage through the town and over to the other side of the river.

The rearguard, composed of Marchand's and Mermet's divisions, deployed on the open ground to the south of the town, occupying a slight rise, facing the Allied advance. Marchand's division was subsequently withdrawn from in front of Redinha and placed on the opposite bank to provide cover for the withdrawal of Mermet's troops. Mermet was supported by six guns of the artillerie légère (Bonnal and Oudinot record it as 14 guns) and cavalry from the 3e hussards, commanded by *colonel* Levesque, comte de la Ferrière, and the 6e and 11e dragons.[100] The 27e and the 59e ligne were placed on the French left, while the 25e légère and the 50e ligne formed the right; the cavalry was also formed towards the right. Loison's division was at Rabaçal but was later moved to Fonte Coberta, and with the VIII corps at Condeixa, could provide support to Ney's forces.

The advance by the Allied forces took place over gently undulating and relatively open ground to the south-west of the bridge, described by Kincaid as a, '... table land in front of the town in the most imposing shape.'[101] Captain Fergusson of the

96   Schaumann, *On the Road with Wellington*, p.287.
97   Pelet, *The French Campaign in Portugal*, p.211.
98   Bonnal, *La Vie Militaire du Maréchal Ney*, vol.3, p.487.
99   Emmanuel Frédéric Sprünglin, 'Souvenirs d'Emmanuel-Frédéric Sprünglin, Publiés Par G. Desdevises du Dezert', *Revue Hispanique*, 1904, p.467.
100 Bonnal, *La Vie Militaire du Maréchal Ney*, vol.3, p.489; Sprünglin, 'Souvenirs', p.467.
101 Kincaid, *Random Shots from a Rifleman*, p.135.

The Bridge at Redinha – The hills behind the village were those upon which Marchand's troops were posted.

43rd Foot described it as, '… an open plain surrounded with wood'.[102] The wooded terrain restricted the space available for the deployment of Wellington's forces in the style he wanted, and he was required to wait until the French were pushed back sufficiently to bring the troops into line. The Allied advance did not necessarily proceed as smoothly as might be expected. As the French rear guard fell back to Redinha, the Light and 5th Divisions, '… with some difficulty … drove them from the wood on the left of the Road, whilst the 3rd with General Pack's [Brigade] succeeded in the same way on the Right. The Enemy still occupied the plain and seemed determined to resist.'[103] Lieutenant Harry Smith of the 95th described how:

> The Light Companies of the 3rd Division came up. I asked, 'Are you going to attack that wood?' A Captain of the 88th Light Company, whom I knew, quite laughed at my question. I said very quietly, 'You will be beat back, and when you are, I will move on the edge of the wood and help you.' How he laughed. My prediction was very soon verified: he was wounded, and picked up by my company, which I moved to the right flank of the French and stopped them immediately.[104]

Pushing the enemy rearguard back across the plain allowed space for the main body of the Allied army to be formed into the required battle order. Despite Wellington's

102   Gareth Glover and Robert Burnham, *The Men of Wellington's Light Division: Unpublished Memoirs From the 43rd Light Infantry in the Peninsular War* (Barnsley: Frontline Books, 2022), p.77.
103   TNA: WO 37/7a, Scovell, *Diary*, p.23.
104   G.C. Moore Smith (ed.), *The Autobiography of Lieutenant-General Sir Harry Smith Baronet of Aliwal on the Sutlej G.C.B* (London: Murray, 1903), p.42.

reputation as a careful general, the plan for the attack at Redinha was unsophisticated but practical. Aware that Loison's division was currently in the vicinity of Rabaçal and could threaten his right flank, he was understandably cautious about bringing on a general action. He formed his army into three separate columns with each of the divisions formed in two lines. The Light Division formed the left, with the 3rd Division established at the edge of a wood on the right of the line, accompanied by Captain Bull's troop RHA, with the cavalry following the division. The 3rd was to move around the French left via Charneca to threaten their left flank and line of retreat. The 4th Division under Major General Sir Lowry Cole was formed in the centre. Pack's Brigade was to occupy the wooded heights to the right of the road, maintaining communications between the 3rd Division and the 4th.[105] In the rear were the 1st, 5th, and 6th Divisions forming the reserve. The general advance was led by Lieutenant General Spencer.[106] Forming the lines took time once the battalions had moved up, and Wellington did not order the advance until the reserve divisions were in place. The 95th, skirmishing in front of the advancing Allied line, was split into two wings approximately along the line of the road. The left was commanded by Major Stewart, the right by Major Gilmore.[107] French artillery opened fire on the advancing Allied line, causing casualties, but did not hinder progress.

Ney has been criticised for withdrawing Marchand's division across the river before it was necessary, and several French authors have described how this prompted the Allied advance.[108] However, it is clear from the orders issued to the Allied army that the attack was going to take place regardless of the French dispositions. The objective was to move the 3rd Division behind the French position, aiming to cut the road to Condeixa-a-Nova and isolate Ney's forces. Picton wrote, 'The third division was ordered to march to the right, through difficult woods, to attack the left of the enemy's position'.[109] He makes the point in the same letter that the enemy, '… retreated across the river by a bridge with which, unfortunately, we were not acquainted.'[110] This would indicate poor reconnaissance by the Allied army, a lack of good maps of the region, or a want of communication between Wellington and Picton. Wellington was provided with very good maps of the region, and the army had retreated over the same road the previous year. The conclusion is probably that Picton did not receive, or was not sent, information about the position the French occupied. Observing that Wellington's progress was gradual and deliberate, Ney manoeuvred his forces in a careful withdrawal in the face of the Allied advance. He wrote to Massena that the Allied manoeuvres, '… took place before my eyes with unimaginable slowness'.[111]

105 TNA: WO 37/11/25, 'Original Orders (in Pencil) by Sir George Murray for the Attack at Redinha', 12 March 1811.
106 Wellington to Liverpool. Villa Secca, 14th March, 1811, Gurwood, *Dispatches*, vol.4, p.666.
107 Verner, *History & Campaigns of the Rifle Brigade*, vol.2, p.224.
108 Koch, *Mémoires de Massena*, vol.7, p.364; Oudinot, 'Souvenirs', p.28.
109 Philadoze, fifty miles in advance of Coimbra, 24th March 1811 ; and Guarda, 29th. Robinson, *Picton*, vol.2, p.382.
110 Robinson, *Picton*, vol.2, p.382.
111 Bonnal, *La Vie Militaire du Maréchal Ney*, vol.3, p.489.

The flags of each of Mermet's regiments were placed at points over the river to indicate the positions to be taken by each battalion once across. Aware that the Light and 3rd Divisions were advancing around his flanks, Ney began to extract Mermet's division through the town and onto the heights above. At a given signal, each battalion was to move quickly, covered by the guns of Marchand's division. Fririon described it thus: 'Mermet performed his retreat in echelons in the greatest order, stopping the enemy with platoon, battalion and cannon fire. He carried out a bayonet charge … and moved through the defile without disarray.'[112] Lieutenant Cox of the 95th wrote, with something akin to admiration, how the French broke from contact, '… by retreating in battalions from the right.'[113] Smith described how, '… no rearguard was ever drawn off in more masterly style, while I thought our attack in lines was heavy [and] slow'.[114]

Despite this initially orderly withdrawal, the manoeuvre soon descended into disorder as the French pressed over the bridge and retreated through the town. Costello wrote:

> I remember to have seen one of the finest views of the two armies I ever witnessed. The rifles were extended in the distance for perhaps two miles, and rapidly on the advance to the enemy's position. These were followed by our heavy columns, whose heads were just emerging from a wood about a quarter of a mile in our rear. Everything seemed conducted with the order and regularity of a field day. Meanwhile the rear columns of the French were slowly retiring, but in a few minutes the scene became exceedingly animated by our artillery opening their fire upon the retreating forces … The enemy, however, although they slowly retired, continually turned, making temporary stands, whenever the ground seemed favourable.[115]

One battalion each of the 27e and 50e ligne were noted by Guingret as performing one of these temporary stands, covering the retreat of some guns in the face of a determined Allied attack.[116] This particular stand was intended to allow a battery of artillerie légère to withdraw from its vulnerable position in front of Redinha. Prompted by Ney, *général de brigade* Charbonnel, commander of the artillery of VI corps, had to order his overly eager officers to move as many guns back as possible. *Adjudant-commandant* Béchet, ADC to *maréchal* Ney, described how Ney, fearing the guns might be captured, shouted to Charbonnel, 'Eh, damn it, General, what is your artillery doing?' but then added, 'Ah! Sorry, General, I lost my temper.'[117] Ney ordered his infantry and cavalry to allow the artillery to withdraw across the narrow bridge. The stand by the 27e and 50e was accompanied by determined resistance from the light cavalry. The 3e hussars fought bravely against the oncoming Allied

112 Fririon, *Journal Historique*, p.147.
113 Glover and Burnham, *Riflemen of Wellington's Light Division*, p.105.
114 Smith, *Autobiography*, p.42.
115 Costello, *Memoirs*, p.94.
116 Guingret, *Relation Historique*, p.146; Pelet, *The French Campaign in Portugal*, p.445.
117 Béchet, *Souvenirs*, p.364.

troops to enable the withdrawal over the bridge to take place: four officers of the 3e are recorded as being wounded. The leaders of Ney's rear guard were fighting in the front line, in the tradition of French arms. *Colonel* Laférière-Levêque of the 3e hussards was seriously wounded in the left hand and the right arm.[118] However, this officer appears in a dispatch from *maréchal* Ney as receiving these wounds at Casal Novo on the 14th.[119]

Wellington observed the Allied skirmishers crossing the bridge with the enemy, and Lieutenant Simmons of the 95th recalls that the final retreat of the French over the bridge was followed so closely by the Allied light troops, '… the bridge was completely blocked up, numbers fell over its battlements, and others were bayoneted; in fact, we entered pell-mell with them.'[120] The French fugitives retreated through the town, with the Allied light infantry pursuing and mixed in.[121] The description of the French retreat as being chaotic is at odds with that provided by French observers and participants in the fighting, who all report that the retreat was undertaken in good order with little or no panic. Marchand's division, in position on the right bank of the river, was well placed to cover the retreat of Mermet's troops, however it was conducted. As the French retreated, the town was put to the torch, with both sides suffering from the heat from burning buildings. As the town began to clear of enemy forces, Wellington dispatched the 3rd Division across the bridge and ford under fire from the French guns positioned on the heights above the village.

Wellington ensured that he had sufficient numbers of troops across the bridge and formed up before advancing on Marchand's position. Picton's men again threatened the French left, while the light infantry from his division, commanded by Lieutenant Colonel William Williams of the 5/60th Rifles, along with the 4° Caçadores under *Coronel* do Rego, pushed the French back.[122] The Light Division again moved to the left, with the 5th Division and Pack in the centre. Picton sent Colville's Brigade forward to attempt to ford the river upstream of Redinha, but found it too deep and rapid.[123] Ney considered that he had held the Allies for long enough and began to pull his troops back. Some Allied soldiers who had been taken prisoner at Pombal the day before were released from captivity when the village was occupied. Following this combat, the 50e and 59e received acclaim from Ney: '… it is impossible to fight with more vigour and to manoeuvre with greater composure and precision before the enemy.'[124] Ney also mentioned that, 'The captains (of artillery) Graillât, Coquart, and Binner deserve the highest praises and rewards … it was with

118 Martinien, *Tableaux Des Officiers*, p.618; Oudinot, 'Souvenirs', p.29.
119 Bonnal, *La Vie Militaire du Maréchal Ney*, vol.3, p.500. No officer appears as commanding the 3e in the *situation*.
120 Wellington to Liverpool, Villa Secca, 14th March 1811, Gurwood, *Dispatches*, vol.4, p.667; George Simmons, Willoughby Verner (ed.), *A British Rifle Man* (London: A. & C. Black, 1899), pp.140–141.
121 John Kincaid, *Adventures in the Rifle Brigade, in the Peninsula, France and the Netherlands from 1809 to 1815*, 3rd edn (London: Boone, 1847), p.52.
122 Wellington to Liverpool. Villa Secca, 14th March, 1811, Gurwood, *Dispatches*, vol.4, p.667.
123 Robinson, *Picton*, vol.2, p.382.
124 Rapport au Marechal Massena, prince d'Essling, Refança, 12th March 1811, Girod de l'Ain, *Vie Militaire du Général Foy*, pp.488–492.

the greatest difficulty that I could extract these brave officers from amidst the skirmishers, and they withdrew, at a steady pace, under the protection of the infantry.'[125]

The Allied army pursued the French until nightfall. The chase was limited by the speed with which the cavalry could be moved across the bridge at Redinha.[126] Scovell explains that a delay in pursuing the French was also experienced as, 'Some difficulty was found in getting the Guns across the Ford'.[127] Despite this, Captain Leach of the 95th recollected, 'No respite was allowed them; and the Light Division, with some cavalry, stuck close to their heels until night.'[128] The 6th Division marched in the evening to Soure, accompanied by one squadron of dragoons.[129] The French rear guard withdrew, Mermet's division taking up a position in front of Arrifana and that of General Marchand remaining at Presa.

Several stories of near misses in combat are recorded from Redinha. Wellington, on a reconnaissance during the battle, was escorted by 24 Hussars of the King's German Legion. He seemed immune to the fire of the French, but the hussars were unfortunate in losing several horses.[130] Major Charles Napier of the 50th, chatting to a Mr Winterbottom, resting his hand on the pommel of his friend's horse, had a cannon ball pass between the two men. Although neither was hit directly, Napier's friend was grazed across his leg and was hospitalised for several months.[131] A close call also happened to Simmons. He and Lieutenant Kincaid moved through a gap in a hedge, followed by a Portuguese grenadier. As they descended from the hedge, the grenadier was hit squarely in his body by a cannon ball. Simmons wrote, 'Very likely during the day a person might have a thousand much more narrow escapes of being made acquainted with the grand secret, but seeing the mangled body of a brave fellow so shockingly mutilated in an instant, stamps such impressions upon one's mind in a manner that time can never efface.'[132] There were to be many who became acquainted with the grand secret in the coming days and weeks.

125 Bonnal, *La Vie Militaire du Maréchal Ney*, vol.3, p.491.
126 Schaumann, *On the Road with Wellington*, p.288.
127 TNA: WO 37/7a, Scovell, *Diary*, p.22.
128 Leach, *Rough Sketches of the Life of an Old Soldier*, p.198.
129 Tomkinson, *Diary*, p.82.
130 Schaumann, *On the Road with Wellington*, p.288.
131 George Napier, William Napier (ed.), *Passages in the Early Military Life of General Sir George T. Napier, K.C.B.* (London: Murray, 1884), p.178.
132 Simmons, *A British Rifle Man*, p.141.

3

The Bridge at Coimbra

Coimbra

Général de division Montbrun had been sent north to establish a crossing of the Mondego at Coimbra, but was facing significant difficulties in the attempt. With Montbrun was *colonel* Valazé, *capitaine* Beaufort, the 15e and 25e dragons and three companies of *sapeurs*.[1] Montbrun's forces appeared in the afternoon of the 11th at Santa Clara near the Convento São Francisco. They found the main stone bridge at Coimbra had one arch destroyed, leaving a gap of some 40 feet, and another damaged. Montbrun sent cavalry west to reconnoitre the river out to Vila Nova de Anços and up to Pereira. A detachment of *dragons* attempted to cross the river at the ford at Pereira. *Général de division* Lazowski was ordered to build a trestle bridge below Coimbra if it was possible; however, the river was in flood, which meant that no fords would be passable and temporary bridges would be unable to withstand the current.

Coronel Trant occupied Coimbra, but had issued orders to evacuate the city, the militia being no match for veteran French regulars. Trant had set out northwards for the Vouga River on the night of 12/13 March. Wellington had indeed expected him to retreat in the face of Montbrun's approach.[2] Nevertheless, Trant had left a small detachment of infantry and artillery in Coimbra to make a show of defending the bridge. Further upstream on the Mondego, *Coronel* Wilson's militia was positioned at the confluence with the Alva near Penacova with 1,200 men to prevent French foragers from making incursions along the Mondego's banks. As with Trant, Wilson withdrew his militia towards the Vouga.

Given time and no interruptions, the *sapeurs* could have patched up the bridge, but the rearguard of Trant's militia was making very visible demonstrations in the area and could threaten the *sapeurs* if they tried to carry out the necessary repairs. Another option was to try downstream around Pereira. There, the river split into four branches separated by three islands. Valazé considered access over the first three was viable, but the fourth would need bridging. Koch observed, 'It would be easy to construct a bridge with 10 trestles, as there was no shortage of wood in Pereira. Therefore, to cross the Mondego, only one bridge was needed, which would

1   Pelet, *The French Campaign in Portugal*, p.437.
2   Wellington to Gen. Bacellar. Thomar, 8th March, 1811, Gurwood, *Dispatches,* vol.4, p.657.

require 36 hours of work.'[3] The true situation, however, was that Montbrun feared any attempt to build a bridge at Periera would receive a similar reaction from Trant as would repairing the bridge at Coimbra.

One source records that during the afternoon of the 12th, there was intense but indiscriminate firing from Coimbra which lasted until the early hours of the 13th.[4] Around eight o'clock in the morning of the 13th, a French representative presented himself at the bridge with a letter from Montbrun to the Governor of Coimbra, requesting the surrender of the city. Montbrun promised not to assault the city if there was no resistance. *Sargento* José Augusto Correia, commander of the artillery detachment in Coimbra, replied that his general was out of Coimbra at that time performing an inspection and would not return until the following day. Only then would it be possible to give an answer to so important a question.[5] Correia also threatened that if the French were to try to force the bridge, he had orders to blow it up. Montbrun believed his forces were too weak to force a crossing against what he thought was the whole of Trant's militia. He knew that the delay of a full day would be too late. *Sargento* Correia, knowing he had only a small force, was bravely prepared to bluff for as long as possible.

The river was in spate, meaning existing fords would be almost impossible to use until the river level dropped, which would also scupper Valazé's plan for a bridge. After delaying on the left bank, Montbrun had so far been unable to gain a crossing. If the situation continued, this would lead to a significant upsetting of Massena's plans. The original plan to take up positions on the right bank of the Mondego, in relatively fertile countryside, would be beyond reach. The only alternative was to march the *armée de Portugal* along the left bank towards Celorico and the Spanish frontier. However, this required secure river crossings at Foz de Arouce and Ponte da Mucela, amongst others. Massena received a letter from Drouet, informing him that he had successfully taken control of the latter bridge. He reported that the bridge had been damaged, but he had his troops cross the river using a ford while the bridge was being repaired. This was a critical moment. If Massena delayed for too long, and there was no available crossing point over the Mondego, Wellington could interpose his army between the *armée de Portugal* and their withdrawal route. The urgency behind these manoeuvres was aimed at preventing the *armée de Portugal* from being trapped against the Mondego and the Alva. If he were to face the approaching Allied army with no secure line of retreat, Massena could be forced to surrender his army or face defeat on the battlefield.

Massena made the decision to keep his options open for as long as possible. Condeixa was the key to giving Massena his choices. If Ney could hold at Condeixa, this might allow Montbrun to push a bridge across the Mondego around Pereira, water level permitting, or capture and repair the main bridge at Coimbra. VIII and II corps, along with one division of IX corps, could cover the alternative route through Miranda do Corvo, and be able to move northwards to cross the Mondego if Ney's action and Montbrun's activities were successful. However, Montbrun's failure to

3   Koch, *Mémoires de Massena*, vol.7, p.367.
4   Soriano, *Historia Da Guerra Civil*, vol.3, p.360.
5   Soriano, *Historia Da Guerra Civil*, vol.3, pp.360–361.

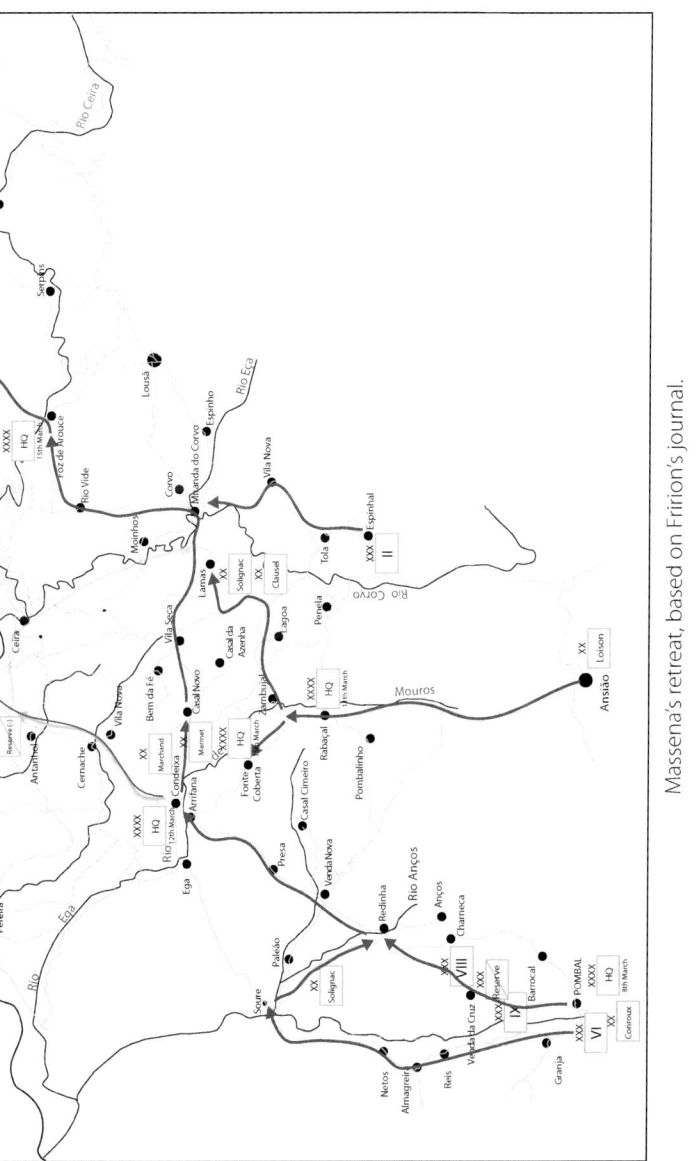

Massena's retreat, based on Fririon's journal.

secure a crossing of the Mondego would put paid to Massena's preferred option. He thus would have no alternative but to move the army eastwards. Nonetheless, the retreating French would need to cross the Corvo (also known as the Dueça) and Ceira before reaching the Alva at Ponte da Mucela. Crossing the River Alva in time was crucial for Massena's forces to avoid being cut off. The successful crossing would enable the French to continue their withdrawal, with an almost direct route back to Celorico. The army would then retreat between that river to its right and Mondego to the left. The terrain beyond the Alva rose into the Serra d'Estrela and would be unsuitable for wheeled transport and cavalry. This funnelled the French retreat towards Celorico along one or two usable roads.

Ney received orders from Massena on the evening of the 12th that he should try to hold the enemy at Condeixa for at least 24 hours to allow crossings over the Mondego and Alva to be established.[6] Massena flattered Ney's record of defeating his enemies, invoking the defeat of the Prussian army at Jena, and bullying him by saying that VI corps had suffered little on the retreat. He finished by reassuring Ney, 'Hold for 24 hours, and we will have bridges at Coimbra and on the Alva. Solignac's division will be in reserve two kilometres behind Condeixa; your left flank is covered by Loison, Clausel, and Reynier. Count d'Erlon will remain tomorrow at Miranda de Corvo, and you will defeat Wellington.'[7]

Pelet was under the impression that Ney had agreed to hold Condeixa for two days. Discussions took place between Pelet, Ney, Massena and Béchet about the risks of holding the position, and Ney's fears of being outflanked via Fonte Coberta. But the description of the situation at Condeixa is enlightening. Pelet wrote, '... all Condeixa was full of artillery, baggage, herds, commissariat, sick, and the regiments. There was terrible confusion, but no remedy at first because of our uncertainty about the direction to follow, the perilous roads, and then because of the nature of the terrain surrounding Condeixa.'[8]

But orders issued later in the day seem to indicate that the decision to withdraw eastwards had already been taken. Massena wrote, 'Maréchal, we have agreed to hold the position in front of Condeixa as long as possible, and throughout the entire day tomorrow if feasible ... P.S. — It is crucial that we hold in front of Condeixa all day tomorrow to give our baggage time to proceed towards Miranda de Corvo.'[9]

The baggage was indeed on its way to Miranda do Corvo. Montbrun had concluded that his objective was unattainable. While Massena's orders to Ney were being issued, a new rearguard was constituted under the command of *général de division* Ferey, who had been newly promoted from Loison's division. This consisted of Labassée's brigade of the 25e légère and 27e ligne, the 39e ligne from Marcognet's brigade, the 3e hussards and *capitaine* Binner's 5e companie, 2e artillerie à cheval.[10]

6   Koch, *Mémoires de Massena*, vol.7, p.369.
7   Koch, *Mémoires de Massena*, vol.7, p.369.
8   Pelet, *The French Campaign in Portugal*, p.448.
9   Masséna au Ney, 12 mars, 8 heures du soir, de Condeixa. Bonnal, *La Vie Militaire du Maréchal Ney*, vol.3, p.496.
10   Bonnal, *La Vie Militaire du Maréchal Ney*, vol.3, p.495.

Condeixa – 13 March

Allied patrols ranged ahead of the army to Rabaçal and Condeixa, looking for the main body of the *armée de Portugal*. Summing up the situation presented to him on 13 March, Wellington wrote:

> We found the whole [French] army … with the exception of the 2d corps, which was still at Espinhal, in a very strong position, at Condeiza; [sic] I observed that they were sending off their baggage by the road of Ponte da Murcella. [sic] From this circumstance I concluded that Col. Trant had not given up Coimbra, and that they had been so pressed in their retreat, that they had not been able to detach troops to force him from that place.[11]

Wellington had instructed his commanders, 'If the enemy is found in position at Condeixa, or at any other point during the march, an operation for dislodging him will be combined by the two columns of the army'.[12] The 6th Division under Major General Campbell would approach Condeixa along the Soure road, whilst the balance of the army would move forward from Redinha. As Wellington had seemed to anticipate, the French rearguard was indeed in position along the low ridges in front of Condeixa.

In preparation for the expected Allied attack, Ney issued orders for Mermet's division to take up position on the heights to the left of the road leading to Condeixa. Trelliard's division of *dragons* and *capitaine* Grailla's 5e companie, 5e régiment à pied would support Mermet. Marchand's division was positioned to the right of Mermet with its right on the town. Ferey was positioned in front so as to cover the other divisions of VI corps.[13] Loison was near Póvoa de Pegas and Fonte Coberta escorting the artillery of VI and VIII corps, but also protecting Ney's left flank. Guingret described the French position at Condeixa:

> Piles of wood were placed on the main road and set on fire as the English approached; further back, large trees had been felled to form barricades. Our troops were arranged to make the most advantageous use of the terrain, which was already highly favourable to us due to its configuration. In short, we prepared to resist the enemy should they come at us.[14]

As VIII corps withdrew along the road to Miranda do Corvo, it was visible to the advancing Allies. Wellington understood the strength of the French deployment but saw an opportunity to cut off the rearguard. This would also remove the necessity of attacking the well-defended position at Condeixa. Picton's 3rd Division, supported by the 5th, was to move on the French left and would aim to cut off their retreat

11   Wellington to Liverpool. Villa Secca, 14th March, 1811, Gurwood, *Dispatches*, vol.4, p.667.
12   Redinha, 12th March, 1811, Gurwood, *Dispatches*, vol.4, p.663.
13   Sprünglin, 'Souvenirs', p.469.
14   Guingret, *Relation Historique*, p.151.

along the road through Casal Novo to Chão de Lamas,[15] along which the baggage of the *armée de Portugal* could already be seen moving.

The 3rd Division was to establish observation posts on the high ground to the south-east of Condeixa to keep a watch on the retreating French and also to secure the right flank of the Allied Army against any threat that might develop from the French forces. If Picton could reach the Casal Novo road before Ney withdrew his corps he could block the only route through the valley that could serve as an escape route for Ney. The Light Division and Pack's Brigade would attack to the left of the 3rd, and the 6th Division would move to turn the French right. A strong screen of skirmishers would provide cover for the Light Division as it negotiated some difficult terrain to its front. The 4th Division would connect the Light Division with the 6th. The infantry would have cavalry support along the width of the attacking line, with artillery placed on the heights and able to fire at the French on the opposite side of the valley.[16] Picton described the actions of the 3rd Division in a letter to Colonel Pleydel,

> … the third division made a forced march over a tract of difficult rocky mountains, to make a demonstration in the rear of the enemy's left flank; which had the desired effect, as they immediately abandoned the position with considerable precipitation, and fell back several miles. The division crossed the river at an extremely difficult pass the same evening, and took up a position within a mile of the enemy's rear-posts.[17]

Ney wrote to Massena around 5:00 p.m., warning that a strong Allied force was going to cut him off if he did nothing and would therefore be withdrawing.[18] Massena's concern regarding the enemy's movements was evident in his message to Ney late in the afternoon of the 13th. He wrote, 'Marshal, you have not yet told me what the enemy is doing. Don't forget that I'm in Ponte Cuberta [sic]. You order movements without telling me. It is necessary that you hold the position at Condeixa to give our baggage time to withdraw'.[19] Ney was troubled; he had learned that Montbrun was marching on Miranda do Corvo and that Trant's forces, freed from the threat of action, were manoeuvring on Ponte da Mucela.[20] Montbrun's movements would leave VI corps exposed to the militia forces to the north. When he saw the Allied forces begin their outflanking manoeuvre to his southeast, he decided to withdraw immediately, otherwise his Corps could be caught in a trap and surrounded. Guingret expressed his concern, and then relief, at the position of VI corps:

---

15   Casal Novo is marked on some modern maps as Beiçudo.
16   Disposition for the attack of the enemy at Condeixa on the 13th of March, 1811. Murray, *Memoir Annexed to an Atlas*, p.47.
17   Picton to Colonel Pleydel, Philadoze, fifty miles in advance of Coimbra, 24th March 1811 ; and Guarda, 29th. Robinson, *Picton*, vol.2, p.381.
18   Bonnal, *La Vie Militaire du Maréchal Ney*, vol.3, p.497.
19   Fonte Cuberta, le 13 mars 1811. Bonnal, *La Vie Militaire du Maréchal Ney*, vol.3, p.497.
20   Bonnal, *La Vie Militaire du Maréchal Ney*, vol.3, pp.500–501.

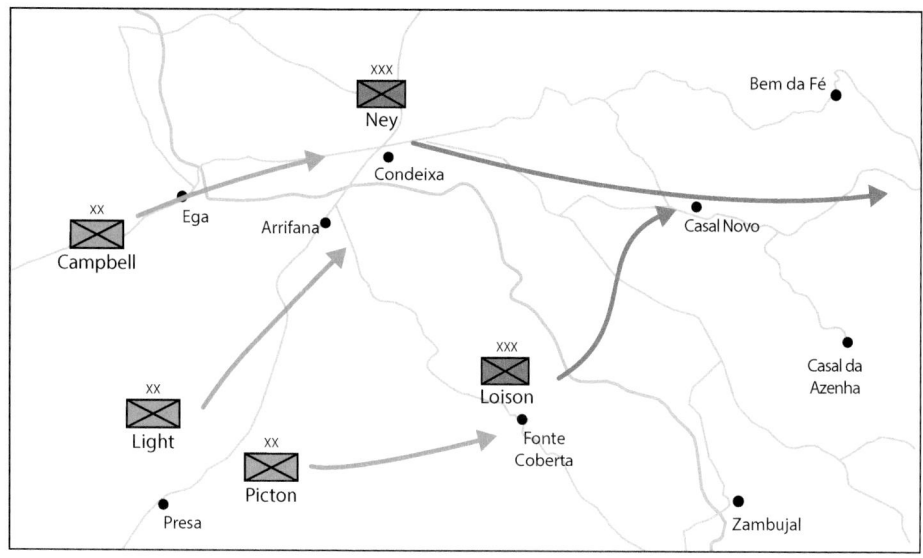

Manoeuvres around Condeixa.

In the evening, we took up position a league and a half from La Condeixa, on favourable heights ... I had been oppressed by a strong apprehension lest the enemy take better advantage of the circumstances ... for the first time, it seemed to me that we could only choose between death and captivity, if a less slow enemy had attacked us vigorously. Such had been our situation during the morning: it had required all the composure of our leaders, and the most prompt determination, to successfully free the army.[21]

Ney sent a message to Massena at approximately 6:00 p.m.: 'I am evacuating Condeixa; the enemy is manoeuvring on my left and directing a strong column towards Fonte Coberta.'[22] Guingret recalled the conditions of the retreat: 'The roads were continually clogged with baggage and pack animals; Most companies had up to twenty mules or donkeys following them, to drag their crews, their sick and their provisions.'[23]

Condeixa was put to the torch as the French withdrew; Ney ordered his troops to set fire to the last houses of Condeixa as he saw the head of Picton's column threatening his left flank. He told a hesitant *chef de bataillon* Girard, who was charged with setting the fire, 'What do you want? Everything is painful in war. I had to burn this town or lose the army. From two evils, I chose the least. I challenge Wellington, now, to risk his caissons through the fire.'[24] The blaze forced the advancing Allied troops to create a path through the stone walls of the town to avoid the flames from

---

21   Guingret, *Relation Historique*, pp.155–156.
22   Oudinot, 'Souvenirs', p.30.
23   Guingret, *Relation Historique*, p.157.
24   Quoted in Natalia Griffon de Pleineville, 'Les Derniers Combats d'arrière-Garde', *Gloire & Empire*, 70 (2017), p.33.

the burning buildings. As the troops waited for a path to be cleared, some were involved in rescuing the inhabitants, with one soldier throwing civilians bodily over a wall to save them from danger.[25] Scovell records that towards evening, the army moved up to Condeixa and the Light Division pushed through the town onto the routes taken by the French rearguard.[26]

Massena replied to Ney's withdrawal by writing to the *maréchal*:

> I have just received your note, informing me that you have evacuated Condeixa. I am very angry to hear this. I am unsure if our baggage will have enough time to move to Miranda de Corvo. Moreover, the most troubling aspect of this situation is that General Montbrun, retreating before Coimbra, will signal Trant and Sylveira [sic] to move towards the bridge at Murcella. [sic] The burning of Condeixa is another unfortunate event, as it will cast a negative light on the French army.
>
> The divisions of the 8th corps will depart early on the 14th to take positions in front of and behind Miranda; they will be preceded by Loison's division, which will then return under Marshal Ney's command.
>
> He will need to position his troops two leagues ahead of Miranda to hold the line all day on the 14th, to give the baggage time to move towards Foz d'Aronce [sic].[27]

As Ney began his retreat from Condeixa, Massena and his staff were sitting down to eat in the small hamlet of Fonte Coberta. *Chef de bataillon* Girbault was instructed to take four dragoons and reconnoitre the surrounding heights to ascertain if VI corps was still in position at Condeixa. Disturbingly for Massena Allied cavalry patrols could be seen on the road to Miranda do Corvo, along which the French would have to retreat. However, Girbault's small force met a squadron of the 1st KGL Hussars and was chased back to Fonte Coberta, with Girbault calling 'To Arms!' The Allied cavalry, wisely, on seeing Loison's division, beat a rapid retreat. Noël recalls, 'At about six in the evening, English [sic] cavalry had surprised and sabred several dragoons; general headquarters was promptly evacuated.'[28] This may have been the reconnaissance of, '… some mountains on our right …' mentioned by Scovell.[29] After such a close call, Massena decided to push on for Miranda do Corvo as quickly as possible. The tail of the rearguard of VI corps, which itself formed the rearguard of the army, was composed of four companies of voltigeurs and 30 troopers of the 3e hussards under the command of Sprünglin.[30] This small force observed the Allies' movement as Clausel's and Solignac's divisions, along with the headquarters, were assembled and marched that night to Miranda do Corvo.

---

25   Costello, *Memoirs*, pp.99–100.
26   TNA: WO 37/7a, Scovell, *Diary*, p.24.
27   Fonte Cuberta, le 13 mars. 1811. Bonnal, *La Vie Militaire du Maréchal Ney*, vol.3, pp.497–498.
28   Noël, *With Napoleon's Guns*, p.114.
29   TNA: WO 37/7a, Scovell, *Diary*, p.23.
30   Sprünglin, 'Souvenirs', p.470.

These events led Massena to accuse Ney of trying to get him captured by abandoning Condeixa without warning. The bad feeling between Massena and Ney, amplified by the withdrawal, now surfaced in the most problematic way. Rumour spread in the army that Ney had deliberately abandoned Condeixa to force Massena to discard the idea of crossing the Mondego at Coimbra and impose a retreat along the left bank of the river back to Spain.[31] Some French authors have perpetuated this story.[32] However, there appears to be no evidence to support either of these accusations against Ney. His actions seem reasonable from a military perspective, regardless of whether his personal feelings towards Massena had deteriorated. Had Ney not moved with the swiftness he did, he certainly risked being surrounded. Although messages were sent to Massena, the rapid pace of events meant that they were not always received in time. Despite Ney's explanation and the plan of attack implemented by Wellington, the ever-loyal Pelet denied that VI corps was in any danger of being outflanked. However, the movement of the 3rd Division clearly threatened the routes from Condeixa to Casal Novo and Fonte Coberta. Wellington's plan of attack would have pinned Ney against Condeixa whilst cutting these roads. Montbrun had failed to secure a crossing of the Mondego, and had VI corps been forced to fight a longer holding action against the whole Allied army, the result would have been disaster for Ney, and possibly the whole *armée de Portugal*.

Both Guingret and Pelet reproached Wellington for manoeuvring the French from their positions rather than attacking with more aggression. This criticism is understandable from a French perspective. French doctrine under Napoleon was very much one of aggressive manoeuvring and the destruction of the enemy's main army. Wellington's approach, which was far more cautious, fitted into the overall Allied strategy of husbanding its forces, especially Britain's main field army. However, those in the British Army also criticised Wellington's attacking style. Harry Smith wrote, 'I thought our attack in lines was heavy, slow, and not half so destructive as a rush of many contiguous columns would have been.'[33]

Ney's withdrawal from Condeixa also posed a threat to Montbrun's retreat from Coimbra. When Montbrun received the news of Ney's departure from Condeixa, he realised that the bridge over the Mondego was no longer part of Massena's plan. The only route available for Montbrun to return to the army was a demanding path that led to Miranda do Corvo. After destroying several wagons and caissons and being pursued by Allied cavalry patrols, Montbrun eventually guided his division of cavalry, horse artillery, and infantry to relative safety at Chão de Lamas.[34]

As Wellington established communication with the Portuguese militia in Coimbra, he understood that Massena now had no choice but to retreat north-eastwards towards Celorico.[35] The Allied advanced guard also kept contact with the retreating French. Kincaid described the night of 13/14 March: 'We lay by our arms

---

31   Noël, *With Napoleon's Guns*, p.115.
32   Koch, *Mémoires de Massena*, vol.7, p.368.
33   Smith, *Autobiography*, p.42.
34   Koch, *Mémoires de Massena*, vol.7, p.376.
35   Wellington to Liverpool. Villa Secca, 14th March, 1811, Gurwood, *Dispatches*, vol.4, p.667.

until towards evening, when the enemy withdrew to Casal Nova, [sic] and we closed up to them. There was continued popping between advanced posts all night.'[36]

Casal Novo – 14 March

On the road from Condeixa to Miranda do Corvo stands Casal Novo. To the west of Casal Novo, the ground is open, but the road proceeds into a valley as it moves eastwards. The road, as described by Sprünglin, ran, '… for more than two leagues, [and] presented a narrow pass between two high mountains.'[37] However, Pelet records that the road, '… meandered across those various summits, and towards Lamas it was very muddy'.[38] The likelihood is that there were tracks along the ridges as well as a more formed road in the valley, where the present road runs. Although Sprünglin might be exaggerating the extent of the heights between which the road ran, they were significant enough for Ney to use them effectively to aid his retreat to Miranda do Corvo. The closing part of Massena's orders to Ney on the 13th insisted that the rearguard remain, '… two leagues in front of Miranda do Corvo …' to allow the baggage to be withdrawn.[39] This would also allow space behind the rearguard for Montbrun's force to move to Chão de Lamas, and for Reynier's II corps to link up at the same place. Blocking access to the valley would stop the advance of the Allied army until the rearguard could withdraw to safety.

VI corps' deployment began at Casal Novo and then reached back to Chão de Lamas via several occupied positions. Ney carefully arranged his forces along the heights which dominated the road the Allies would use to advance. Ferey's brigade was positioned on the heights in front of Casal Novo. Ney deployed the brigades from Mermet's divisions in support of Ferey's troops, with Marchand's as the third line, and *général de division* Trelliard's *dragons* placed in support of Marchand.[40] VIII corps was placed on the heights behind Chão de Lamas, covering Miranda de Corvo and serving as a reserve.

These dispositions were unknown to the Allied army as a thick fog covered both armies. Wellington issued some rather qualified instructions for the 14th, which are worth quoting at length:

> Major Gen. Sir W. Erskine will put the advanced guard in motion soon after day break, and will follow the enemy along the road towards Miranda do Corvo.
>
> The 3d division will be prepared to take its place in the column immediately behind the advanced guard; but Major Gen. Picton will not move into the line of march until it has been ascertained that the enemy has retired to

36   Kincaid, *Adventures*, p.54.
37   Sprünglin, 'Souvenirs', p.470.
38   Pelet, *The French Campaign in Portugal*, p.455.
39   Massena au Ney, Fonte Cuberta, le 13 mars. 1811. Bonnal, *La Vie Militaire du Maréchal Ney*, vol.3, p.498.
40   Bonnal, *La Vie Militaire du Maréchal Ney*, vol.3, pp.500–501.

such a distance, and in such a direction, as renders it no longer necessary to occupy in force the heights connected with the Serra where the division now is.

The Royals and the 14th light dragoons will follow the advanced guard under Sir William Erskine, leaving room, however, for the 3d division in their front, if it should be ordered to enter the column.

The 6th division will follow the Royals and 14th light dragoons; and the 4th division, and the other troops in rear of it, will follow in the same order as they have taken up their ground this evening along the great road.

Capt. Lawson's brigade of 9 pounders will take its place in the line of march at the head of the 1st division.

The baggage of each division, or separate regiment, must be collected together and kept clear of the road until its turn comes to enter the line of march in the situation above pointed out. The reserve of ammunition which was attached during this day's march to the troops under Major Gen. Hoghton will move, till further orders, with the 5th division.

The Royal Staff corps will march from Redinha at daybreak, and will proceed towards the head of the column. It is to be allowed to pass, as also the mules attached to the corps.[41]

Picton remained on the heights to the south of the road, having moved there as part of the manoeuvres the day before. Wellington was still concerned about the possibility of an attack from French units which had been in the region of Zambujal and Espinhal. Meanwhile, Nightingall, with help from Colonel Hawker's cavalry brigade, received instructions to pursue II corps from Espinhal to Miranda do Corvo. Major General Cole was directed to take his 4th Division to Penela and establish contact with Nightingall. Cole was instructed that if the French had left Espinhal, '… or have an inconsiderable rear-guard only in it, Major-General Cole will march there, and take possession of Espinhal, or he may combine his movement, for that purpose, with Major-General Nightingall, if necessary.'[42]

As the rest of the army moved towards Miranda do Corvo, the movement of Cole and the advance of Nightingall could trap II corps and possibly the rearguard as well. If that failed, then the Allied army would occupy Espinhal and take the bridge at Miranda do Corvo. This would open the route to Foz de Arouce and position a strong force to pursue the enemy further. These instructions gave Wellington a chance to squeeze the French from two directions and force them further from any chance of establishing a passage over the Mondego.

At around 5:30 a.m. the advanced picquet of the Light Division reported to Erskine that the enemy was in strength around Casal Novo, but despite this warning, Erskine ordered the Division to advance. Harry Smith recalled that a small patrol of the 16th Light Dragoons returned and reported that they had, '… seen naught.'[43] The report was received with suspicion by Beckwith as the Light Dragoons had said

41   Head-Quarters, Ega, 13th March, 1811. Murray, *Memoir Annexed to an Atlas*, p.48.
42   G. Murray, QMG, Villa Seca, 14th March, 1811, Murray, *Memoir Annexed to an Atlas*, p.50.
43   Smith, *Autobiography*, p.44.

they had patrolled for a league and a half, some seven kilometres, ahead of the Allied advanced guard, in thick fog. Erskine is reported to have arrived,

> ... and asked why we were not in march and following the enemy. Colonel Ross [of the 52nd Foot] said because the enemy were not gone, but were within cannon shot of us at that very moment, for the captains of the pickets, [William] Napier, 43rd, and Dobbs, 52nd, had patrolled up to their sentinels a short time before, and reported that the enemy was still in position. This did not satisfy Sir William Erskine, who kept blustering and swearing it was all nonsense and that the captains of the pickets knew nothing about the matter and that there was not a man of them there.[44]

As the Light Division advanced, the heavy fog that had been present that morning began to lift, '... when was displayed to our longing eyes the glorious sight of the whole French rear-guard in martial array, in position, with the sun brightly glittering on their arms.'[45] Marchand's division, still very much in place despite Erskine's assertions, was presented with the Light Division advancing in close column-of-march along the road. The French opened fire with their artillery, causing substantial casualties among the Allied troops. Major George Napier described the effects:

> ... bang came a shot from a twelve-pounder which struck the head of our column and made a lane through it killing and wounding many men; immediately a second and third, and then commenced a regular cannonade. Still the wise Sir William was sure it could be nothing but a single gun or two and a picket of the enemy ...[46]

Major Stewart of the 95th commanded the skirmishers, which were pushed forward to engage the enemy, and Rifleman Costello remembered, '... their skirmishers, at times, making short stands to keep our rifles in check, and a few of their rear sections occasionally pouring a running fire into us. We drove them, however, through the village of Casal Nova [sic].'[47]

Montbrun arrived with his cavalry and infantry and took up a position on the right of Chão de Lamas, where Massena had his headquarters. As the Allies advanced on the initial positions at Casal Novo, Sprünglin wrote, 'The first line withdrew and reformed behind the third. The brigades moved in succession and were placed in positions designated in advance which were indicated by staff officers.'[48] Mermet's division was turned out of its position between Casal de Azenha and Villa Seca and there was particularly difficult fighting disputing the

---

44   Napier, *Passages*, p.180.
45   John Cowell-Stepney, *Leaves from the Diary of an Officer of the Guards* (London: Chapman and Hall, 1854), p.57.
46   Napier, *Passages*, p.181.
47   Costello, *Memoirs*, p.101.
48   Sprünglin, 'Souvenirs', p.471.

village of Chão de Lamas.[49] Much of the contest took place amongst the walled enclosures and lanes of the village and surrounding areas. George Napier recalled ordering his company to jump a wall to protect his troops from nearby French *dragons* that were using some trees as cover.[50] The Napier brothers, William and George, were both wounded in bitter fighting through the enclosures and woods around the village. The men they commanded were constantly engaged with enemy skirmishers, both infantry and cavalry. French skirmishers put up fierce resistance against the frontal attacks of the Light Division, taking cover behind stone walls, but withdrew when they were outflanked.[51] However, during the latter part of the day, '... the British guns and the skirmishers got within range of his masses, and the retreat became more rapid and less orderly'.[52] The fighting was so intense that ammunition needed to be brought up for the Light Division, the skirmishers of which were at risk of running out.

Wellington reported to the Secretary of War, the Earl of Liverpool, that his manoeuvres, '... obliged the enemy to abandon all the positions which they successively took in the mountains, and the corps d'armee [sic] composing the rear guard were flung back upon the main body, at Miranda do Corvo'.[53] However, the French writers, and some Allied, concur that Ney's commanding presence and planned manoeuvres allowed the rearguard to withdraw with minimal loss regardless of the Allied manoeuvres. Pelet described it in the following terms: '... the Marshal started to march, retiring the first line from the village and moving it behind the second line on the height. In this way he continued his withdrawal, echeloned by brigades, stopping the enemy at each position.'[54]

Tomkinson explained that, 'The enemy held their ground as long as they could, and then retired to another ridge of high ground in their rear.'[55] Referring to the numerous places that were successively occupied and defended, the French soldiers named this battle the, 'day of positions.'[56] *Lieutenant* Oudinot, one of Massena's ADCs, recorded that Ney handled his Corps,

> ... with such skill and precision that both armies were filled with admiration. The 1st and 2nd divisions, as well as the cavalry, successively supported the retreat and defended the ground step by step until evening, only abandoning one position to take another, where they received the enemy with well-directed fire and executed movements in perfect order. The various arms of the 6th Corps all proved worthy of their illustrious leader.[57]

---

49   Pelet, *The French Campaign in Portugal*, p.456.
50   Napier, *Passages*, p.182.
51   Costello, *Memoirs*, p.101.
52   Thomas Garrety, *Memoirs of a Sergeant, Late in the Forty-Third Light Infantry Regiment during the Peninsular War* (London: John Mason, 1835), p.123.
53   Wellington to Liverpool. Villa Secca, 14th March, 1811, Gurwood, *Dispatches*, vol.4, p.668.
54   Pelet, *The French Campaign in Portugal*, pp.455–456.
55   Tomkinson, *Diary*, pp.83–84.
56   Koch, *Mémoires de Massena*, vol.7, p.378.
57   Oudinot, 'Souvenirs', p.30.

Ney wrote in his report to Massena, '... my troops had fought the enemy by ceding the ground to him, not by force, but following the required manoeuvres'.[58] The action was not without loss however: several of the 3e hussards were casualties. Three officers from the 27e ligne were wounded, three from the 39e, six from the 76e, three from the 86e, and two from the 25e légère.[59] The Allied losses were recorded as 115 officers and men killed, wounded and missing.[60] Major Stewart was killed as a direct consequence of Erskine's incompetence, pushing the skirmishers forward despite warnings of French troops nearby. Of George Napier's company of 66 rank-and-file, three sergeants and three subalterns, one officer, one sergeant and 12 soldiers were killed, and 19 wounded.[61] As evening fell, Costello described the scene: 'The sun had set, its light had been supplanted by burning villages, and fires that on vale and mountain, correctly pointed out where the hostile divisions were extended.'[62]

With only one road through some difficult terrain and crossing the Rio Corvo, the *armée de Portugal* had to move more than 40,000 troops with over 5,000 sick and wounded, plus the baggage train. Ney ordered the destruction of baggage, wagons and other equipment. Sprünglin explained that only the strictly necessary transport was kept: 'To get rid of everything that might have delayed his march, he burned his own vehicles and ordered that, following his example, everything that was useless or of luxury should be burned, and that the soldiers employed in transporting the baggage should return to the ranks.'[63] Béchet was instructed by Ney, '... to burn all the baggage, starting with his own, without sparing Massena's, who I believe was not very pleased about it, leaving only a few wagons to transport the wounded and sick who absolutely could not ride mules.'[64]

Ney and Massena once again argued over the withdrawal of the rearguard from Condeixa. Ney insisted he was being outflanked, but Massena was concerned at the speed with which the withdrawal was proceeding. Oudinot suggested that Massena actively considered replacing Ney in his command at the time but limited himself to expressing his displeasure.[65] Conversely, Ney accused Massena of trying to break the back of the VI corps, and a fierce argument broke out between the two men in front of their soldiers.[66]

With Montbrun's return, 'The baggage that had initially been directed towards Coimbra had also gathered at Miranda; there was therefore a frightening congestion there'.[67] However, now that the *armée de Portugal* was reunited, the French forces could withdraw more securely through Miranda do Corvo and on to Ponte de Mucela. In the evening, Sprünglin's small command took up position on a conical

---

58   Au prince d'Essling, 14 mars 1811. Bonnal, *La Vie Militaire du Maréchal Ney*, vol.3, p.501.
59   Martinien, *Tableaux Des Officiers*.
60   Oman, *A History of the Peninsular War*, vol.4, p.615.
61   Napier, *Passages*, p.185.
62   Costello, *Memoirs*, p.103.
63   Sprünglin, 'Souvenirs', p.470.
64   Béchet, *Souvenirs*, p.367.
65   Oudinot, 'Souvenirs', p.30.
66   Pelet, *The French Campaign in Portugal*, pp.456–457.
67   Béchet, *Souvenirs*, p.367.

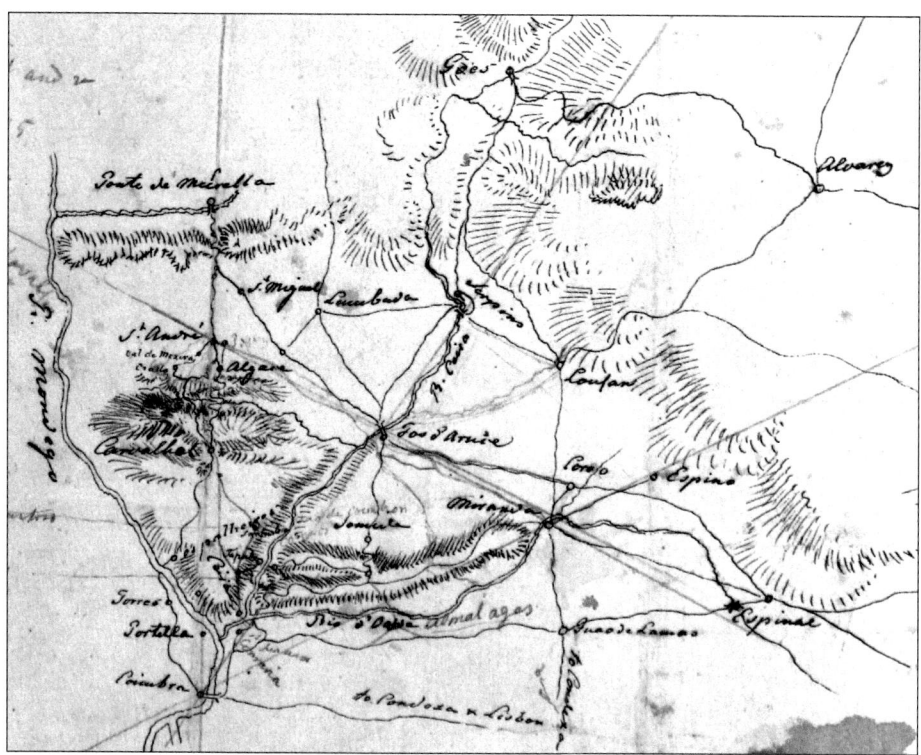

Sketch map of the area south and east of Coimbra as far as the river Zezere, 1810 (North is to the left). (TNA: MPH 1/1007/11)

hill in front of Miranda do Corvo, covering the withdrawal of the rest of the French troops.[68]

Supply problems were again making themselves felt in the Allied regiments. Cooper of the 7th Fusiliers recalled that he had, '... nothing to eat but boiled bean tops. I could not relish them. The officers were just as badly off as ourselves. The cause was we had outmarched our stores.'[69] Wellington summed up the situation as he understood it in a letter to the Earl of Liverpool.

> The result of these operations has been that we have saved Coimbra and Upper Beira from the enemy's ravages; we have opened the communications with the northern provinces; and we have obliged the enemy to take for their retreat the road by Ponte da Murcella, [sic] on which they may be annoyed by the militia acting in security upon their flank, while the Allied army will press upon their rear.[70]

---

68   This is likely the hill around which the N342 road runs, one kilometre west of the road junction into Miranda do Corvo, posted at 275 metres. Bonnal, *La Vie Militaire du Maréchal Ney*, vol.3, p.505.

69   John Spencer Cooper, *Rough Notes of Seven Campaigns in Portugal, Spain, France, and America, During the Years 1809-15* (London: John Russel Smith, 1869), p.53.

70   Wellington to Liverpool. Villa Secca, 14th March, 1811, Gurwood, *Dispatches,* vol.4, p.668.

But Wellington still faced a multitude of troubles, not least of which was the erratic behaviour of Erskine. Charles Napier commented, '… the ignorance and imprudence of Sir Wm. Erskine [was] said to have been conspicuous'.[71]

The majority of Wellington's army continued its pursuit of the *armée de Portugal*, which was now clearly heading along the left bank of the Mondego away from Coimbra. Presently, Major General Houghton received orders to take his brigade away from the pursuit of Massena to reinforce Hill.[72] Massena's forces would need to cross several more rivers before reaching the open terrain beyond the Alva. Pelet considered it a missed opportunity to delay the Allied advance by destroying some segments of the road into Miranda do Corvo, but this would have taken time the French did not have. A night march was then ordered to move the army along the road to Foz de Arouce. The *armée de Portugal* started withdrawing at 10:00 p.m. An advanced guard of *dragons* was followed by the II corps and VIII corps marching at midnight. VI corps with Ferey's rearguard then began its retreat at 1:00 a.m. on the 15th.[73] In the early morning, Sprünglin's detachment withdrew through the town, setting Miranda do Corvo afire as they finally abandoned it.

Wellington now felt secure enough to send Cole's 4th Division and de Gray's cavalry brigade southwards to join Beresford's force.[74]

Foz de Arouce – 15 March

The bridge at Foz de Arouce had three arches, of which the one towards the right bank was slightly damaged. The bridge was repaired quickly by French engineers, allowing the retreat to continue with II corps crossing first, followed by VIII corps. Some fords offered crossings above and below the bridge, however, Pelet reported, 'The Ceira, sixteen to twenty yards wide, was deeply embanked and its bottom was full of rocks, resulting in some difficult fords.'[75] The recent rains now made some fords almost impossible to use and others were so bad that men had drowned whilst trying to cross.

Wellington had issued orders on the 14th for the advance on the 15th. The left column was composed of the 3rd Division, a brigade of 9-pounders and the Royal Staff Corps. Picton described the terrain around Foz de Arouce as being, '… abrupt woody heights, connected by narrow gorges …',[76] which was particularly favourable for defence. The right column was formed by the 1st, 5th and 6th Divisions. Nightingall's brigade was to advance on Miranda do Corvo, but was not to press onwards if they met significant resistance. Hawker's cavalry would establish communications between the main Allied forces and Nightingall. Pack was to take

---

71   Sir William Napier, *The Life and Opinions of General Sir Charles James Napier, G. C. B.* (London: Murray, 1857), vol.1, p.159.
72   Murray, *Memoir Annexed to an Atlas*, p.49.
73   Pelet, *The French Campaign in Portugal*, pp.457–466.
74   Villa Secca, 14th March. Murray, *Memoir Annexed to an Atlas*, p.50.
75   Pelet, *The French Campaign in Portugal*, p.465.
76   Robinson, *Picton*, vol.2, p.384.

The bridge at Foz de Arouce showing heights on the French side of the river. (Author's photo)

his brigade, half a brigade of mountain guns, and a squadron of light cavalry across the river below Miranda do Corvo and ascend the ridge of Nossa Senhora da Serra.[77] The aim was for Pack to threaten the road to Foz de Arouce from the north, as Nightingall did the same from the south. The Allied army, encamped along the road from Casal Novo to Miranda do Corvo, found the dawn of the 15th foggy, preventing an early start, except for Pack, who began his march promptly.[78] Uncertain of where the enemy rearguard was located, and with the experience of the previous day fresh in his mind, Wellington waited for the fog to clear before ordering the main advance. Tomkinson commented that, 'Lord W. was said to be much disappointed, as he intended to have attacked them, and, from the nature of the ground, much might have been done.'[79] The Light Division moved through Miranda do Corvo, which was still burning.[80] Thus, it was late in the afternoon before the Allied advanced guard came into direct contact with VI corps, which meant that the divisions following were further delayed. According to Captain William Stothert, adjutant of the 3rd Foot Guards, the 1st Division passed through Miranda do Corvo about 3:00 p.m.[81]

Despite orders from Massena to follow VIII corps across the bridge and take up a position on the right bank, Ney had left the larger portion of his corps on the left

77   Villa Secca, 14th March. Murray, *Memoir Annexed to an Atlas*, pp.50–51.
78   Murray, *Memoir Annexed to an Atlas*, p.51.
79   Tomkinson, *Diary*, p.84.
80   Leach, *Rough Sketches of the Life of an Old Soldier*, p.200.
81   William Stothert, *A Narrative of the Principal Events of the Campaigns of 1809, 1810, & 1811, in Spain and Portugal* (London: P Martin, 1812), p.228.

bank of the Ceira to cover the retreat and allow the bridge to be mined. Pelet, never a staunch supporter of Ney, described how the *maréchal* said the position on the left bank was preferable and that he would even move some of his troops back over the bridge from the right bank.[82] Béchet recalled that Ney, '... seeing that he was not being pursued, halted before crossing the Ceira'.[83] This would turn out to be a significant mistake. However, it appears Ney did not consider an attack likely on the 15th, and that he would have plenty of time to withdraw his corps before the Allied forces began moving again. Wellington's apparent timidity in their previous encounters had perhaps lulled Ney into a sense of false security. With the Ceira in flood and the fords too deep to use, the only route for an organised retreat was via the repaired bridge. To speed the retreat, orders were repeated to destroy the transport animals, and this was carried out by the river. *Chef de bataillon* Noël, commanding Clausel's artillery, recalls they, '... were killed near the bridge, which was immediately named the "Bridge of Assess" but this was soon altered to "Bridge of Defeat".'[84]

Ney was convinced that Wellington would not attack his position on the 15th but would prepare to receive an attack on the morning of the 16th.[85] Marchand's division, and *général de brigade* Bardet's brigade of Mermet's division, were posted on the left bank, with Loison's division and Labassée's brigade on the right. *Général de brigade* Gourlez, *baron* de Lamotte, took the light cavalry of the rearguard onto the left bank of the river in search of fodder.[86] During the day troops continued crossing the bridge, with the priority given to II and VIII corps and the artillery.[87] Pelet wrote: 'Around the bridge there were other ... [d]etachments made up of all flags and of all nations – for we had Prussian, Irish, Swiss, Hanoverians, and Portuguese troops with us – were pushing each other, shouting and swearing in every language. The unfortunate wounded ... waited sadly for their turn to cross.'[88]

After reviewing the situation at Foz de Arouce, Massena retired to his headquarters. The troops were settled and preparing food as the Allied troops arrived on the heights overlooking the river.[89] As the Light Division approached the French campfires were clearly visible to them.[90] Perhaps smarting from his experience of over-zealous pursuit the previous day at Casal Novo, Erskine had brought the Light Division to a halt, and the troops also began preparing their evening meal. Wellington arrived and immediately ordered an attack.[91] Leach recalled, 'The day was drawing to a close, and the troops were cooking their suppers, when a sudden order reached the bivouac for them to fall in, and to attack the French rear-guard.'[92] According to Simmons, an order was given by Wellington directly to Lieutenant

82   Pelet, *The French Campaign in Portugal*, pp.466–467.
83   Béchet, *Souvenirs*, p.367.
84   Noël, *With Napoleon's Guns*, p.115.
85   Koch, *Mémoires de Massena*, vol.7, p.384.
86   Béchet, *Souvenirs*, p.368.
87   Pelet, *The French Campaign in Portugal*, p.468.
88   Pelet, *The French Campaign in Portugal*, p.469.
89   Guingret, *Relation Historique*, p.164.
90   Costello, *Memoirs*, p.105.
91   Cowell-Stepney, *Leaves from the Diary of an Officer of the Guards*, p.60.
92   Leach, *Rough Sketches of the Life of an Old Soldier*, p.201.

Colonel Beckwith; 'Fall in your battalion and attack the enemy; drive in their skir-mishers, and I will turn their flank with the 3rd and 1st Divisions.'[93]

Wellington was clear in his orders for the battle that, 'It is not intended to attempt any thing against the enemy's position beyond the Ceira, but only to drive the troops on the left bank across the river.'[94] He ordered Picton's 3rd Division on the right to take some wooded hills at Relvios and secure that flank of the army, supported by the 1st Division and Nightingall's Brigade. The Light Division on the left was to advance on the high ground near Pousafoles, with a troop of Royal Horse Artillery accompa-nying it, supported by the 6th Division and Anson's Brigade of cavalry. Once the 5th Division had arrived, it would also support the Light Division. Hawker's cavalry and a troop of Royal Horse Artillery would remain in reserve on the right of the road. Pack's Brigade was directed to move to the left to turn the French from any position they took up on the left bank of the Ceira.[95]

Ney had received little intelligence about the movements of the Allied forces. His light cavalry was on the right bank, and there were no vedettes placed on the approach roads to Foz de Arouce. *Capitaine* Marcel recorded:

> ... the 39e was assigned to rear-guard duty. After the bridge had been repaired and during the crossing, we heard some gunfire. As we were already on the other side of the Ceira and preparing to bivouac, a violent exchange of gunfire broke out towards the bank we had just left. The enemy, apparently aware of our predicament, had sought to be more aggressive than usual; they attacked the 39e fiercely, causing confusion in two other battalions.[96]

Simmons described the initial advance of the 95th: 'The approach was through a pine wood, and the branches were rattling about our ears from the enemy's bullets. Lieutenant Kincaid got shot through his cap, which grazed the top of his head.'[97] Costello recalled that his company had just received a batch of recruits, none of whom had seen action before. Major O'Hare gave the recruits some sound advice: '"Do you see those men on that plain?" asked the Major, as he pointed to the French camp. On several of the men answering "Ees, Zur!" Major O'Hare, with a dry laugh, continued, "Well then, those are the French, and our enemies. You must kill those fellows, and not allow them to kill you."'[98]

The 95th were sent forward along with some of the light companies of the Guards from the 1st Division. Ensign Cowell-Stepney of the Coldstream Guards described how the Royal Horse Artillery supporting the left, '... galloping forward to a rising ground, opened their fire with a sudden and great effect.'[99]

93   Simmons, *A British Rifle Man*, pp.144–145.
94   Extracts from the instructions communicated by the Q.M.G., Arrangement for the attack of the enemy's rear guard, at Foz d'Arouce, 15th March, 1811, Gurwood, *Dispatches,* vol.4, p.670.
95   Wellington to Liverpool. Louzão, 16th March, 1811, Gurwood, *Dispatches,* vol.4, p.676.
96   Marcel, *Campagnes du Capitaine Marcel*, pp.128–129.
97   Simmons, *A British Rifle Man*, p.145.
98   Costello, *Memoirs*, p.106.
99   Cowell-Stepney, *Leaves from the Diary of an Officer of the Guards*, p.60.

As soon as the Allied attack began to develop, Ney issued orders to move the remaining troops from the left to the right bank of the Ceira, across the bridge. Covering the withdrawal were several regiments formed in a semicircle on the heights. Pelet commented that he saw Ney position the, '… 25e ligne and then the 39e ligne.'[100] It is probable here that Pelet meant the 25e légère, which was part of Ferey's rearguard along with the 39e ligne. These regiments occupied the left of the semicircle. The 1e brigade of the 1e division, commanded by *colonel* Fririon in the absence of *général de brigade* Maucune, who was injured, also remained on the left bank. Comprising the 6e légère and 69e ligne, it was placed in some woods and held the right of the semicircle.[101] Skirmishers from these regiments were sent forward to support the picquet, but were driven back, causing confusion in the 39e ligne. The 39e was presumably on the right of the 25e, as Fririon records the action taking place behind the left flank of Fririon's (Maucune's) Brigade. This would imply the Allied attack aimed to break through the centre of the French position. Thomas Garrety of the 43rd described how on Ney's right wing (the Allied left) the terrain was rugged and wooded, and the combat there, '… resolved itself into a skirmish, and thus Ney was able to use some battalions to check the pursuit of his left'. Yet the French left, '… being surprised and overthrown by the first charge, dispersed in a panic, and fled in such confusion towards the river'.[102]

Colonel Lamour of the 39e ligne was wounded and taken prisoner. The loss of command proved critical at this point. 'The *chef de bataillon* who was in command [of the 39e] dared not take it upon himself to give orders which were becoming urgent; he wanted to wait for the Colonel. The 39e retreated and was soon fleeing in disarray.'[103] Nightingall recorded the events in a matter-of-fact way: 'We had a skirmish on the 15th afternoon, the light companies only of my brigade were engaged, at Foz do Arouce [sic] and the enemy's rearguard was driven from the ground with some loss. A Colonel of the 39th was taken prisoner by my light infantry.'[104]

This was indeed an understatement, demonstrated by Cowell-Stepney's contrasting description from the perspective of the Coldstream Guards: '… in spite of all our efforts, we arrived only in time for Nightingale's [sic] brigade of our Division to take a share in the fray, which was a sufficiently heavy one.'[105]

VIII corps was deployed on the right bank of the river, and seeing troops approaching, took them for the Allies, and opened fire. However, they turned out to be French troops retiring, but the mistake only served to increase the confusion in the French ranks. According to Ney's report, the 50e and the 59e ligne were withdrawing in good order towards the bridge, but panicked when an artillery battery seemed as if it was going to block their retreat. Ney wrote to Massena, 'At that moment, the 50e, marching behind the 59e, mistakenly believed that our artillery

100 Pelet, *The French Campaign in Portugal*, p.466.
101 Fririon, *Journal Historique*, p.155.
102 Garrety, *Memoirs*, p.123.
103 Sprünglin, 'Souvenirs', p.472.
104 Letter 6, Sarcedo, on the banks of the river Alva. 22nd March, 1811. Glover, 'The Nightingall Letters', p.140.
105 Cowell-Stepney, *Leaves from the Diary of an Officer of the Guards*, p.61.

was being driven back by the enemy. This caused them to be seized with panic and they dragged the 59e into the most terrible disorder imaginable, up to the bridge where, in their extreme fear, these unfortunate soldiers rushed at once'.[106]

Additionally, Lamotte's cavalry blocked the exit of the bridge on the right bank, impeding the movement of troops from the left bank.[107] Pelet reported that the 25e légère and 39e ligne were pushed back onto the 50e and 59e, mixing the troops up. The confusion was communicated to the rest of Marchand's and Mermet's divisions, and with the troops so tired and hungry from their retreat, discipline broke and many of the soldiers ran for the bridge. Some officers feared for Ney's safety at this critical time as he positioned himself in the places of greatest danger. *Général de division* Mermet was wounded by a bayonet thrust to his thigh, indicating the closeness of the fighting. Ross's and Bull's batteries were moved forward into the fight, causing more confusion in the French ranks. Marcel continued, 'The Anglo-Portuguese division that had attacked was advancing rapidly; the bridge was immediately congested, despite all the wagons having passed, and several soldiers who had fallen into the water drowned. Marshal Ney ordered Colonel Fririon to immediately send Commander Duthoya [sic] with his battalion to restore order.'[108]

Fririon led the 3e bataillon of the 69e ligne, and three companies of the 6e légère, in a counterattack, providing a little respite for the retreating French troops. This attack pushed back some companies of the 95th that had advanced almost to the bridge.

The 52nd was closely in pursuit of the French, and Captain Dobb's and Madden's companies, '… pressed upon them so closely that their rear was seized with a panic, and in their impatience to escape, great numbers were drowned and trampled upon'.[109] Ensign William Grattan of the 88th recalls, 'The village of Foz d'Aronce [sic] was warmly contested, and more than once taken and retaken.'[110] Kincaid was knocked unconscious by a musket ball to the head and was nearly looted by a soldier of the 5/60th, thinking him dead from his wound.[111]

As French troops rushed for the bridge, others plunged into the river in an attempt to swim across. The fragility and diminished morale of many French troops during the retreat was revealed by experienced units breaking in battle. These were veteran units, described by Pelet in May 1810 as being, '… magnificent, truly elite units … most of them had taken part in the campaigns of 1805 and 1806'.[112] Indeed, Ney had praised the 50e and 59e for their composure and precision at Redinha. In his report, Ney recounted how the French defence halted the Allied attack, causing the Allies to retreat at 6:00 p.m. Nevertheless, Ney was also open about the chaos occasioned

106   Les hauteurs de Foz de Aronze, à 4 heures du matin, du 16 mars, Bonnal, *La Vie Militaire du Maréchal Ney*, vol.3, p.506.

107   Bonnal, *La Vie Militaire du Maréchal Ney*, vol.3, p.513.

108   Marcel, *Campagnes du Capitaine Marcel*, pp.128–129.

109   William Moorsom, *Historical Record of the Fifty-Second Regiment (Oxfordshire Light Infantry)* (London: Richard Bentley and Son, 1860), p.135.

110   William Grattan, Charles Oman (ed.), *Adventures with the Connaught Rangers, 1809-1814* (London: Arnold, 1902), p.58.

111   Kincaid, *Adventures*, pp.59–60.

112   Pelet, *The French Campaign in Portugal*, p.22.

during the afternoon. The rout of the 50e and 59e, '… necessarily dispersed all the skirmishers on our flanks, but I had fortunately positioned several battalions on the heights astride the road crossing the village, which contained the enemy so effectively that they did not notice our partial rout.'[113] He reported to Massena that at 3:00 a.m. the following morning, he had ordered the destruction of the bridge, causing a gap of some 25 metres.[114] The number of dead caused by the destruction of the bridge indicates it might have been blown earlier than 3:00 a.m., even as French troops were still trying to cross. Several witnesses from the Allied side, such as Costello and Leach, wrote that the bridge was blown while still occupied by French infantry. A French witness described how, 'A sergeant of artillery, who had been left at the bridge with orders to blow it up after all the retreating army had crossed, became so confused that he set fire to the mine when a considerable number of men were still on the enemy's side of the river'.[115]

Nevertheless, Simmons may have the answer for the different reports. He wrote that at 2:00 a.m. on the morning of the 16th, '… the enemy had the arches of the bridge more effectually blown up.'[116] This implies that the early attempt witnessed by others on the Allied side had not been too successful, although it had resulted in the deaths of many French soldiers. The early morning explosion then rendered the bridge unusable. However, the Light Division forded the river the next day, the water level having lowered. On 17 March, Commissary Schaumann recorded the consequences of the destruction of the bridge:

> Here we began to see evidences of the appalling consequences of too hasty a flight. Prisoners assured us that the crowd on the bridge was so thick at the time it was blown up that a number of men had been flung into the air, and about 500 had been drowned in crossing the river. The banks were still covered by dead bodies.[117]

In addition to the human debris, Allied witnesses recorded the sight of several hundred mules, unable to be driven along quickly enough, that had been hamstrung and left to die.[118] The duty had been given, '… to two companies of the marine battalion, tasked with hamstringing and killing them.'[119] This had become a common occurrence, as George Napier had recorded during the pursuit:

> … we found sixty or seventy poor donkeys who had been hamstrung by the French in a shamefully cruel manner, cutting the sinews of the hind-legs just above the hocks, and leaving the poor animals to die by inches. Now

113 Bonnal, *La Vie Militaire du Maréchal Ney*, vol.3, p.507.
114 Rapport au prince d'Essling, 16th March 1811, Bonnal, *La Vie Militaire du Maréchal Ney*, vol.3, pp.506–507.
115 Doisy de Villargennes, *Reminiscences*, p.61.
116 Simmons, *A British Rifle Man*, p.146.
117 Schaumann, *On the Road with Wellington*, pp.289–290.
118 Costello, *Memoirs*, p.109; Simmons, *A British Rifle Man*, p.146.
119 Nicolas Marcel, *Campagnes du Captaine Marcel du 69e de Ligne En Espagne En Portugal (1808-1814)* (Paris: Plon-Nourrit, 1913), p.128.

it might have been necessary to prevent the animals from falling into our hands, but why not have shot them at once, and not maim them in that cruel manner?[120]

Grattan wrote, '... the road ... was covered with a number of horses, mules, and asses, all maimed; but the most disgusting sight was about fifty of the asses floundering in the mud, some with their throats half cut, while others were barbarously houghed [hamstrung] or otherwise injured.'[121]

The answer to Napier's question might have been as simple as a lack of ammunition. *Capitaine* Marcel describes the problem from the French perspective:

> ... upon reaching the bridges over the Ceira, we found them cut. The river is fordable, but so steep that the artillery could only pass over one bridge; thus, it was necessary to repair it, which took a lot of time. While we waited, the order came to get rid of all our donkeys and hand them over to two companies of the marine battalion, tasked with cutting their tendons and stunning them. It was with profound sorrow that we witnessed the massacre of these poor animals, for these unfortunate donkeys had been our saviours ...[122]

Controversy arose within the French headquarters regarding Ney's actions at Foz de Arouce. Guingret, a *capitaine* in the 6e légère of Ney's Corps, was interrogated by Massena's aide-de-camp, Pelet, in connection with this matter. 'The latter came to visit the post where I was on duty and seemed to want to question me ... I told him frankly what had happened and it was soon known to the General Staff that the trouble was far from being as great as it had first been reported.'[123]

One prize for the Allies was the eagle of the 39e ligne, thrown into or lost in the river during the crossing. Pelet records that the eagle-bearer drowned in the river.[124] However, Marcel wrote that the eagle-bearer himself was retrieved from the river by soldiers of the 6e légère. He had apparently thrown himself into the river to save the regimental standard and eagle, and despite a meticulous search, the soldiers of the 6e légère could not find either.[125] The Allies were luckier in their search, and Wellington wrote to Liverpool on 4 July, 'I send to England by Mr Sydenham ... the eagle of the 39th regt., which was thrown into the river Ceira, near Foz d'Arouce [sic]'.[126] Another benefit obtained more directly by the Allied soldiers was the food left by the French during their withdrawal. After the problems of supply encountered by the troops, the meals being prepared by the French were welcome. On finding some biscuit, Simmons wrote, 'We had been very ill-off for some days for bread, so that some of these proved a great luxury.'[127]

120   Napier, *Passages*, p.174.
121   Grattan, *Adventures with the Connaught Rangers, 1809-1814*, p.57.
122   Marcel, *Campagnes du Capitaine Marcel*, p.128.
123   Guingret, *Relation Historique*, p.172.
124   Pelet, *The French Campaign in Portugal*, p.470.
125   Marcel, *Campagnes du Capitaine Marcel*, p.130.
126   Wellington to Liverpool, Quinta de S. João, 4 July 1811. Gurwood, *Dispatches*, vol.5, p.136.
127   Simmons, *A British Rifle Man*, p.146.

During their retreat, the French continued to rely on scavenging for food along their line of march. Although not as dire as the French predicament, Wellington was also facing supply difficulties. Staff officer Lieutenant Colonel Benjamin D'Urban wrote, 'The Army rested and (waited) for the arrival of Biscuit which from the nature of things had been a little behind.'[128] Even at this late stage of the campaign, the Portuguese troops were ill-fed and provisioned despite repeated attempts to make the Portuguese government reorganise their commissary. In a forthright manner, Wellington wrote to Liverpool:

> The destruction of the bridge at Foz d'Arouce, [sic] the fatigue which the troops have undergone for several days, and the want of supplies, have induced me to halt the army this day … the Portuguese troops had no provisions, nor any means of conveying any to them … it is literally true, that Gen. Pack's brigade, and Col. Ashworth's, had nothing to eat for 4 days, although constantly marching or engaged with the enemy. I was obliged either to direct the British Commissary Gen. to supply the Portuguese troops, or to see them perish for want; and the consequence is, that the supplies intended for the British troops are exhausted, and we must halt till more come up, which I hope will be this day.[129]

Food was scarce for officers and men alike. Some, '… got a portion of donkey-flesh, cut from the corpses of those respectable animals left behind by the enemy, but minus salt, biscuit, or other addenda; however, it was something, which was better than nothing.'[130] Lieutenant George Brown of the 43rd reported on the 16th, '… we are halted today to refresh the men and get up provisions, not having had bread for three days.'[131] On the 17th, *Brigadeiro* Pack was moved to write a letter to Murray, the quartermaster general:

> The bearer, our Commissary, says there is nothing to be got in Coimbra, and I wish to God you could tell him, or me, what to do. The men have had neither bread nor meat yesterday nor to-day, and very little indeed the day before. They live, literally, upon what they pick up in the fields, and consequently they are falling sick, and are becoming daily more disorganized. Our mules are gone back, I am told, to a great distance, and I really dread our coming to a complete stand still. Indeed, honestly to speak, I do not see how the men can march.[132]

---

128 15 March, Benjamin d'Urban, I.J. Rousseau (ed.), *The Peninsular Journal, 1808-1817* (London: Greenhill, 1988), p.194.
129 Wellington to Liverpool, Louzão, 16th March 1811, Gurwood, *Dispatches*, vol.4, p.676.
130 Cowell-Stepney, *Leaves from the Diary of an Officer of the Guards*, p.62.
131 Glover and Burnham, *The Men of Wellington's Light Division*, p.63.
132 Letter from Pack to the QMG, dated Venda Nova, 17th March, 1811. Quoted in Murray, *Memoir Annexed to an Atlas*, p.52.

Pack was not the only officer in Portuguese service to despair at the state of supply to the troops. Wellington wrote to Charles Stuart, the British ambassador in Lisbon, on the 18th, stating:

> One consequence, therefore, of omitting to feed the troops, will be to throw us again upon the defensive in this part of the country; another consequence, also, which I seriously apprehend, is, that the British officers serving with the Portuguese troops will resign their situations: one of them spoke to me seriously upon the subject of the state of the troops this day, and declared his intention to resign if a remedy was not applied.[133]

Wellington thus halted his army at Foz de Arouce and awaited the expected supplies. It was not until 5:00 a.m. on the 17th that orders were issued to resume the pursuit of the French. Only the Light, 1st and 3rd Divisions of infantry were instructed to move across the Ceira. Hawker's and Anson's cavalry were to move in support. The second of those brigades was to advance along the road to Ponte de Mucela to reconnoitre the route. 'The divisions that first pass the river will be prepared to form, should it be necessary, to cover the passage of the rest of the army. All the troops not mentioned … and all the baggage of the army, will remain upon the left bank of the Ceira till further orders.'[134]

Two hours later, orders were issued for the movement of the other divisions, and more detailed directions for the first formations which crossed the Ceira.[135] The pursuit continued.

133 Wellington to Charles Stuart, Esq. Pombeiro, 18th March, 1811, Gurwood, *Dispatches*, vol.4, p.679.
134 Arrangement for passing the river Ceira. Head-Quarters, Louzao, 17 March, 5 A.M. Murray, *Memoir Annexed to an Atlas*, pp.52–53.
135 17 March, 7 A.M. Murray, *Memoir Annexed to an Atlas*, p.53.

4

Retreat

Ponte de Mucela – 18 March

A large stone bridge, capable of taking cavalry and wheeled transport, crossed the Alva at Ponte de Mucela. The bridge was positioned in a double bend, and the heights overlooking it, the Serra da Atalhada, are an extension of the landform that includes the Serra do Buçaco. The bridge had recently been damaged severely by the *Ordenança* of Trant and Silveira. The main arch had been cut, making any repair time-consuming.[1] This was a significant part of the reason Ney's withdrawal of the rearguard after Casal Novo had been cautious: he was acutely aware of gaining time for the damaged bridge to be repaired and had received orders from Massena on the 15th to delay the enemy as much as possible to allow the repair to be completed.[2] Ney was having a difficult time, and the pressures of commanding the rearguard were taking their toll. Pelet described Ney as, '… anxious and moody.'[3] Ney became more nervous about his position and the vulnerable left flank, and his general frame of mind only added to his anxiety and heightened his reactions to any problem or apparent criticism. After the confusion at the battle at Foz de Arouce he was in a rage. When *général de brigade* Lamotte complained about the situation, Ney became so angry that he seized a pistol and threatened to blow out Lamotte's brains if he did not withdraw immediately. Lamotte was placed under arrest and sent back to France charged with negligence.[4] *Colonel* Pierre Mourier of the 15e chasseurs à cheval was given command of the rearguard light cavalry.[5] Sprünglin recalled that Lamotte was not the only recipient of Ney's ire:

> I have never seen Marshal Ney in such a bad mood as that day. He held a grudge against the 39e ligne for the disorder of the previous day and the loss of its eagle and colonel; he was furious with General Lamotte, whose incomprehensible conduct had caused the congestion on the bridge and the resulting disaster. He refused the company of grenadiers from the 39e,

---

1   Noël, *With Napoleon's Guns*, p.116.
2   Bonnal, *La Vie Militaire du Maréchal Ney*, vol.3, p.508.
3   Pelet, *The French Campaign in Portugal*, p.484.
4   Béchet, *Souvenirs*, p.367.
5   Marechal Ney au prince d'Essling, 17 mars. Bonnal, *La Vie Militaire du Maréchal Ney*, vol.3, p.512.

Ponte de Mucela from the heights above the town. (Author's photo)

which came to form the guard for his bivouac, removed General Lamotte from the command of the light cavalry.[6]

Béchet described the scene on the 16th:

> ... a grenadier company came as usual to form the Marshal's guard at his bivouac. It was precisely the company whose eagle-bearer [of the 39e] had drowned the previous day. The Maréchal, who was particularly irritated as he felt he had some blame for the previous day's events and deeply regretted the loss of the eagle, said to the company: 'Grenadiers, you have lost your eagle, you will not guard me.' The captain lowered his sword and withdrew; I had never seen such gloomy and sad faces; even a few tears fell on these sunburnt and eminently martial faces.[7]

Despite the vehicles and most of the troops waiting for the bridge repairs to be finished, some had been crossing using the fords on foot. They were described by Pelet as, '... an unending procession, descending on one side and climbing on the other.'[8] The fords were dangerous, and as the river rose, so the danger increased. The cavalry had difficulty using them, and no wheeled transport could cross by this method. More could be got across if the bridge was repaired. Massena had been cajoling and persuading Drouet for several days to remain with the *armée de Portugal*, or to at least maintain communications over the Alva towards Celorico and Guarda. He had almost pleaded with Drouet to

---

6   Sprünglin, 'Souvenirs', p.473.
7   Béchet, *Souvenirs*, p.370.
8   Pelet, *The French Campaign in Portugal*, p.477.

remain at Ponte de Mucela and repair the bridge. Drouet remembered the situation slightly differently:

> I pointed out to Marshal Massena that the English, having established their military route to Almeida via the Alva and Celorico, a much more direct route than that of Coimbra, I believed it more appropriate and prudent to follow the Almeida route so as not to be overtaken in Spain by the English. But in any case, it was urgent to send a division to the Alva to restore the bridge that had been cut by the enemy, which forced me to ford this river when I had come to Portugal. This was all the more necessary as even a slight rain could swell the torrent and prevent the army from crossing.
>
> Marshal Massena, appreciating my observations, tasked me with preceding the army on the Alva, having the bridge restored, and gave orders to follow this direction.[9]

Drouet had thus been working with *colonel* Valazé, *commandant le génie* of VIII corps, and *capitaine* Beaufort from the *état-major général* of the army, with their *sapeurs*, to repair the bridge since the 15th. These *sapeurs* had previously been involved in the unsuccessful venture to repair the bridge at Coimbra. When Massena and Pelet visited to check on progress, they were told the repairs would not be completed until the 17th. However, the work was hastened sufficiently that troops were able to cross in the late afternoon of the 16th.[10] The strength of the repair was successfully tested by sending the *sapeurs'* equipment and a heavy forge across. Once this had been done, the troops could cross with dry feet.

II corps, which had spent the 15th at Forcado, some five kilometres north-east of Foz de Arouce, moved to new positions on the 16th. The vanguard and 1e division were placed on the heights to the right of Ponte de Mucela, with the 2e division further along the road from Ponte de Mucela to Arganil. VIII corps began its movement to the plateau east of Ponte de Mucela at 2:00 a.m. on the 16th. Concerned by the threat from Trant's and Silviera's *Ordenança* north of the Mondego, close observation was kept on the routes leading towards that river. Loison's and Mermet's divisions were spread out between the positions occupied by II and VIII corps. Marchand's division remained on the heights behind Foz de Arouce to allow time to repair the bridge over the Alva. Massena established his headquarters over the river at Sobreira. In the evening of the 16th, after the bridge over the Alva was repaired, the artillery and baggage began crossing. Some had crossed the river with difficulty by fording earlier in the day, and the whole finished passing during the night. The cavalry reserve covered the movement of VI corps as it withdrew.[11]

There were several accessible fords across the river further upstream, as well as several bridges, and Reynier was instructed to take his corps and position it along the Alva at Sarzedo and Arganil to protect Ney's flank from encirclement. II corps

---

9   Jean Baptiste Drouet, *Le Maréchal Drouet, Comte d'Erlon. Vie Militaire Écrit Par Lui Même* (Paris: Barba, 1844), p.65.
10   Pelet, *The French Campaign in Portugal*, pp.473–474.
11   Fririon, *Journal Historique*, p.159.

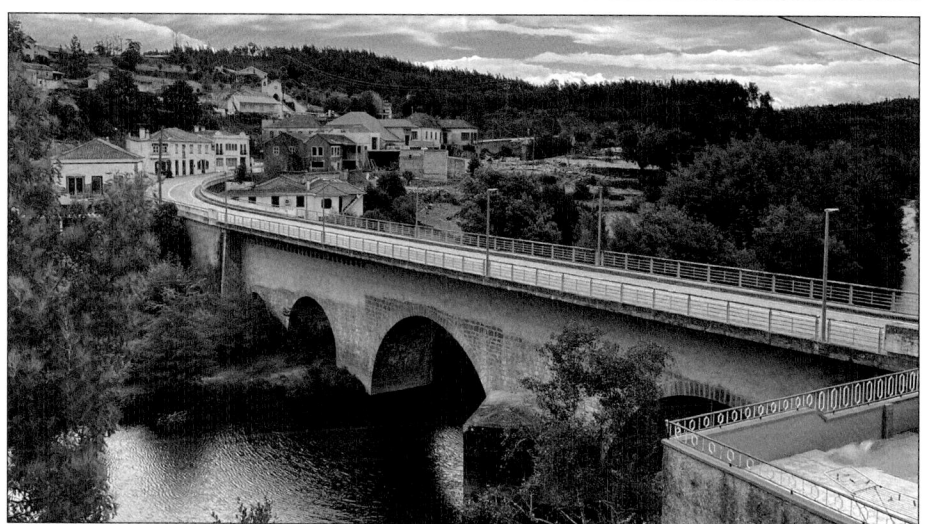

Ponte de Mucela bridge, showing heights on the right bank. (Author's photo)

crossed the Alva via the fords there and took up its position on the heights of Sarzedo, the 1e division located, '... to the right of the path which will join the main road, and the 2e division on the left.'[12] The rear-guard occupied Arganil.[13] VIII corps continued its march and arrived in the morning of the 18th at Galizes.

The rear-guard of VI corps covered the main retreat to Ponte de Mucela. This corps took up position on the right bank of the Alva but retained a small post on the left bank to protect the bridge. Ney wrote to Massena:

> I have the honour to report to Your Excellency that the troops of the 6th Corps have just taken up positions on the right bank of the Alva, as I have informed Your Excellency, and are deployed from the plateau overlooking the Murcilla [sic] bridge on the Alva, extending through Carievailha, to near Carticado, so as to cover the directions of Pinheiro de Azère and those of Gallices. The division of General Ferey, is responsible for the defence of the Murcilla bridge and the fords on the army's front.
>
> Mermet's and Loison's divisions are deployed as a second line, in support of General Ferey's division. Finally, Marchand's division is in reserve. An enemy cavalry detachment has been following the general rear-guard since 10 o'clock in the morning and has exchanged pistol shots with our outposts on the crest of the heights on the left bank.[14]

The ground at Ponte de Mucela offered a fine defensive position if the line of the Alva was held in force and the vulnerable flanks were sufficiently protected: the area around Sarzedo being particularly flat and the river easily fordable. Despite

---

12   Fririon, *Journal Historique*, p.160.
13   Koch, *Mémoires de Massena*, vol.7, p.391.
14   Bonnal, *La Vie Militaire du Maréchal Ney*, vol.3, pp.511–512.

this weakness, Massena considered holding the position for a time, placing Reynier's II corps in position to defend the left flank. However Reynier, instead of coordinating with Ney to cover the position at Ponte de Mucela as he had been ordered, wasted time questioning and disputing his instructions with Ney and Massena.[15] Massena sent a sharply worded message to Reynier to maintain communications with Ney:

> I have learned that you have moved on Galices [sic]. I expected you to remain on the line of the Alva the whole day. I am scarcely able to believe that you placed yourself so far from the Duc d'Elchingen, exposing his left. I declare that your manoeuvre will cause a serious calamity and I order you to move in line regardless of the hour. It is very important that you observe the general orders in the future.[16]

Seeing the strength of the position at Ponte de Mucela, Wellington was not willing to commit to a frontal attack over the bridge. By turning the French left flank at Sarzedo, he sought again to manoeuvre the French from a strong position. On the 18th, he marched his troops towards the Alva in two columns. The left column under Major General Erskine, comprising Pack's and Ashworth's brigades, the Light and 6th Divisions and Anson's brigade of cavalry, along with a brigade of British 9-pounders, advanced along the road towards Ponte de Mucela.

> The left column … will halt before descending to the bridge, and wait for further orders. If, however, the enemy has abandoned the ground on the opposite side of the bridge, the advanced guard of the left column will take possession of it, and the General officer at the head of the column will cause the bridge to be repaired without delay.[17]

The right column, comprising the 1st, 3rd and 5th Divisions and Hawker's brigade of cavalry, was to approach the Alva further upstream near Pombeiro da Beira and the bridge at Vale de Espinho.[18] The main body of the *armée de Portugal* was assembling on the Serra de Moita, and Wellington's aim was to intercept and cut VI corps off by moving around Ney's left flank before a junction could be made with the rest of the army. Cavalry from Hawker's brigade reconnoitred towards Arganil, and the presence of these troops indicated to Massena that Ney's position around Ponte de Mucela was about to be outflanked. Reynier's troops should have been covering the fords around Sarzedo, with an outpost at Arganil, but were nowhere to be seen. Ney had already realised what Wellington intended. He wrote to Massena:

---

15   Oudinot, 'Souvenirs', p.31.
16   SHD: General Reynier au prince d'Essling, 17 mars, 1811. *Correspondance*, 7C12.
17   Extracts from the instructions communicated by the Q.M.G., Arrangement for the movement of the army on the 18th March, 1811, Gurwood, *Dispatches*, vol.4, p.680.
18   Murray, *Memoir Annexed to an Atlas*, p.54.

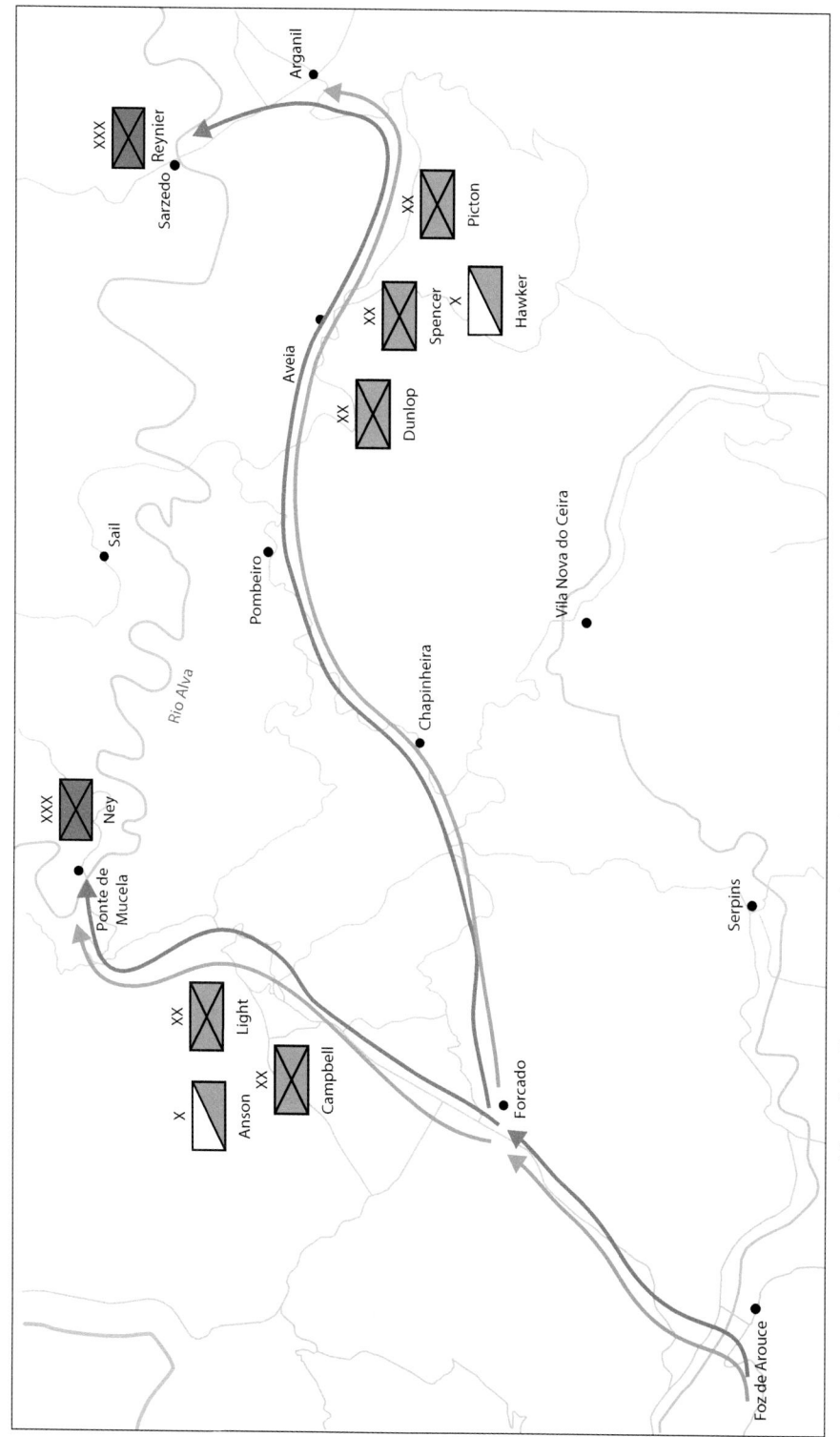

Map of the Alva positions and general routes of the French and Allied units on 18 and 19 March.

Prince, the enemy has begun to fire on the position at the Murcilla [sic] Bridge.

My left is completely exposed. General Reynier is very far from me, since my troops, in their reconnaissance, have not encountered his. The enemy can thus occupy me on the front by a demonstration and come in force to turn my left and even cut my retreat on Gallices. [sic] Consequently, it is urgent that Your Excellency decides to withdraw the troops, not only because we are unable to remain on this defensive position, the various bodies being dispersed there, but also because the soldiers are truly hungry and that I fear that by staying here they will scatter under the pretext of providing for their subsistence.[19]

Ney wrote that he would withdraw his forces to Galizes if he did not receive orders to retreat. Treussard, an officer of engineers, was sent to assess the situation at the fords near Pombeiro and reported the approach of Allied cavalry. Ney again wrote to Massena, complaining that he was now facing 15,000 Allied troops and would have to withdraw or be outflanked.[20] Pelet, seemingly intent on disparaging Ney's behaviour, suggested that there were no troops in front of Ney's position and that his desire to withdraw was to ensure VI corps was at the front of the retreat.[21] He does Ney a serious injustice, as there was indeed a large Allied force to his front, as well as one clearly visible and threatening his left, intended to separate his corps from the rest of the army. Ney had correctly discerned that the Light Division would be used in a holding action to pin his troops in place, whilst the Allied right column outflanked him. To make Ney's situation more vulnerable, on receiving news of the approaching Allied cavalry, Reynier ordered a retreat to Serra de Moita without informing his commander. Reynier had observed enemy troops moving at Avelar around noon and vacated his position.[22] Ney justifiably asked Massena, 'How is it that General Reynier has left his position?'[23] Thus, VI corps seemed to be at serious risk of being isolated from the main *armée de Portugal* before it could withdraw. Massena dispatched several ADCs and his *chef de l'état-major général* Fririon to find Reynier. At approximately 4:00 p.m., Fririon encountered a battalion of the 2e légère that was on its way to rejoin II corps, already at the Serra da Moita. Reynier, through the absence of communication with Massena and Ney, had exposed the entire left flank of the *armée de Portugal*.

From the Allied dispositions and movement orders, Wellington's intention was to envelop Ney's left flank and cut his line of retreat through Cortiça and on to Carapinha, but this would also have the effect of splitting the French line and placing the right column of the Allied army between Ney and Reynier. Reynier had seen the approaching troops and feared for his line of retreat, hence his rather hasty withdrawal. Massena issued orders for VI corps to retire to Venda do Porco, leaving

19   SHD: *Correspondance*, 7C12; Bonnal, *La Vie Militaire du Maréchal Ney*, vol.3, p.515.
20   Bonnal, *La Vie Militaire du Maréchal Ney*, vol.3, pp.516–517.
21   Pelet, *The French Campaign in Portugal*, p.484.
22   Koch, *Mémoires de Massena*, vol.7, pp.395–396.
23   18 mars 1811. Bonnal, *La Vie Militaire du Maréchal Ney*, vol.3, p.516.

its rearguard at Venda do Vale.[24] Despite being left exposed and vulnerable, Ney was able to withdraw his troops before the Allied outflanking movement could trap him. Simmons, as part of the 95th Rifles, was in the advanced guard on the 18th of March. He noted:

> Advanced early this morning to the river Alva, found the bridge blown up, and the enemy in position on very strong ground at Ponte de Mucela with some guns in position commanding the approach to the river. We formed opposite the enemy and had a fine view of a large body of them. Some nine pounders were soon got up, and commenced pounding their columns. I never saw Johnny go off in such confusion.[25]

Tomkinson, with the 16th Light Dragoons, wrote:

> We pushed on to the hill above the Ponte Murcella. [sic] The enemy's small infantry piquet was driven across by a detachment from the Light Division. The place is very strong either way, and the enemy hold the opposite banks with the whole of their 6th Corps d'Armée.[sic] Our nine pounders came up to the nearest ground they could to the river and fired a few shots, and, although at their utmost range, the enemy moved off, not intending to keep it longer than was necessary to get everything away.[26]

The right Allied column approached the fords upstream of Ponte de Mucela by the road through Pombeiro. Stothert noted that the Guards crossed the Alva on the 19th at about 5:00 p.m. via a ford where the river was '… mid-deep …'.[27] The Allied army now had the Light, 6th and 7th Divisions, along with Pack's, Ashworth's and *Tenente-coronel* Barbacena's Brigades around Serra da Moita and Carapinha.[28] The 1st and 5th Divisions were around Sarzedo, and the 3rd at Secarias. The cavalry of Anson's Brigade formed the advanced guard at Venda da Serra.[29] Wellington concluded that the French had intended staying in the position around Ponte de Mucela, 'As the greatest number of the prisoners taken … had been sent out on foraging parties towards the Mondego, and had been ordered to return to the position on the Alva'.[30] According to Sprünglin, several hundred French were captured, '… returning to the bivouac which had just been abandoned, and where they believed they would find their regiments.'[31] This situation was to be repeated during the following days as the French retreat accelerated, leaving numerous stragglers and foragers behind in their haste.

---

24   Bonnal, *La Vie Militaire du Maréchal Ney*, vol.3, p.518.
25   Simmons, *A British Rifle Man*, p.147.
26   Tomkinson, *Diary*, p.86.
27   Stothert, *A Narrative of the Principal Events of the Campaigns of 1809, 1810, & 1811, in Spain and Portugal*, p.230.
28   The report shows the village as Carrapichana, but this village is many miles to the east.
29   Extracts from the instructions communicated by the Q.M.G., Gurwood, *Dispatches*, vol.4, p.680.
30   Wellington to Liverpool. Oliveira do Hospital, 21st March, 1811, Gurwood, *Dispatches*, vol.4, p.688.
31   Sprünglin, 'Souvenirs', p.473.

The Allied engineers laid a bridge across the Alva, and the pursuit continued.[32] Simmons wrote that, 'A wooden bridge having been thrown across the river during last night, we passed over this morning [19th] and advanced through Sobreira.'[33] Nevertheless, the pursuit would be a stuttering affair. On the 18th, Wellington wrote to Charles Stuart in Lisbon:

> There are 2 brigades of [Portuguese] infantry and one of cavalry with this part of the army … none of whom have received any provisions since the troops marched from the Rio Maior river, excepting what have been issued to them by the British Commissary Gen., and the consequence has been, that the army has been obliged to halt; and I am unable to carry into execution the arrangement which I lately proposed.[34]

Major General Slade, with two brigades of cavalry and a troop of horse artillery, was instructed to pursue the French along '… the great road leading to Pinhanços.'[35] Wellington was struggling with the interminable problem of keeping his forces supplied. He wrote to Spencer on the 20th, 'I am concerned to hear you are badly off for provisions. I think we shall have a large supply of all kinds up this evening; if we have not, however inconvenient and disadvantageous it is to halt again, I shall send an order to countermand the march to-morrow, as it will not do to destroy the troops.'[36] The general orders issued on the same day stated bluntly:

> The want of supplies will prevent any general movement of the army taking place to-morrow; but Major Gen. Slade will march at daybreak … in pursuit of the enemy … If supplies can be procured in the course of to-night, one division of infantry will be pushed forward a short march to-morrow, as a support for the cavalry to fall back upon in case it should become necessary.[37]

An instruction was issued criticising some units in the rear of the army for seizing provisions meant for the units at the front:

> Those who stopped and seized those supplies should reflect that it is most easy to supply the troops nearest to the magazine, while those nearest the enemy require the supplies with the greatest urgency. It is besides quite irregular, and positively contrary to the orders of this army, for any Commanding officer to seize supplies of any description; there is a commissary attached

---

32   Schaumann, *On the Road with Wellington*, p.291; Simmons, *A British Rifle Man*, p.148.
33   Simmons, *A British Rifle Man*, p.148.
34   Wellington to Charles Stuart, Esq. Pombeiro, 18th March, 1811, Gurwood, *Dispatches*, vol.4, p.679.
35   Extracts from the instructions communicated by the Q.M.G., Arrangement for the 20th March, Gurwood, *Dispatches*, vol.4, p.682.
36   Wellington to Spencer, Arganil, 20th March, 1811, 1:30 p.m., Gurwood, *Dispatches*, vol.4, p.683.
37   Extracts from the instructions communicated by the Q.M.G., Arrangement for the 20th March, Gurwood, *Dispatches*, vol.4, p.682.

to every part of the army, and there is no individual, much less regiment, for whom some commissary is not obliged to provide.[38]

Despite this, some Allied troops were found plundering villages, and their officers subject to an inquiry.[39] This indiscipline occurred as Wellington was wrestling with the problems of the continued failure of the Portuguese commissary to supply their troops. Food from the British commissary was being given to the Portuguese, and this led to a general lack of victuals and supplies, resulting in the immobility of the army. He had written again to Charles Stuart in Lisbon, complaining of the failure of the Portuguese government to feed its own troops.

> Among other good qualities, [the Portuguese troops] possess that of being patient under privations in an extra ordinary degree. But men cannot perform the labor [sic] of soldiers without food. Three of Gen. Pack's brigade died of famine yesterday on their march, and above 150 have fallen out from weakness, many of whom must have died from the same cause ... I cannot bear to see and hear of brave soldiers dying for want of common care.[40]

The French had withdrawn at some speed after crossing the Alva, and this coincided with the pause in the Allied advance. The three *corps d'armée* marched in separate columns with Reynier's on the right flank and the baggage in the middle. Marching along the edges of the Serra da Estrela through villages whose occupants had fled, the French made good progress but suffered still from a lack of food and forage. Those marauders who left the retreating columns to look for food were met with armed resistance by the locals. Ney, with his corps between Galizes and Venda Nova, proposed a clear route to take his forces to Celorico to, '... avoid confusion and for the march of the columns to have a military aspect, that the army corps be sent off a few hours apart and even that the stops be regulated. By this means, the stragglers and transports could join their respective bodies'.[41]

The terrain began to flatten as the corps passed Gouveia, easing the burden on the men and remaining horses. Massena established his headquarters at Celorico on 21 March and began to consider his next moves. The *armée de Portugal* benefitted from the improvements to the roads completed under Wellington's orders the previous year. Pelet recorded, 'The result ... was an undulating road that was very good almost everywhere'.[42] Nevertheless, abandoned caissons and wagons littered the road, and the speed of the retreat was such that foraging parties continued to be abandoned and captured.

---

38   G.A.O., Arganil, 20th March, 1811, Gurwood, *Dispatches*, vol.4, p.681.
39   The A.G. to Major Gen. Dunlop, 5th division. 22d March, 1811, Gurwood, *Dispatches*, vol.4, p.690.
40   Wellington to Stuart, Pombeiro, 18th March, 1811, Gurwood, *Dispatches*, vol.4, pp.679–680.
41   Chamusca, le 19 mars 1811, à 5 heures du soir. Bonnal, *La Vie Militaire du Maréchal Ney*, vol.3, p.520.
42   Pelet, *The French Campaign in Portugal*, p.487.

On the 21 March Wellington wrote, 'The enemy retired from the position of Moita in the night of the 18th, and have continued their retreat with the utmost rapidity ever since: I imagine their rear guard will be at Celorico this day.'[43] Indeed, VIII corps had reached and marched through the town, but II and VI corps were stretched between Folgosino, Cortiço and the approaches to Celorico. The rearguard, now comprising a brigade of the 2e division of VI corps and the light cavalry, was positioned on the road at Carrapichana, some 10 kilometres from Celorico.[44] Picton was generous in his praise of Ney's handling of the French rear guard. He wrote:

> The enemy's rear-guard, during the whole course of the retreat, was commanded by Marshal Ney in person; and all his movements afforded a perfect lesson in that kind of warfare. Moving at all times upon his flank, I had an opportunity of seeing everything he did; and I must be dull in the extreme if I have not derived some practically useful knowledge from such an example.[45]

The difficulties of supply continued for the Allies, with the divisions moving in short marches, if at all. The Light Division and Slade's cavalry had acted as the vanguard of the Allied army but had struggled to keep up with the enemy rearguard. Wellington's headquarters moved to Oliviera do Hospital on the 21st, reaching Santa Marinha on the 23rd and halting there until the 25th. Orders were issued from Gouveia on the 28th for the final push of the Allied army to Celorico. The Light Division was ordered to press on past Celorico and occupy the area between that town and Ribiera, whilst the rest of the army was strung out between Gouveia and Celorico. The 3rd Division was directed to move over the difficult terrain of the Serra da Estrela with the clear intent of coming up on the French flank or rear.[46]

Notwithstanding problems of supply, the situation now was such that Portugal was no longer threatened, as it had been only a few months before. Wellington was confident that Portugal was safe. The *armée de Portugal* was between Celorico and Guarda, having suffered greatly from a lack of food for both the men and horses. On 20 March 1811, he requested that Beresford order the *Ordenança*, and *Milícia* in the Lines, to return to their homes, but to be ready at short notice to return to arms. Additionally, Vice Admiral Berkeley was instructed to send home the bulk of the transports from Lisbon, keeping only the, '… ships of war fitted for the conveyance of troops [and] coppered transports for the conveyance of 3000 infantry [and] 300 horses, all the hospital ships, and the baggage ships'.[47]

---

43   Wellington to Liverpool, Oliveira do Hospital, 21st March 1811, Gurwood, *Dispatches*, vol.4, p.688.
44   Fririon, *Journal Historique*, p.163.
45   To Colonel Pleydel, Philadoze, fifty miles in advance of Coimbra, 24 March 1811 ; and Guarda, 29th. Robinson, *Picton*, vol.2, p.387.
46   Arrangement for the movement of the army, 28 of March. Head-Quarters, Goveia, 27 March. Murray, *Memoir Annexed to an Atlas*, pp.55–56.
47   Wellington to Berkeley, Arganil, 20th March 1811, Gurwood, *Dispatches*, vol.4, p.684.

5

Disobedience and the Return to Spain

Having collected his forces in the region between Celorico and Guarda, most of the commanders of the *armée de Portugal*, and indeed the soldiers, expected the withdrawal into Spain to be completed in the next few days. This feeling was reflected in Massena's dispatch to Berthier, dated 19 March. He wrote, '… it is in the interests of his majesty to withdraw the army to our base of operations … it seems impossible to feed our troops in the mountainous country exhausted by the two armies'.[1] However, on 21 March, Massena began to issue a series of orders which would lead to the most significant confrontation between him and his most unruly subordinate, *maréchal* Michel Ney. He wrote to Ney to inform him that, '… the army will remain two or three days in the positions it occupies; it needs this in order to take some rest, repair its armaments, collect the stragglers and baggage. Please give your orders accordingly.'[2] Massena instructed his commanders that, after these few days' rest, the army was to move south from around Celorico and Guarda and to make for Belmonte and Alfayates. The artillery and its logistics would be brought up to Guarda, and all the sick and wounded would be returned to Spain.[3] All information regarding the bridges at Alcantara, Almaraz, and Alconetar was to be collected, as well as intelligence regarding the area around Badajoz, Plasencia and Coria.[4]

As this dispatch was on its way to Ney, he was writing a report to Massena on the position and condition of VI corps. The 1e division was placed behind and to the left of Cortiço da Serra, occupying Linhares, observing the roads to Gouvea and Guarda. The 2e division, with the light cavalry brigade, was spread from Carrapichana to Cortiço da Serra, maintaining observation of the road to Pinhanços. The 3e division, to the right and behind Cortiço, was observing the road to Vizeu. *Général de division* Trelliard's *dragons* were positioned between Celorico and Cortiço da Serra. Ney expressed his concern that the Allied army would continue to attack, and that Massena should indicate a fall-back position for the army. Ney also requested that the detachments that had been taken from VI corps be returned. More emphatically

---

1   SHD: *Correspondance,* 7C12; Also quoted in Pelet, *The French Campaign in Portugal*, p.488; Oman, *A History of the Peninsular War*, vol.4, p.173.
2   Celorico, le 21 mars 1811. Bonnal, *La Vie Militaire du Maréchal Ney*, vol.3, p.524.
3   Fririon, *Journal Historique*, p.165.
4   Jean Baptiste Koch, *Mémoires de Massena Rédiges d'apres les Documents Qu'il a laissés et Sur Ceux du Dépôt de la Guerre et du Dépôt de Fortifications* (Paris: Paulin and Lechavelier, 1848), vol.7, p.402.

expressed was the need for food, clothing, and shoes for his men. Ney knew that continuing in this region would be difficult, as it was almost devoid of supplies for the army, which had already suffered much. He wrote:

> I have just received the order for the army which specified that it will have a few days of rest. The position I occupy is by no means suitable to support the troops. Besides, the enemy will probably attack me tomorrow, and it is not in such a position that one can hope to take rest. I therefore believe that the safety of the army requires that Your Excellency determine a different position from the one I occupy.[5]

Clearly dismayed at this turn of events, Ney then sent several letters in quick succession in addition to his original response to Massena's order. He began with a reasoned reply based on the condition of the army, describing the area between Carrapichana and Celorico as a '… dreadful desert.'[6] He wrote that a single division, along with the light cavalry, would be sufficient to observe the defile at Cortiço da Serra, allowing the rest of the corps to disperse to collect food. Ney's generals were complaining to him that their troops were in a dire situation and needed food. *Général de division* Marchand, commander of the 1e division, wrote to Ney, 'For a few days our troops have had nothing to eat; I am convinced that in the vicinity of my division one would not find enough to feed a regiment for a day. The troops are bivouacked in the rain, without any means of building shelters and almost without wood to make a fire.'[7] To add pressure to the French position Allied cavalry now occupied Villa Cortês, as well as pushing reconnaissance out to Ney's flanks, posing a direct threat to his formations.

Ney wrote again, including Marchand's observations. Massena replied to Ney's letter in high dudgeon. Massena wrote, 'I have received your letter, including that of General Marchand, which I find very inappropriate … There is no question of going to Salamanca, but rather to Coria, Plasencia, and the surrounding areas to be able to sustain ourselves.'[8] He had decided on a plan, and no amount of argument, however realistic and logical, would move Massena from it. Ney and Reynier had first-hand experience of this region, and *maréchal* Victor had suffered there in 1809. Pelet suggests that Reynier had approved of the plan, but with the qualification that the army, '… would have great difficulties finding food in that area'.[9] Despite Ney's insistence that he had, '… travelled this country and nothing comes close to its sterility …'.[10] Ney wrote, at 2:00 p.m. on the 22nd:

---

5   Cortizo, le 21 mars 1811, 6 heures du soir. Bonnal, *La Vie Militaire du Maréchal Ney*, vol.3, p.525.

6   22 mars, dans la matinée. Bonnal, *La Vie Militaire du Maréchal Ney*, vol.3, p.526.

7   21 mars, au duc d'Elchingen par le général Marchand. Bonnal, *La Vie Militaire du Maréchal Ney*, vol.3, pp.526–527.

8   Bonnal, *La Vie Militaire du Maréchal Ney*, vol.3, pp.530–531.

9   Pelet, *The French Campaign in Portugal*, p.489.

10   22 mars, au prince d'Essling par le maréchal Ney, à 4 heures du soir. Bonnal, *La Vie Militaire du Maréchal Ney*, vol.3, p.532.

Prince, with the arrangements Your Excellency has just established, which direct all artillery equipment to Guarda and send the wounded or sick men to Spain, it seems that Your Excellency is prepared to move by the left to approach the Tagus towards Alcantara ... This manoeuvre seems very extraordinary to me at this moment. Your Excellency will have the kindness to tell me if you have received particular orders from the Emperor on these dispositions, which once again compromises the army and, by removing it from all its means of clothing and footwear, exposes at the same time, without a reason, the borders of Spain and Castile without achieving any essential goal of military operations.[11]

Massena remained unmoved:

I have received your three letters. You must not doubt my surprise. Their content forces me to take an extreme measure that I have sought to avoid until now. Your disobedience is too pronounced to not require from me a response commanded by the authority that His Majesty the Emperor has given me over the Army of Portugal by appointing me its commander.[12]

Ney's reply crossed the line from informed disagreement to disobedience: 'I persist in not allowing the VI corps d'armée to march on Coria and Plasencia, as Your Excellency has given me notice in your letter of this day, unless you inform me of the orders of the Emperor in this regard'.[13]

This refusal to obey the direct order from Massena resulted in his being relieved of his command. Massena wrote:

... it is with regret that I see you persist in formally disobeying my orders. As Commander-in-chief of the *armée de Portugal*, no one has the right to require me to inform him of the instructions which I may have received from His Majesty the Emperor ... I order the generals of division Loison, Marchand and Mermet, of the 6th corps, not to obey, as of present, any other than my direct orders or to those which will be transmitted to them by the senior general of division, M. le Comte Loison, and I order you to go to Spain to await the orders of His Majesty there.[14]

Loison was sent a letter informing him of Ney's dismissal, and another which made him commander of VI corps. That evening, Massena sent Pelet, his ADC, to Paris with a letter explaining Ney's dismissal.[15] Ney sent word to Massena that only the Emperor could remove him from command of VI corps, but that he

---

11   Cortizo, le 22, à 2 heures de l'après-midi. Bonnal, *La Vie Militaire du Maréchal Ney*, vol.3, p.528.
12   Bonnal, *La Vie Militaire du Maréchal Ney*, vol.3, pp.532–533.
13   22 mars, à 9 heures 30 du soir. Bonnal, *La Vie Militaire du Maréchal Ney*, vol.3, p.533.
14   22 mars 1811, 10 h 30 du soir. Bonnal, *La Vie Militaire du Maréchal Ney*, vol.3, pp.533–534.
15   SHD: Celorico, le 22 mars, 1811. Lettre du Marechal Massena, au prince Berthier. *Correspondance*, 7C12.

would grudgingly accede to Massena's instructions. On the morning of the 23rd, as Ney was preparing to leave with an escort of two companies of voltigeurs, he was informed of Allied troop movements in front of VI corps. He wrote to Loison that he was resuming command of the corps. Loison replied that he could not accede to Ney's suggestion. Ney then appealed to Massena again that only the Emperor could remove him from command, and that he should issue unambiguous orders for Ney to leave the army. Massena replied that Ney should, '… go immediately to Spain to await the orders of His Majesty.'[16]

Ney's removal caused upset in the army generally, but especially in VI corps. Sprünglin suggested that Ney briefly considered arresting Massena and taking command of the army, but sensibly refrained. However, Sprünglin described how, '… the French army was appalled. VI corps especially, formed by the Marshal, in 1804, at the Montreuil camp, led by him since that time and of which he knew every soldier, was deeply dejected.'[17]

Massena's troubles were not over with Ney's dismissal. Drouet informed him that his role with the armée de Portugal had ceased, and that the Emperor's intention was not for IX corps to enter Portugal. 'I have consequently given to all the troops which I command the order to fall back on Rodrigo and Salamanca.'[18] Without waiting for Massena's reply, he moved Conroux's division to Ciudad Rodrigo and recalled général de division Claparède from Guarda.

Massena's plan seems to have been to outmanoeuvre the Allies and push the armée de Portugal south across the Tagus. The decision to move his tired and starving army southwards rather than eastwards proved problematic. Although it would allow the army to link up with the forces of Soult and Mortier south of the Tagus and possibly approach Lisbon from the southeast, there were problems. Junot, still not recovered from his face-wound, and having suffered two reversals in Portugal, did not hide his antipathy to the expedition. Massena knew that Wellington's army was closing on his rearguard, but was not aware that the 3rd and 5th Divisions were moving across to Guarda over the Serra da Estrela. Regardless of the unruliness of his high command and contradictory orders from Paris, Massena drove his army towards Guarda, and then on to Belmonte, with piquets pushed out to observe the Estrada Nova and routes towards Castello Branco. II corps occupied Guarda and posted picquet on the road to Belmonte, with VIII corps between Celorico and Guarda around Ratoeira, having sent a detachment to observe the bridge at Ponte do Ladrão.

Predictably, the sparse mountainous environment proved too much for the army. As Ney had warned, the area was devoid of supplies to support the forces. Reynier reported the region was empty of provisions to keep the army fed: 'From Guarda to Plasencia the army would find no resources; this misery would cause it to commit the same horrors as in Portugal, and, supposing this difficulty is solved, there remains the passage of the Tagus.'[19]

16   23 mars à 11 h. 30 du matin. Bonnal, La Vie Militaire du Maréchal Ney, vol.3, p.537.
17   Sprünglin, 'Souvenirs', pp.474–475.
18   Koch, Mémoires de Massena, vol.7, p.414.
19   Koch, Mémoires de Massena, vol.7, p.418.

On 24 March, II corps' advanced guard approached Belmonte, the 1e division at Sortelha and the 2e around Águas Belas and Pousafoles do Bispo. VIII corps took position on the road from Guarda to Belmonte, with VI corps covering the artillery in its descent of the mountain of Tintinolho.[20] In the following days, VI corps closed up on Guarda, with Marchand's division in the town and Ferey's 3e division at Rapoula. Mermet's division, the 25e légère and a cavalry brigade were positioned around Gouveias and Freixedas. VIII corps sent patrols along the road towards Castello Branco and on the Estrada Nova.[21] Its artillery was left at Guarda because the roads were too bad for it to proceed with the rest of the formation.

Supplies continued to be a problem for Wellington, causing pauses in his pursuit of the French. The Light Division had reached Celorico on the 25th, and, like the 3rd Division, had only received one issue of bread in the last four days. Wellington wrote, 'The French have gone towards the Côa. Their left will cross at Sabugal, I should think, and their right about Pinhel and Almeida. We have been a little distressed for provisions, which has prevented us from pressing them so hard for these last days as I should have wished.'[22]

Two days later, he wrote that the army must halt, '… till the supplies which had been sent round from the Tagus to the Mondego should arrive.'[23] Cowell-Stepney of the Guards commented, 'Neither Indian corn, bread, nor biscuit, was to be seen; and I remember giving a dollar for a ship's biscuit to a sergeant of the 42nd, who was coming up from the rear'.[24] The Portuguese troops were in a precarious situation as well, still having no food at all from their own commissariat.[25]

By the 26th, the *armée de Portugal* had gone as far as it could. Reynier's II corps was in particular difficulty, having reached the mountains between Sortelha, Benquerença and Penamacor. VI corps was in Guarda, and the main body of VIII corps in Belmonte. All formations were suffering from a lack of supplies and difficulty moving along bad roads. Massena finally issued orders to stop, and, '… take advantage of the halt to produce bread and biscuits.'[26] For three days, the *corps d'armée* were halted in this desolate region without additional provisions. Junot wrote, 'It is therefore essential that Your Excellency promptly makes a decision, if you do not want to run the greatest risks, because troops that are starving are not capable of presenting themselves for battle.'[27] As Massena's troops paused, Wellington's were approaching from the west and north.

Wellington had not been idle while Massena procrastinated. On the 27th, he issued orders for the main body of the army to march via Celorico and then onto Guarda. The 3rd and 5th Divisions were to cross the mountainous territory between Linhares and Guarda, taking with them the mountain guns, whilst the field artillery

20   Fririon, *Journal Historique*, p.172.
21   Fririon, *Journal Historique*, pp.172–173.
22   Wellington to Beresford, Santa Marinha, 25th March, 1811, Gurwood, *Dispatches*, vol.4, p.695.
23   Wellington to Liverpool, Gouvea, 27th March 1811, Gurwood, *Dispatches*, vol.4, p.706.
24   Cowell-Stepney, *Leaves from the Diary of an Officer of the Guards*, p.65.
25   Wellington to Stuart, Gouvea, 27th March 1811, Gurwood, *Dispatches*, vol.4, p.705.
26   Fririon, *Journal Historique*, p.173.
27   Koch, *Mémoires de Massena*, vol.7, p.421.

followed the rest of the army. Specific information was sent to Picton to explain the movements Wellington required of his Division:

> The movements, ordered to take place to-morrow, are made with the view of acting against Guarda on the following day, should the enemy continue to maintain that post. I think it right to put you in possession of what is intended in that case, with regard to your division, and I therefore enclose an extract from the draft of the general instruction prepared for the 29th inst. I send also a sketch and a report, which I beg you will return to me along with your acknowledgment of the receipt of this letter.[28]

Wellington indicated that two of the brigades of the 3rd Division should cross the Mondego near Corujeira and move towards Guarda, with the intention of taking the fortress in the village of Vale de Estrela, which had been constructed by the Marquis d'Alorna in 1801. The remaining brigade would approach Guarda via the bridge at Faia and on through Cubo.

A small cavalry action took place towards Guarda involving a patrol of Allied cavalry of the 16th Light Dragoons under Lieutenant Persse, and Royal Dragoons under Lieutenant Foster. French prisoners were taken, adding to Wellington's intelligence of the condition of the enemy and providing some idea of their intentions.[29]

Guarda

Approaching Guarda from the north, the Light Division was to occupy the heights between Rocamondo and Guarda, with the 6th Division on its right. To their right would be Picton's 3rd Division approaching over the mountains from Linhares via Mizarela. Both armies had problems moving their artillery on the roads leading to Guarda. Wellington sent much of his artillery along the paved roads, protected by a battalion of the 3rd Division.[30] VI corps artillery had taken an entire day to ascend some particularly difficult heights at Tintinolho. Thus, the forces of both sides were without artillery or significant mounted forces when they faced one another at Guarda.

The French dispositions around Guarda left a lot to be desired, given the proximity of the Allied forces. Ney's experience as the commander of the rear guard was sorely missed on this occasion. Only one battalion from VI corps covered the northwest approaches to Guarda. When the advance of the Allies was reported by a patrol of *hussards*, the French quickly began to move their wagons and guns, followed by the cavalry and infantry, along the road to Alfaiates and Sabugal. One of Maucune's brigades narrowly escaped being surrounded and was withdrawn into

---

28 Instructions communicated by the Q.M.G. to Major General Picton. Gouvea, 27th March, 1811, Gurwood, *Dispatches*, vol.4, p.706.

29 Wellington to Liverpool. Gouvea, 27th March, 1811, Gurwood, *Dispatches*, vol.4, pp.707–708.

30 Arrangement for the movement of the army, 29 March, 1811 : Celorico. 28 March, 1811, Gurwood, *Dispatches*, vol.4, p.708.

Guarda from its vulnerable position. Ensign Grattan noted that the 3rd Division had approached Guarda without meeting any French picquet. He regretted the lack of artillery, considering that having a battery with the 3rd would have meant disaster for the French. He complained that:

> ... we had the mortification to witness the French getting out of [Guarda], bag and baggage, as quick as they could. The scene of confusion that the streets presented was great ... Our cavalry came up shortly after the enemy had evacuated the place, but too late to do much good. Some prisoners and baggage and a few head of cattle were captured, and we took up our quarters in the town for the night.[31]

Picton recorded:

> Massena himself, with full twenty thousand men, was on the heights and in the city of Guarda when I made my appearance at nine o'clock in the morning, with three British and two Portuguese regiments. This famous general certainly showed little determination or talent on the occasion; with his great superiority of force, he should immediately have attacked me, notwithstanding the excellence of my position, which, independent of its strength, had a most commanding appearance; but he allowed me to remain within four hundred yards of his main body, threatening his rear, for above two hours before the other [Allied] columns made their appearance ...[32]

Picton regretted that other divisions were not able to reach the French position at Guarda as speedily as he had done. He had to wait two hours before the 6th Division closed up on his left and considered that the day would have been decisive had the full force of the Allies been available in a coordinated fashion. Béchet recorded that, through the unexpected arrival of Picton's troops, the French were extremely vulnerable.[33] It may be that Wellington was concerned about attacking a strongly held position, especially as he believed the French to have the advantage in numbers. Wellington's intelligence, on this occasion, was faulty. On the 30th of March, he wrote,

> I don't know what to make of the French army. They had yesterday, some say, the whole force, but certainly not less than 2 corps, under Massena himself, upon Guarda, which is one of the strongest positions in the country. We manoeuvred them out of it, in 5 columns, without firing a shot; and they went off towards the Coa in considerable confusion, except the rear guard, which retired in excellent order. They were much stronger than we.[34]

---

31   Grattan, *Adventures with the Connaught Rangers, 1809-1814*, p.61.
32   Robinson, *Picton*, vol.2, p.386.
33   Béchet, *Souvenirs*.
34   Wellington to Stuart, Celorico, 30th March, 1811, Gurwood, *Dispatches*, vol.4, pp.712–713.

Rather than there being two entire Corps in the town, only a part of VI corps was in Guarda, and was outnumbered by the Allies' three divisions. Additionally, Picton's advance had caught the French by surprise. Some blamed Loison's slowness and lack of charisma for the poor performance of the VI corps at Guarda. Béchet wrote, 'Since the departure of Marshal Ney, we noticed in the movements of the army a lot of uncertainty and letting go; the illustrious marshal was far from having been replaced by general Loison, and each day increased the regret caused by his absence. That confidence between the leader and the soldiers, which inspires extraordinary feats, no longer existed.'[35]

Godart suggests that the delay in leaving Guarda was due to waiting for Massena's mistress to pack.[36] Whatever the real reason, the withdrawal was so rushed that the Allied troops found food already prepared on tables in the houses; one cooked mule's head had a note in its mouth that read, 'For Mr John Bull'.[37] Massena, finally realising the folly of his manoeuvres, had ordered a concentration of the army between Sabugal, Rapoula-do-Côa and Alfaiates.[38] He wrote to Berthier, 'Compelling circumstances which I must no longer conceal from Your Highness have forced me to give up the project of operating in Portugal. I have done everything in my power to keep the army out of Spain for as long as possible'.[39] He then blamed his commanders for causing unrest, which had been communicated to his soldiers and caused their morale to collapse.

In addition to following Massena, Wellington was handling other matters. On the 31st, he wrote to the Earl of Liverpool requesting 150,000 pairs of large, well-made shoes for the army. Footwear was in short supply, and that which was available was often of poor quality. He complained, '… as the soldiers pay for the shoes they receive, it is but just towards them that they should be of the best quality for their purpose, and should fit them.'[40] The army had marched far, and shoes were crucial to the soldiers' well-being. The rough Portuguese roads meant that their shoes wore out quickly, and at times they had to march barefoot. Lack of essentials such as food, water and shoes could quickly stop an army from moving. The Allied army was again stationary due to a lack of means to transport food and supplies, further delaying the pursuit of the French.[41] Charles Napier was moved to write to his mother that:

> We have now, for one month, been up at three a.m. marching at four, and halting at seven o'clock at night, when we eat all we can get, from shoe soles to bread and butter … we are on biscuits full of maggots, and though not a bad soldier, hang me if I can relish maggots … there! my biscuit has run away on maggots' legs.[42]

35   Béchet, *Souvenirs*, pp.374–375.
36   Roch Godart, J-B Antoine (ed.), *Mémoires Du Général Baron Roch Godart (1792-1815)* (Paris: E. Flammarion, 1895), p.162.
37   Natalia Griffon de Pleineville, 'L'évacuation du Portugal', *Gloire & Empire*, 70 (2017), p.71.
38   Fririon, *Journal Historique*, pp.173–175.
39   Alfayatès, le 31 mars 1811. Fririon, *Journal Historique*, p.177.
40   Wellington to Liverpool, Celorico, 31st March, 1811, Gurwood, *Dispatches*, vol.4, p.716.
41   Head-Quarters, Celorico, 31st March, 6:00 p.m., Murray, *Memoir Annexed to an Atlas*, p.59.
42   Alfayates, April 6th. Napier, *The Life and Opinions of General Sir Charles James Napier*, vol.1, p.166.

As much as Wellington was managing the minutiae of his army's progress, Napoleon was completely out of touch with the situation in Portugal. On 31 March, he dictated a letter to *maréchal* Berthier, planning the destruction of the British forces in Portugal. Massena was to, '… remain at Coimbra, and threaten Lisbon, which will be attacked after the harvest by 70,000 men belonging to the army of Portugal'.[43] Napoleon still only counted 30,000 British troops as the size of the enemy army to be defeated, ignoring the Portuguese. By the time the letter was written, Massena's army was straggling back to the Portuguese-Spanish border, unable to threaten Portugal anymore.

The capability of Wellington's intelligence is demonstrated in a single sentence in his dispatch to Beresford on 30 March. He notes, almost in passing, 'Ney is gone to Salamanca, it is said in arrest.'[44] Wellington knew that Loison had taken command of VI corps. He had missed the chance, however, of cutting off Junot's corps during its retreat from around Belmonte. Although it had been pursued by Erskine's cavalry, only small skirmishes had occurred.[45]

On 31 March, Massena wrote to Berthier, partly to excuse his latest manoeuvres, to inform him that the army must be removed from Portugal and be given rest. 'The desire that the army has long manifested to go to rest leaves me in no doubt that it would be dangerous to await battle or to offer it.'[46] On 1 April, Reynier wrote to Massena explaining the problems he was facing as a direct consequence of the abortive move southwards:

> … the troops, especially the horses, suffer greatly; they have nothing to eat, and nothing can be found in this position. You could see that all the land around Sabugal is uncultivated. The few villages within a two- or three-league radius are exhausted or occupied by VI Corps … Unable to feed the army in this position, it seems to me that there are only two choices: move forward and occupy the position … or move back, that is to say, into Spain … I hope you make a decision today. The cavalry officers all say their horses cannot survive in this position; I am sending part of the cavalry to fetch forage two leagues from here.[47]

The French had now moved beyond the Côa, with VI corps south of Sabugal on the Côa between Ponte de Sequeiros and Bismula. VIII corps was at Alfaiates, with the II corps acting as the main rear-guard watching the bridges and fords across the Côa near Sabugal itself. The cavalry reserve occupied Navas-Frias, Casillasde-Flores and Fuente-de-Guinaldo.[48] Reynier sent information to Massena, warning him of the approach of the Allied army along the road from Urgueira and requesting orders to

43   17531, au Prince de Neuchatel et de Wagram, Major Général de l'Armée d'Espagne, a Paris. Paris , nuit du 29 Au 30 Mars 1811, *Correspondence de Napoléon I*, vol.21, pp.525–529.
44   Wellington to Beresford, Celorico, 30 March, 1811, Gurwood, *Dispatches,* vol.4, p.710.
45   Wellington to Liverpool. Marmeleiro, 2 April, 1811, Gurwood, *Dispatches,* vol.4, p.720.
46   Alfayatès, [sic] le 31 mars 1811. Fririon, *Journal Historique*, pp.177–179.
47   SHD: *Correspondance du Général Reynier*, 1814, C8-251; Also quoted in Béchet, *Souvenirs*, pp.372-373.
48   Fririon, *Journal Historique*, p.178.

withdraw. In response to these increasingly worried dispatches, Massena reassured him that the army would begin its retreat on the 4th, continuing:

> You are on the spot and capable of judging the enemy's movements. I have nothing to add to your observations, and if I were to make any, I would say that I don't think the enemy wants to attack you. He positioned himself on the Penamacor road to observe if we want to take it. Moreover, the army is free from its artillery and baggage and ready to manoeuvre without hindrance; the 6th corps is on your right, the 8th behind you, and either will support you if necessary. By starting your movement during the night, it would be admitting to the enemy that he forced you to leave your position, and to tell you the truth, I don't believe that Lord Wellington is in front of you. Furthermore, the army is departing the day after tomorrow, and we must hold tomorrow.[49]

Reynier continued to be concerned about his position. On 2 April, Massena wrote to him, 'If you believe you cannot hold out without compromising yourself, warn the Sixth Corps which is on your right at [Ruvina] of your movement; Loison will do the same with regard to you, if he is obliged to begin the retreat'.[50] Reynier wrote to Loison for reassurance that he would send a warning of any rearward movement of VI corps, and stated:

> … if the enemy attacks me seriously, my posts will cross back over the river, and I expect to be able to defend the passage if the Allies attempt it, regardless of their attack, and to resist them until evening. I prefer to fight in this position, since the Prince has decided to remain here today, rather than to carry out my retreat in daylight, pursued by the enemy; I shall depart tonight.[51]

Wellington issued orders for 1 April instructing the 1st Division to close up to the Côa between Seixo do Côa and Porto de Ovelha, taking possession of the bridge at Ponte de Sequeiros. The recently formed 7th Division would support the 1st, positioned near Pínzio. The 6th Division, supported by the 5th, would occupy Rapoula do Côa but keep in touch with the 1st Division on its left. The Light Division, accompanied by the 3rd, would move on to Pega and thence to Sabugal. Wellington wrote to Beresford that, in response to the presence of British cavalry patrols, the enemy had destroyed the bridge over the Côa at Almeida. Patrolling aside, because of a shortage of supplies, the movement described above was suspended, and then set in motion on the 2nd.[52] The Light Division, nevertheless, marched to Adão on the road from Guarda to Sabugal to keep in contact with the French rearguard.[53] Even though

49   Koch, *Mémoires de Massena*, vol.7, pp.429–430.
50   Koch, *Mémoires de Massena*, vol.7, p.431.
51   Koch, *Mémoires de Massena*, vol.7, p.432.
52   Head-Quarters, Celorico, 28th March, 1811. Murray, *Memoir Annexed to an Atlas*, pp.58–59.
53   Head-Quarters, Celorico, 31st March, 6:00 p.m. Murray, *Memoir Annexed to an Atlas*, p.59.

they kept moving, the Light Division suffered from a lack of supplies as much as the rest of the army. Lieutenant John Paul Hopkins of the 43rd Foot, recalled on 1 April that, 'The Light Division suffered very much for want of bread during the last days of operations.'[54]

At midday on the 2nd, Reynier informed Massena that, within view of his outposts, a column of infantry, squadrons of cavalry and 10 cannon were moving along the road from Urgueira to Sabugal. These troops appeared to be taking position with their right on the Penamacor road. More troops could be seen around Quintas de São Bartolomeu and Vale Mourisco.[55] The 6th Division moved into Rapoula do Côa and had seized a mill defended by a company of the 82e ligne. This was almost immediately retaken, but the fighting continued until nightfall. Ferey ordered the Légion du Midi and the Légion Hanovrienne to guard the mill and the ford.[56] This small action caused uncertainty for Massena as to where the next blow would fall.

Reynier's Corps had occupied the ridges above Sabugal on the right of the Côa, covering the bridge in the village and the fords upstream. Voltigeurs from II corps were posted to guard the fords across the Côa above Sabugal, and the 25e dragons were posted to the left of the French position to observe that flank. Reynier placed Sarrut's brigade of *général de division* Merle's division, consisting of the 2e légère, 36e ligne and 4e légère, on the low plateau overlooking the Alfaiates road. At the same time, he ordered *général de division* Heudelet, as well as the troops at Sabugal, to prepare to march. VI corps kept its positions on the Haute-Côa around Nave, with VIII corps towards Alfaiates. The cavalry reserve was located across the border around Navasfrías, Casillas de Flores and Fuenteguinaldo.[57] Concerned about the threat developing at Sabugal, early on the morning of 3 April Massena ordered II corps artillery to fall back on Alfaiates.

Wellington issued orders for an attack. He had received intelligence from an officer of Reynier's staff captured nearby that II corps was alone on the other side of the Côa.[58] The Light Division and attached cavalry under Anson and Hawker would be employed in a flanking manoeuvre around the French left. The orders for Erskine describe in some detail where he was expected to pass his troops across the Côa:

> Major Gen. Sir W. Erskine will have the troops under his orders formed in close columns behind the top of the heights which form the left bank of the Coa above Sabugal, so as to be prepared at 8 o'clock A.M. to move down towards the river (if so ordered), and to pass it about one mile above the little chapel which there is on the left bank of the Coa a mile higher up than the bridge of Sabugal. If Sir W. Erskine is directed to pass his infantry at the place here mentioned, he will make the cavalry pass farther up the river, so

54 John Paul Hopkins Description of the action at Sabugal. Glover and Burnham, *Riflemen of Wellington's Light Division*, p.79.
55 Koch, *Mémoires de Massena*, vol.7, p.428.
56 Koch, *Mémoires de Massena*, vol.7, p.430.
57 Fririon, *Journal Historique*, pp.178–179.
58 TNA: WO 37/7a, Scovell, *Diary*, p.28.

as to cover the right of the infantry and gain the open country, by leaving the woods upon the opposite side of the Coa to their left.

As circumstances may, however, render it desirable that the cavalry, and the Light Division also, should turn the enemy by even a wider circuit, Sir William Erskine will be prepared, in that case, to move to his right, along the left bank of the Coa, in order to pass it as far up as Quadrasayes, [sic] or at any intermediate point that may be ordered. He will be so good, therefore, as to have the roads in that direction reconnoitred as soon as possible.[59]

These orders leave a certain degree of flexibility for Erskine and are presumably dependent on verbal orders given at the last minute. The normally accepted version of the advance of the Light Division is that, because of the weather conditions, the commanders became disoriented and were to cross at fords closer to Sabugal, rather than those that Wellington had indicated. This may not be the case. Erskine, not being the most stable and attentive of officers, may have become confused by the conditional nature of the orders. Indeed, the cavalry moved much further along the river. However, if a contemporary map held at the National Archives in Kew is accurate, then the Light Division crossed approximately at the position given in the first paragraph, some two miles upriver of the bridge at Sabugal, and a mile upstream of the chapel of Nossa Senhora da Graça.[60] Additional instructions expanded the detail of Wellington's plan and clearly show the anticipated points of attack:

> As soon as the Light Division and 3rd Division have moved down to pass the river, the light infantry of the 5th Division will drive in the enemy's posts which are upon the left bank of the Coa opposite Sabugal … As soon as the enemy begins to give way at the town and the bridge, in consequence of the movements of the Light and 3rd Divisions round his left and rear, and of the fire of the 9-pounders upon his front, the 5th Division will move forward and pass the river.[61]

The expectation from these additional orders seems to be that the 3rd Division would attack the French left, and the Light Division would be positioned at the French rear. It may be that whatever reconnaissance of the French line was carried out on 2 April failed to reveal the full extent of Reynier's line, or that it was extended during the night, undoing the conclusions drawn from information gathered by previous reconnaissance. Whatever the reason, the Light Division advanced into the left of the French line, rather than moving past it, and the 3rd Division hit the left-centre of the enemy line.

The 3rd Division was to cross a mile upstream of the bridge. The 5th Division was to form up on the road from Pega to Sabugal. The 6th Division was to be at Pega, prepared to move to its right and cross the Côa in support if required. Campbell

---

59   Head-Quarters, Marmaleira, 2 April. Murray, *Memoir Annexed to an Atlas*, p.60.
60   TNA: WO 78/5974, T. Mitchell, *Sketch of the Action at Sabugal, 3 April 1811*.
61   Additional Instructions. 3 April, near Sabugal. Murray, *Memoir Annexed to an Atlas*, pp.61–62.

was to make sure he had reconnoitred the roads to Sabugal and the fords between Rapoula do Côa. The 1st Division was to move to Vale Mourisco, to be followed by the 7th Division. Barbacena's cavalry would cover the left flank of the Allied army, observing the crossings of the Côa between Ponte Sequeiros and Castello Bom. The Allied army thus converged towards Sabugal in a position to outflank the French around Sabugal and Quadrazais, whilst also threatening the French right towards Rapoula do Côa. If II corps could be fixed long enough for the Light Division to cut the road to Alfaiates, it would be trapped.

Sabugal

Sabugal, like many battles, reflects Wellington's view that individual events may be recalled, but the order in which they occurred can vary based upon who is recounting them.[62] Thus, an outline of the action can be provided, and specific events recounted, but the overall sequence of events cannot be described with absolute certainty.

On the morning of 3 April, there was a thick mist and occasional showers of rain. The Light Division and attached cavalry advanced towards the fords across the Côa that they had been told to use. Beckwith's brigade comprised the 1/43rd Foot, three companies of the 3° Caçadores, and four companies of the 1/95th.[63] Why only three companies of the 3° Caçadores were present is uncertain. The brigade was moved forwards early on the 3rd and halted to await orders. Lieutenant Hopkins recalled the 43rd waiting in column of companies, under arms, for orders to cross the Côa.[64] A staff officer rode up and abruptly asked why the brigade had not begun the attack.[65] Immediately, Beckwith ordered his troops over the river via a ford where the water came up to the men's armpits, significantly slowing down their advance.[66] Kincaid described the initial advance: 'We instantly uncorked our muzzle-stoppers, off with our lock-caps, and our four companies of riflemen, led through the river, (which was deep and rapid,) followed by the 43d, driving in the enemy's picquet which defended it.'[67] The crossing was somewhat disorganised because of the appalling weather. The cavalry became separated from the infantry, and the two brigades of the Light Division were out of sight of each other in a sudden downpour. Fergusson of the 43rd mentions that the 3° Caçadores also became separated, although others mention their presence.[68] The poor weather conditions had delayed or caused the diversion of Drummond's Brigade. The Division advanced in a driving rain with the enemy positions obscured by mist, so the mistake was not identified immediately. Beckwith's brigade was alone, at least for the moment. The French picquet, voltigeurs

---

62   A dam was built near Sabugal in 1994 which has inundated the area where the allies crossed the Côa and part of the battle was fought.
63   Wellington to Beresford, Sabugal, 4 April, 1811, Gurwood, *Dispatches*, vol.4, p.723.
64   Glover and Burnham, *The Men of Wellington's Light Division*, p.60.
65   Garrety, *Memoirs*, p.125; Kincaid, *Adventures*, p.164.
66   Simmons, *A British Rifle Man*, p.161.
67   Kincaid, *Random Shots from a Rifleman*, p.165.
68   John Paul Hopkins Description of the action at Sabugal. Glover and Burnham, *Riflemen of Wellington's Light Division*, p.79.

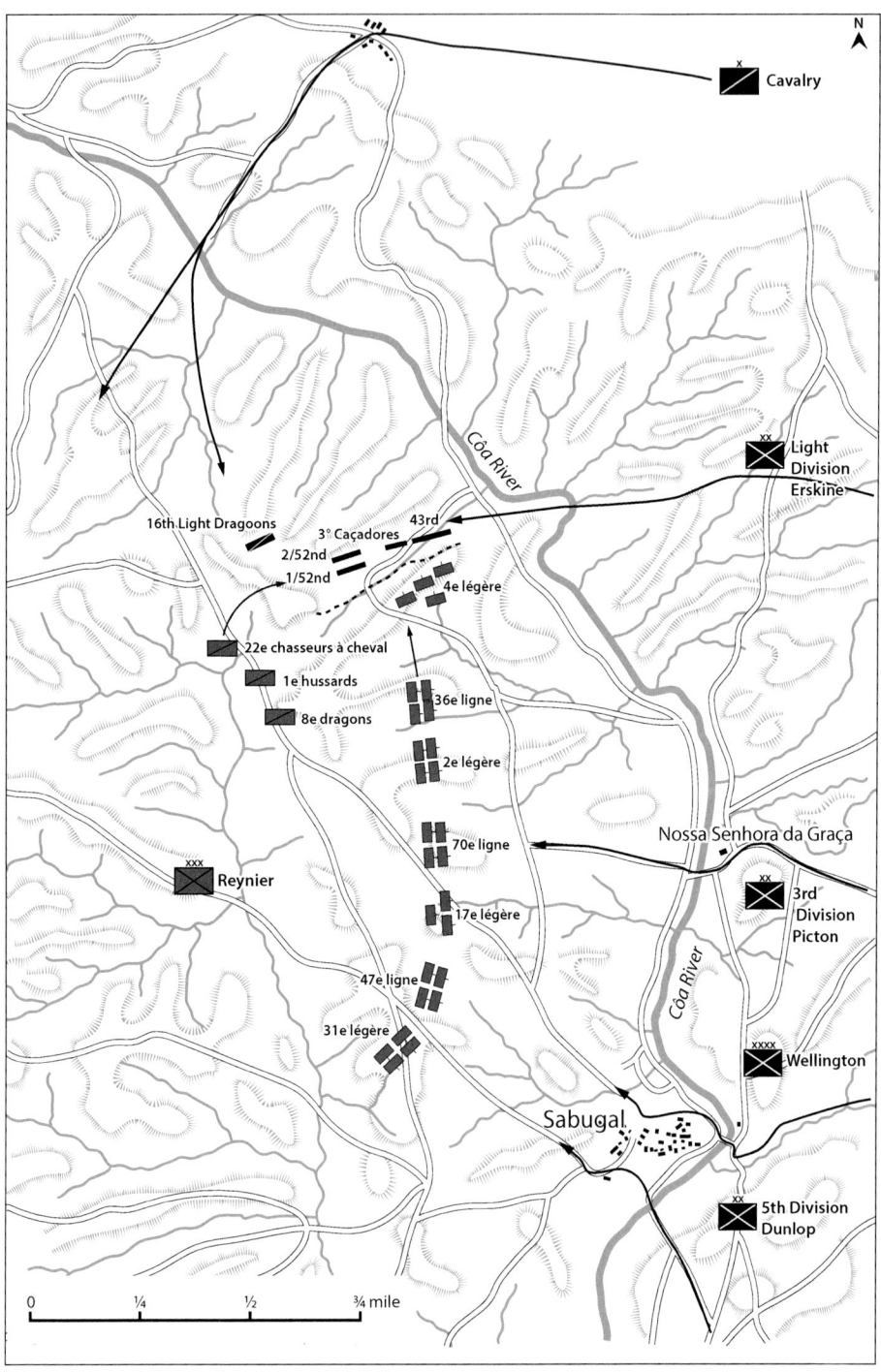

The Battle of Sabugal, 3 April 1811.

from the 17e légère, kept up a fire on the advancing British until they were driven in by the companies of the 95th and 3° Caçadores advancing ahead of the 43rd.[69] As the companies of the 43rd cleared the river, they advanced piecemeal towards the French line, '... each company getting into line as it arrived.'[70] Tomkinson may add some information regarding the order in which the 43rd crossed the river. He wrote, 'Much was said of the impropriety of the division crossing left in front. As it attacked immediately on passing, it was correct; had it marched as intended, some distance before it met an enemy, it ought to have moved by its right, and so would have been ready on the march to form line in a moment.'[71]

The order of march, or 'left in front', refers to the junior company of the regiment being at the head of the column. The order of companies in line is by seniority from right to left. In a regular British battalion, the grenadier company, the senior, stands on the right of the line, and the light company on the left. In a light battalion, not having a grenadier or separate light company, the order of deployment was probably based on the captain's seniority. According to the 1792 regulations, if a battalion is expecting action to its left, it should march right in front, thus allowing a turn to the left into the correct order.[72] This may be why the companies of the 43rd were fed into the battle individually, in order to reorder them correctly. However, Hopkins of the 43rd recalled that the battalion advanced right in front, and as an infantryman as opposed to a cavalryman, as was Tomkinson, Hopkins' description seems the most likely. The piecemeal advance of the 43rd may simply be a result of disorganisation caused by the weather and crossing the ford, following which the companies would require time to reform before proceeding.

Merle's division was on the left of the French position, at the end of a ridge running from Sabugal along the Côa. The 4e légère, comprising four battalions, was on the far left of the position, with the 2e légère (four battalions) and 36e ligne (four battalions) under *général de brigade* Sarrut to their right. Thus, Merle could bring 12 battalions to the fight. Heudelet's division formed up on Merle's right, and comprised *général de brigade* Godart's 1e brigade of the 17e légère (three battalions) and 70e ligne (four battalions) on the left and *général de brigade* Arnaud's 2e brigade of the 31e légère (four battalions) and 47e ligne (four battalions) on the right. *Général de brigade* Soult was instructed to protect the left flank with his cavalry brigade, comprising the 1e hussards, 22e chasseurs à cheval, 8e dragons and the chasseurs Hanovrienne.[73] Having been warned of the approaching Allied forces, Merle initially brought the 4e légère into battle, advancing in column of divisions.[74] Lieutenant John Cox of the 95th described the scene: 'In front was a wood of large horse chestnut trees which was warmly disputed by the 4th [Cox misidentified them

69   Michel Molières, *Les Expéditions Françaises En Portugal de 1807 à 1811* (Paris: Publibook, 2007), p.365.
70   Glover and Burnham, *Riflemen of Wellington's Light Division*, p.79.
71   Tomkinson, *Diary*, p.93.
72   *Rules and Regulations for the Formations, Field Exercise and Movements of His Majesty's Forces* (London: Adjutant General's Office, 1812), pp.94–95.
73   Fririon, *Journal Historique*, p.179.
74   Auguste Braquehay, *Le Général Baron Merle, 1766-1830* (Montreuil-sur-Mer: A. Becquart, 1892), p.160.

as the 14th] French Light Infantry, but the galling fire of the 95th Rifles at point blank range soon compelled them to retire, but rallying with strong supports, the wood again became the scene of sharp work and close-firing.'[75]

Costello recorded, '… through some mistake, we were left almost unsupported; after crossing the river, we advanced up the hill, on the other side, and under a fleecy shower of rain, soon became hotly engaged with the French.'[76] With visibility of only a few tens of metres, Kincaid remembered, 'As soon as we gained the summit of the hill, it became as clear as the mist that we were regularly in for it.'[77] At this point, Simmons mentions that the 43rd and Caçadores had joined and moved up with the 95th.[78] The 95th were driven back by the 4e légère and formed in column on the flanks of the 43rd, who then fired on the advancing French columns. Three enemy columns were counted by Cox, and given that the 4e légère had four battalions, keeping one in reserve would make sense, and provide three for the attack. An exchange of musketry followed, and Beckwith led his troops in a charge which forced the 4e back to the top of their hill. A lack of space stopped the 4e from deploying into line, forcing them to fight in column of divisions.

Hopkins was in command of the right-most company of the 43rd as the battalion advanced upon the French positions to its front. Seeing some French approaching from his right rear, he detached his company and moved to occupy a small hillock, fighting off repeated attempts by the enemy to gain it. He recalled, 'I reserved my fire until they neared the summit of the hill, when I opened upon them, causing them to retire in some disorder to the plain. They again formed and advanced as before, but were checked, retreating to a greater distance.'[79]

Private Thomas Garrety described that Hopkins, '… with admirable presence of mind seized a small eminence close to the French guns and commanding the ascent by which the French troops were approaching.'[80] Major Christopher Patrickson of the 43rd recalled Alexander Cameron, then of the 95th Foot, bringing his company to join the 43rd's left flank during the fight.[81] It is apparent from Hopkins' testimony that the French were not solely occupying the low ridge running along the Côa, but were also positioned to the rear, or east, of that ridge. As such, the 43rd was exposed to attack from both its right flank and its front, but Reynier appears to have been unaware of the weakness of the first Allied attack.

The 2e légère and 36e ligne, which had been brought up by *général de brigade* Sarrut, covered the withdrawal of the 4e, firing into the advancing British. Two guns from Merle's divisional artillery were brought into action and supported Sarrut's

---

75   Glover and Burnham, *Riflemen of Wellington's Light Division*, pp.92–121.
76   Costello, *Memoirs*, p.112.
77   Kincaid, *Random Shots from a Rifleman*, p.165.
78   Simmons, *A British Rifle Man*, p.176.
79   Garrety, *Memoirs*, p.126; Description of the action at Sabugal. Glover and Burnham, *The Men of Wellington's Light Division*, p.60.
80   Garrety, *Memoirs*, p.126.
81   Letter dated 1845 [?] from Patrickson to Sir Alexander Cameron, 95th Foot, regarding the action at Sabugal, 1811, and the Côa on 24 July 1810. Glover and Burnham, *The Men of Wellington's Light Division*, p.38.

infantry as they charged with bayonets and pushed Beckwith's Brigade back.[82] Sarrut's men then returned to the plateau where they continued to defend their position, assisted by the artillery of the 1e division. A howitzer under the command of *lieutenant* Lamorinière of the 3e régiment d'artillerie à cheval became the focus of fighting for a while, as its possession alternated between the French and Allied troops. Garrety described the action: '... a second charge cleared the hill, a howitzer was taken, and the British skirmishers were even advanced a short way down the hill, when small bodies of French cavalry came galloping in from all parts, and obliged them to take refuge in the main body of the regiment.'[83]

Guingret recalled how Lamorinière, '... fought determinedly and met a glorious death trying to reclaim his piece. We might have managed to take it away if our infantry had understood anything about manoeuvring cannons.'[84] This may be the officer noted by Harry Smith when he mentioned the fighting over the guns: 'A French officer on a grey horse was most gallant. Old Beckwith, in a voice like thunder, roared out to the riflemen, "Shoot that fellow, will you?" In a moment he and his horse were knocked over'.[85] Lamorinière's death is recorded by Martinien, and two other officers from the same regiment were wounded.[86] One of Garrety's comrades, '... having previously passed the howitzer, took a piece of chalk from his pocket, and, as he said, marked it as our own, and we were determined to keep it.'[87] Later, there was controversy over who had taken the gun, some claiming the 52nd and others the 43rd. Patrickson wrote some 34 years later: 'Colonel Gurwood, I understand, has published a pamphlet among his friends stating that the 52nd came up towards the close of the business, and took the howitzer at Sabugal, which is all a farce. They hardly lost a man, their first battalion three men and their second battalion none at all.'[88]

Gurwood, who had served in the 52nd, may be excused for overzealous devotion to his former regiment. The history of the 52nd records that the regiment retook the gun, even naming Lieutenant J. Frederick Love as the commander of the company.[89] But it was indeed the 43rd who took the gun, confirmed by a dispatch to the Earl of Liverpool in which Wellington attributes the taking of the gun directly to that battalion.[90]

According to a manuscript quoted by Oman, Drummond had received an order from Erskine not to engage. However, '... the staff officer who carried it, and Drummond, seeing how matters stood, took the liberty of forgetting the message'.[91]

82   Braquehay, *Merle*, p.160.
83   Garrety, *Memoirs*, p.127.
84   Guingret, *Relation Historique*, p.189.
85   Smith, *Autobiography*, p.46.
86   Martinien, *Tableaux Des Officiers*, p.649.
87   Garrety, *Memoirs*, p.127.
88   Letter dated 1845 [?] from Patrickson to Sir Alexander Cameron, 95th Foot, regarding the action at Sabugal, 1811, and the Côa on 24 July 1810. Glover and Burnham, *The Men of Wellington's Light Division*, p.38.
89   Moorsom, *Historical Record of the Fifty-Second Regiment (Oxfordshire Light Infantry)*, p.138.
90   Wellington to Liverpool. Villar Formoso, 9 April, 1811, Gurwood, *Dispatches*, vol.4, p.734.
91   Oman, *A History of the Peninsular War*, vol.4, n.194.

We might imply from this that Drummond was not lost, but in fact holding a position behind Beckwith's Brigade. Marching to the sound of the gunfire, Drummond brought his second brigade of the Light Division into action to the right of Beckwith's. He advanced the companies from the 95th Rifles and the 1° Caçadores in a screen in front of the 1/52nd, with the 2/52nd in reserve. This unexpected assault caught those French who were attacking the right of the 43rd on their left flank and drove them back once again. Hopkins wrote:

> I perceived the 2nd Battalion of the 52nd advancing rapidly. I went to the commanding officer, pointing out the enemy near and we agreed it would be best for him to form his regiment on the right of my company and make an immediate advance upon the French, which we did. As we advanced, they retired … extending all my men as skirmishers; the 52nd doing the same to my right, we all commenced skirmishing amid the trees in unabated rain.[92]

The 1e brigade of Heudelet's division were now fed into the battle, with seven battalions of the 17e légère and 70e ligne under *général de brigade* Godart attacking the Light Division. *Général de brigade* Soult charged Drummond's Brigade with a squadron of the 1e hussars and the 22e chasseurs à cheval, forcing the riflemen of the 95th and the skirmishers of the 52nd to form up on the main body of the brigade.[93] The attacks were eventually beaten off by a combination of furious musketry from behind any obstacle available, and a squadron of the 16th Light Dragoons which had found its way onto the right flank of Drummond's Brigade.[94] Many infantrymen fought from behind the stone-walled enclosures, with at least one soldier of the 52nd using a tree stump for protection.[95] The to-and-fro nature of the battle was recalled by Costello: 'They were at least four or five times our number, and compelled us to retire twice before their overwhelming masses.'[96] During the firefight, Beckwith was wounded by a musket ball on the right side of his face next to his eye, but continued to lead his men.

As the rain began to clear, Reynier saw the threat to his line developing as the 3rd and 5th Divisions crossed the river. The only force available to Reynier now was Heudelet's 2e brigade. This would not be able to hold back the advancing Allied columns. He knew his position was hopeless and ordered his forces to retreat toward Alfaiates.[97] Godart's brigade was to hold the ridge and keep back the Light Division to enable the other units to withdraw, but was unable to prevent the advance of the 3rd and 5th Divisions on their flank. Kincaid recalls:

---

92 Captain John Paul Hopkins Description of the action at Sabugal. Glover and Burnham, *Riflemen of Wellington's Light Division*, p.79.
93 Glover and Burnham, *Riflemen of Wellington's Light Division*, p.80.
94 Tomkinson, *Diary*, pp.93–94.
95 Moorsom, *Historical Record of the Fifty-Second Regiment (Oxfordshire Light Infantry)*, p.139.
96 Costello, *Memoirs*, p.112.
97 Paul Charles Thiébault, *Memoires du General Baron Thiébault* (Paris: E Plon, Nourrit, 1895), vol.4, p.318.

... a French column occupied the top of what seemed to be almost a preci-
pice overlooking the river; but I observed some of the 60th rifles clambering
up the face of it on all fours, and, to see their astonishment, when they
poked their heads over the brink, to find themselves within a couple of yards
of a French column! They, of course, immediately concealed themselves
under the bank; but it was curious to observe that they were unseen by the
enemy, who were imprudent enough either to consider themselves secure
on that side, or to give all their attention to the fight going on between their
comrades and us; but certain it is they allowed the riflemen to gather there
in formidable numbers.[98]

This was the leading edge of the 3rd Division, which had crossed the Côa by a ford
close to the chapel of Nossa Senhora da Graça. The 5th Division had begun to
advance across the bridge in the town. Meanwhile, the Allied cavalry appeared on
the French left, heading along the same road as the leading guns of the French reserve
artillery. The Allied cavalry had swept widely to the right of the Light Division and
a squadron of Hussars reached the baggage, taking that of the unlucky *général de
brigade* Pierre Benoît Soult, younger brother of the *maréchal*.[99] The French withdrawal was becoming disorganised under pressure from the three converging Allied
divisions. Heudelet had organised cover for the retreat from the 31e ligne and his
artillery.[100] Nonetheless, Wellington, acting on reports that VIII corps was coming
to Reynier's aid, and with deteriorating weather, ordered the army to halt.[101]

Godart recorded simply, 'The II Corps, attacked by the enemy, was forced to
retreat after losing approximately 400 men.'[102] On the night of 3/4 April, the *armée
de Portugal* began its withdrawal into Spain. At the same time, an order was given to
extract cadres of officers and non-commissioned officers to send them to the depots
in France to pick up conscripts awaiting deployment. Along with these cadres, a
number of dismounted cavalrymen would also return. *Chef de bataillon* Olivet of
the 31e légère was given command of the column.[103]

The choice by Reynier to make a stand at Sabugal is questionable. The decision to
withdraw into Spain had already been made, and Massena had even ordered II corps'
artillery to withdraw. It would have made sense for the main body of the corps to
have left at the same time. Koch suggests that Reynier misrepresented orders received
from Massena and that authorisation to withdraw arrived earlier than Reynier
claimed.[104] However, he appeared confident in his corps' ability to defend the river
line.[105] That confidence was misplaced despite the bravery and tenacity of the French
troops. Regarding the Battle of Sabugal, Wellington wrote, with some restraint, that:
'Although the operations of this day were, by unavoidable accidents, not performed in

98   Kincaid, *Random Shots from a Rifleman*, p.171.
99   Tomkinson, *Diary*, p.94.
100   Koch, *Mémoires de Massena*, vol.7, p.435.
101   Tomkinson, *Diary*, p.94.
102   Godart, *Mémoires du Général Baron Roch Godart (1792-1815)*, p.163.
103   Lemonnier-Delafosse, *Souvenirs militaires*, p.128.
104   Koch, *Mémoires de Massena*, vol.7, p.436.
105   Koch, *Mémoires de Massena*, vol.7, p.432.

the manner in which I intended they should be, I consider the action that was fought by the Light division, by Col. Beckwith's brigade principally, with the whole of the 2d corps, to be one of the most glorious that British troops were ever engaged in.'[106]

Erskine, joining Wellington following the battle, remarked that he claimed no merit for the victory, but that it was all down to Beckwith.[107] Scovell remarks only that the 3rd Division arrived late because of delays imposed by traversing difficult ground. It was this, '… want of combination in the columns made the victory at the time doubtful, but the Gallantry of the Light Division overcame every difficulty.'[108] Thus, it seems that it was not that the Light Division crossed at the wrong point, but that the cavalry went too far to provide the necessary support, and the 3rd Division was delayed.

Casualties reflected which regiments had been most hotly engaged. The Light Division suffered 17 killed and 139 wounded.[109] Surprisingly, the 43rd had eight soldiers killed, surely light casualties considering the severity of the combat. The Portuguese casualties were one soldier killed and five wounded.[110] The French regiments most heavily engaged were those of the 17e légère and 70e ligne, with 177 and 244 casualties, respectively, out of a total of 760 French casualties.[111] The presence of the chasseurs Hanovrienne is confirmed by a single officer casualty recorded in Martinien's list.[112] Private Timewell of the 43rd vividly described the outcome:

> The enemy's wounded that lay on the ground they burned before they would let them fall in the hands of the Portuguese. The number [that] engaged us that day was 21,000, and our division, that is the 43rd, 52nd, 95th, two Portuguese regiments [1° and 3° Caçadores], Captain Ross's Flying [Horse] Artillery, and King's 1st German Light Dragoons [Hussars], all only [a] mounted to 7,000 men; and those 21,000 men was the rearguard of the French army that could not get out of the way.[113]

Kincaid makes an interesting observation regarding the different formations used by the opposing sides. When the lines of the 43rd confronted the French columns Beckwith, '… had but single companies to oppose to the enemy's battalions; but, strange as it may appear, I saw him twice lead successful charges with but two companies of the 43d, against an advancing mass of the enemy. His front … was equal to theirs'.[114] This seems to confirms that the French remained in columns during the battle due to the limited space available to deploy.

---

106 Wellington to Liverpool, Villar Formoso, 9 April, 1811, Gurwood, *Dispatches*, vol.4, pp.733–735.
107 Kincaid, *Adventures*, p.172.
108 TNA: WO 37/7a, Scovell, *Diary*, p.30.
109 Oman, *A History of the Peninsular War*, vol.4, p.616.
110 Tomkinson puts the Portuguese wounded at nine. Tomkinson, *Diary*, p.94; Soriano, *Historia Da Guerra Civil*, vol.3, p.380.
111 Appendices VII and VIII, losses at Sabugal, April 3rd, 1811. Oman, *A History of the Peninsular War*, vol.4, pp.616–617.
112 Légion hanovrienne (Cavalerie). Martinien, *Tableaux Des Officiers*, p.503.
113 Private John Timewell, Journal. Glover and Burnham, *Riflemen of Wellington's Light Division*, p.220.
114 Kincaid, *Random Shots from a Rifleman*, p.167.

Wellington later wrote of Sabugal:

> We have given the French a handsome dressing, and I think they will not
> say again that we are not a manoeuvring army. We may not manoeuvre so
> beautifully as they do; but I don't desire better sport than to meet one of
> their columns en masse with our lines. The poor 2d corps received a terrible
> beating from the 43d and 52d on the 3d.[115]

The withdrawal of the *armée de Portugal* proceeded swiftly, and on 4 April the
French took up position on what would become the battlefield of Fuentes de Oñoro.
II corps was established around the villages of Poço Velho, Fuentes de Oñoro and
Espeja. The corps artillery moved directly to Ciudad Rodrigo along with that of
VI corps. That corps was positioned around Fuente de Guinaldo. VIII corps took
up position at Ituero and Campillo de Azaba. Montbrun's cavalry and the attached
artillery occupied Fuente de Guinaldo and El Bodón. The 6e dragons, posted around
Castillejo de Azaba, observed the pursuing Allied army. The 11e and 15e dragons
were pushed forwards along the road towards Ciudad Rodrigo.[116]

Reynier was nervous that his corps would be caught on the wrong side of the
Agueda and isolated by an attack that would cut him off from the bridges at Ciudad-
Rodrigo and Barba de Puerco (now called Puerto Seguro). Perhaps the action at
Sabugal had unsettled him. He sent a message to Massena expressing his concerns,
noting that the fords across the Agueda had been measured at up to 1½ metres deep,
meaning they could only safely be crossed with cavalry. Massena seems to have lost
patience with him and replied to Reynier's message:

> The more I have read and reread your letter, the more incomprehensible
> it has become to me. Don't you know that the Agueda flows at the foot of
> the fortress [Ciudad Rodrigo], and that the troops that could be positioned
> there are completely sheltered under its artillery? Since you are so fright-
> ened of your position, Conroux's division of the 9th corps will relieve you
> tomorrow, and you will go to San Felices.[117]

The Allied cavalry probed the French along their entire front, occasionally
exchanging shots and capturing a few prisoners. On 7 April, Claparède's division, responsible for maintaining communications between Almeida and Ciudad
Rodrigo, was threatened in its position by Slade's cavalry, Bull's troop of Royal Horse
Artillery and Trant's militia. The 6th Division was held on the high ground above
Val de Mula as a reserve.[118] The 6e de ligne provisoire was assembled at the Fuerte
de la Concepción. Claparède ordered the 5e de ligne provisoire, stationed at Val
de Mula, to stand to, and instructed the 2e légère provisoire to join him. Once the

---

115 Wellington to Capt. Chapman, Royal Engineers. Villar Maior, 8th April, 1811, Gurwood,
     Dispatches, vol.4, p.727.
116 Fririon, *Journal Historique*, p.184.
117 Koch, *Mémoires de Massena*, vol.7, p.446.
118 Wellington to Beresford, Villar Formoso, 10th April, 1811, Gurwood, *Dispatches*, vol.4, p.739.

fighting began Claparède directed a second *bataillon* to Val de Mula and pushed two others from the 5e forward to meet the 2e légère provisoire. Two *bataillons* from the 6e légère provisoire were also moved to Val de Mula. Lacking cavalry and artillery, once Claparède had gathered his troops they moved towards Aldea del Obispo and withdrew across the Agueda.[119] The Allies had thus cut communications between Almeida and Ciudad Rodrigo, and inflicted more casualties and loss of prisoners upon the French. Wellington summed up the action by writing to Charles Stuart in Lisbon, 'We knocked a division of the 9th corps, from Almeida, out of Portugal very handsomely yesterday, and I believe the whole army have crossed the Agueda this day.'[120] The slow but steady dissipation of strength would have a detrimental effect on French morale and effectiveness as veteran soldiers were replaced by recruits.

On the 7th, Massena sent a message to *général de brigade* Brenier in Almeida, warning that the army could no longer find food in its positions, would move across the Agueda completely, and would be quartered around Salamanca, Toro and Ledesma. Meanwhile, the cavalry reserve moved across the Agueda to Ciudad Rodrigo to rest its exhausted horses and look for fodder. IX corps alone would remain near the Côa around San Felices de los Gallegos. Drouet complained that his corps had not received any bread and would be unable to move. Massena denied Drouet access to the supplies until his orders had been obeyed. He sent *adjudant commander* Delosne to IX corps with instructions to see that it moved as ordered.[121] The next day, II corps crossed the Agueda, and VI corps took the road to Salamanca, with Marchand's division arriving on the 10th. The army remained quartered between Salamanca, Valladolid and Ciudad Rodrigo until the beginning of May, conducting reconnaissance and observing the Allies as they became established between the Côa and the Agueda rivers.

Wellington placed the Light Division in a position to cut off Almeida. Although the fortress was still occupied by Brenier's troops, Wellington was confident it would not take long to retake. He wrote on the 9th that reports had been received of the low morale of the French and their plans to blow up Almeida. Despite this, he urged the Earl of Liverpool to send more horses because, 'I am very desirous not to be found in an incomplete state, if we are to be attacked.'[122] The Allied army took up position along the Portuguese frontier and awaited the French.

On 10 April, Wellington felt confident enough to issue a proclamation announcing the liberation of Portugal.

119   SHD: Claparède à Drouet, 7 mai, *Correspondance*, 7C12; Wellington to Liverpool. Villar Formoso, 9th April, 1811, Gurwood, *Dispatches*, vol.4, p.735.
120   Wellington to Charles Stuart, Esq. Villar Maior, 8 April, 1811, Gurwood, *Dispatches*, vol.4, p.731.
121   Koch, *Mémoires de Massena*, vol.7, p.473.
122   Wellington to Liverpool, Villar Formoso, 9 April, 1811, Gurwood, *Dispatches*, vol.4, pp.735–736.

6

Behind the Scenes

At the end of the retreat from Portugal, both armies had suffered losses of horses, clothing, and even men due to starvation. However, the ability to recover from such privations was to mark the difference between the two national and local strategies.

The French Army

The *armée de Portugal* comprised three corps d'armée: *général de division* Reynier led II corps; *maréchal* Ney commanded VI corps; and *général de division* Junot VIII corps. IX corps under *général de division* Drouet was not directly under the command of Massena until after the retreat had begun.

At the beginning of the campaign in 1810, II corps, '… consisted of excellent troops, having received no conscripts for more than two years.'[1] It was a restructured version of the former II corps from the *armée d'Espagne* and comprised over 16,000 soldiers and 18 guns. Many of Reynier's troops had already fought against the British and faced Wellington in the earlier invasion of Portugal and Soult's occupation of Oporto. Reynier had fought alongside Massena in Italy and been present at the Battle of Wagram in 1809. He had been beaten by the British at the Battle of Maida in 1806. At Buçaco II corps had attacked at the pass above San Antonio do Cantaro, were repulsed and suffered considerably. During the retreat from Santarém, II corps had only one serious engagement, at Sabugal, and had experienced significant casualties and a blow to their morale.

VI corps was established from the two infantry divisions of *maréchal* Ney's Corps of the Grande Armée. It originally consisted of over 27,000 men and 30 artillery pieces and was primarily composed of seasoned soldiers who had served under Ney for several years. One of Napoleon's most pugnacious battlefield commanders, he was usually to be found in the thick of the fighting. Leading VI corps since its establishment in 1804, Ney had garnered the loyalty of his troops, and he demonstrated significant tactical skill as the rear-guard commander during the retreat from Santarém. At the beginning of the campaign Ney received reinforcements totalling 6,000 troops under *général de division* Loison. These formed an additional division to add to the experienced units of the 1e and 2e divisions. A significant

---

1 Pelet, *The French Campaign in Portugal*, p.23.

portion of these reinforcements consisted of foreign units, such as the Légion Hanovrienne, raised from German troops, and the Légion du Midi, formed in the annexed *departments* of northern Italy.[2] Some battalions, formed as recently as 1809, were sent directly to Spain and consisted of raw conscripts. VI corps fought against the Light Division at Buçaco and had been pushed off the mountain with significant casualties.

VIII corps was originally composed of a large number of conscripts and less reliable troops, initially assembled for rear-area security during the 1809 Franco-Austrian War, comprising predominantly fourth battalions and the reconstituted 65e ligne. It was placed under Junot's command in June 1809 and officially designated as VIII corps later that summer. Upon its march to Spain, several additional units were added to its ranks, including the 15e and 86e ligne, and a battalion of the 15e légère. The elements of the 1e division led by Clausel comprised inexperienced 4th battalions from various regiments, except for the 3e brigade, which consisted of four battalions exclusively from the 22e Ligne.[3] The corps was filled out with other foreign troops such as the Légion Irlandaise and Régiment de Prusse. Despite appearing to have Irish or Prussian origins, these units comprised individuals from various nationalities, including prisoners of war and deserters from Wellington's army.[4] Many of the French troops were from regions that had been recently incorporated into the French Empire, and might therefore be less committed in their loyalty to the Emperor. There were troops from Italy, the Low Countries and parts of Germany, even troops of the artillery train from Wurtzburg.[5] Pelet described Junot's command as being, '… made up almost entirely of new or foreign regiments and one third of the infantry in the fourth battalions had been formed up very recently.'[6] Many of these troops had been collected from various depots in France and had seen little fighting.[7] This corps sat out the Battle of Buçaco but later made the only serious attempt to break the first line of defences around Lisbon at Sobral. Junot possessed an unpredictable nature but displayed great courage in battle. He sustained a facial wound during a reconnaissance of the Lines of Torres Vedras near Pernès, and it is believed that this injury, along with several previous ones, contributed to his eventual mental breakdown.[8]

IX corps, commanded by *général de division* Jean-Baptiste Drouet, *comte* d'Erlon, although not officially a part of the *armée de Portugal* at the beginning of the campaign, was eventually placed under Massena's command. These orders were sent by Napoleon on 6 February 1811, but they would not be received until

---

2   Digby George Smith, *Napoleon's Regiments: Battle Histories of the Regiments of the French Army, 1792-1815* (London: Greenhill, 2000), pp.219–220.

3   Pelet, *The French Campaign in Portugal*, pp.520–521.

4   Ernest Picard and Louis Tuetey (eds), Louise Seymour Houghton (trans.), *Unpublished Correspondence of Napoleon I Preserved in the War Archives* (New York: Duffield and Company, 1913), vol.3, p.790; Smith, *Napoleon's Regiments*, pp.218–219.

5   Etat de Situation des Troupes au 15 Septembre 1810. (Presents sous les armes.) Fririon, *Journal Historique*, p.68.

6   Pelet, *The French Campaign in Portugal*, p.23.

7   Koch, *Mémoires de Massena*, vol.1, p.27.

8   Noël, *With Napoleon's Guns*, p.108.

several weeks later.[9] The corps comprised a number of 4e bataillons composed of recruits or soldiers with little service time, as well as returning injured soldiers. It functioned largely as a temporary holding formation for these battalions until they could be reunited with their parent regiments. These 4e bataillons were formed into provisional units called *régiment de ligne provisoire* or *régiment légère provisoire*, but were also referred to as *demi-brigade de ligne* or *légère*. For example, at the Battle of Fuentes de Oñoro, the 2e demi-brigade légère consisted of the 4e bataillons of the 54e ligne, 21e and 28e légère. IX corps included *général de brigade* Fournier's cavalry, comprising the 7e, 13e, 20e chasseurs à cheval. Battalions that had been separated from their regiments in the *armée de Portugal*, the 6e and 25e légère, 27e, 39e, 59e, 69e, and 76e ligne, were reunited with their parent units in April.

One consequence of the increasing number of inexperienced troops was a rise in officer and NCO casualties. Oman comments on the increased number of officer casualties at Sabugal, noting that 61 officers had been lost against 699 rank and file, a ratio of one to 11, compared with a standard ratio of one to 20.[10] The *armée de Portugal* suffered heavy officer casualties in the fighting because of the habit of the officers encouraging their often inexperienced troops, urging them on from the front. Simmons recalled that during the fighting at Almeida, the, '… French officers like mountebanks running forward and placing their hats upon their swords, and capering about like madmen'.[11] Some of the units in the *armée de Portugal*, however, had considerable experience and demonstrated what would now be called strong unit cohesion. Even those units, such as the fourth battalions, which may be considered lower quality, had been together since June 1809. During that time, they had marched across much of Germany, continuing on to Portugal in 1810. But the loss of experienced officers, or soldiers, could not be replaced easily, and as time went on, more of the veteran troops would be siphoned off for the campaigns in Russia and of 1813 and 1814. The French armies in Spain became less able to fight against a more capable enemy.

Logistics

Before the retreat from Santarém, the appearance of the French soldiers was described thus: '… our regiments which had nothing left but their uniform coats for parade days, and what a uniform … troops of harlequins, the diversity of colours of greatcoats and trousers was obvious.'[12] The situation had deteriorated further by the time the army was back in Spain. Noël wrote, 'Our supply situation was deplorable; we lacked everything – food, ammunition, clothing, boots, money and horses.'[13] All of the corps had lost a considerable number of men, and those that were left were starving and riddled with disease and vermin. Many soldiers had fallen into the hands of the Allied army while out foraging, while others had simply surrendered. The lucky ones were taken by the British soldiers; the unlucky ones fell into the hands of the Portuguese.

---

9   17335, Au Prince de Neuchatel et de Wagram, Major Général de l'armée d'Espagne , a Paris, 6 February 1811, *Correspondence de Napoléon I*, vol.21, p.387.
10   Oman, *A History of the Peninsular War*, vol.4, p.617.
11   Simmons, *A British Rifle Man*, p.77.
12   Lemonnier-Delafosse, *Souvenirs militaires*, p.111.
13   Noël, *With Napoleon's Guns*, p.117.

By 1 April 1811, the number of effectives was reduced to approximately 40,000 men, including officers.[14] Massena was deeply concerned by the losses of men and materiel during the retreat, and on 3 April, as Reynier was struggling with the Light Division at Sabugal, he issued a decree offering the *armée de Portugal*, '... distributions which will be made to it regularly; consequently marauding is expressly forbidden, and marauders will be punished according to all the rigour of the law.'[15] Fririon states that this was also intended to reduce the impact of foraging on Spanish peasants, who were supposed to be under French protection. The simple act of issuing orders like these indicates the deplorable situation which had obtained during the retreat.

The army was not just in need of food, shoes and uniforms but was desperately in need of horses. Noël recorded that the artillery of VIII corps had started the campaign in September 1810 with 142 wagons and 891 horses (Fririon records the VIII corps artillery and engineers had 1,151 horses)[16] By the time the corps returned to Spain in April 1811, it had only 49 wagons and 182 horses.[17] Overall, between 16 September 1811 and 1 March, the *armée de Portugal* lost 4,597 horses: this was before the retreat from Santarém began.[18] Pelet recorded that before the Battle of Fuentes de Oñoro, '... the artillery had been brought near the battlefield by oxen, in order to spare the horses, which were in very poor condition.'[19] Replacing horses in Spain and Portugal was problematic, not least because even if there were replacements to be had they were smaller and weaker than those from France and Central Europe, and fodder was always difficult to come by. Thus, the losses sustained by the army were significant, yet Massena, his subordinates, and historians more recently, have sought to minimise them. On 19 March, he wrote to Berthier that:

> Our retreat was carried out with the utmost order; we did not leave behind a single sick or wounded person, nor a single artillery piece or baggage wagon. The enemy was repelled every time they attacked, always suffering losses. Finally, since the army regrouped at Pombal, it has only travelled 2 leagues per day and has never been driven back by the English.[20]

One eminent French historian wrote, '... from October 1810 to March 1811 Massena had lost but a single cannon.'[21] This may be true, but that period was when the French were stationary around Santarém.

---

14   Fririon, *Journal Historique*, p.179.
15   Fririon, *Journal Historique*, p.184.
16   Fririon, *Journal Historique*, p.69.
17   Noël, *With Napoleon's Guns*, p.117.
18   Pièces justificatives No XI. Summary of horse losses suffered by the armée de Portugal from September 16, 1810, the time of the invasion, until March 1, 1811, five days before the retreat. Koch, *Mémoires de Massena*, vol.7, p.590.
19   *Victoires, Conquêtes, Désastres, Revers Et Guerres Civiles Des Français, De 1792 À 1815* (Paris: C.-L.-F. Panckoucke, 1820), vol.21, p.341.
20   No XXXVI. Le Maréchal Prince d'Essling à S. A. le Prince de Wagram et de Neufchâtel, Major Général. Maceira, le 19 Mars, 1811, Gurwood, *Dispatches*, vol.4, p.839.
21   Georges Blond, Marshall May (trans), *La Grande Armée* (London: Arms and Armour Press, 1995), p.275.

Command and Control

The dysfunctional French command structure led to what Clausewitz called 'friction'. He wrote, 'Friction is the only conception which, in a general way, corresponds to that which distinguishes real war from war on paper.' He likened it to moving in water: 'Activity in war is movement in a resistant medium.' In summing up the problem, he wrote, 'Everything is very simple in war, but the simplest thing is difficult.'[22] Massena was faced with several elements of his command that made the simple difficult. Amongst the most significant were his cantankerous and self-willed subordinates, making coordination between formations, an essential element for a successful military operation, difficult. Ney and Bessières were to prove openly obdurate, whilst Junot and Reynier were less vocal but equally as troublesome. Under the command of Napoleon, these *maréchaux* and *généraux* had performed well, but without his guiding will, the commanders bickered to the detriment of the overall objective of defeating the Allied armies.

Massena and Bessières had recently commanded *corps d'armée* in the campaign against Austria in 1809. Massena's actions in the campaign had earned him plaudits from Napoleon, but he had been seriously hurt in a fall from his horse. His situation was so bad that for part of the Battle of Aspern-Essling he commanded from a horse-drawn carriage. At the same battle, Bessières had almost come to blows with *maréchal* Lannes, and only Massena's intervention to separate bodily the two men had prevented a serious incident. As a result of a serious wound received at the Battle of Wagram, Bessières was sent home to recuperate. During Napoleon's divorce from Empress Josephine and the courting of *Erzherzogin* Marie-Louise, Bessières' support for Josephine earned him Napoleon's disfavour. Whether as an act of conciliation or to humble Bessières, Napoleon gave him the task of welcoming the Empress-to-be Marie-Louise on her journey to Paris.[23] Once he was again considered fit to campaign, physically, militarily and politically, Bessières was appointed commander of the new *armée du Nord* in Spain in January 1811.

Friction was present in the *armée de Portugal* from the moment Massena took up his appointment. Foy observed at the time:

> Our army in Portugal is rife with discord. Ney wants to act but does not know how to obey; he constantly fails to show the respect he owes to the prince. Junot, rightfully humiliated to find himself third, where he was once first, wholeheartedly wishes for the expedition to fail. Reynier, whose interests currently align with the public good, plays his cards well; but the prince does not like him.[24]

As early as the siege of Ciudad Rodrigo in July 1810, Massena and Ney were at loggerheads over control of the siegeworks and planning.[25] Ney's repeated displays of insolence and then of outright insubordination led ultimately to his dismissal. However,

---

22   Clausewitz, *On War*, book 1 Chapter 7.
23   Marie Élie Guillaume de Baudus, *Études Sur Napoléon* (Paris: Debécourt, 1841), vol.1, p.148.
24   Girod de l'Ain, *Vie Militaire du Général Foy*, p.101.
25   White, *The Key to Lisbon*, p.104.

this did not stop other commanders from being critical of Massena's behaviour, but most acquiesced grudgingly to the *prince's* orders. Following Ney's removal, Loison was appointed commander of VI corps, but his behaviour mirrored the drop in morale in the *corps d'armée*. He was not a leader or tactical commander of the same calibre as Ney. He complained repeatedly of the situation of the army, indicating a wish to return to France at the earliest opportunity, citing poor health.[26]

French Fighting Techniques

In 1808, Napoleon announced a decree to restructure the composition of infantry regiments and battalions. This entailed reducing the number of companies in a battalion from nine to six. Additionally, the overall configuration of a regiment, each with a total strength of 3,970 personnel, inclusive of officers, was adjusted to include five battalions.[27] However, the prescribed limit of five battalions was occasionally exceeded, as is evident from army lists in Appendix 2. Notably, certain units, like the 26e ligne in Simon's brigade, included a sixth battalion.[28]

Some historians have perpetuated the notion that the French always favoured attacking in column formations to break through enemy lines. This generally derives from the works of Oman and Fortescue. Oman delivered a lecture, published in his work *Studies in the Napoleonic Wars,* entitled *Column and Line in the Peninsula.*[29] This lecture and subsequent publication set the standard in English language history for the interpretation of French tactics in the Peninsular War.

This misunderstanding has been so influential that the idea of 'attack columns' as the only means of attack by the French in the Peninsula still holds sway. There is the perception that the French *fought* in columns. The evidence is clear that the French *manoeuvred* in column but attempted to *fight* in line. Moving in column was faster since there was a reduced need to maintain the alignment essential to a linear formation. French doctrine was that the infantry would advance in column and then attempt to deploy into line out of musket range just before engaging the enemy. Deploying into line meant the number of muskets available to fire was maximised, aiming to bring troops swiftly into action and unleash volleys of fire.

When moving in a column, the practice was to maintain a gap between each company. This gap, known as the 'full distance', was equal to the frontage of the company. However, it was a regular practice to close up this gap, reducing it to half distance or even closer, to enhance the column's manageability on the battlefield and boost the morale of the soldiers. If the column is closed up so that there are no gaps between companies, it is termed a 'close column,' referred to as *en serrée* or *en masse*.

Columns could be organised by division, platoon, or section. In this context, confusingly, a division indicated two companies, while a platoon denoted one company. The form of deployment was to be determined by the presence, or absence,

26   SHD: Correspondence de Loison, *Armée de Portugal: Correspondance*, 1811, 7C20
27   Composition de l'infanterie de ligne et légère, Decree, Palais des Tuileries, 18 February 1808, *Correspondance de Napoléon I*, vol.26, p.338.
28   État de situation des troupes au 15 Septembre 1810, Fririon, *Journal Historique*, p.64.
29   Charles Oman, *Studies in the Napoleonic Wars* (London: Methuen, 1929), pp.82–108.

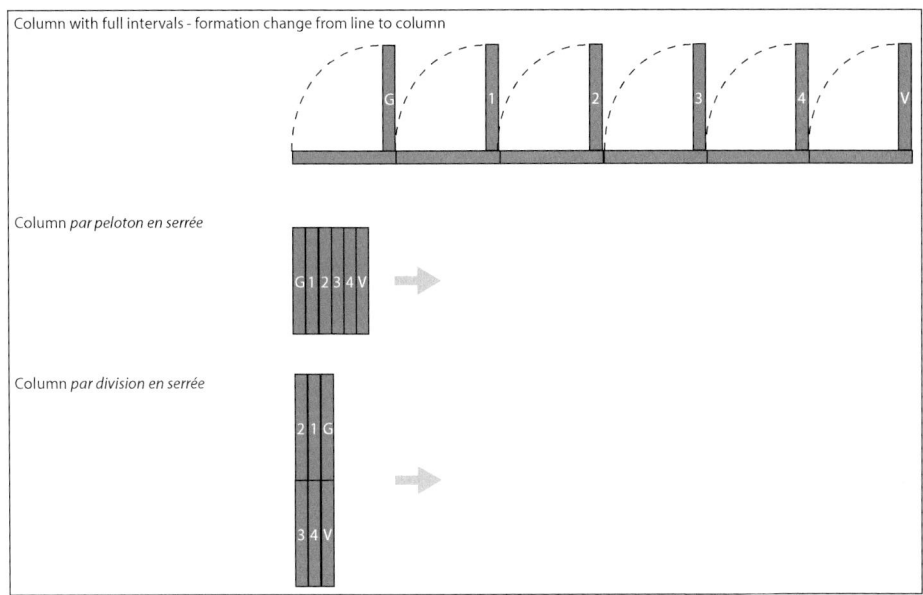

Column with full intervals - formation change from line to column

Column *par peloton en serrée*

Column *par division en serrée*

French infantry battalion formations.

of the complement of companies. Therefore, a French battalion of six companies in a column of divisions would be two companies wide and three companies deep. If the grenadiers and/or voltigeurs were detached, then the battalion would deploy in *colonne d'attaque*, one company wide.

In the British Army, known for its linear fighting formations, manoeuvres would also be performed in column, as Wellington noted in his orders of 3 May 1811.[30] Speed of movement was key, as his instruction demonstrates. Wellington commented that most armies facing the French were already demoralised, and their infantry, pounded by artillery and harassed by skirmishers, had no real answer to the attack. According to John Croker, then Secretary to the Admiralty, in a conversation with the then Sir Arthur Wellesley, the French and their tactics were described in these terms:

> I have not seen them since the campaign in Flanders, when they were capital soldiers, and a dozen years of victory under Buonaparte must have made them better still. They have besides, it seems, a new system of strategy, which has out-manoeuvred and overwhelmed all the armies of Europe. 'Tis enough to make one thoughtful; but no matter: my die is cast, they may overwhelm me, but I don't think they will outmanoeuvre me. First, because I am not afraid of them, as everybody else seems to be; and secondly, because if what I hear of their system of manoeuvres be true, I think it a false one as against steady troops. I suspect all the continental armies were

---

30   Instructions communicated by the Q.M.G., Heights near Fuentes de Onoro, 3 May, 1811, 10:00 a.m., Gurwood, *Dispatches*, vol.4, p.784.

more than half beaten before the battle was begun. I, at least, will not be frightened beforehand.[31]

The continental armies alluded to, in many cases, broke and ran and did not wait for the enemy to come close enough to deploy. The appearance would be of an attack in column, but the outcome was based more on the limited ability of the continental armies to stand than on any doctrinal employment by the French.

French tactics relied on a mass of light infantry to weaken the enemy line before the main weight of the attack developed. The approaching French columns were preceded by swarms of skirmishers whose goal was to weaken the enemy line by constant attrition, aiming to kill officers and NCOs where possible. The intention was to unnerve the defending troops as much as possible and weaken their resolve. These skirmishers would also keep the enemy skirmishers away from the advancing columns, denying the enemy the ability to inflict the same kind of attrition on them. This would also allow the columns to deploy with minimal interference.

The Allied army had the answer to this problem by fielding not only the light companies of each brigade, but attached rifle companies and entire battalions of *Caçadores* and light infantry, such as the 43rd and 52nd. By countering the French skirmishers with their own, their effect would be to a large degree neutralised. This caused a tactical crisis for the French. Meeting an enemy in a defensive position who took shelter behind the crest of a ridge and, most importantly of all, did not turn and run meant the French needed to try to deploy into line. Allied artillery and skirmishers would take their toll of the French columns as they advanced. Because the Allied main battle line was generally hidden behind a hill crest, the moment to deploy would be difficult to estimate. By the time it was clear that the column needed to deploy, it was presented with a line of Allied troops. Once the Allied line lowered its muskets to fire, and then charged with the bayonet, panic would quickly set in. The deploying column would be hit by disciplined volleys from the British and Portuguese troops. The column would briefly lose its momentum, its organisation, and most probably many of the officers at the head of the column who had been enthusiastically urging the men forward. The precise moment to deploy would easily be missed. The Allied line would charge with the bayonet, and a swift retreat would follow.

When the French infantry attempted to form line, the French officers had difficulty convincing soldiers to move out from the relative safety of the column into the line of fire. In the attacks at the pass of San Antonio do Cantaro at Buçaco, the 31e légère attempted to deploy into line after advancing in column, even though they were under heavy fire from the Allied position. Lemonniers-Delafosse wrote:

> ... the heads of the columns arrived ... within range of the enemy line: A rise in the terrain gave the 31e légère the opportunity to try to form a battle line ... a few regiments managed to form and line up, but in mine, only part of the first battalion was able to carry out the command. Captain of the

31   14 June, 1808. Croker, *The Croker Papers*, vol.1, pp.12–13.

fourth company, I never had more than four files formed; all those arriving were shot down.[32]

The impression would be given that the column had halted in the process of its attack, when in fact it had stopped to change formation. From French accounts, we can see that the *expectation* on the part of French officers was that they would deploy into line to fight. The fact that events were different speaks to the successful tactics of the Allied army and that the French were unable to find a solution to the tactical problem they faced. The impression of French attacks in column is reinforced by Wellington's comments after Sabugal. He wrote, '... really these attacks in columns against our lines are very contemptible.'[33] Additionally, his dispatch to Captain Chapman of the Royal Engineers, mentioned above, demonstrates the problem faced by the French and the failure of their battlefield doctrine to adjust to the Allied tactics.[34]

French armies normally had a preponderance of artillery on the battlefield. Napoleon, as an artillery officer, understood the effects of massed artillery and the benefit it provided to the morale of inexperienced troops. Standard equipment for each compagnie comprised eight guns for *artillerie à pied* and six for *artillerie à cheval*. Each Corps should have a compagnie attached from a *régiment d'artillerie à pied* for each infantry division, usually of 8-pounder guns, and one from a *régiment d'artillerie à cheval* for cavalry armed with 4-pounders. In addition, each corps would have a *reserve parc compagnie* of *artillerie à pied*, armed with 12-pounders. Each *compagnie* would have two howitzers of comparable calibre to the main guns. However, in 1811, the artillery available to the *armée de Portugal* was below what would be considered a minimum in central European battles.

The state of the French artillery had suffered over the course of the campaign because of the quality of the roads, as well as a reduction in the number of horses available to pull the guns and caissons. The army had gone into the campaign in 1810 with a full complement of artillery *compagnies*. For example, VI corps had a compagnie for each division, including the cavalry, and a reserve Parc.[35] The return of 1 March 1811 showed that the artillery was reduced to nineteen 8-pounders, thirty 4-pounders, and four 3-pounders, with eighteen 6-inch howitzers, totalling 71 guns. This was reduced to 52 guns by 25 March, and by the Battle of Fuentes de Oñoro, down to 42 guns of various calibres.[36] There were no 12-pounders recorded as being with the army after the stay at Santarém and before the retreat began.[37]

---

32   Lemonnier-Delafosse, *Souvenirs militaires*, p.70.
33   Wellington to Beresford, Sabugal, 4 April, 1811, Gurwood, *Dispatches*, vol.4, p.723.
34   Wellington to Chapman, Royal Engineers. Villar Maior, 8 April, 1811, Gurwood, *Dispatches*, vol.4, p.727.
35   Koch, *Mémoires de Massena*, vol.7, p.569.
36   Tableau de l'organisation de l'artillerie à l'époque du 25 mars 1811, lorsque l'armée se préparait a marcher sur Alcantara. Koch, *Mémoires de Massena*, vol.7, p.577.
37   État de la composition du matériel d'artillerie à l'époque du 1e mars 1811 (cinq jours avant la retraite), après la réduction nécessitée par la perte des chevaux. Koch, *Mémoires de Massena*, vol.7, p.587.

These reductions combined meant that at Fuentes de Oñoro the Allied army, unusually, had the advantage in artillery.

Having suffered severely during the retreat from Portugal, the artillery and cavalry horses had been drastically reduced in number and condition. Without sufficient fit horses to pull the guns, Massena was forced to compromise. According to the French *Situation* of 1 May, II corps had 16 guns, VI corps had 17, VIII corps and IX corps both had 12. However, there were insufficient horses to pull all of them despite Bessières bringing additional teams with him. Massena wrote to Napoleon on 7 May:

> In my letter of April 30, I had the honour of informing your Highness that each corps of the army could barely manage to harness three artillery pieces. Thanks to the teams brought by the Duke of Istria, we now have 30 pieces for the entire army, not including the six of the Imperial Guard—a number significantly lower than what would be necessary to match the enemy's artillery.[38]

Massena seems to be deliberately understating the number of guns. For the battle, Fririon recorded that II corps brought eight pieces, VI corps had 12 pieces, and VIII corps had four guns.[39] The divisions of VI corps were allotted four pieces each and had their gun teams provided by the horses brought along by Bessières. The distribution of guns is only detailed for VI corps. Montbrun had six guns attached to the cavalry division, although there is no confirmation that these guns were brought along.[40] This gives a confirmed total for the *armée de Portugal* of 24 guns. It would seem that Bessières had the elite *artillerie à cheval de la garde impériale* with six pieces allocated to Montbrun's cavalry. Thus, it is likely (although not certain) that Massena had 30 guns with the *armée de Portugal* (including Bessières guns), eight guns with IX corps and two guns in reserve.

The weight of the guns taken is also difficult to assess. However, by deduction, it is possible to make an educated guess for some of the corps. II corps probably took six 4-pounders and two 6-inch howitzers.[41] VIII corps may have taken either four 4-pounders or two 4-pounders and two howitzers. The other corps are more difficult to assess. VI corps had a variety of combinations available, but the most likely might be one full company of 8-pounders (six 8-pounders and two howitzers), and one full light artillery company of four 4-pounders and two howitzers. This would then tally with Koch's numbers, but is slightly over Fririon's allocation. If that is correct, and the distribution between the divisions influenced the allocation of guns, then each division may have had two 8-pounders and two howitzers.

The cavalry available to Massena was composed of some reliable troops, but their organisation left much to be desired. Many were experienced troopers under veteran

---

38   Wellington, *Supplementary Despatches*, vol.13, p.630.
39   Fririon, *Journal Historique*, p.202.
40   Koch, *Mémoires de Massena*, vol.7, p.602.
41   SHD: Matériel de l'Artillerie. *Armée de Portugal: Situation Des Troupes Composant Armée de Portugal à l'époque du 1er Mai 1811*, 7C28.

Maréchal Bessières, by Ernest Meissonier. (Public domain)

officers such as Montbrun, Pierre Soult and d'Ornano. The cavalry brigade of II corps is a good example of the structure of the cavalry units. It comprised the four squadrons of the 1e hussards, three of the 22e chasseurs à cheval, four from the chasseurs Hanovrienne and two squadrons of the 8e dragons. The *dragons* formed the core of the cavalry brigades and made up the majority of the reserve cavalry division. The cavalry played an important role in the retreat from Santarém, covering the movements of the infantry and acting as flank guards.

Provisional cavalry regiments were formed in a similar way to the infantry. The third and fourth squadrons of *dragon* regiments already in Spain were detached from their parent regiments and organised into three provisional regiments as part of VIII corps. The provisional regiments did nothing to improve the morale of troops who were now expected to serve with different units in a new organisation. Despite this, the *armée de Portugal* had a distinct advantage in cavalry numbers, which Massena was to attempt to exploit during the coming battle.

Bessières brought more experienced cavalry with him, commanded by the veteran *généraux de brigade* Watier and Lepic. 800 brought to Fuentes de Oñoro from the *armée du Nord* were the much-vaunted *garde impériale*, comprising the chevau-légers lanciers, chasseurs à cheval, grenadiers à cheval and mamluks. They could exert an influence far beyond their small numbers if they were used at the right moment.

The Allied Army

During the retreat to La Coruña in 1808, the British Army had suffered significantly. Upon returning to Britain in January 1809, efforts to restore it to combat readiness began immediately. While this was happening, other troops were sent to Portugal under Wellesley's command. These were largely inexperienced units, mostly second battalions, which had not served abroad and were below their full strength. Most British battalions were supposed to have a regulation strength of 1,000 soldiers, but some had establishments of 800 or even fewer, and many of those dispatched to Portugal were significantly understrength. Moreover, second battalions were often made up of less able or poorly trained soldiers. Furthermore, some troops earmarked for Portugal had been diverted to the unsuccessful Walcheren expedition, reducing the already small number of experienced troops and available transports for Wellington.

The organisation of the British Army, which successfully defeated the French, was an evolutionary process. During the Porto campaign, Wellington had mixed British and Portuguese regiments in the brigades.[42] This would allow the Portuguese troops to fight alongside British forces that had already been engaged with the French. Following the successful conclusion of the campaign, Beresford collected the Portuguese troops together for training while the British Army, with a small number of Portuguese attached, moved into Spain.[43]

---

42   Murray, *Memoir Annexed to an Atlas*, pp.11–12.
43   Wellington to Major General Mackenzie, Abrantes, 18 June, 1809, Gurwood, *Dispatches*, vol.4, p.436.

In the British Army, the battalion, usually commanded by a lieutenant colonel, was the tactical unit; the regiment being administrative only. Sometimes, as casualties were inflicted, the command of a battalion could be in the hands of the senior major. British battalions were organised into 10 companies, one of which was designated as grenadiers, and one as light infantry. The other eight companies were known as centre companies. When deployed into line, the grenadiers would occupy the right end of the line, and the light company the left. The battalion could be divided into two 'wings' of five companies each, commanded by a major, or the senior captain, for independent action.

King George III as Elector of Hanover offered a home for displaced Hanoverian soldiers in the British Army after the invasion of their state by the French. They formed a separate legion, the King's German Legion, and fought under British command throughout the Peninsular War. Their soldiers were steadfast, and their cavalry renowned for bravery and outstanding outpost duty. Other foreign units included the Brunswick Oëls Jägers, originally from the German state of Braunschweig, and Chasseurs Britanniques, a French émigré unit. Neither unit was regarded very highly because of their reputation for indiscipline and tendency to desert. The poor reputation of the Chasseurs Britanniques would be moderated, at least temporarily, during the coming campaign. The poor reputation of the Oëls seems to be partially borne out by the casualty returns for the Oëls after Fuentes de Oñoro, where eight men were killed or wounded, but 10 were reported missing.[44]

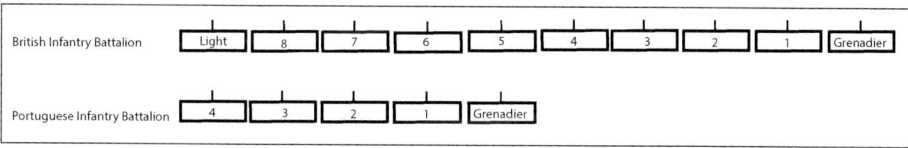

Allied infantry battalion formations.

The Portuguese army had been hard at work, organising and training new troops. As with the British, the regiment was administrative, and the tactical formation was the battalion. The Portuguese *regimento de infantaria* internal structure had been reorganised by a decree of 13 July 1808. The light infantry, or *caçadore* companies, were discontinued, so that each Portuguese regiment comprised two battalions, each of four fusilier companies and one of grenadiers.[45] The two battalions of a regiment were usually brigaded and fought together, unlike in the British Army. To provide the light infantry, initially six *Caçadore* battalions were formed separately, each comprising six companies and armed with a mix of muskets and rifles.

The higher organisation of the army was set out in a general order of 18 June 1809, dividing the army into four divisions.[46] Despite the losses of the Talavera campaign,

44   Otto von Pivka, *The Black Brunswickers* (Reading: Osprey Publishing, 1973), p. 16.
45   Estevão Brocardo (ed.), *Observador Portuguez, Historíco e Político de Lisboa*, (Lisbon: Impressão Regia, 1809), p.462; Manuel A. Ribeiro Rodrigues and Carlos Alberto Santos (eds), *Infantaria: 1806-1815* (Lisbon: Ed. Destarte, 2001), p.57.
46   Abrantes, 18 June 1809. Wellington, *Supplementary Despatches*, vol.6, p.288.

reinforcements to the British Army continued to arrive so that by the end of 1809 it was stronger than at the outset. The general order of 4 May 1810 formed the Light Division by dividing the Light Brigade, originally consisting of the battalions of the 43rd Foot, the 52nd Foot and companies of the 95th Rifles, into two brigades, one commanded by Lieutenant Colonel Beckwith of the 95th, containing the 43rd, 4° Caçadores and four companies of the 95th, the other commanded by Lieutenant Colonel Barclay of the 52nd containing the 52nd, 1° Caçadores and four companies of the 95th.[47]

Each line division incorporated additional light troops, with companies of the rifle-armed 5/60th or 95th attached to the brigades. The light infantry of the regular line brigades performed an important role in protecting the main battle line. Following a general order issued on 4 May 1809, when battalions were formed for battle, their light companies and the rifle companies attached to each brigade were to be formed into a unit commanded by a field officer or captain of light infantry.[48] At Fuentes de Oñoro, the light battalions in the village were formed from the light companies of each brigade from Picton's Division, and those from Nightingall's and Howard's Brigades, under the command of Lieutenant Colonel Williams of the 5/60th.[49]

Some Portuguese brigades were not formally part of higher formations, and this gave Wellington flexibility when reinforcing or adjusting the structure of the army. He made extensive use of independent Portuguese brigades to strengthen existing formations. Hill's 2nd Division operated with several independent Portuguese brigades under his command, but they were not officially part of the division. This meant Hill commanded what would, in the French army, be regarded as an army corps. The independent Portuguese brigades could be attached to different divisions as necessary. This provided a benefit to Craufurd: because of his rank, a brigadier general of lower seniority, Wellington kept the official structure of the Light Division small and flexible. He wrote:

> I have been thinking for some time of reinforcing your division, and you see what I have been able to do in this way this day. The truth is, that if I should make you as strong as I could wish, there will be other claimants for the command of the division; and I think it much better to keep a Portuguese brigade in reserve and unattached, to be attached to you when it is necessary to reinforce you, than to place one permanently under your command which would give claims to others.[50]

This attached brigade was usually *Brigadeiro* Pack's, consisting of the 1° and 16° infantaria de linha, and the 4° Caçadores. The working relationship between Pack's Brigade and the Light Division was very good, and Wellington frequently commended the Portuguese troops on their fighting spirit. Occasionally, Coleman's

---

47   Adjutant General's Office, Celorico, 4 August, 1810. *General Orders. Spain and Portugal* (London: Egerton, 1811), vol.2, p.124.

48   General Order, Coimbra, 4 May 1809. *General Orders. Spain and Portugal*, vol.1, p.11.

49   Wellington to Liverpool. Villar Formoso, 8 May, 1811, Gurwood, *Dispatches*, vol.4, pp.794–795.

50   Wellington to Craufurd, Pero Negro, 12 November, 1810, *Dispatches*, vol.4, p.415.

(7° and 19° infantaria de linha) or Ashworth's (6° and 18° infantaria de linha and 6° Caçadores) brigade might be attached in addition to Pack's. As part of the flexibility provided by the independent Portuguese brigades, their allocation of artillery gave them an added punch, however small. Pack's Brigade had a battery of 3-pounder mountain guns attached, and Ashworth had 3-pounder carriage guns.[51] Mountain guns were light in construction and could be dismantled and carried on mules. Alexander Dickson, whose Portuguese artillery was attached to Hamilton's Division, writing later in the war, considered them to be good for the morale of the infantry to which they were attached, but, '… ruins many animals, and the only advantage it possesses … is that the Ordnance can be conveyed by the narrowest footpaths, and up the most difficult steeps.'[52] This capability would have been of great benefit to formations such as Pack's, attached as it was so often to the Light Division, entailing the need for mobility in difficult terrain.

By the time of Buçaco, Wellington could field six divisions consisting of the originals, 1st to 4th, the Light Division, and a new, 5th Division under the command of Major General Leith. Unusually, Leith's division began with two Portuguese brigades and only one British. This was changed after Buçaco when a newly formed British brigade replaced one of the Portuguese. The army continued to expand while it was safe behind the lines around Lisbon during the autumn and winter of 1810–1811. A reorganisation of infantry regiments was undertaken, and the first of two new divisions, the 6th under Major General Campbell, was formed following a general order of 6 October 1810.[53] Campbell had been wounded in the leg at Talavera but recuperated sufficiently to command this new division. It was initially to comprise the brigade of British infantry formerly commanded by him, and a brigade of Portuguese infantry under Baron Eben, but would be expanded to two British brigades by the time of the Battle of Fuentes de Oñoro. Hulse was appointed commander of the 1st Brigade, previously commanded by Campbell, in November 1810, with Burnes' Brigade added on 5 March 1811.

Sufficient reinforcements were received from England that a 7th Division could be formed. Initially, this was to be composed of Major General Alten's and Brigadier General Long's British brigades, and *Brigadeiro* Coleman's Portuguese Brigade.[54] The Division was to be commanded by Major General Sir William Houston. Its structure was soon modified so that it comprised one British brigade under Major General John Sontag and one Portuguese brigade under *Brigadeiro* John Milley Doyle, while Houston remained in command. Sontag had previously been given command of the troops, '… destined for the defence of the redoubts constructed at and in the neighbourhood of Torres Vedras and extending from thence along the river to the sea.'[55] This was an extremely important command, and it shows the

---

51   Wellington to Beresford, Celorico, 30 March, 1811, Gurwood, *Dispatches*, vol.4, p.711.
52   Letter to Major General J. Macleod, Head Quarters, St Jean de Luz, 28 November 1813. Alexander Dickson, John H. Leslie (ed.), *The Dickson Manuscripts: Being Diaries, Letters, Maps, Account Books, with Various Other Papers, for the Year 1813* (Godmanchester: Trotman, 1987), vol.5, p.1120.
53   Adjutant General's Office. Rio Major, 6 October, 1810. *General Orders*, vol.2, pp.178–179.
54   Adjutant General's Office. Cartaxo, 5 March 1811. *General Orders*, vol.3, p.49.
55   Wellington to Major Gen. Sontag. Rio Maior, 6 Oct. 1810, Gurwood, *Dispatches*, vol.4, p.319.

level of trust Wellington already had in him. Sontag had then been on sick leave, but on 8 March 1811 Wellington wrote informing him of the chance of a more active command once his health had recovered. In a general order of 31 March, he was appointed to command the brigade comprising the 51st Foot, 85th Foot, Chasseurs Britanniques, and eight companies of the Brunswick Oëls.[56] The British units were composed of many raw or unfit troops, having served in the Walcheren campaign. The 51st, having no second battalion to draw replacements from, was not fit to proceed on active service until the end of 1810.[57] The battalion eventually disembarked at Lisbon on 5 March 1811 with 33 sergeants, 19 drummers and 613 other ranks.[58] The Portuguese brigade under Doyle consisted of the 7° Infantaria (two battalions), 19° Infantaria (two battalions) and the 2° Caçadores. The 7th Division would be roughly handled by the French at Fuentes de Oñoro, taking several months to recover and reorganise. Despite this, the seven-division organisation that was established would remain unchanged throughout the Peninsular War.

The Allies had few cavalry compared to the *armée de Portugal*, although the quality was exceptional. The British fielded some four regiments at Fuentes de Oñoro, amongst the most noteworthy were the men of the King's German Legion, regarded by such veterans as Kincaid of the 95th as:

> … thorough-bred soldiers, for they were as singularly intelligent and useful on out post duty, as they were effective and daring in the field … The first regiment of hussars were associated with our division throughout the war and were deserved favourites. In starting from a swampy couch and bowling along the road long ere dawn of day, it was one of the romances of a soldier's life to hear them chanting their national war songs some three or four voices leading and the whole squadron joining in the chorus … If we saw a British dragoon at any time approaching in full speed, it excited no great curiosity among us, but whenever we saw one of the first hussars coming on at a gallop it was high time to gird on our swords and bundle up.[59]

Kincaid's comments regarding the British cavalry reflected Wellington's view of the dependability of that arm. He concluded in 1812 that their unreliability was, '… occasioned entirely by a trick our officers have acquired of galloping at everything, and then galloping back as fast as they gallop at the enemy. They never consider their situation, never think of manoeuvring before the enemy …'.[60] Scovell supported this view of British cavalry with first-hand experience at Fuentes de Oñoro, commenting that, '… our Cavalry want Conduct not Courage'.[61]

56   General Order, Adjutant General's Office. Celorico, 31 March, 1811. *General Orders*, vol.3, p.71.
57   A.F. Mockler-Ferryman (ed.), *The Life of a Regimental Officer During the Great War, 1793-1815* (London: Blackwood, 1913), p.143.
58   TNA: WO 17/2467, Return of 25 of March 1811. Remarks. 'Monthly Returns to the Adjutant General, January to June', 1811.
59   Kincaid, *Adventures*, pp.161–162.
60   Wellington to Hill, Salamanca, 18 June 1812, Gurwood, *Dispatches*, vol.5, p.712.
61   TNA: WO 37/7a, Scovell, *Diary*, p.41.

The Portuguese cavalry was rather poor in comparison to the British, but this can at least in part be blamed on the inadequate supply system provided by the Portuguese commissariat. *Brigadeiro* Sir George Madden, commanding a brigade of Portuguese cavalry, regarded them somewhere near their Spanish equivalents, and with those he was unimpressed.[62] There were also problems in recruitment for the regiments, never achieving the levels required. However, some Portuguese were subject to the same misplaced fervour as their British counterparts:

> The undisciplined ardor [sic] of the 13th dragoons, and 1st regt. of Portuguese cavalry, is not of the description of the determined bravery and steadiness of soldiers confident in their discipline and in their officers. Their conduct was that of a rabble, galloping as fast as their horses could carry them over a plain, after an enemy to whom they could do no mischief after they were broken ...[63]

Much of the artillery was provided by the Portuguese, with three Royal Horse Artillery troops and five Royal Artillery or KGL artillery brigades available. However, not all of these units were deployed in the campaign. The troops of the Royal Horse Artillery were generally attached to the Light Division and the cavalry brigades, with the foot brigades attached to various infantry divisions.

Command and Control

Wellington could not choose which general officers he had in his army, as they were appointed by Horse Guards. He wrote to Lieutenant Colonel Sir Henry Torrens, the Military Secretary at Horse Guards in London, with responsibility for appointing officers, protesting that, 'When I reflect upon ... the general officers of this army, and consider that these are persons on whom I am to rely to lead columns against the French generals, and who are to carry my instructions into execution, I tremble.' He added, 'I only hope that when the enemy reads the list of their names, he trembles as I do.'[64] Despite these misgivings, Wellington had in his army some capable and talented divisional and brigade commanders. Craufurd and Picton were constantly engaged against the French rearguard during the retreat, manoeuvring their divisions with assurance. Craufurd had applied for leave to go back to England, but Wellington was reluctant to let him go. Several senior officers had asked to return to England 'on business', and he was loath to let another, mostly reliable, officer leave the army. He wrote, in frustration that, 'I may be obliged to consent to the absence of an officer, but I cannot approve of it.'[65] However, Craufurd persisted, and Wellington issued his permission, but with a word of caution:

62   Wellington to H. Wellesley. Cartaxo, 23 Feb. 1811, Gurwood, *Dispatches*, vol.4, p.615.
63   Wellington to Beresford, Celorico, 30 March, 1811, Gurwood, *Dispatches*, vol.4, p.710.
64   Special Collections, Hartley Library, University of Southampton (UoS): The Wellington Papers, WP 1/312.
65   Wellington to Craufurd. Cartaxo, 28 Jan. 1811, Gurwood, *Dispatches*, vol.4, p.558.

I shall be very happy to attend to your wishes; but I would beg you to reflect whether, considering the situation in which you stand in the army, it is desirable that you should go home upon leave. Adverting to the number of General officers senior to you in the army, it has not been an easy task to keep you in your command; and, if you should go, I fear that I should not be able to appoint you to it again, or to one that would be so agreeable to you, or in which you could be so useful.[66]

In view of Craufurd's temporary return to England, Major General Erskine was assigned the '… duties of the outpost.'[67] This particular officer caused Wellington considerable concern. He had previously contested Erskine's appointment to the army in the Peninsula, writing to Henry Torrens, military secretary to the Duke of York in London, 'I have received your letter announcing the appointment of General Erskine to this army, who I generally understood to be a madman'.[68] Torrens replied wittily, '… no doubt General Erskine is sometimes a little mad, but in his lucid intervals he is an uncommonly clever fellow; and I trust he will have no fit during the campaign, though he looked a little wild as he embarked'.[69]

During the campaign, Erskine demonstrated disobedience and incompetence on several occasions, committing several serious mistakes with significant consequences. At one moment he would be cautious, at the next reckless. Wellington's description to Beresford of Erskine was that, 'He is very blind … but very cautious.'[70] Sabugal demonstrated his lacklustre command of the Light Division, saved only by the behaviour of his brigade commanders and the doggedness of the troops. Wellington expressed his annoyance at Erskine's subsequent failure to intercept a French relief convoy bound for Ciudad Rodrigo.[71] On the same day, he wrote to Craufurd in frustration: 'You will find your division in your old quarters, Gallegos, and the sooner you can come up to them the better.'[72] Fortunately, Craufurd returned in time to command the Light Division at the Battle of Fuentes de Oñoro. However, Erskine must have had some qualities desired by Wellington, as he would go on to be appointed to command the 5th Division, and then the 2nd Cavalry Division.[73]

Two Divisions, the Light and 3rd, with their attached units, were employed almost continuously as the advanced guard in pursuit of the French. Wellington indicated, once the campaign had finished, the disruption that rapid movement and constant fighting had caused. He wrote to Spencer:

---

66   Wellington to Craufurd. Cartaxo, 9 Dec. 1810, Gurwood, *Dispatches*, vol.4, pp.455–456.
67   General Order, Cartaxo, 6 Feb. 1811, Gurwood, *Dispatches*, vol.4, p.582.
68   UoS: The Wellington Papers, Wellington to Torrens, 29 August 1810.
69   UoS: The Wellington Papers, Torrens to Wellington, 19 September 1810, WP 1/315.
70   Wellington to Beresford, Elvas, 24 April, 1811, Gurwood, *Dispatches,* vol.4, p.772.
71   Wellington to Beresford, Villar Formosa, 14th April, 1811, Gurwood, *Dispatches,* vol.4, p.749.
72   Wellington to Brig. Gen. R. Craufurd. Villar Formoso, 14th April, 1811, Gurwood, *Dispatches*, vol.4, p.747.
73   Adjutant General's Office. Alameda, 22d April, 1811. *General Orders*, vol.3, p.78. Adjutant General's Office. Quinta dos Banos, 19th June, 1811. *General Orders*, vol.3, p.112.

When the army were employed on the pursuit of the enemy out of Portugal, the Light division of infantry and the cavalry were placed under the directions of Major Gen. Sir W. Erskine, which has led to an alteration of the organization of the army that may be very inconvenient.

Although the cavalry may at times be joined to one or more divisions of the army for particular services, and that the senior officer present would of course command the whole, still each division, as well as the cavalry, must be considered as a separate body, under its own Commanding officer, for all matters of interior regulation, having its Staff officers and departments exclusively attached to it, and employed under the directions of the General officer commanding the division, in the duties of the division to which they are attached. In all duties of a general nature, of course the senior officer of the 2 or 3 divisions acting together, would give his directions, and would be responsible, leaving the execution of the duty to be performed by each division, under the direction of its Commanding officer, who would be responsible to him for it. As the Light division and the cavalry were a good deal jumbled together on the late service, I had determined to draw this line, but I forgot it before I came away; and I shall be obliged to you if you will communicate this letter to Sir S. Cotton and Gen. Craufurd.

As for our advanced guard, at present I think it ought to consist of the Light division and 4 squadrons of cavalry, and Pack ought to have 2 squadrons of Portuguese cavalry with his post at Barba de Puerco, &c.[74]

From February to May, the Light Division's 1/43rd and 1/52nd lost some 20 percent of their effective strength, whilst the 3rd Division's battalions lost between 10 percent and 30 percent. The 1/45th Foot of MacKinnon's Brigade recorded 539 effectives in February, with only 396 in May.[75] Those returned as sick included wounded men, and this number would fluctuate as wounds healed and soldiers returned to the ranks. The 1/95th recorded 75 sick in February, but after the pursuit of the retreating French and the Battle at Sabugal, this number rose to 114.[76] The loss, even temporarily, of these elite troops would be a worry for Wellington as he had to conserve the strength of his army, even though he was receiving reinforcements.

Many of the reinforcements arriving in 1810 and 1811 had been involved in the Walcheren campaign, a misguided attempt to open another front against France by securing navigation in the Scheldt, which would enable access to Antwerp. Many of those who returned from Walcheren suffered from 'Walcheren Fever,' a combination of malaria with typhus, typhoid and other diseases.[77] Several units had been made

---

74   Wellington to Lieut. Gen. Sir B, Spencer, K.B. Sabugal, 16th May, 1811, Gurwood, *Dispatches*, vol.5, p.24.

75   These data are available from The National Archives, Kew, under WO 17 – Office of the Commander in Chief: Monthly Returns to the Adjutant General.

76   Verner, *History & Campaigns of the Rifle Brigade*, vol.2, p.301.

77   John Lynch, 'The Lessons of Walcheren Fever, 1809', *Military Medicine*, 174.3 (2009), pp.315–319.

unfit for active duty, and many soldiers were sick.[78] Indeed, some units suffered so much that they were only good for garrison duty.

Two battalions that were to provide good service during the 1811 campaign were the 71st and 85th, both of which had returned seriously under-strength from Walcheren. Both battalions had been retrained as light infantry in 1809. Only five companies of the 85th, totalling some 30 sergeants, 13 drummers and 416 rank-and-file, disembarked at Lisbon on 5 March.[79] The battalion lasted less than a year before returning home. The 71st went to Portugal with only six companies, but as the remaining companies were brought up to strength, they were sent to join their parent battalion.[80] As the survivors of the Walcheren campaign were again fit for service, they were sent to Portugal.

Logistics

Wellington wrote at the beginning of 1811, 'There is an old military proverb respecting these operations which is strictly and invariably true, and that is, that "if they are attempted with small numbers they must fail; if with large, the army must starve."'[81] He now had a relatively large army, and much of his attention in the coming months would be focused on keeping his army fed, watered and clothed. Wellington frequently returned in his dispatches to the problem of supplies for the Portuguese troops. The problems with the Portuguese commissariat, which Wellington and Beresford had encountered during the previous year, had not been solved. Wellington wrote to Charles Stuart, the ambassador to Lisbon, about the problems of supply in the Portuguese army. He noted Pack's Brigade had been forced to stop during the pursuit of the French because of supply issues.

> I have the honor [sic] to enclose you a report from Sir W. Erskine, of the want of bread by the Portuguese brigade of infantry at Marmeleira, under the command of Brig. Gen. Pack, which I request you to lay before the Portuguese government. It was settled by Marshal Sir W. Beresford that there should always be 6 days' bread for the troops in their cantonments, especially those on the advanced post, as these are; but instead of that they have not one day's bread, and in every week receive none for 2 or 3 days. I have also a complaint from 2 companies of caçadores at Rio Maior, who have received no bread for a week. The Portuguese government, however, will expect that these troops should march when ever an opportunity shall offer for them to make an exertion.[82]

78   Wellington to Marquis Wellesley, Merida, 28th August 1809, Gurwood, *Dispatches*, vol.3, p.456.
79   TNA: WO 17/2467, Return of 25th of March, 1811. Remarks. 'Monthly Returns to the Adjutant General, January to June'.
80   TNA: WO 17/2467, Return of 25th of April, 1811. Remarks. 'Monthly Returns to the Adjutant General, January to June'.
81   Memorandum of Operations in 1810. 23d Feb. 1811, Gurwood, *Dispatches*, vol.4, p.624.
82   Wellington to Charles Stuart, Esq. Cartaxo, 26th Feb. 1811, Gurwood, *Dispatches*, vol.4, p.637.

Pack's Brigade, often attached to the Light Division, was a veteran formation that was frequently commended by Wellington. He wrote on 1 May that the Brigade, '... has always been distinguished on service'.[83] Because of the pitiful state of the troops, it is reasonable to suggest that Pack's Brigade was chosen for the blockade of Almeida as it was not properly fit for battle. His soldiers had already been left behind once through lack of food, and some had even died of starvation.[84] Wellington noted that the British commissariat purchased rice in the markets of Lisbon, and this supply was just as available to the Portuguese as it was to the British. In a memorandum to Charles Stuart, he mentioned that officers and soldiers of the British Army had subscribed to purchase rice to make soup for the starving inhabitants of Portugal.[85] The Portuguese Army's supply of food, '... north of the Tagus was desperate, even if great quantities of rice and cod fish were stored at Peniche. The Governing Junta had no money (notwithstanding the fact that from January 1810 to February 1811 they had received £1,820,000 from the British government, twice what had been agreed).'[86] Wellington wrote again regarding the problems with Portuguese supply to their troops. He strongly suggested that it should be brought to the notice of the British government:

> His Majesty supplies not only the pay, but money to pay for the provisions of 30,000 men; yet these men are not better provided than others, for the whole army is absolutely without food. I would also beg to observe, that in consequence of the want of food, and the want of means in the hospitals, the effective strength of the Portuguese army diminishes every month, while that of His Majesty's troops increases.[87]

Picton observed, 'Two regiments attached to my division, the establishment of which is two thousand five hundred men, do not bring one thousand two hundred into the field, and this is pretty generally the proportion throughout the army.'[88] The situation with the Portuguese *Junta de Víveres* (Board of Victuals) was so poor that Wellington instructed it should be abolished and a board of commissariat be appointed to provision the Portuguese army.[89] The Junta had been heavily criticised by Wellington, who complained their returns held, '... not one line of truth ...'[90] Soon after joining the 6° Caçadores, part of Ashworth's Independent brigade, in 1811, *Capitão* Richard Brunton wrote,

---

83 Wellington to Liverpool. Villar Formoso, 1st May, 1811, Gurwood, *Dispatches*, vol.4, p.782.
84 Wellington to Charles Stuart, Esq. Pombeiro, 18th March, 1811, Gurwood, *Dispatches*, vol.4, p.679.
85 Wellington to Charles Stuart, Esq. Cartaxo, 26th Feb. 1811, Gurwood, *Dispatches*, vol.4, p.637.
86 Gabriel Espírito Santo and Pedro de Brito, *A Logística Do Exército Anglo-Luso Na Guerra Peninsular: Uma Introdução* (Lisboa: Tribuna da História, 2012), p.95.
87 Wellington to Charles Stuart, Esq. Cartaxo, 3d March, 1811, Gurwood, *Dispatches*, vol.4, p.648.
88 Robinson, *Picton*, vol.2, p.14.
89 Wellington to Charles Stuart, Esq. Gouvea, 26th March, 1811, Gurwood, *Dispatches*, vol.4, p.702.
90 Wellington to Charles Stuart, Esq. Thomar, 26th March, 1811, Gurwood, *Dispatches*, vol.4, p.658.

... we had more than our share of hardship and suffering for we were continually without supplies and in an exhausted Country, being an independent Brigade the British Commissariat took little note of us, and our own was wretchedly supplied, however by occasionally attaching us to one or other of the British Divisions we sometimes got supplies, and kept up 'till we arrived on the ground of Fuentes D'Onor, [sic] in a half starved 'tho tolerably effective state.'[91]

Due to the shortcomings in Portuguese administration and at times blatant corruption, Wellington claimed that, in contrast to the 30,000 that the British government paid for, there were fewer than 11,000 soldiers in the Portuguese army.[92] In writing to the Earl of Liverpool at the beginning of May, he reported:

The 12 Portuguese regiments of infantry, 5 battalions of cacadores, one battalion of the Lusitanian Legion, and 2 regiments of cavalry, which are with this part of the army, and which ought to amount to 21,800 R[ank]. and F[ile]., don't amount to 11,000 fit for duty. Some regiments, which ought to have 1400 men, have only 300 for duty, others 400; and Gen. Pack's brigade, which has always been distinguished on service, and of which the General has taken the utmost care, which ought to have 3400 R. and F., has only 1545, by a return sent me this day. The brigade of Portuguese cavalry, which ought to have 1000 R. and F., has only 400![93]

However, Wellington knew corruption and inefficiency were not confined to the Portuguese administration, especially in the commissariat. Several commissariat officers in British service were sent home or dismissed through failure or financial impropriety.[94] Indeed, as S.G.P. Ward commented, 'There can have been few professions ... which could point, as the Commissariat could, to two men of the highest rank who were serving a sentence in Newgate Gaol.'[95]

Manoeuvring across Portugal was problematic for both armies. The condition of the roads left a lot to be desired, and guiding troops across the country was difficult because of the lack of truly reliable maps. A general order instructed:

... for route-marches each company in every battalion of infantry may be told off in threes; when the column is to be formed for the march the companies must be wheeled up or backward by threes, and each stand in

---

91   National Army Museum (NAM): 1968-07-461, Richard Brunton, 'Narrative of the Service of Lt Col Richard Brunton', n.d., The National Army Museum, NAM 1968-07-461.

92   Wellington to Beresford, Villar Formoso, 30th April, 1811, Gurwood, *Dispatches*, vol.4, p.780.

93   Wellington to Liverpool. Villar Formoso, 1st May, 1811, Gurwood, *Dispatches*, vol.4, pp.782–783.

94   See, for example, Wellington to Col. Gordon, Commissary in Chief. Niza, 18th April, 1811, Gurwood, *Dispatches*, vol.4, p.756; To J. Murray, Esq., Commissary General. Celorico, 28th May, 1810, Gurwood, *Dispatches*, vol.4, p.92.

95   In 1810, they were Commissary-Generals Alexander Davidson and Valentine Jones. S.G.P Ward, *Wellington's Headquarters* (Barnsley: Pen & Sword Military, 2017), p.72.

column of three men in front, which is as large a number as the greater proportion of the roads in Portugal will admit.[96]

Items, such as shoes, for men and horses, were quickly worn out while marching on the rough roads of Portugal and Spain. Wellington sent a request to the government, '… to order to Lisbon without loss of time 100,000 pairs of soldiers' shoes of the best quality, and that orders should be given to continue the manufacture of them.'[97] The quality was not always the highest. He was moved to write, '… there is no use in sending to this country any articles which are not of the best quality for service. They are of no use to the troops, are an [sic] useless expense to the public'.[98] All sorts of equipment, including shoes, was also provided to the Spanish forces, but Wellington had to insist that, '… shoes sent by the British commissariat are for the British troops.'[99] Other simple items, the replacement of which might make the life of the soldiers a little better, also came under scrutiny. Cloth overalls for the cavalry were to replace the uncomfortable and inconvenient leather breeches and stiff boots they had previously worn. In wet weather, the breeches became sodden and chafed, whilst the stiff cavalry boots were not suited to field duty.[100]

That other necessity for any army, ammunition, was generally plentiful for the Allies, but there was sometimes difficulty in transporting it. Ammunition depots were established in locations such as Elvas and Abrantes, with a constant reserve carried by the army. Soldiers normally carried up to 60 rounds in their cartridge boxes. The usage of ammunition in battle could be prodigious. After the Battle of Fuentes de Oñoro, Wellington wrote:

> In the actions of the 3d and 5th the quantity of ammunition expended by the Portuguese brigade of artillery engaged very nearly amounted to the whole quantity they carried with them; and I was obliged to have recourse to the expedient of picking up the enemy's shot which had been fired into our camp, and of making it up into ammunition with powder and materials drawn from the British artillery.[101]

The 43rd almost ran out of ammunition at Casal Novo but were resupplied during the action.[102] Given the amount of ammunition expended in some combats, the number of casualties could be surprisingly small. At Sabugal, the 43rd was heavily engaged for several hours but suffered eight killed and 72 wounded. In other actions, the losses could be considerable: the 79th suffered over 30 percent casualties in the fighting in the village of Fuentes de Oñoro.

---

96 Adjutant General's Office. Lousaõ, 16th March, 1811. *General Orders*, vol.3, p.59.
97 Wellington to Liverpool. Pero Negro, 30th Oct. 1810, Gurwood, *Dispatches*, vol.4, p.348.
98 Wellington to Liverpool. Cartaxo, 15th Dec. 1810, Gurwood, *Dispatches*, vol.4, p.462.
99 Wellington to Beresford, Celorico, 30th March, 1811, 6 P.M, Gurwood, *Dispatches*, vol.4, p.711.
100 Wellington to the Adjutant General of the Forces. Nisa, 18th April, 1811, Gurwood, *Dispatches*, vol.4, p.756.
101 Wellington to Liverpool. Villar Formoso, 8th May, 1811, Gurwood, *Dispatches*, vol.4, p.791.
102 Garrety, *Memoirs*, p.123.

Discipline

At times, Wellington had serious difficulties with criminal behaviour, desertion and absence in his army. During the retreat to Lisbon in 1810, there was looting and desertion by the Allies. When the army was suffering from adversity, looting was commonplace, and reports of murder were seen sporadically.[103] However, the army settled down somewhat once it was on the offensive or established for any length of time in one place. The historical cliché that capital punishment was common is somewhat misplaced. Although there is a steady record of capital sentences, some were commuted and others simply not carried out. The hanging of a British and a Portuguese soldier in Leiria during the retreat from Coimbra is an indication that, broadcast as a warning in a general order, this was an uncommon event used to deter further plundering.[104] Many soldiers were sentenced to transportation or to serve in unpleasant postings such as the West Indies. Officers were not immune to punishment for the actions of their men. After some soldiers were found six miles from their camp with mules loaded with plunder, an inquiry was instituted immediately, '… into the fact of the officers named detaching soldiers in so irregular a manner, so often prohibited by every instruction; and should you find these officers as responsible as they appear to be, you will cause them to be placed in arrest'.[105]

An example of a unit that suffered serial desertions was the Chasseurs Britanniques. This regiment was initially composed of French émigrés, but as attrition reduced their numbers, replacements were drawn from French deserters and prisoners of war who volunteered to fill their ranks. Despite this reputation, the regiment was to fight well at Fuentes de Oñoro.

The locations of the armies meant those wishing to desert or return to the *armée de Portugal* would have opportunities as they manoeuvred in close proximity. Wellington attributed the high levels of desertion among foreign recruits to the stern discipline that existed in the British Army. He requested that once enemy troops had been encouraged to desert, especially those non-French units in the *armée de Portugal*, they should be formed into battalions and sent for service in locations where the lure of desertion would not be so obvious.[106]

Massena was having difficulties with desertion from his ranks, much like that of the Allies. Significant numbers came from non-French recruits into the army, something that had grown with the expansion of the French Empire. Fririon tells us that, on 20 April, 'Major Fitz-Henri [sic], commanding the Irish Battalion, passed over to the enemy taking with him 100 men of his battalion.'[107]

As the *armée de Portugal* returned to Spain, the decree issued by Massena warned that marauders would be punished according to the law. Soldiers were not allowed to go more than half a league, one and a half miles or two and a half kilometres,

---

103 General Order, Pero Negro, 10th Nov. 1810, Gurwood, *Dispatches*, vol.4, p.405.

104 Adjutant General's Office, Leiria, 3d Oct. 1810., Gurwood, *Dispatches*, vol.4, p.311.

105 The A.G. to Major Gen. Dunlop, 5th division. 22d March, 1811, Gurwood, *Dispatches*, vol.4, pp.690–691.

106 Wellington to Lieut. Gen. Graham, Elvas, 23d April, 1811, Gurwood, *Dispatches*, vol.4, pp.767–768.

107 Fririon, *Journal Historique*, p.199.

from their cantonments without written authorisation. Limiting the distance the troops could wander meant that concentrating the army would be easier, and there would be fewer losses during any movement. Losing soldiers to capture by the advancing Allies had happened frequently on the retreat from Portugal as soldiers became detached from their units while foraging for food. The officers, up to corps commanders, would also be held responsible for the offences of their troops, and would be punished accordingly. Most worryingly for them, the names of offending officers would be reported to the Emperor.

The value Wellington placed on his men, and in particular some of his most reliable troops, is shown in the commuting of death sentences and the release of those found guilty, as well as the unwillingness, '... to order the punishment of any soldier of the 1st Hussars'.[108] Despite this, one particular offender, John Wagener, who had conspired to desert, was to be given 800 lashes and a dishonourable discharge from that regiment. Discipline in the Light Division was amongst the strictest in the army. However, there was always an opportunity to improve, as described by Kincaid:

> I was one of a crowd of skirmishers ... when I found myself all at once within a few yards of one of [the French] regiments in line, which opened such a fire, that had I not, riflemanlike, taken instant advantage of the cover of a good fir tree, my name would have unquestionably been transmitted to posterity ... And however opposed to it may be the usual system of drill, I will maintain from that day's experience, that the cleverest method of teaching a recruit to stand at attention, is to place him behind a tree and fire balls at him as, had our late worthy disciplinarian, Sir David Dundas, himself, been looking on, I think that even he must have admitted that he never saw any one stand so fiercely upright as I did behind mine, while the balls were rapping into it as fast as if a fellow had been hammering a nail on the opposite side, not to mention the number that were whistling past within the eighth of an inch of every part of my body, both before and behind, particularly in the vicinity of my nose, for which the upper part of the tree could barely afford protection.[109]

Kincaid, like many others, was able to see the humour in an otherwise dark situation.

Military Intelligence

Information is useless if it cannot be used quickly. Thus, the speed of its collection, analysis and employment is paramount. The process of gathering intelligence is not consistently reliable. Analysing the gathered intelligence entails sorting through vast amounts of information, much of which may be irrelevant, contradictory, or simply of no use, in order to extract the facts. Timeliness is also a critical factor. Outdated information is just as worthless as inaccurate information, and sometimes it is hard to distinguish between the two. For information to be valuable to commanders on the ground, it must be analysed swiftly and communicated to them

---

108   Adjutant General's Office. Lousaõ, 16th March, 1811. *General Orders*, vol.3, p.57.
109   Kincaid, *Adventures*, p.51.

for effective use. Both armies in this campaign faced challenges related to these aspects. Wellington had an abundance of information to sift through and disseminate. In contrast, Massena had limited information, some of which was quickly proven to be inaccurate.

The complexity of Allied intelligence collection included cavalry patrols, prisoners, spies, the local population and the guerrillas.[110] The intelligence network covered large parts of the country.[111] Wellington had information in some abundance, even to the extent of knowing where Massena had slept.[112] In addition, the guerrillas provided Wellington with numerous enemy dispatches. He also had access to a telegraph system for the transmission of information quickly between selected sites.

During the retreat from Santarém, Wellington required accurate information about the location of the French and the route they might be expected to take. In the time preceding the Battle of Fuentes de Oñoro, he acquired some idea of their strength, location and direction of movement. Much information was obtained from dispatches captured by the guerrillas, including the *situations* (returns) taken each month, which provided the strength of the French units and sometimes their location.[113] Less tangible information was obtained by spies. The type available can be gauged by his letter to the Earl of Liverpool on 9 April 1811:

> I enclose a letter which I have received this day from one of my correspondents at Salamanca, which shows the state in which they are. The whole army is dispirited and dissatisfied. Ney left them about a fortnight ago, it is said, in arrest; and I understand that the other Generals are equally dissatisfied with Massena's operations. It was reported that they intended to blow up Almeida …[114]

The correspondent in question was Father Patrick Curtis, serving as the Rector of the Irish College in Salamanca, along with his role as a Professor of Natural History and Astronomy at the university. Given his social standing, he enjoyed the freedom to move around the university town, allowing him to observe the movements of French troops. Furthermore, he could associate with some of the senior French officers, learning snippets of information directly.

Massena had little intelligence of the scale available to Wellington. Although he could gather information using his cavalry as scouts, the Allied army was experienced in screening its movements. However, much information was published in the press in Britain and would find its way to the French. Wellington wrote to the Earl of Liverpool, 'It is very desirable that you should not publish the details of my dispatches to your Lordship. You cannot conceive how very deficient the French are

---

110 Wellington to Beresford, Gouvea, 10th September 1810, Gurwood, *Dispatches*, vol.4, p.272.
111 TNA, PRO 30/43/52, 'Sir Galbraith Lowry Cole: Papers', 1810.
112 Wellington to Beresford, Torres Novas, 7 March, 1811, 11:30 a.m. Gurwood, *Dispatches*, vol.4, p.656.
113 For example, see dispatch to Hill. Celorico, 18 June, 1810, Gurwood, *Dispatches*, vol.4, p.123.
114 Wellington to Liverpool. Villar Formoso, 9 April, 1811, Gurwood, *Dispatches*, vol.4, p.736.

in information. All the dispatches from me which are published are sent to Massena from Paris, and they thus acquire the information of what is going on.'[115]

Cavalry was employed extensively for gathering intelligence and for reconnaissance. The word reconnaissance comes from Old French, *reconoistre*, to explore or recognise. This reflects its use as describing observation of troops and terrain and scouting to identify enemy formations or positions. Cavalry can also be used to deny an enemy information by screening the main body of the army and blocking the opportunity for the enemy to perform their reconnaissance patrols. General picquet duties and keeping an eye on the opposition were carried out principally by the cavalry. However, this duty significantly reduced the effectiveness of the cavalry, as small units were sent to observe and, in the British Army, to escort observing officers as they roamed the countryside. Prisoners could be taken by patrols sent out with this in mind. Cornet Strenuwitz of the 1st KGL Hussars captured an enemy picquet larger than his own force but was still able to bring them back to Allied lines, unharmed, for questioning.[116] Prisoners were a rich source of information, presuming the guerrillas did not kill them first. Those taken in open battle or by the Allied regular troops would be treated relatively well. The *Ordenança* were instructed explicitly to treat prisoners well, and were offered 1,200 *Reis* for the safe delivery of French deserters or prisoners.[117] If the prisoners had been treated badly, those responsible would, '… be punished in the most severe way'.[118] Some prisoners were brought in by the *Ordenança* in December 1810, who indicated they were from a formation in Drouet's IX corps, comprising 11 battalions assembled in Nantes during the previous summer.[119] This information would be very useful to Wellington to establish the strength and capability of enemy formations.

Wellington often asked for intelligent and capable officers to gather information, but finding men of intellect in the army was not always easy. Known as 'exploring officers' this role was often fulfilled by educated men engaged on daring missions. What Wellington wanted was an officer who could act independently, take risks, and gather as much information as possible. For instance, he asked Lieutenant General Cotton, commander of the Allied cavalry, to leave an officer like Captain Krauchenberg, Cordemann, or Major Cocks on the Mondego to keep an eye on enemy movements between the Dão and the Mondego, and to maintain communication with these officers throughout the time they were away.[120]

Wellington built an effective intelligence network, which included these officers, who made maps and took notes on the terrain, helping to plan troop movements and

---

115 Wellington to Liverpool. Portalegre, 25 April, 1811, Gurwood, *Dispatches*, vol.4, p.777.
116 Wellington to Liverpool. Cartaxo, 16 Feb. 1811, Gurwood, *Dispatches*, vol.4, p.604.
117 This amounted to approximately 16 days' pay for a labourer in British service. Wellington to Major General Leith, Gouvea, 6th September 1810, Gurwood, *Dispatches*, vol.4, p.259.
118 Arquivo Histórico Militar (AHM): PT/AHM/DIV/1/14/270/09, Ajutante-General do Exercito Portuguez Mosinho Manoel de Brito, 'Ordem Do Duque Wellington Para Serem Recompensadas as Pessoas Que Entregaram Desertores e Castigados Os Que Trataram Mal' (Headquarters at Lagioza, 17 August 1810).
119 Wellington to Liverpool. Cartaxo, 5 Jan. 1811, Gurwood, *Dispatches*, vol.4, p.503.
120 Wellington to Lieutenant General Cotton, Cortiçó, 20 Sept. 1810, Gurwood, *Dispatches*, vol.4, p.291.

logistics. Colquhoun Grant was perhaps the most famous of these officers.[121] There were others, including Majors John Waters and Edward Cocks, who would dress in full uniform while operating behind enemy lines to avoid the accusation that they were spies. Wellington held these men in high esteem and was troubled when they were captured, wounded, or killed.

Tactical intelligence was vital for the commanders of the outposts, as well as the commanders of the armies. The Allied forces boasted regiments of Light Dragoons and Hussars, while the French had *chasseurs à cheval* and *hussards*. Renowned for their flamboyant uniforms, the hussars in both armies were seasoned troops. The *chasseurs à cheval* and light dragoons, though less ostentatious in attire, were equally effective in their roles. In the Allied army, the advanced guard consisted of a cavalry brigade, which invariably included the 1st KGL Hussars, supported by Craufurd's Light Division, a brigade of Portuguese infantry, usually Pack's, and a troop of Royal Horse Artillery. Reports from the picquet could go directly to headquarters for examination. Throughout the campaign, both armies utilised their light cavalry extensively for reconnaissance. However, as Tomkinson wrote, the continuous employment of the light cavalry in these duties had a bad effect: 'We never unsaddle excepting in the evening, merely to clean the horses; and at night the men sleep in their appointments, with their bridle reins in their hands, ready to turn out in an instant.'[122] These duties had the consequence of reducing the numbers available for general service in each individual regiment. Wellington was aware that continuous patrols and advanced-guard action were having on his cavalry, especially with the infrequent supply of fodder for the horses. He wrote, '… our excellent cavalry are falling off very fast.'[123]

Gathering intelligence was markedly more challenging for the French, and the process of delivering this intelligence to its intended recipients was equally difficult. Unlike their British counterparts, French officers did not have the freedom to roam the countryside individually or in small groups. Instead, the French armies in the Peninsula depended heavily on spies for obtaining general information or conducted reconnaissance operations in the immediate vicinity of their forces to gather tactical intelligence. Pelet, among other officers and ADCs, spent much time reconnoitring the ground ahead of the army and trying to establish their location. The French had inadequate knowledge of the topography of the country despite their best efforts. Pelet tells us that he, '… spared no trouble nor pains to collect information from all sides.'[124] On the advance into Portugal he noted that the army, '… never had a single guide. Everywhere the inhabitants had fled to hard to access places, chasing their cattle before them, and taking away from their houses what might be of some use to us.'[125] The situation was worse as the French withdrew, because this time the Portuguese knew of what extreme actions the French soldiers were capable.

---

121   TNA: PRO 30/43/53, For example, see Lecor to Cole, Castello Branco, 19th June 1810, 'Sir Galbraith Lowry Cole: Papers', 1810.
122   Tomkinson, *Diary*, p.25.
123   Wellington to Stuart, Villar Maior, 8 April, 1811, Gurwood, *Dispatches*, vol.4, p.731.
124   Pelet, *The French Campaign in Portugal*, p.142.
125   Jones and Jones, *Journals of Sieges*, vol.3, pp.185–186 Rapport de l'intendant général Lambert au Prince Berthier, major-général , sur la situation de l'armée de Portugal, Viseu, 23rd September 1810.

7

Pause

The French

The *armée de Portugal* had paused at the border while Massena decided on his next step. Almeida was still garrisoned by French troops, among them the 5e bataillon 82e ligne, various artillerymen and provisional units, numbering some 1,400 men. It was clear that before any offensive operations could be undertaken that the army required rest, and, above all else, food. This meant that the army needed to be provided with regular supplies. Massena thus instructed the army to withdraw to the comparative safety of Spain around Salamanca. Massena expected that Bessières, following an exchange of letters, was collecting supplies to send up to the army. There was ill-feeling between the two *maréchaux*, and although Bessières promised much, Massena was repeatedly disappointed by the lack of support he received. Bessières wrote on 9 April to the Minister of War:

> The state of the Army of Portugal is difficult to describe: demoralised, without cavalry, without artillery horses or equipment. The Emperor should not count on this army to take the offensive for some time; because it is an army that needs to be completely reorganised. Everything I hear about it boggles the mind, but truly it is in a state of total deficiency, without horses, without coherence, with disobedience.
>
> I had not waited for Your Highness's orders to put the entire 9th corps at the disposal of the Prince d'Essling, nothing has been neglected to send him provisions, but scarcely had I learned of his plan to return to Spain than he was already near Ciudad-Rodrigo.[1]

On the same day, Napoleon dictated a letter, showing concern over the dislocation of communications between Massena and Paris, but also interfering in operational details:

> I wish you to send off this evening Senator Lecoulteux's son, aide-de-camp to the Prince of Essling; he will take with him several copies of the 'Moniteur' of to-day addressed to the Prince of Essling, to the Duke of

---

1   Koch, *Mémoires de Massena*, vol.7, p.476.

Istria, and to General Caffarelli. Tell the Prince of Essling that an express has been intercepted, and it is to be feared that it contained despatches from him, since between those which Colonel Pelet brought, and the one written from Guarda, none have been received from him.

You will send the Prince of Essling by his aide-de-camp a duplicate of yesterday's despatch; you will let him know that I have given the command of the 1e division of the 6e corps to General Foy; that therefore there is no occasion to appoint General Maucune general of division; that he should arm Almeida as soon as possible, since it appears that it would take a long time to destroy the place and to remove the artillery.

Desire him to hasten the departure of General Drouet and his corps for Andalusia ...[2]

Massena would be moved to write to the minister in Paris again on the 17th, explaining the situation with the army and the lack of cooperation he was receiving from Bessières:

The cavalry, although quartered, daily loses a great number of horses which have been exhausted by lack of food and their fatigues in Portugal. The trains and the artillery are, for the same reasons, in a state of absolute uselessness ... The summary of my letter is that, of all the promises that the Duke of Istria made to me, none have been fulfilled; that I see only an extremely unfortunate future; that I have done and am doing everything in my power; that I can only make representations, write, and expose the true situation of things, without having advanced any further so far.[3]

Massena's ADCs, *chef de bataillon* Pelet, *capitaine* Delavillé and Briqueville, had been sent in turn to Bessières to obtain supplies. Eventually, Massena informed him that 200,000 rations of biscuit would be taken from Ciudad-Rodrigo, which would need to be replaced as soon as possible. A commissioner was sent to Salamanca to find ways to replenish the army's supplies, and the *intendant général* received orders to send flour and wheat to Ciudad-Rodrigo, in the absence of biscuits, to replace those that had been taken. Disappointed, on 6 April, *intendant général* Lambert wrote to the war ministry that the resources intended for the army had been devoured by others and his treasury depleted. The reserves of hospital supplies and clothing had been reduced to the point where there were only 600 pairs of breeches and fewer than 5,000 pairs of shoes left in the stores.[4]

Two events now occurred, one of which improved the morale of the *armée de Portugal*, and the other which caused Wellington some concern. The first was the announcement of the birth of Napoleon's son, the King of Rome, on 20 March. Finally, he had an heir to inherit the Empire, and the event was celebrated with

---

2   *The Confidential Correspondence of Napoleon Bonaparte*, vol.2, p.177.
3   Fririon, *Journal Historique*, p.194.
4   SHD: *Correspondance*, 7C12.

a salute of 101 cannon shots.[5] The second event was deeply worrying. Lieutenant Colonel John Waters of the Royal Scots was an exploring officer who epitomised the stereotype of the dashing, devil-may-care British officer. However, by a miscalculation on his part whilst on reconnaissance without an escort near the Côa, he was taken prisoner. Surrounded by French *hussards*, he had no choice but to surrender. The loss of Waters was a serious blow to Wellington's intelligence-gathering network. Wellington was concerned enough to write to Beresford:

> You will be concerned to hear that Waters is at last taken prisoner. He crossed the Coa alone, I believe, yesterday morning, and was looking at the enemy through a spying glass, when 4 hussars pounced upon him. Nobody has seen him since yesterday morning; and we have the account from the prisoners, who tell the story of an officer attached to the Staff, a Lieut. Colonel, blond, with a petit chapeau. They saw him with Regnier. [sic][6]

There was relief a few days later when Waters returned, having refused parole and escaped from captivity.[7]

Général de division Thiébault, governor of Salamanca, was alarmed about the state of his administrative region once the *armée de Portugal* reached it. He wrote to Bessières, 'The return of the army makes all administration impossible. Requirements will be out of all proportion to resources; waste and disorder of every kind will go on, and all efforts will be ineffective.'[8] As Massena established his headquarters at Salamanca, he found more than 18,000 infantry and nearly 1,700 horses gathered to join the *armée de Portugal*.[9] These had been accumulated from reinforcements and recuperating sick and wounded whilst the *armée de Portugal* had been out of contact. However, as Bessières had pointed out, the main body of the army was in poor condition. The *corps d'armée* were dispersed over a wide area for rest and the collection of food. Wellington summed up the situation:

> We have given the French some terrible beatings, and they are completely dispirited and disorganised. We have cut off the communication with Almeida, in which place there is a month's provision; and I have desired Don Julian to distress the communication with Ciudad Rodrigo, in which there may be as much. I hope we shall be able to stay here, to get at least the first mentioned of these places …[10]

Fririon, Massena's chief of staff, was sent to Ciudad Rodrigo to assess the feasibility of getting a convoy of supplies into the fortress. Should the opportunity present itself,

5   Noël, *With Napoleon's Guns*, p.117.
6   Wellington to Beresford, Sabugal, 4 April, 1811, Gurwood, *Dispatches*, vol.4, p.724.
7   To Beresford, Villar Formoso, 13th April 1811, Gurwood, *Dispatches*, vol.4, p.745.
8   Paul Charles Thiébault, Arthur Butler (trans), *The Memoirs of Baron Thiébault (Late Lieutenant-General in the French Army)* (London: Smith, Elder & Co, 1896), vol.2, p.320.
9   Thiébault, *Memoires du General Baron Thiébault*, vol.4, p.448.
10 To H. Wellesley. Villar Formoso, 10 April, 1811, Gurwood, *Dispatches*, vol.4, p.740.

he was ordered to use Marchand's division and the 10e dragons to escort 100,000 rations of biscuit and as much flour as possible into the fortress. If the Allied forces near Almeida were too strong for this force, he was instructed to use IX corps and Fournier's cavalry to force the convoy through.[11] However, both Reynier and Drouet declared the operation impossible.[12] This seems to have provided Massena with the motivation to bring the entire army into play to push the convoy into Almeida.

II corps established its headquarters at Ledesma, with its vanguard at Villamayor and Lamata. The 1e division occupied Carbellino and Alameda; the 2e division was around Almenara and San-Pelayo. VI corps had the 1e division at Caridad and the suburbs of Ciudad-Rodrigo; the 2e division was at Alba de Tormes, Salvatierra and Fuentes, having a brigade at Baños, Bejar and Monte-Mayor for observation purposes; the 3e division was at Salamanca, guarding the road to Ciudad Rodrigo. VIII corps remained on the Douro; the 1e division at Toro and the 2e division at Boveda. The artillery equipment was based at Salamanca, but the horses needed to be moved to Madrigal in the province of Avila to obtain sufficient fodder.[13] IX corps was at San Felices de los Gallegos and Vitigudino, and orders had finally arrived from Paris placing Drouet's IX corps under Massena's direct orders, having been sent on 6 February.[14] The cavalry reserves were sent to the region north of Salamanca around Castronuevo, Villanueva del Campo, Villafáfila and Villalpando to find fodder and to rest.

On 27 of April, a substantial reorganisation was undertaken within the *armée de Portugal* and IX corps. The 4e battalions of the 6e and 25e Légère, and the 27e ligne from Conroux's division, and those of the 39e, 59e, 69e and 76e ligne from Claparède's were returned to their respective regiments in other corps.[15] These reinforcements were incorporated into their respective regiments to bring the first two or three battalions up to strength, and a cadre was then sent back to France for recruiting and training new replacements. As an example, the 76e ligne of Marchand's division under *chef de bataillon* Castillon received the 4e battalion of the regiment, bringing 636 men, including 19 officers.[16]

According to Fririon, the 27e, 50e and 69e ligne each also received a company of regimental artillery. Eble's previous returns of 25 March show the number of guns reduced to approximately six per division because of the lack of draught horses.[17] These losses had to be made up before Massena could take the field again, but there were no replacements for the guns, and few for the horses.

Overall, this reorganisation had a beneficial effect on the II and VI corps and Solignac's division of VIII corps, but meant that Clausel's division was reduced

---

11   Fririon, *Journal Historique*, p.194.
12   Koch, *Mémoires de Massena*, vol.7, p.489.
13   Fririon, *Journal Historique*, pp.191–193.
14   Koch, *Mémoires de Massena*, vol.7, p.473; 17335 au Prince de Neuchatel et de Wagram, Major Général de l'armée d'Espagne, a Paris. Paris, 6 février 1811. Plon and Dumaine, *Correspondence de Napoléon I*, vol.21, pp.387–388.
15   Fririon, *Journal Historique*, p.198.
16   Henri du Fresnel, *Un Régiment à Travers l'histoire Le 76e* (Paris: Flammarion, 1894), p.496.
17   Pièces Justificatives No VII, Tableau de l'organisation de l'artillerie a l'époque du 25 Mars Koch, *Mémoires de Massena*, vol.7, p.577.

to just over 3,000 men. IX corps was equally depleted and reduced to 18 orphan 4e battalions.[18] When the army advanced towards Almeida, Massena left Clausel behind to protect his lines of communication, calculating that the denuded division would not be useful in the battle line.

Massena was conducting a review of II and IX corps on 1 May when Bessières arrived, bringing the long-promised reinforcements. But he was to be extremely disappointed with the number of troops that came. Bessières led *général de brigade* Watier's light cavalry brigade, a detachment of the Imperial Guard cavalry, six pieces of guard artillery, and 30 artillery teams numbering some 1,636 men.[19] Massena had expected more than 6,000 troops from Bessières' *armée du Nord*.[20] Thiébault considered that Bessières never intended to provide the infantry, claiming it would take too long to collect them.[21] According to Marbot, on seeing the forces Bessières had brought along, Massena commented, 'He would have done much better to have sent me a few more thousand men with ammunition and provisions, and to have remained at the centre of his province than to come examining and criticising what I am going to do.'[22]

For a *maréchal* to command so few men possibly indicated that Bessières wanted to share in the glory of a victory. He is recorded as saying, 'I am come, like a French cavalier, at the head of a handful of heroes.'[23] He could always, if a defeat was the outcome, place the blame squarely on to Massena's shoulders whilst claiming shares in any victory. Rumours and stories of the situation in the *armée de Portugal* circulated in the Allied camp. There were concerning reports that Bessières had brought, '... 50,000 infantry and 5,000 cavalry.'[24] Charles Stewart, Wellington's Adjutant General, wrote from his first-hand observation:

> Rumours of [Massena's] excessive unpopularity began also to make their way within our camp. We were told a variety of tales touching a quarrel which had occurred between the Prince of Esling [sic] and Marshal Ney, into which, it was added, that the whole army had entered, with a decided leaning towards the latter officer; and it was repeatedly rumoured, that Massena was on the eve of his recall, and that some new chief would shortly appear upon the stage to supply his place.[25]

18   Order of Battle, 3 May 1811. Koch, *Mémoires de Massena*, vol.7, p.600.
19   Fririon, *Journal Historique*, p.200.
20   Koch, *Mémoires de Massena*, vol.7, p.443.
21   Thiébault, *The Memoirs of Baron Thiébault*, vol.2, p.323.
22   Jean-Baptiste-Antoine-Marcelin Marbot, Arthur Butler (trans.), *The Memoirs of Baron De Marbot: Late Lieutenant-General in the French Army* (London: Longmans, Green, 1913), vol.2, p.462.
23   Thiébault, *The Memoirs of Baron Thiébault*, vol.2, p.323.
24   Camp on the Heights before Alameda: 8 May 1811, Sir William Gomm, Francis Carr-Gomm (ed.), *Letters and Journals of Field Marshal Sir William Maynard Gomm, G.C.B. &c, &c, from 1799 to Waterloo, 1815* (London: Murray, 1881), p.213.
25   Charles William Vane (formerly Stewart), *Narrative of the Peninsular War from 1808 to 1813* (London: Colburn, 1828), p.500.

The Allies

The Allied army had followed up the retreating French but had been seriously hindered by a lack of supplies. Wellington now had an opportunity to bring his forces together, re-establish his logistical system to re-equip and resupply, and integrate new units into his army. During the pursuit of the retreating French, some units, most notably the Portuguese brigades, had been left behind through lack of food, water and shoes. Wellington wrote to Charles Stuart expressing his frustration at the situation of some of his best Portuguese troops: 'There is a note from Gen. Pack this morning, whom I have been obliged to leave behind. He has had one day's rice, and one day's Indian corn or bread … since I saw him, 12 days ago!! It is really a joke to talk of carrying on the war'.[26]

The Portuguese commissariat was persistently failing their own troops. Additionally, Wellington complained that the muleteers, most of whom were Spanish, would not take supplies to the Portuguese troops. The muleteers would supply the British formations, and in some cases, where Portuguese troops were attached to British units, this information was kept from the muleteers to ensure a continuous supply of matériel. Wellington wrote to Stuart, complaining that he had, '… been obliged to leave Gen. Pack's brigade at Mangualde for want of food, and that Col. Pamplona's brigade receives nothing but beef, with which they are supplied by the British Commissaries.'[27] He stated, 'Barbacena's [sic] brigade will soon be annihilated.'[28] The condition of the Portuguese troops was subject to serious decline whenever the British commissariat was unable to supply them. Additionally, the lack of fit cavalry would be a problem in the coming weeks, against a French army well supplied with that arm. Wellington, despite his subsequent reputation, did not stint in his praise for the Portuguese officers and men. He wrote to *Tenente-General* Bacellar:

> I beg leave to take this opportunity of congratulating you upon the evacuation of your country by the enemy, and to return you my thanks for the assistance which I have received from you in the operations which have been carried on throughout the year, and have been brought to this result.
>
> … I likewise request you to convey to the officers, non-commissioned officers, and soldiers, who have served under your directions, and under the immediate command of Gens. Silveira and Trant, and Col. Wilson, the expression of the high sense which I entertain of their gallantry and discipline as soldiers, of their patriotism, and of their loyalty to their Sovereign, and my assurances of confidence in the ultimate result of the just cause in which we are engaged, if they, and others in similar situations, continue their exertions, and to act in a manner worthy of the ancient reputation of their country.[29]

---

26   To Charles Stuart, Celorico, 30 March, 1811, Gurwood, *Dispatches*, vol.4, p.712.
27   To Charles Stuart, Villar Maior, 8 April, 1811, Gurwood, *Dispatches*, vol.4, p.727.
28   To Charles Stuart, Villar Maior, 8 April, 1811, Gurwood, *Dispatches*, vol.4, p.731.
29   To Bacellar, Villar Formoso, 10 April, 1811, Gurwood, *Dispatches*, vol.4, pp.736–737.

The *milícia* through some misunderstanding had been sent home by Beresford. However, Wellington required they be held in readiness, '… because I don't think that affairs are yet in such a decided state as to enable me to say that in the course of 2 or 3 months it may not be necessary to call out the whole again.'[30] Wellington sent Don Julian's forces across the Agueda to interfere with French communications into Ciudad Rodrigo. He was instructed to, '… render the communication with Ciudad Rodrigo difficult by the right of the Agueda, while our cavalry shall do it by the left.'[31] Wellington believed that both Ciudad Rodrigo and Almeida had small garrisons with provisions for about a month.

Almeida is Blockaded

The border fortress of Almeida was constructed around a medieval castle, and surrounded by star-shaped, low defences in the Vauban style.[32] It mirrored Ciudad Rodrigo on the Spanish side of the border. The fortress had surrendered to the French on 27 August 1810, after an explosion in the powder magazine destroyed a large proportion of the town. Massena left 1,600 men under the command of *général de brigade* Brenier, who worked tirelessly to repair the damaged fortifications and provide supplies for the town's garrison. From October 1810, Silveira's *milícia* attempted to blockade the garrison, and it took the arrival of IX corps in December 1810 to drive them away. However, the corps' stay in this impoverished region was only possible by using the already scarce supplies from the fortress. Consequently, by 2 February 1811, the garrison had only 36 days' worth of food left. On 20 February, Brenier wrote to Berthier, 'If no one comes to my aid, there will be no way left for me to keep this place and I will have no other recourse than to blow up the fortifications.'[33] When Drouet had reached Almeida in March, he was surprised at the lack of food and warned Massena that the fortress was down to 15 days' supplies. However, the true state was not as poor as Drouet had claimed, as there was some 40 days' worth in stock.[34] Despite the discussion concerning food, there was a plan for Almeida to be slighted and abandoned. Brenier had, on 27 March, received an order from the Emperor to proceed with the demolition and evacuation of Almeida.[35] Massena also sent him instructions to prepare the destruction of the fortress, and ordered Drouet to establish a line of communication to Ciudad Rodrigo.

Meanwhile, the *armée de Portugal* retreated from its abortive advance southwards and took up position between Almeida and Ciudad Rodrigo. On 7 April, Massena warned Brenier that the army could no longer find food in its current positions and

---

30   To Beresford, Villar Formoso, 10 April, 1811, Gurwood, *Dispatches*, vol.4, p.738.

31   To Beresford, Villar Formoso, 10 April, 1811, Gurwood, *Dispatches*, vol.4, p.738.

32   João Campos, *Almeida: Três Pontas Notáveis Numa Estrela Singular* (Almeida: Câmara Municipal, 2010).

33   Brenier, quoted in Jean Sarramon, 'Campagne de Fuentes de Oñoro, 15 Avril–11 Mai 1811', *Carnet de La Sabretache*, 425 (1962), p.7.

34   Oman, *A History of the Peninsular War*, vol.4, p.181.

35   Koch, *Mémoires de Massena*, vol.7, p.417.

would withdraw into Spain, thus exposing Almeida to the full weight of the Allied army.[36] Because he lacked transportation, Massena had to leave his siege artillery behind at the fortress, which was to have unfortunate consequences. As the *armée de Portugal* withdrew across the Agueda, Wellington wrote to Charles Stuart in Lisbon, 'I am trying to frighten Regnier [sic] out of Almeida.'[37] The attempt failed, and Wellington was forced to invest Almeida in a formal siege. Wellington reported to his brother that on 10 April, 'We have cut off the communication with Almeida, in which place there is a month's provision'.[38] The Allied army pushed outposts along the Agueda, aiming to monitor Massena's movements in anticipation of an attempt to get supplies into the fortress.

The 6th Division surrounded Almeida, with other divisions spread between Almeida and Fuerte de la Concepción. The Light and 5th at Fuerte de la Concepción were acting as the advanced guard of the Allied army, keeping an eye on the French, but Almeida was now the focus. Major General Campbell's 6th Division, Pack's Portuguese brigade and *Visconde* de Barbacena's brigade of Portuguese cavalry were given the task of blockading the town.[39]

While Almeida was being surrounded, Wellington ordered the Light Division with cavalry support to attempt to stop Ciudad Rodrigo from being resupplied. Wellington wrote to Beresford that, 'The French have but little provisions in Ciudad Rodrigo, as well as in Almeida, and I have sent some troops over the Agueda to shut up the former.'[40] However, the orders were not carried out to Wellington's satisfaction, and Massena was able to get supplies into the town twice in quick succession. This persuaded Wellington that a blockade of the town would be useless, and he was to focus his army's efforts on Almeida. He wrote in evident frustration to Beresford:

> Sir W. Erskine did not send a detachment over the Agueda in time, as I had desired him, and the consequence was that the French got their convoy into Ciudad Rodrigo yesterday morning. At all events I was not very sanguine of the result of the blockade of that place, and indeed had determined not to make it in any strength; and now it is useless to keep any body on the other side of the Agueda, excepting for the sake of food and observation. I confine myself, therefore, to the blockade of Almeida ...[41]

At first, responsibility for the blockade of Almeida was assigned to the 6th Division under Campbell, stationed around Freineda, Naves, Junça, and São Pedro to the south; the 5th Division stationed in Vale-de-Coelho and Malpartida to the north-east; and Trant's Brigade of *milícia* to the north and west. Following the resupply of Ciudad Rodrigo, and before his journey south to see Beresford, Wellington wrote to Spencer:

36   Fririon, *Journal Historique*, p.185.
37   To Charles Stuart, Villa Maior, 6 April, 1811, Gurwood, *Dispatches*, vol.4, p.726.
38   To H. Wellesley, Villar Formoso, 10 April, 1811, Gurwood, *Dispatches*, vol.4, p.740.
39   Memorandum for Spencer, Villar Formoso, 14 April, 1811, Gurwood, *Dispatches*, vol.4, p.747.
40   Wellington to Beresford, Villar Formoso, 13 April, 1811, Gurwood, *Dispatches*, vol.4, p.745.
41   To Beresford, Villar Formoso, 14 April, 1811, Gurwood, *Dispatches*, vol.4, p.749.

… we should confine ourselves to the blockade of Almeida, which operation should be given over to Major Gen. Campbell's division and Gen. Pack's brigade; and that the remainder of the army should be so posted as to cover and protect that operation, to get green forage for the horses and cattle of the cavalry and artillery, and to be able to collect the whole in a short space of time, as hereafter pointed out. Orders will be given respecting the positions to be taken by the 6th division, and Gen. Pack's brigade, for this operation.[42]

Wellington's freedom of action was limited as most of his siege train was still in Lisbon and would not reach the army until the autumn.[43] Lieutenant Colonel Charles Bevan of the 4th Foot, part of Dunlop's Brigade of the 5th Division, wrote to his wife on 15 April, 'We have been for the last two or three days very much harassed in blocking Almeida which is about 5 miles from hence … our men stand much in need of repose for we are 150 short since we left Torres Vedras.'[44]

Kincaid described the direct measures taken by the Allies to reduce the already limited resources available: 'The garrison of Almeida was blockaded with a fortnight's provision only, and two companies of ours under Colonel Cameron were immediately dispatched to shoot their bullocks while grazing on the ramparts, which still further contracted their means of subsistence.'[45]

Wellington summoned the garrison of Almeida on 15 and 17 April but was firmly rejected by Brenier. The French governor maintained the training of the garrison, and each night at a different time he had cannons fired, a measure which was to prove its usefulness shortly afterwards.[46]

In order to stop Massena from revictualling Almeida, Wellington chose a location from which he could block the approaches to the town from Ciudad Rodrigo. He left instructions for the deployment of the army with Spencer while he was at Badajoz with Beresford. Campbell, Pack and Barbacena were to continue the blockade of Almeida, with part of Barbacena's cavalry observing along the Agueda. Pack had issued clear orders to his brigade as early as 17 April regarding their duties around Almeida:

… commanding officers will hold their regiments in readiness to march at a moment's notice, by day or night. They will be under arms every morning half an hour before daylight, and remain so for half an hour after … The garrison of Almeida is supposed to be about 1400 men, and the probability is that after blowing up the place they will make an attempt to escape, which ought to be guarded against by every possible means, and must be frustrated by the attention, zeal, and care of the Field officers who may be

42   Memorandum for Spencer, Villar Formoso, 14 April, 1811, Gurwood, *Dispatches*, vol.4, p.747.
43   Oporto, August 6, 1811. Dickson, *The Dickson Manuscripts*, vol.3, pp.438–439; To the Officer commg. the Artillery, Lamego. Fuente Guinaldo, 21 August 1811. Gurwood, *Dispatches*, vol.5, p.226.
44   Archie Hunter, *Wellington's Scapegoat: The Tragedy of Lieutenant-Colonel Charles Bevan* (Barnsley: Leo Cooper, 2003), p.129.
45   Kincaid, *Random Shots from a Rifleman*, p.183.
46   Sarramon, 'Campagne de Fuentes de Oñoro, 15 Avril – 11 Mai 1811', p.23.

on duty with the piquets, which may be always certain of assistance from the brigade and other troops in readiness to support them.[47]

The Light Division was tasked with observing and defending the crossings over the Agueda; the 5th Division was to be positioned at Fuerte de la Concepción and provide support for the Light Division. The cavalry was to move to Fuenteguinaldo and El Bodón, and the remaining divisions were to be positioned around Nave de Haver. Wellington wrote, 'If the enemy are determined to raise the blockade of Almeida, it is probable that they will move their whole army, or the greatest part of it, upon Ciudad Rodrigo, from whence they would turn the heads of the ravines of the Azava, Dos Casas, and Turon, [sic] on which we might take a position to protect the blockade.[48]

This position ran along a ridge between two small rivers which ran into the Agueda. The region situated between the Agueda and Côa features moderately undulating terrain, characterised by extensive rounded plateaus covered in moorland and intersected by woods and forests, particularly in the southern areas. The topography of the position is dominated by the north-south ridge that runs between the two small streams, the Rivera del Campo O del Barrocal and Rio Tourões, both of which run almost parallel to the Rio Côa. The Barrocal runs into the Dos Casas around Alameda. To add confusion to this description, however, at the time of the battle, the Barrocal was also known as the Dos Casas.[49]

To Badajoz and Back

Given the relative inactivity of the *armée de Portugal*, Wellington saw an opportunity to go south to confer with Beresford. He left detailed instructions with Lieutenant General Sir Brent Spencer, the senior divisional commander, regarding actions to be taken if the French advanced to relieve Almeida while he was absent. The memorandum explains the dispositions of the enemy and the threat they might pose to the Allies. It finishes by predicting the possible movements of the French and what response Spencer should make:

> If the enemy are determined to raise the blockade of Almeida, it is probable that they will move their whole army, or the greatest part of it, upon Ciudad Rodrigo, from whence they would turn the heads of the ravines of the Azava, Dos Casas, and Turon, [sic] on which we might take a position to protect the blockade.
>
> If the enemy should make this movement, it would be necessary to raise the blockade of Almeida …[50]

---

47   Brigade order by Pack, Cinco Villas, 17 April, 1811, Gurwood, *Dispatches*, vol.5, n.16.
48   Memorandum for Spencer, Villar Formoso, 14 April, 1811, Gurwood, *Dispatches*, vol.4, p.748.
49   For the description of the battle in the coming pages the river which runs in front of Fuentes de Oñoro will be referred to as the Dos Casas.
50   Memorandum for Spencer, Villar Formoso, 14 April, 1811, Gurwood, *Dispatches*, vol.4, pp.747–748.

The withdrawal routes were specified clearly, allowing for no misunderstanding. On the same day, he wrote to Major General Charles Stewart in a calming manner, 'We are blockading Almeida, in which there may be provisions for about a month; and as the French army are gone towards the Douro, I don't think they are inclined, or able, to interrupt this undertaking.'[51]

Napoleon seemed spellbound when he received news of Wellington's movements, making unfounded assumptions regarding the activities of the Allied army. He wrote to Berthier:

> I am sending the translation of the English newspapers. You will see there that on 18 April Wellington had crossed the Tagus. I beg you to have these despatches copied and to send them this evening to the Dukes of Istrie and Ragusa, and even to General Beliard. Thus it appears that there was only half the English army left on the side of Castile. The events which will have passed on the side of Almeida will have already informed the generals of the army of this news and will enable them to take the proper course, to press on the Tagus.[52]

Napoleon assumed that Wellington had taken troops with him to Estremadura, when in fact he took only a small entourage, including George Scovell, in order to reduce any delays. His itinerary indicated how fast he would be moving. He left Villar Formoso on 15 April and later that day wrote to Cotton from Sabugal, 'I am going into the Alentejo, but intend to return to the army in less than 3 weeks.'[53] The route would be by Castello Branco on the 17th, Portalegre on the 19th, and then Elvas.[54] Writing to Spencer on the 16th, he explained that if he left his baggage behind, '… supposing a communication from you should be 48 hours going to Elvas, I should be with you in 60 hours after I should receive it.'[55] On the following day, he indicated to Spencer the route to be taken to enable the fastest and most efficient means of contacting him during his trip:

> In case you should wish to communicate any thing [sic] to me, and to be quite certain that it reaches me as soon as it can, I recommend to you to send a Staff officer, on his own horses, to Sabugal, and to order him to proceed on with the horses of the guides by the following route from Sabugal:

> Memoa, leave Penamacor on the left.

---

51   To Major Gen. C. Stewart, Villar Formoso, 14 April, 1811, Gurwood, *Dispatches*, vol.4, pp.746–747.
52   17701 – Au Prince de Neuchatel et de Wagram, Major Géneral de l'armée d'Espagne , a Paris. Saint-Cloud, 7 mai 1811, Plon and Dumaine, *Correspondence de Napoléon I*, vol.22, p.146.
53   Wellington to Lieutenant General Sir S. Cotton, Bart. Sabugal, 15 April, 1811, Gurwood, *Dispatches*, vol.4, p.750.
54   Wellington to Beresford, Sabugal, 15 April, 1811, Gurwood, *Dispatches*, vol.4, p.751.
55   Wellington to Spencer, Pedrogão, 16 April, 1811, Gurwood, *Dispatches*, vol.4, p.752.

Pedrogão, from Sabugal about	27 miles
S. Miguel d'Arche	8
Escalhos de Cima	10
Castello Branco	10
Sarnadas	10
Villa Velha, across the Tagus	10
Niza	11
Portalegre	24
Elvas	36

P.S. I received last night your letter of the 16th, and am much obliged to you. I conclude that the rain of yesterday has reached you, and puts out of the question all possibility of crossing the Agueda by either side.[56]

Throughout his journey, he also dealt with the mundane tasks of leadership and command, in one instance indicating the correct accounting for the purchase of shoes.[57] Once again, he had to warn the Government about publishing confidential dispatches in British newspapers. Writing to the Earl of Liverpool, he stated, 'It is very desirable that you should not publish the details of my dispatches to your Lordship. You cannot conceive how very deficient the French are in information. All the dispatches from me which are published are sent to Massena from Paris, and they thus acquire the information of what is going on.'[58]

As can be seen from Napoleon's correspondence above, Wellington's fears were not misplaced. In reply, Liverpool reassured Wellington, 'I have used every caution in my power on this subject, and have almost invariably confined the publication of them to statements of facts, without observation or prediction as to the future.'[59] He suggested that subsequent dispatches be marked with which sections could be used for publication.

Wellington reached his destination as intended on the 20th after travelling more than 130 miles. On the 22nd, Wellington rode to reconnoitre the road to Badajoz and was fired upon by the French picquet. A detachment was sent to provide cover for Wellington, but the situation escalated, and approximately 18 men of the detachment were killed.[60] After instructing Beresford on the forthcoming siege of Badajoz and campaign in the region,[61] he returned north. What is clear from the itinerary is that French assertions that he took troops with him, or that he returned when urged to by Spencer, are erroneous. Infantry could not cover the distances that a mounted man could achieve. Massena mentioned these phantom troops in his dispatch to

---

56   Wellington to Spencer, Castello Branco, 17th April, 1811, 2 p.m., Gurwood, *Dispatches*, vol.4, p.754.
57   Wellington to Beresford, Castello Branco, 17 April, 1811, Gurwood, *Dispatches*, vol.4, p.754.
58   Wellington to Liverpool, Portalegre, 25 April, 1811, Gurwood, *Dispatches*, vol.4, p.777.
59   Liverpool to Wellington, 7 May, 1811, *Supplementary Despatches*, vol.7, p.120.
60   TNA: WO 37/7a, Scovell, *Diary*, p.38.
61   Memorandum to Beresford, Elvas, 23 April 1811, Gurwood, *Dispatches*, vol.4, pp.763–765; Memorandum to Beresford, Col. Fletcher, and Major Dickson, Elvas 23 April 1811, Gurwood, *Dispatches*, vol.4, pp.765–766.

Berthier on 7 May.[62] *Général de division* Oudinot even went so far as to suggest that the troops Wellington brought back from Elvas increased the numerical imbalance between the two armies, and this led to the failure to relieve Almeida.[63]

On 22 April, Lieutenant General Sir Stapleton Cotton rejoined the army and was appointed commander of the cavalry, '… and the advanced posts of the army.'[64] On the 23rd, and again on the 27th, the French had attacked the Allied outposts on the Rivera de Azaba. The outposts, comprising troops from the 52nd and 95th, drove off the attackers on both occasions. However, they noticed that on the 27th, a strong reconnaissance force of eight squadrons of cavalry and three battalions of infantry reconnoitred the line of the river but made no attempt to cross.[65] Marchand's division and the 10e dragons had conducted a reconnaissance towards Carpio. Finding the enemy in position on the banks of the Azaba, they had withdrawn without engaging. On the same day, a detachment from II corps had reconnoitred the Allied picquet guarding the Barba de Puerco bridge and observed the Allied forces deployed there. Wellington reported to Beresford that, 'The river is not yet fordable, at least not for infantry, and they have hitherto made no movement, excepting two of reconnaissance towards the bridge on the Azava [sic] near Marialva [sic].'[66]

Massena moved his headquarters to Ciudad Rodrigo on the 25th, and in the evening of that day, Spencer wrote to Wellington with the news that the French were on the move. Wellington received this dispatch on the road back to the army. The *corps d'armée* were moving into their concentration points in preparation for Massena's orders to move towards Almeida. Wellington passed this news to Beresford on the 27th and was back at his headquarters in Villar Formoso on the 28th.[67] Scovell wrote in his diary of a forced march from Pedrogão to Alameda, but on reaching the destination, '… found everything quiet but with the Enemy collecting fast above Ciudad de Rodrigo [sic].'[68]

Wellington had already indicated to Spencer his thinking regarding the coming campaign. He wrote on 16 April, '… that so long as we can maintain ourselves upon the line of the Dos Casas, the enemy cannot interrupt the blockade of Almeida.'[69] His intention now was to implement this plan, whilst retaining as much flexibility in his dispositions as possible. Although the army was strung out between Fuerte de la Concepción and Nave de Haver, it could quickly concentrate at any point along the Dos Casas. Or, if necessary, the army could withdraw out of harm's way, but leave Almeida exposed.[70] The southern part of the landscape provided favourable

62   Le Maréchal Masséna, Prince d'Essling, à S. A. le Prince de Wagram et de Neufchatel, Major Général. Au camp de Fuentes de Onoro, le 7 Mai, 1811, Gurwood, *Dispatches*, vol.4, p.849.

63   Marc Oudinot, 'Souvenirs intimes et militaires du général Victor Oudinot, duc de Reggio Campagnes de Portugal : 1810 et 1811', *Napoleonica La Revue*, 5.2 (2009), p.36.

64   General Order, Alameda, 22 April 1811. Wellington, *Supplementary Despatches*, vol.7, p.620.

65   Wellington to Liverpool. Villar Formoso, 1 May, 1811, Gurwood, *Dispatches*, vol.4, p.781.

66   Wellington to Beresford,, Villar Formoso, 30 April, 1811, Gurwood, *Dispatches*, vol.4, p.779.

67   Wellington to Beresford, Villar Formoso, 30 April, 1811, Gurwood, *Dispatches*, vol.4, p.779.

68   TNA: WO 37/7a, Scovell, *Diary*, p.39.

69   Wellington to Spencer, Pedrogão, 16 April, 1811, Gurwood, *Dispatches*, vol.4, p.753.

70   Memorandum for Spencer, Villar Formoso, 14 April, 1811, Gurwood, *Dispatches*, vol.4, pp.747–748.

conditions for manoeuvring bodies of cavalry. The region along the Agueda was covered by the outposts of the Light Division and the light cavalry. Captain Edward Cocks noted that the French had, '… made several reconnaissances [sic] over the Agueda and there have been one or two sharp skirmishes at the Puente de Marialva [sic].'[71] Scovell recorded the concentration of French forces was visible from '… above the Bridge of Marialva'.[72]

On 30 April, Massena wrote to Berthier:

> The army could only be assembled yesterday, instead of the 26th, as I had hoped. I reviewed a large part of it, and I would have started my movement towards Almeida this morning if I had not been informed that Maréchal Duc d'Istrie had arrived in Salamanca with cavalry and artillery teams. I wrote to him to hasten the arrival of these reinforcements, which are so essential to us. I expect them tonight, and tomorrow I plan to march towards the enemy.[73]

Both armies recorded their numbers on 1 May, the British in their regular returns, and the French in their situations. According to Oman, the Anglo Allied army totalled some 37,504 men.[74] Some very small battalions were present. The 85th fielded only some 198 men, but the battalion did not have all its companies present. Although Oman shows this unit as fielding 365 men, the returns from Kew show that the battalion recorded 155 sick. The next smallest was the 2/88th fielding only 262 effectives. The largest regiments belonged to the Portuguese. The 12° Regimento totalled some 1,222 men, but it is worth remembering that this was a two-battalion regiment and included all the officers and men combined. The Allied cavalry comprised only 1,745 men, some five percent of the army total.

The *armée de Portugal*, on the other hand, could field approximately 4,200 cavalry, 800 of which were veterans from the *garde impériale*. The situation of 1 May, excluding the *armée du Nord*, gives the total cavalry as 6,231, but with only 4,622 horses.[75] The order of battle for Fuentes de Oñoro given in Koch shows only 2,606 cavalry and 800 grenadiers à cheval de la garde impériale, totalling 3,406.[76] Finding a true account of the number of cavalry available is therefore rather difficult, but for the purposes of this account, the original *situation* of 1 May will be taken as the most accurate, rather than Koch's interpretation of it. According to this, for example, Montbrun's division had 2,362 horses, and thus could only mount that number as a maximum. This also includes the *etat-major*

71   Edward Charles Cocks, Julia V. Page (ed.), *Intelligence Officer in the Peninsula: Letters and Diaries of Major the Hon. Edward Charles Cocks, 1786-1812* (Tunbridge Wells: Spellmount, 1986), p.102.
72   TNA: WO 37/7a, Scovell, *Diary*, p.39.
73   Appendix No. XLV, Gurwood, *Dispatches*, vol.4, p.849.
74   Oman, *A History of the Peninsular War*, vol.4, pp.618–621.
75   SHD: Situation de l'armée de Portugal au 1er mai 1811. *Armée de Portugal: Situation 1er Mai 1811.*
76   Ordre de bataille de l'armée de Portugal, commandée par le maréchal Massena, dans les journées de Fuentes de Onoro (3 et 5 mai 1811). Koch, *Mémoires de Massena*, vol.7, pp.600–602.

who were not combat troops. The location of VIII corps' 1,030 *dragons*, which are missing from other army lists, is explained by a note in the situation which reads, 'The Provisional Brigade of Dragoons composed of the 1st, 2nd and 3rd regiments received the order to leave the 8th Corps on April 22 and to go to Salamanca to come under the orders of [General] of Brigade Soult and to join the 9th Corps with this general officer. The movement was executed the same day.'[77] Soult's transfer from II corps to command this brigade is confirmed in the *rapport* section of the *situation*.

An overall figure of 40,636 rank-and-file present and under arms is given for the French, but this includes Clausel's division of 2,156 men, which had been left behind to guard the lines of communication as it was considered too weak to take the field. It does not include IX corps, which, according to Oman's source, fielded 11,098 men. This is slightly different from the order of battle in Koch, which gives 13,417 men, including artillery and train, but only some 9,171 infantry. The overall calculation for the troops under Massena's command comes to approximately 50,000 men. For a full breakdown of both armies, see the appendices.

The Pause Ends

On 1 May, Kincaid, with 30 riflemen and some dragoons, was posted to observe a ford across the Agueda on which the French had an outpost. On the morning of the 2nd, the French had gone. Seeing a Spanish peasant on the opposite bank, Kincaid had one of the dragoons cross and bring him over the river. The peasant told Kincaid the French were on the move. Informing headquarters, Kincaid then rejoined his battalion in its position between Gallegos and Alameda.[78]

On the night of the 1st/2nd, the *armée de Portugal* began crossing the Agueda over the bridge at Ciudad Rodrigo. The *ordre généraux*, issued on 2 May, provided clear instructions for moving the army forward. The VIII and IX corps would form, '... les corps de bataille ...',[79] or the main body of the army, where Massena would be located. VI corps would take the left flank, with II corps in the centre providing communication between the two flanks. By dawn, the army was positioned firmly on the left bank of the river. A report from Reynier indicated that the route to Almeida would be clear and that the Allied army would be concentrated around Fuentes de Oñoro and São Pedro de Rio Seco.[80] Intelligence on the Allied side indicated that Massena sought a diversion whilst he threw the supplies into Almeida. The Allied cavalry picquet, positioned between Puerto Seguro and Fuenteguinaldo, turned out to observe and slow the French advance. Cocks speculated in his diary that, 'I think it is imprudent for Massena, with an army not very superior in numbers, inferior in

---

77   SHD: Situation de l'armée de Portugal au 1er mai 1811. *Armée de Portugal: Situation 1er Mai 1811*.

78   Kincaid, *Random Shots from a Rifleman*, p.190.

79   SHD: Ciudad Rodrigo, le 2 mai 1811. Ordre Généraux. *Correspondance*, 7C12.

80   Koch, *Mémoires de Massena*, vol.7, p.522.

artillery, of late often beat ... to attack our army in the spirits it now is ... If he had not so much cavalry it would be madness.'[81]

Montbrun was ordered to send a regiment via Fuentes de Oñoro to Castelo Bom, and another to São Pedro de Rio Seco. The advanced guard under Montbrun was led by *général de brigade* Fournier's cavalry. This brigade consisted of two squadrons from each of the 7e, 13e, and 20e chasseurs à cheval. Montbrun also had the *dragon* reserve at his disposal and was supported by half a troop of *garde impériale artillerie à cheval*. Montbrun pushed the advanced guard along the route of advance to Alameda and along the road to Espeja. VI corps, on receiving the report of what enemy could be found in front of the cavalry advanced guard, would set out to go to São Pedro de Rio Seco via Fuentes de Oñoro.[82] II corps was to advance on the right to Gallegos and carry out a reconnaissance along the road to Aldea del Obispo. IX corps and Solignac's division from VIII corps would be in the centre, advancing towards Carpio de Azaba. *Général de brigade* Watier's light cavalry brigade, consisting of the 5e hussards and 4 squadrons from the 11e, 12e and 24e chasseurs à cheval, reinforced the left flank, while the cavalry of the Guard remained to the rear. The 1e and 2e divisions of II corps, with six artillery pieces, six artillery and two musket ammunition caissons, advanced via Marialba to Alameda.

VI corps advanced in the morning, while its 3e division crossed the Azaba on the Espeja road. In the evening, the corps resumed its march towards Espeja, where it took up position covering the roads to Fuentes-de Oñoro, Nave de Haver and Gallegos. The 1e and 2e divisions encamped in the woods near Espeja. The light cavalry brigade established itself on the south of Espeja to the Nave de Haver road. Each division was accompanied by four pieces of artillery. The corps then pressed on, taking position to the left of II corps. The cavalry reserve took up position to the rear of the VI corps near the edge of a wood.[83]

The convoy of supplies for Almeida followed the 2e division of VIII corps commanded by *général de division* Solignac. It comprised 120,000 rations of biscuit, 80 quintals (20 quintals equals one ton) of vegetables, 80 quintals of salted meat, and 100,000 rations of brandy, and was under the direct protection of the 4e battalion of the 15e ligne and 200 men of the 103e ligne.[84]

Solignac's division, supported by IX corps, would move to the left of Alameda with the intention of isolating it from the rest of the line, while VI corps moved through Fuentes de Oñoro.[85] According to French sources, Massena intended VI corps to push the Allied army back, or outflank it, and reach Castello Bom, trapping it against the Côa.[86] IX corps, with Solignac's division attached, would act as support for VI corps if needed, or as flank cover for II corps as it moved towards Almeida. Koch, in his biography of Massena, indicates that, 'The direct route from

81   2 May. Cocks, *Intelligence Officer in the Peninsula*, p.102.
82   SHD: Par ordre du Maréchal Prince d'Essling, Ciudad Rodrigo le 2 Mai 1811. *Correspondance*, 7C12.
83   Fririon, *Journal Historique*, pp.201–202.
84   SHD: Par ordre du Maréchal Prince d'Essling, Ciudad Rodrigo le 2 Mai 1811. *Correspondance*, 7C12.
85   Koch, *Mémoires de Massena*, vol.7, p.527.
86   Fririon, *Journal Historique*, p.201.

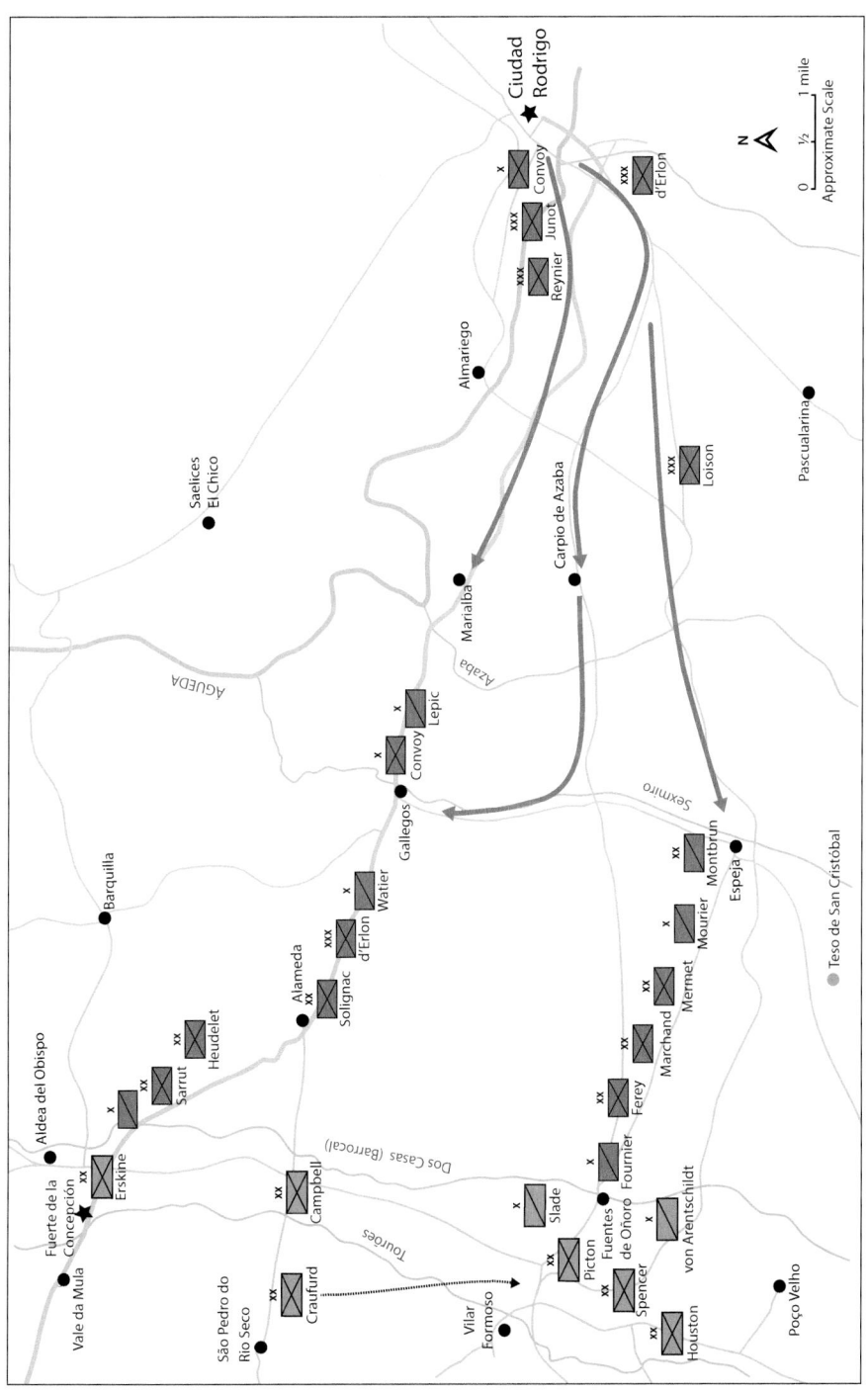

Map of the advance from Ciudad Rodrigo.

Ciudad-Rodrigo to Almeida passes through Fuentes de Oñoro. The one that leads to Marialva and Gallegos, besides being much longer, has the disadvantage of crossing the two bridges of Alameda and Val de Mula [sic]; moreover, it is commanded between these two villages by the fort de la Concepcion.'[87]

The suggestion that the route via Fuentes de Oñoro is somehow more convenient or direct is misleading. We might conclude that French intelligence gathering was faulty, or that the maps they were using were inaccurate. This would be difficult to understand, however, as the *armée de Portugal* had recently spent time in this region and must have known the area well. Contemporary maps show the main route between the two fortresses as being along the Gallegos – Alameda – Vale da Mula road, which is also the most direct route.[88] This road may have been in poor condition, however its selection for the approach of the convoy to Almeida challenges this interpretation. There are as many waterways to cross on the road through Fuentes de Oñoro as there are on the Gallegos-Alameda road. From Massena's own instruction, the original intention placed the principal weight of forces on the road via Alameda. Koch may be simply attempting to explain why the battle occurred at Fuentes de Oñoro. Massena's orders of 2 May were specifically that VI corps would pass through Fuentes de Oñoro on its way to São Pedro de Rio Seco. Massena, on the heights of Gallegos, awaited the report from Montbrun before issuing his next set of orders.

Wellington had originally placed the 5th Division on the French main line of advance, in support of the Light Division, which was acting as screening guard for the Allies on the Agueda.[89] The 5th Division covered the approach to Fuerte de la Concepción during the battle. Wellington issued orders for the general deployment of the Allied army on 30 April:

> In the event of the enemy passing the Agueda, and moving forward in force, the Allied army will oppose his progress by occupying the high country, of which the left is between the Dos Casas and the Turon [sic] rivulets, and the right extends by Navé d'Aver [sic] behind Almedilla [sic], towards Furcalhos [sic]. The body of the army will be drawn towards the right, or towards the left of this line of country, or will be concentrated at any particular part of it, according to the direction which the enemy appears to give to the principal part of his force. It is not intended to dispute the country in front of the line of position above-mentioned.

In this order, Wellington's intentions are quite clear. He does not intend to defend the whole line of the Dos Casas, but to concentrate his forces according to the movements of the enemy. However, the position along which the army is deployed extends further than Nave de Haver, with Forcalhos being some 24 kilometres due south of Fuentes de Oñoro. The order continues:

---

87   Koch, *Mémoires de Massena*, vol.7, p.526.
88   For example, see Biblioteca Nacional de Portugal (BNP): 'Carta Militar Das Principaes Estradas de Portugal' (Romão Eloy, 1808), l, cota CC-1226-R.
89   Memorandum for Spencer, Villar Formoso, 14 April, 1811, Gurwood, *Dispatches*, vol.4, p.748.

The area around Espeja as it is today. (Author's photo)

When it appears that the enemy is decidedly moving forward in force, there-fore, Sir Stapleton Cotton will give orders to the troops in front to retire, the Light Division falling back from Gallegos and Espeja, by the direct roads from these two places to Fuentes d'Oñoro [sic], and the cavalry falling back towards the line of position in such direction as circumstances may at the time require; continuing, however, to watch and delay the progress of the enemy's columns, but without committing themselves or harassing the troops. The order for the retreat of the 38th regiment from Barba de Puerco [sic] is also to be given by Sir Stapleton Cotton, as soon as he finds that the enemy is advancing in such force as to make it expedient to withdraw the troops from Gallegos, and from the posts upon the Agueda, to the left of that village.

The Light Division, acting as the rearguard, was ordered to retire on Fuentes de Oñoro, and this would seem to indicate Wellington's expectation of the French main thrust. The cavalry is given a broader remit to fall back on the position more generally, rather than the village itself. The order concludes with a warning to the staff officers: 'It is very necessary that the staff-officers attached to the several divi-sions should make themselves acquainted with the general line of the position above pointed out, with all the roads in its neighbourhood, and with the names of the villages; in order that no mistake or delay may occur in the execution of any move-ment that may be directed.'[90]

90   Villa Formoso, April 30, 1811. Murray, *Memoir Annexed to an Atlas*, p.64.

Cotton was instructed to reduce the number of cavalry on the left of the line and to reinforce the right. Two squadrons would be sufficient to observe the enemy and keep the line of retreat of the 38th at Barba del Puerco open. Cotton was to maintain small cavalry posts at Puebla de Azaba and out towards Fuenteguinaldo to observe any advance in that direction by the French. Murray wrote:

> I do not know exactly what the distribution of the cavalry is at present, but Lord Wellington seems to think we have rather too much of it on the left. I am inclined to think it is advisable, in case of the enemy advancing in force, that we should be prepared to collect our people towards the right. All we can do to the left of this place is, to observe the enemy…[91]

The main concern expressed by Murray was to keep the line of retreat via Alfaiates and Vilar Maior open. The choice of this route served a dual purpose; it provided a safe route in case of a reverse, but also allowed the Allied army to threaten the French lines of communication back to Ciudad Rodrigo. As the French route of advance became clear, Wellington was able to refine his plans and made the following dispositions on the evening of 2 May:

> Major-General Campbell will move the 6th Division to-morrow morning at daybreak, and will take post to the right of the 5th Division, near that part of the general line of position which overlooks the bridge over the Dos Casas river, coming from the village of Alameda towards St. Pedro. One battalion of the division, and two guns, are to be left, however, near Val de la Mula, as a support to Brigadier-General Pack.[92]

A soldier of the 71st wrote, 'The enemy having resumed the offensive, we quitted our cantonment, and arrived on the plains of Fuentes de Honoro [sic] on the 3d of May.'[93] This particular soldier will have been glad of the distribution of food ordered by the QMG on 2 May, '… cattle sufficient to furnish two days' meat in advance are to be retained near the divisions. Whatever bread there may be in reserve is to be issued to the men, and the commissariat mules are to be sent to the rear for a fresh supply.'[94]

As the Allies withdrew before the French advance, the two armies' outposts kept contact with each other. The dispositions on 2 May placed the cavalry under Cotton between the Espeja rivulet and Fuentes de Oñoro. Beckwith's brigade of the Light Division was to extend southwards from the cavalry position, maintaining communication with Nave de Haver. Beckwith was to keep a picquet on the hill of San Christoval for as long as possible. To the north of the cavalry, the remaining part

91   Gallegos, 30 April, 1811. Viscountess Combermere and Knollys, *Memoirs and Correspondence of Field-Marshal Viscount Combermere*, vol.1, p.194.
92   Villa Formosa, 2 May, half-past 9, P.M., Murray, *Memoir Annexed to an Atlas*, pp.65–66.
93   Anonymous, *Vicissitudes in the Life of a Scottish Soldier* (London: Colburn, 1827), p.151.
94   Hill of San Christoval, behind Espeja, 2nd May, 3 P.M. Murray, *Memoir Annexed to an Atlas*, p.65.

of the Light Division, Drummond's and Ashworth's brigades and the Caçadores battalions, would keep communications open with the 5th Division at Alameda.[95]

Beckwith's and Drummond's troops gradually withdrew while skirmishing with the leading units of the French forces. At the Marialba bridge, the advanced troops of II corps were forced to deploy for an attack and exchanged some cannon fire before the Allied rearguard prudently decided to withdraw. The vanguard of the VI corps forced the passage of the stream at Gallegos in a similar fashion. Towards nightfall, Ferey's division and Montbrun's light cavalry pushed the Allied rearguard from Espeja. The Allied rearguard was concerned about the possibility of being flanked on their right side towards Carpio de Azaba. Simmons recalls the Light Division forming column of regiments in a wood, presumably that near Espeja, with Allied cavalry in the plain to their front.[96]

95   Hill of San Christoval, 2nd May, half-past 6 P.M., Murray, *Memoir Annexed to an Atlas*, p.65.
96   Simmons, *A British Rifle Man*, p.166.

8

The 3rd of May

Descriptions of the Battle of Fuentes de Oñoro tend to focus on the activities of 5 May. However, the preceding two days are vital in understanding the full extent of the battle.

The village of Fuentes de Oñoro straggles along the Dos Casas stream as it runs towards Fuerte de la Concepción and into the Agueda. The village, positioned on the Portuguese side of the valley and mostly on the exposed east-facing slope, is open to observation from across the valley. An 1800 map shows the buildings in the village predominantly on the left bank of the stream, with only two identified on the right bank. It is unlikely that many additional buildings were added in the 11 years following the creation of the map. Similarly, a map in the UK National Archives, surveyed by Lieutenant Mitchell of the 95th Regiment in 1811, shows almost no structures on the right bank of the stream.[1] French troops approaching the village would be clearly visible as they descended the opposite slope and crossed the river.

Its scattered houses are constructed principally from local stone, and there are numerous small gardens enclosed by sturdy dry-stone walls. These offered plentiful opportunities for fortification. The walls of the houses and their attached enclosures constrict the roadways, funnelling movement along narrow paths and tracks. More enclosures surround the village on the slopes which lead up to the flatter ground on the ridge and are also scattered on the approaches to the village from the east. A wood is shown on the higher ground on the right bank towards Espeja.[2]

The Allied forces knew this area well. Cocks had written to Cotton in July 1810 describing his experience of outpost duty in the vicinity of Fuentes de Oñoro, Gallegos and Alameda.[3] As the Allied troops took up their positions in May 1811, many were saddened to see the destruction visited upon familiar places and people. Newly promoted Corporal Thomas Garrety of the 43rd Foot wrote, 'The beautiful village of Fuentes d'Onoro [sic] was now destined to suffer. It had escaped all injury during the previous warfare, though occupied alternately for above a year by both sides. Every family in it was known to our division; and it was therefore a subject of deep regret to find that the preceding troops had pillaged it'.[4]

---

1   TNA: MR 1/183/12, T. Mitchell, 'Plan of the Field of Battle of Fuentes de Oñoro 3 & 5 May 1811'.
2   Biblioteca Virtual de Defensa (BVD): 'Croquis de Fuentes de Oñoro', 1800, , Ar.E-T.7-C.3-399.
3   Viscountess Combermere and Knollys, *Memoirs and Correspondence of Field-Marshal Viscount Combermere*, vol.1, pp.137–139.
4   Garrety, *Memoirs*, pp.131–132.

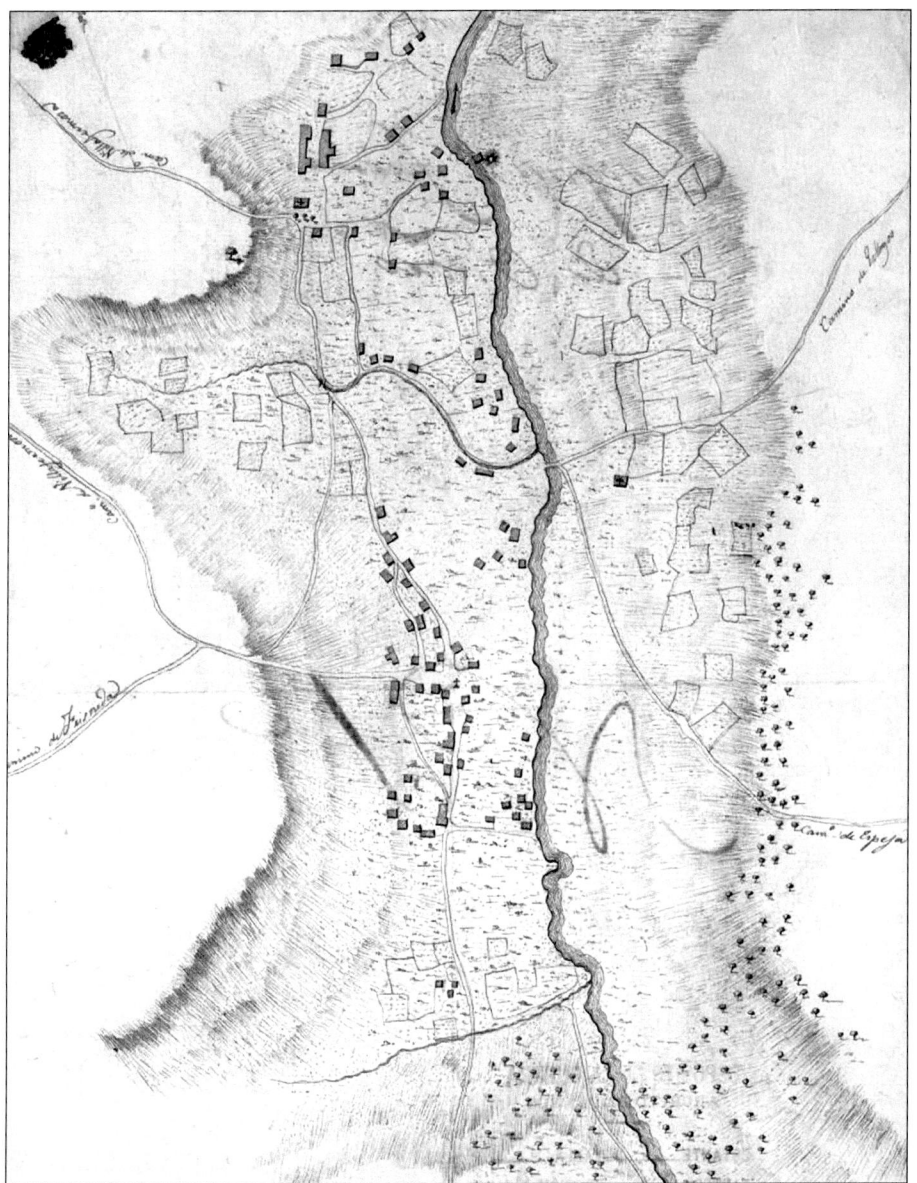

Sketch of Fuentes de Oñoro, 1800. (Biblioteca Virtual de Defensa, Ar.E-T.7-C.3-399)

Napier confirms this story, writing, '… the British troops … had pillaged it, leaving only shells of houses, where three days before a friendly population had been living in comfort.'[5] Kincaid was generous in his praise of the villagers: '… every family so well known to the light division, that no matter into which quarter the billet fell, the individual was received as an old and approved friend.'[6] Captain Fergusson of the 43rd wrote of one family in the village: 'Poor Camillo's family we greatly pitied; a good Spaniard who possessed large flocks and great property as a farmer, his daughter Josepha beautiful & lovely with some fine young men [as] sons, were all driven from the shelter of their homes. We collected a subscription for the poor inhabitants.'[7]

Dispositions

By the end of 2 May, the *armée de Portugal* had advanced to a line running approximately from Alameda through Gallegos to Espeja with piquets out towards the line of the Dos Casas. The Allied force's main body was established upon a line running south from Fuerte de la Concepción with light cavalry and infantry piquets mirroring the French. Captain Jonathan Leach of the 95th recalled that the rearguard of the Light Division, '… bivouacked between Espeja and the Duas Casas, [sic] close to the enemy's advanced guard.'[8] The extreme south of the Allied line was located at the village of Nave de Haver, which Cocks described as occupying a commanding position as the ground rises from Poço Velho. He refers to the Dos Casas around Poço Velho as a morass.[9] This provided little obstruction to infantry movement but required careful navigation by cavalry because of the soft condition of the ground. The ridge separating the Dos Casas and Tourões is fairly open, although some small ravines descend from it on both sides. Of these, some are strewn with rocks while others are barely discernible and would offer almost no protection to troops sheltering from enemy fire. A significant change in the landscape of the Dos Casas valley is evident at Fuentes de Oñoro, where larger isolated rocks begin to pose a military obstacle. Additionally, the sides of the Dos Casas become more pronounced the further north one proceeds, making attempts at fording it very difficult.

Late on the 2nd, Wellington instructed Campbell to move the 6th Division to take position overlooking the bridge over the Dos Casas between Alameda and São Pedro do Rio Seco. This would place it to the right of the 5th Division: Wellington needed to cover the approaches to Almeida along the road from Alameda and Gallegos.[10] Additionally, he needed to be able to withdraw his army in case of a reverse on the battlefield. Orders issued by Murray on 3 May confirmed the route for each division to take in the event of, '… any advantage being obtained by the enemy,

---

5   Napier, *History of the War in the Peninsula*, vol.3, p.147.
6   Kincaid, *Random Shots from a Rifleman*, p.176.
7   Glover and Burnham, *The Men of Wellington's Light Division*, p.83.
8   Leach, *Rough Sketches of the Life of an Old Soldier*, p.211.
9   Cocks, *Intelligence Officer in the Peninsula*, p.102.
10   Villar Formoso, 2 May 1811, 9:30 p.m. Wellington, *Supplementary Despatches*, vol.13, p.628.

which may induce the Commander of the Forces to order the army to retire …' The general direction of withdrawal was to the southwest, apart from Pack, who was instructed to, '… withdraw the troops under his orders either towards Pinhel or by the fords of Junça, and the bridge of Castello Bom, as he may find most expedient under the circumstances of the moment.'[11] The 1st and 7th Divisions were to withdraw along the road leading from Nave de Haver to Aldea da Ribeira; The 3rd and Light Divisions were to withdraw along the Caril road, '… to the turn near where the road to Villar Maior branches off from the Caril road; and if necessary to retire farther, these divisions will pass the rivulet behind them by the fords between Aldea da Ribeira and Villar Maior.'[12]

The Caril road mentioned in the order had a well-made surface and ran from Almeida southwards. The cavalry and two brigades of horse artillery would withdraw along this road with the 3rd and Light Divisions to cover their march. The 5th and 6th Divisions were to withdraw through São Pedro do Rio Seco, Freineda and Malhada Sorda to Vilar Maior, remaining on the heights above that village. They were to withdraw only when it was necessary. These orders, and subsequent instructions to Cotton, seem to indicate Wellington's concern for his right flank. Murray wrote to Cotton on 30 April:

> The lines of retreat which we must always keep open are upon Alfiates [sic] and Villa Maior. If the enemy moves their force from Ciudad Rodrigo towards the right, we might be rather hurried in making a corresponding movement to meet him should he have much of a force to the left. But it will be much easier for us (should he move against our left and direct towards Almaida) [sic] to make a corresponding movement to oppose him in that quarter; and we shall be better placed to have our own lines of retreat perfectly open, and at the same time to threaten his line of retreat upon Ciudad Rodrigo, and to threaten also his left flank as he moves forward.[13]

If this flank was turned, his line of retreat as described in these orders would be blocked. Wellington would then be forced to move the army across the Tourões and Côa via the existing bridges and fords, such as those to the west of Junça. The only route for wheeled vehicles would be over established fords or bridges, such as that at Ponte Sequeiro or Castello Bom, the latter being described as, '… narrow, and of difficult access'.[14]

On the morning of the 3rd, Wellington issued more detailed orders for the deployment of his forces along the ridge between the Dos Casas and Tourões:

> The 1st Division, in two lines, is to form the right; and the 3rd Division, and Colonel Ashworth's brigade, in two lines, are to form the left.

11   Villar Formoso, 3 May 1811, 8:00 a.m. Gurwood, *Dispatches*, vol.4, p.784.
12   Villar Formoso, 3 May 1811, 8:00 a.m. Gurwood, *Dispatches*, vol.4, p.784.
13   Viscountess Combermere and Knollys, *Memoirs and Correspondence of Field-Marshal Viscount Combermere*, vol.1, p.194.
14   Murray, *Memoir Annexed to an Atlas*, p.63.

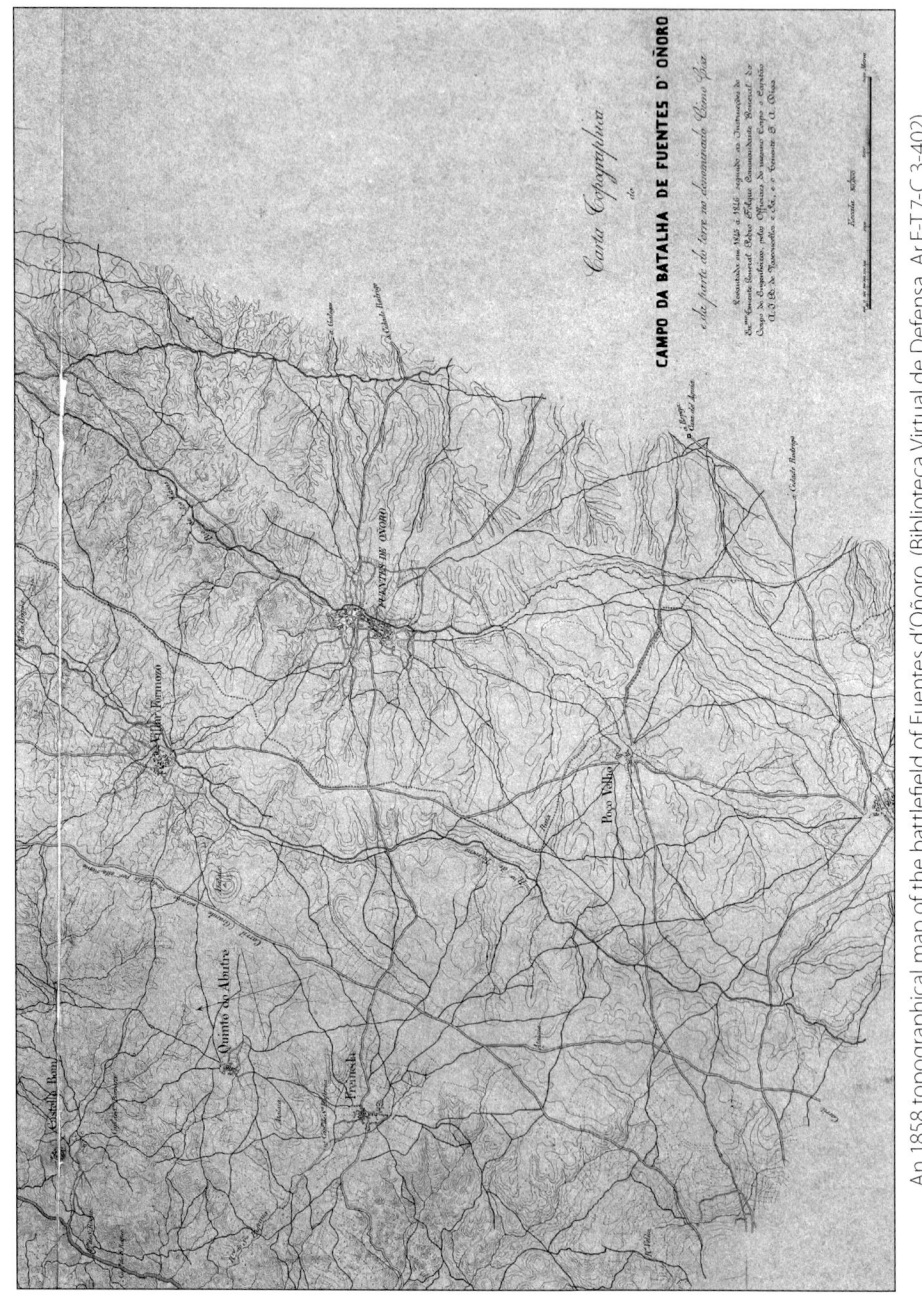

An 1858 topographical map of the battlefield of Fuentes d'Oñoro. (Biblioteca Virtual de Defensa, Ar.E-T.7-C.3-402)

The 7th Division is to be in reserve behind the right of the 1st Division; and the Light Division is to be in reserve behind the left of the 3rd Division.

Each brigade of the two divisions in reserve is to be formed in close column where the ground admits of it, that they may be the better prepared to make any movement which may be directed.

Captain Lawson's brigade of British 9-pounders is to be with the 1st Division; and Major Arentschildt's brigade of Portuguese 9-pounders is to be with the 3rd Division.

The light infantry are to dispute the village of Fuentes d'Onoro, [sic] and the gardens, enclosures, and broken ground along the left bank of the Dos Casas rivulet.

The line of infantry is to occupy, and maintain as its position, the higher parts of the ridge which is between the Dos Casas and the Turon [sic] rivulets.

And the officers of the artillery will place their guns in the most advantageous manner for annoying the enemy in his advance up the slopes to attack that position.

The cavalry will be placed as circumstances may require.[15]

The indication from Wellington's deployment is that the expected thrust would be towards Fuentes de Oñoro. What seems clear from the dispositions above is that the main force of the Allied army is along the ridge to the rear of the village of Fuentes de Oñoro, deployed in echelon. On the extreme right of the Allied position at the village of Nave de Haver was guerilla leader Don Julian Sánchez's force of 1,600 men.

Joseph Donaldson of the 94th Foot recalled moving out of Fuentes de Oñoro in the morning of 3 May, and his regiment, '… took up their position with the rest of the division on a plain, some distance behind it.'[16] Garrety remembered, 'The first and third divisions were concentrated on a gentle declivity, about a cannon-shot behind Fuentes d'Oñoro [sic], where the line of ground occupied by the army turned back, and ended on the Turones [sic].'[17] The high ground between the two streams is a distance from the church, supporting the idea that Fuentes de Oñoro was an outpost of the position, rather than an integral part of the main defensive line. This is confirmed by Charles Stewart's observation that:

Fuentes de Honoro [sic] was not, strictly speaking, embraced in our position, and though occupied by the light troops of the 1st and 3rd divisions supported by the 7th regiment, it was held merely as an advanced post. Yet, in spite of its advanced situation, it possessed so many defensible features, as to form, in point of fact, one of the main bulwarks of our ground …[18]

---

15 Heights near Fuentes d'Onoro, 3 May, 10:00 a.m., Murray, *Memoir Annexed to an Atlas*, pp.66–67.
16 Joseph Donaldson, *Recollections of the Eventful Life of a Soldier* (Edinburgh: Robert Martin, 1847), p.123.
17 Garrety, *Memoirs*, p.132.
18 Vane, *Narrative of the Peninsular War from 1808 to 1813*, p.501.

He continues:

> The village itself is crossed in various directions by walls, which afforded excellent cover for infantry, and were not altogether profitless against artillery; whilst in its rear arise some rocky heights, which at once covered the troops whilst in possession of the place, and afforded them a safe place of retreat, in case they should be driven out. Above these rocky heights was our main line arrayed; from whence, in case of need, reinforcements could be continually sent to the troops in the village; whilst, in the event of the village itself being carried, the conquerors would find that their labours, so far from being completed, were only beginning.[19]

Wellington was in the unusual situation of fielding more guns than the French. The Allied army had two troops of Royal Horse Artillery and two Royal Artillery brigades, each fielding five guns and one howitzer.[20] 'T' troop under Bull was attached to the cavalry, 'A' troop RHA under Ross was attached to the Light Division. Ross records that his battery spent the entire battle on the left of the Allied position, and perhaps it had been left there after the Light Division was moved to the right.[21] Lawson's RA battery was attached to the 1st Division, while Thompson's RA battery was attached to the 5th Division. The Portuguese fielded four brigades, however, two guns had been left with Pack at Almeida.[22] Artilheria n.º 1, comprising Da Cunha Preto's company and Rozières company, and Artilheria n.º 2, comprising De Sequeira's company and Rosado's company, were commanded by Major Victor Von Arentschild.[23] Each fielded six guns. Both companies of Artilheria n.º 2 were attached to the 3rd Division, while Rozières was attached to the 6th Division and Preto's to the 5th Division.[24] This meant Wellington had 46 guns to hand.

The French had spent the night of 2/3 May in their positions as follows: II corps was near Marialba; VI corps and the Reserve cavalry were around Espeja. Cavalry patrols were sent to reconnoitre in the direction of Fuentes de Oñoro and Nave de Haver. Others were sent in the direction of Gallegos to communicate with VIII and IX corps, which were meant to be on the road to Carpio.

The Morning of the 3rd

The day dawned clear and warm and offered the prospect of a hot day ahead. The *armée de Portugal* moved forward at daybreak, pushing cavalry patrols ahead of II corps as it moved along the Marialba road towards Alameda. Massena instructed

---

19   Vane, *Narrative of the Peninsular War from 1808 to 1813*, p.502.
20   Carl E. Franklin, *British Napoleonic Field Artillery: The First Complete Illustrated Guide to Equipment and Uniforms* (Stroud: Spellmount, 2012), p.28.
21   Sir Hew Dalrymple Ross, *Hew Ross of the Chestnut Troop: With the Royal Horse Artillery During the Peninsular War and... at Waterloo* (London: Leonaur, 2020), p.32.
22   Murray, *Memoir Annexed to an Atlas*, p.66.
23   Soriano, *Historia Da Guerra Civil*, vol.3, p.417.
24   Lipscombe, *Wellington's Guns*, pp.168–169.

From the forward Allied positions looking towards the French position opposite Fuentes de Oñoro. (Author's photo)

Reynier to take the bridge over the Azaba as quickly as possible if the enemy retired over it. He was then to ensure his right flank was secure and establish communications with the other Corps as they advanced. VI corps, preceded by Fournier's brigade and followed by the cavalry reserve and a half battery of artillery of the *garde impériale*, waited until the light cavalry had emerged onto the plain around Espeja before advancing on Fuentes de Oñoro. Massena had ordered Loison to head for São Pedro do Rio Seco and occupy the heights near Naves to observe the road to the bridge at Castelo Bom. For the first part of the march, Massena accompanied VI corps as far as Espeja, then he returned to VIII corps.[25]

VIII corps would precede IX corps and would form the main body of the army, advancing towards Carpio and then, '… cross the Azava [sic] at the ford, opposite the farm located slightly to the left.'[26] They would be accompanied by the cavalry and the other half battery of artillery of the *garde impériale*. Massena would take post with these Corps, and the cavalry would maintain communications with VI corps to the left, in the direction of São Pedro do Rio Seco. Very early in the day, II corps passed Gallegos and moved in the direction Alameda, still flanked on its left by VIII corps. According to Pelet, IX corps moved on Gallegos from Carpio but was stopped to serve as a reserve. Massena, he recorded, was concerned for the security of his left as an interval of, '… more than a league …' opened between VIII corps and VI corps.[27] By midday, II corps was positioned to the right of Alameda, with Solignac's division to its left. What is apparent from these orders is that either Massena was not anticipating significant resistance, or he expected it to be in the same form as the last few days – in other words, a rearguard action. Massena hoped to be able to push

25 SHD: Jean Jacques Pelet, *Papiers Pelet* (n.d.), 918/2.
26 SHD: Ciudad Rodrigo, le 2 mai 1811. Ordre Généraux l'armée fera son mouvement le 3 Mai. *Correspondance*, 7C12.
27 SHD: Pelet, *Papiers Pelet*.

the convoy into Almeida without necessarily fighting a large action to accomplish that feat.

The night before, Wellington had deployed his forward picquet in the country between the Rivera de Gallegos and Fuentes de Oñoro. Sir Stapleton Cotton was ordered to place the cavalry here with the two brigades of the Light Division on either side of the road from Carpio de Azaba. Beckwith's Brigade was to be in the woods on the right with Drummond's Brigade on the left. Beckwith was instructed to keep a piquet on the hill of Teso de San Cristóbal to aid communication with Poco Velho and Nave de Haver.[28] This is the, '... conical hill ...' mentioned by Kincaid.[29] Drummond was to establish communications with the 5th Division in Alameda.[30] The main body of the 14th Light Dragoons was engaged in covering the Allied withdrawal from Gallegos.[31] A company of the 95th had been assigned to work as vedettes with the 14th Light Dragoons on the Gallegos road. Costello recollected, '... about half-past 9 o'clock, a.m.; our advance videttes were observed circling, one to the right, and the other to the left, at a trot, by which information was conveyed that bodies of infantry and cavalry were advancing. The bugle immediately sounded the "assemblée," and our division quickly assembled on its alarm post, on the Gallegos road.'[32]

The rearguard had orders to make a fighting withdrawal back to the main positions along the Dos Casas. A short encounter between the cavalry outposts ensued. Major General Slade ordered the withdrawal, covered by the cavalry, alternating by squadrons as the infantry pulled back. According to Kincaid, his party took post in a wood to the rear of Espeja. He wrote that Wellington, '... had ordered us not to dispute the passage of the river; so that when the *armée de Portugal* advanced, on the morning of the 3d of May, we retired slowly before them, across the plains of Espeja, and drew into the position where the whole army was now assembled. Our division took post in reserve, in the left centre.'[33]

Beckwith refused to keep some of his infantry in the woods despite the pleas of the officer commanding a detachment of King's German Legion Hussars.[34] Lieutenant Colonel John Elley, adjutant general of the cavalry, recorded in his private journal:

> About eight or nine a.m. a prodigious force of cavalry appeared at the corner of the wood, leading from Especa [sic] by the road from thence, to Fontes d'Onoro, [sic] which obliged us to fall back gradually to the left [bank] of the rivulet which divides the plain, running from S. to N. The enemy's cavalry remained on the opposite bank, and upon our rear guard opened a cannonade which lost us a horse, killed by reason of the reserve to our

---

28   Marked as the *Teso de San Cristobal* on modern maps, approximately two miles south-west of Espeja.

29   Kincaid, *Random Shots from a Rifleman*, p.191.

30   Hill of San Christoval, 6:30 p.m. Murray, *Memoir Annexed to an Atlas*, p.65.

31   Henry Hamilton, *Historical Record of the 14th (King's) Hussars* (London: Longmans, Green and Co, 1901), p.80.

32   Costello, *Memoirs*, p.117.

33   Kincaid, *Adventures*, p.74.

34   Kincaid, *Random Shots from a Rifleman*, p.191.

skirmishers being improperly placed. The cavalry and light division retired to the high ground between Fontes d'Onoro and Villa Formosa, leaving picquets only on the plain on the right bank of the Dos Casas. About noon the enemy advanced, our picquets retired, and were pressed at the head of the defile leading to Fontes d'Oñoro, the walls of which were occupied by some riflemen of the 60th, who brought some of the cavalry down and checked the remainder.[35]

On the French side, Montbrun did not have a good start to his day. The cavalry under his command was late in starting, and he reported that, although Loison's infantry were supposed to support him, he did not receive the assistance he demanded, and thus lost the opportunity to destroy part of the Allied rearguard.[36]

There was an apparent feint by II corps to the north which was intended to distract and fix Wellington's forces. However, there are no indications in Massena's orders for such a feint, only, '... strong reconnaissance parties along the road to Aldea del Obispo via Villa del Puerco.'[37] Colonel Delagrave, ADC to Junot, asserts that, '... the 2e and 8e Corps occupied the entire enemy line with feigned attacks.'[38] It is certainly possible that the reconnoitring parties could have been misconstrued as a feint. Whatever the reason for the activity on the Allied left, for the early part of the day, Wellington could not immediately identify the main thrust of the French advance, and it was only as the fighting began in Fuentes de Oñoro that both sides began to focus on that village. The weight of the armée de Portugal seemed to be advancing along the road through Alameda. In his report to Berthier on 7 May, Massena mentions fixing the Allied 'centre' with the II and IX corps, but the II corps was in position opposite the northern end of the Allied position. Wellington previously had posted the 5th Division there and sent the 6th Division to support it on the morning of the 3rd.[39] The 6th Division was to form to the right of the 5th and cover the bridge from Alameda to São Pedro do Rio Seco. A result of the activity was that the Light Division was also sent to support the 6th Division, as, '... the enemy were in strength in that quarter ...'.[40] Lieutenant Colonel Elley wrote, 'This morning was ushered in by an early movement of the enemy, commencing evidently by a ruse. Drumming was heard unceasingly on our left, to imply the movement of a considerable force towards Alameda and Barkilla [sic]'.[41] Leach recalled, '... the Light Division was marched off in great haste to support General Erskine's division

---

35 Quoted in Memoirs and Correspondence of Field-Marshal Viscount Combermere, vol.1, pp.194–195.

36 SHD: Pelet, Papiers Pelet.

37 SHD: Armée de Portugal Ciudad Rodrigo le 2 Mai 1811. A M. le General Charbonel, Commandant l'artillerie du 6e Corps. Correspondance, 7C12.

38 Delagrave, Campagne, p.207.

39 Villa Formosa, 2nd May, half-past 9, P.M., Murray, Memoir Annexed to an Atlas, pp.65–66.

40 Wellington to Liverpool. Villar Formoso, 8th May, 1811, Gurwood, Dispatches, vol.4, p.794.

41 Quoted in Viscountess Combermere and Knollys, Memoirs and Correspondence of Field-Marshal Viscount Combermere, vol.1, p.195.

on the left, which was menaced by General Regnier's [sic] corps; but nothing further than an affair of light troops took place at that point.[42]

Fournier's cavalry brigade, at the head of the advanced guard preceding VI corps, was formed into a single column with the 20e chasseurs à cheval, commanded by *major* Barbé, at its head.[43] This column drove in the Allied screen in front of Fuentes de Oñoro, throwing them back into the enclosures on the right bank of the Dos Casas. Captain Brotherton of the 14th Light Dragoons recalled, '… whilst we were retiring in the face of very superior numbers of the enemy, Lieutenant John Townsend … was in charge of the picquet, and he had to bring them in gradually under a heavy cannonade towards Fuentes d'Onor. [sic][44] The French cavalry pressed on into the outskirts of the village, mingled with the Allied cavalry, where they were received by musket and rifle fire from the Allied light infantry posted there and, in their turn, were forced to withdraw.

The Afternoon of 3 May

The Garrison of Fuentes de Oñoro
In Fuentes de Oñoro Wellington had placed:

> … the light infantry battalion belonging to Major Gen. Picton's division, supported by the light infantry battalion in Major Gen. Nightingall's brigade, commanded by Major Dick of the 42d regt., and the light infantry battalion in Major Gen. Howard's brigade, commanded by Major M'Donnell of the 92d, and the light infantry battalion of the King's German Legion, commanded by Major Aly, of the 5th batt. of the line, and by the 2d batt. 83d regt., under Major Carr.[45]

The role of the Portuguese units in the defence of Fuentes de Oñoro on 3 May has been overlooked to a great degree. Oman mentions them in passing, but successive historians have minimised or ignored their presence.[46] In his dispatch of 8 May Wellington wrote that, '… the 6th Portuguese Caçadores, commanded by Major Pinto … the light companies in Col. Champelmond's [sic] Portuguese brigade, under Col. Sutton; and those in Col. Ashworth's Portuguese brigade, under Lieut. Col. Pynn …',[47] were active in the defence of the village on the 5th, although the 6° Caçadores were certainly in the village on the 3rd. There is some confusion, however, about the structure of the Portuguese light infantry and the

---

42   Leach, *Rough Sketches of the Life of an Old Soldier*, p.212.

43   Marcel Dupont, *Fournier Sarlovèze: Le plus Mauvais Sujet de l'armée* (Paris: Librairie Hachette, 1936), XIII.

44   Hamilton, *Historical Record of the 14th (King's) Hussars*, p.80.

45   Wellington to Liverpool, Villar Formoso, 8 May, 1811, Gurwood, *Dispatches*, vol.4, pp.794–795.

46   Napier, *History of the War in the Peninsula*, vol.3; David Buttery, *Wellington Against Massena: The Third Invasion of Portugal, 1810-1811* (Barnsley: Pen & Sword Military, 2007).

47   Wellington to Liverpool, Villar Formoso, 8th May, 1811, Gurwood, *Dispatches*, vol.4, p.797.

The view from the French positions towards the heights of Fuentes and the initial Allied positions.
(Author's photo)

units from which they were taken. It is interesting to note that Wellington refers to the light companies of the Portuguese infantry, despite the reorganisation undertaken by Beresford three years before, which removed them from the battalion structure. The regulations issued by Beresford in 1809 confirmed that the *infantaria de linha* had no light companies: each battalion was to be made up of one *granadeiros* and four *fuzileiro* companies only.[48] The function of light infantry was provided by the *caçadore* battalions. Officially, the 1° to 6° Caçadores were organised from local volunteer battalions: 1° from Volunteers of Castelo de Vide, 2° from Moura, 3° from Vila Real, 4° from Viseu, 5° from Campo Maior and 6° from Porto. Some of the light infantry may have been transferred to the *caçadore* battalions being formed at the time, although there is little evidence to support this. While the titles may have reflected the official recruitment areas, the demographic of the soldiers may not. As recruitment and retention were problematic for the Portuguese forces, the unit compositions may be ideal rather than real. Thus, according to the dispatches, the light 'battalion' in Fuentes de Oñoro was formed from the following regiments' light companies, where they existed:

1st Division (Spencer)
Nightingall's Brigade – 2/24th, 2/42nd, 1/79th Foot, 1 company, 5/60th Rifles
Howard's brigade – 1/50th, 1/71st Foot (no separate light company), 1/92nd Foot, 1 company, 3/95th Rifles
Baron Löw's Brigade – 1st, 2nd, 5th and 7th KGL Line, Detachment 1st & 2nd Light KGL Battalions

---

48   Terceira Parte. Do Batalhão. William Carr Beresford, *Instrucções Para a Formatura, Exercicio e Movimentos Dos Regimentos de Infanteria* (Lisboa: Impressão Regia, 1809), p.6.

3rd Division (Picton)

MacKinnon's Brigade – 1/45th, 1/74th, and 1/88th Foot, 3 companies, 5/60th Rifles

Colville's Brigade – 2/5th, 2/83rd Foot (whole battalion), 2/88th Foot, 94th Foot

Champalimaud's Brigade (Colonel Manley Power) – 9° Line (no light company), 21° Line (no light company)

Light Division

Ashworth's Brigade – 6° Line (no light company), 18° Line (no light company), 6° Caçadores (no separate light company)

The whole battalion of the 6° Caçadores was deployed.[49] Other *Caçadore* battalions may have been sent into the village later in the day, as Donaldson recalls, before the 71st, 79th and 24th were dispatched.[50] Regardless of the nationality of their parent formations, the command of the units in the village was combined under Lieutenant Colonel Williams of the 5/60th. The 71st was a light infantry regiment and thus did not have specialist flank companies, so it may not have detached a company. According to a soldier of the 71st, the battalion was not deployed into the village until after the first French attacks. This is confirmed by Donaldson of the 94th, who mentions the 71st coming into the village as his company was retreating.

The French attack on the village of Fuentes de Oñoro began between 1:00 and 2:00 p.m. Ferey's division formed the head of the column of VI corps. The regiments were formed *en masse*, which means that the battalions would be formed one or two companies wide with no gaps between one company and the following company; the regiments formed solid blocks of men. Indeed, the infantry units may have been marching by threes due to the limited width of the roads. Ferey was supported by Marchand's division deployed on the heights to the left. Mermet's division, concealed on the reverse of the position, remained in reserve.[51] The advance was supported by 11 pieces of artillery.[52]

There is some confusion in the French account as to who was responsible for ordering the initial attack against the village, but perhaps the answer is more mundane than suggestions made in other histories. The fighting in Fuentes de Oñoro was the result of Ferey's advanced guard pushing on to its ultimate destination of São Pedro do Rio Seco. The subsequent attacks escalated the fighting as both armies sought control of the village.

The marching order for 3 May specified that VI corps was to move from Espeja to Naves. This required securing the bridges over the Dos Casas, including the one at Fuentes de Oñoro, to enable the wagons and heavy transport to move towards the Tourões. The Allied picquet fell back in front of the French advance, as they had done for the previous two days. Loison may have presumed he was simply clearing

49   Brunton, 'Narrative of the Service of Lt Col Richard Brunton'.
50   Donaldson, *Recollections of the Eventful Life of a Soldier*, p.125.
51   SHD: Rapport du 6e corps au 15 mai, *Armée d'Espagne: Correspondance*, 1811, C8.
52   Fririon, *Journal Historique*, p.203.

the Allied rearguard from the village. It had withdrawn in front of his advance, and there was little to indicate that the skirmishers would behave any differently if pressed in the village. The main battle line of the Allied army was not visible to the advancing French, being posted to the rear of the crest of the ridge, so the reaction from the Allies, who were intent on stopping the French along the line of the Dos Casas, must have come as an unwelcome surprise to Loison, Ferey, and their men. Thus, an advance along the road from Espeja met unexpected resistance, and the attack developed from this.

Reynier had reported to Massena that the Allied army would be concentrated around Fuentes de Oñoro and São Pedro do Rio Seco, but that the route to Almeida via Alameda would be clear.[53] If Reynier's report was accepted by Massena, the plan of advance through Alameda makes sense, and the attack on Fuentes de Oñoro does not, unless it is a diversion intended to draw most of Wellington's forces southwards. However, in a letter to Berthier on 7 May, Massena accepted full responsibility for the attack:

> … while the Second and Ninth Corps and Solignac's division of the Eighth fixed the enemy's centre, I moved to the enemy's right with the Sixth Corps, pursuing their rear guard, the greater part of which was forced from Fuentes de Oñoro. This village was hidden by the irregularities of the ground, and placed partly on the foot of the hill held by the enemy. I hoped to seize and hold it. I ordered [Loison] to assault the village and occupy it. Lord Wellington, who saw a part of his line cut by the occupation of this important post, never ceased to throw new forces into it, and held it.[54]

Despite this assertion, Massena may not have been with the VI corps at the time, but with II corps. He is recorded as arriving, '… from the right, and found three brigades of the sixth corps engaged.'[55] Thus, it would appear that the French advance was thrown off-balance by the fighting in Fuentes de Oñoro, pulling the attention of both sides southwards towards the village and away from the direct line of approach to Almeida. Pelet wrote, 'General Loison attacked the village of Fuentes de Oñoro without orders, in spite of my representations, fixing the attention of the enemy on this important point.'[56] Jomini concurs with Pelet's judgement: 'Loison, at the head of VI Corps, burning to avenge the affront of the retreat, ordered the attack on the enemy without hesitation.'[57] It may be that Loison felt out of his depth after taking over command of VI corps, and he had certainly failed to perform well during the last stages of the retreat. He has been described as, '… never better than a passable

53   Koch, *Mémoires de Massena*, vol.7, p.522.
54   Rapport du Maréchal Masséna, prince d'Essling, au prince Berthier, major général, Au camp de Fuentes de Oñoro, le 7 mai 1811. Jacques Vital Belmas, *Journaux Des Siéges Faits Ou Soutenus Par Les Français Dans La Peninsule, de 1807 à 1814* (Paris: Didot, 1837), vol.1, p.536.
55   *Victoires*, vol.21, p.339.
56   *Victoires*, vol.21, pp.338–339.
57   Antoine Henri de Jomini, Ferdinand Lecomte (ed.), *Guerre d'Espagne: Extrait Des Souvenirs Inédits Du Général Jomini* (Paris: L. Baudouin, 1892), p.172.

général de division ...' and out of his depth in command of a *corps d'armée*.[58] This may also be hindsight informing the narrative of the battle, but he was not highly regarded by Napoleon. Loison would be arrested in 1813 for failing in his duty during the campaign in Germany.

The 1e brigade, commanded by *général de brigade* Simon, led the advance on the village in three columns: the single battalion of the 32e légère advanced directly towards the village while the Legion du Midi moved on the right; the 82e ligne advanced on the left.[59] However, this short description does not tally with the French order of battle certified by Fririon, the *chef de l'état-major general* (chief of the general staff), and quoted in Koch's work.[60] This placed the 82e in the 2e brigade with the 66e ligne. The 1e brigade consisted of the 32e légère, 26e ligne, the Légion du Midi and the Légion Hanovrienne. An alternative structure is shown in the *situation* of 1 May:

> 1st Brigade – 32e légère (1 bataillon), 82e ligne (2 bataillons), Légion du
> Midi 1 bataillon), Légion Hanovrienne (1 bataillon)
> 2nd Brigade – 26e ligne (3 bataillons), 66e ligne (3 bataillons)[61]

This structure makes more sense given the units used in the attack on the village.

The subsequent attack is recorded as being supported directly by the Légion Hanovrienne and the 2e brigade, which suggests the Légion Hanovrienne had been held back as a reserve for the 1e brigade.[62] There is little doubt that the regiments mentioned in the attack were deployed as described, which seems to indicate the brigading endorsed by Fririon was incorrect. However, this organisation may merely reflect changes in formations dictated by the circumstances at any particular point in time. The 'situations' presented in Koch may simply be the 'official' structure, rather than the tactical command structure adopted on the battlefield. This is interesting nonetheless, suggesting that tactical organisation may have been adjusted temporarily, but leaves no record for the researcher as to why the adjustment took place. It also suggests that second hand accounts should be used only as an indication of actual organisation.

The 32e légère was at the head of the attack but was only a single battalion of 131 men. The French skirmishers were supported by their light cavalry, pushing back the hussars of the King's German Legion. The French advanced through the enclosures on the right bank of the Dos Casas stream, eventually splashing through the shallow water and gaining a lodgement in the houses on the lower slopes of the ridge on the left bank. From the very beginning, the fighting in Fuentes de Oñoro was ferocious, close work. Richard Brunton, a British officer who had recently transferred into the

---

58   Sarramon, 'Campagne de Fuentes de Oñoro, 15 Avril – 11 Mai 1811', p.39.
59   Paul Arvers, *Historique du 82e Régiment d'infanterie de Ligne et du 7e Régiment d'infanterie Légère, 1684-1876* (Paris: Lahure, 1876), p.117; Rapport de Loison à Masséna, *Armée d'Espagne: Correspondance.*
60   Koch, *Mémoires de Massena*, vol.7, pp.600–602.
61   SHD: *Armée de Portugal: Situation 1er Mai 1811.*
62   Arvers, *Historique du 82e Régiment d'infanterie de Ligne et du 7e Régiment d'infanterie Légère, 1684-1876*, p.117.

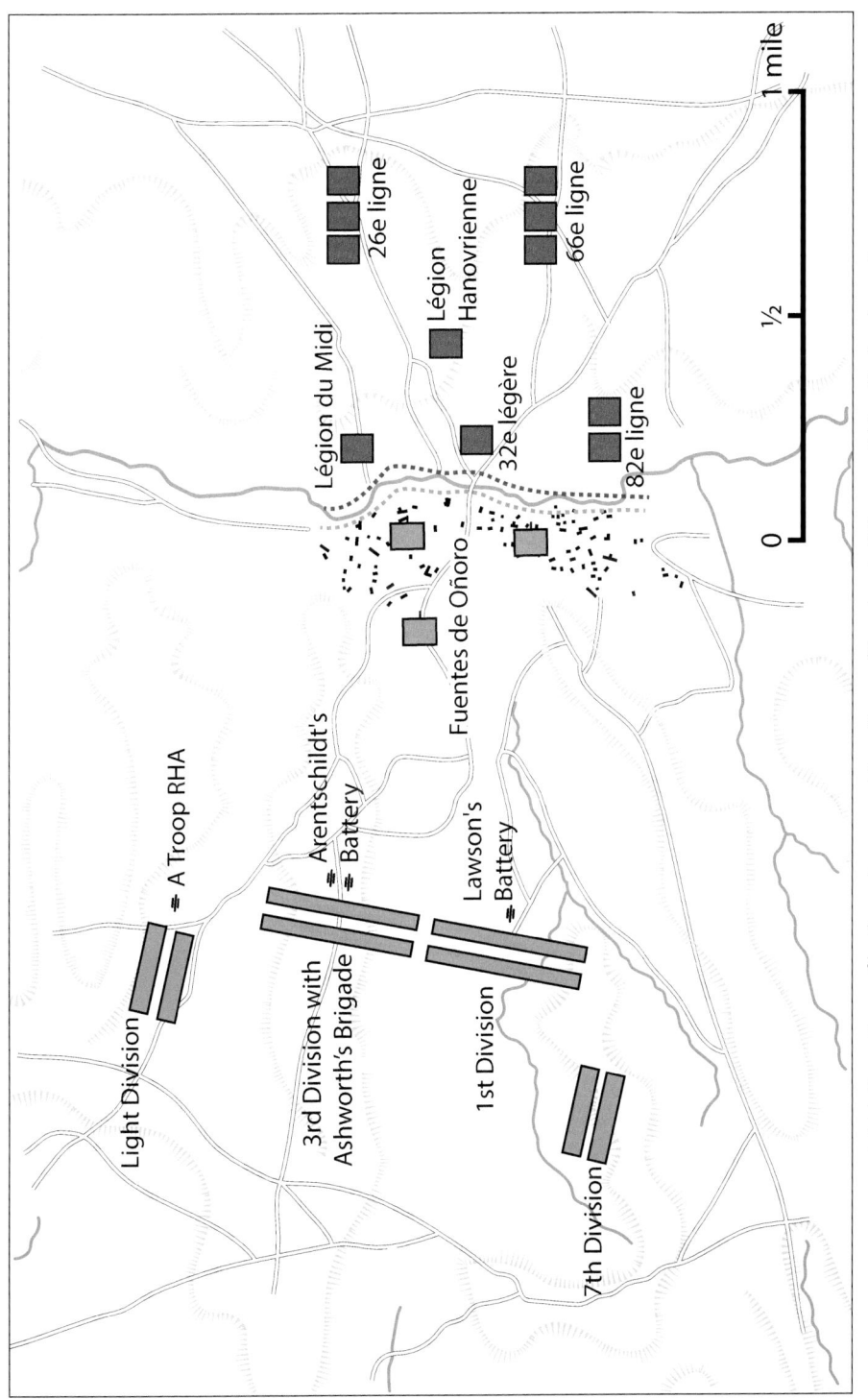

Initial dispositions of both armies around the village of Fuentes de Oñoro on 3 May. (Author's map)

6° Caçadores, wrote, 'On the 3d of May my Battalion and some light companies were … thrown into the village of Fuentes D'Onor [sic], and were hotly engaged in disputing its possession.'[63] The infantry of the 32e légère followed the main street which ran through the village up to the plateau and towards the church. The Légion du Midi advanced through the rockier terrain to the north of the village. The Allied forces, threatened with being outflanked, fell back, disputing each building and enclosure as they did so. Williams rallied his troops, counter-attacked and pushed the French back over the Dos Casas. This left the village in Allied hands, but by now the troops on both sides were tired and disorganised.

Ferey then reinforced the troops from the initial attack. The 32e, the Légion du Midi, and the 82e formed up as they had in the morning, but this time they were supported by the Légion Hanovrienne and the 2e brigade comprising the 26e and 66e ligne.[64] There was some confusion caused by the Légion Hanovrienne, dressed as they were in red coats. They were able to approach the Allied line and deliver a volley before the defenders realised they were not British.[65] Their luck did not last, and the advancing 66e, moving up to support the Légion Hanovrienne, in the dust and smoke, confused their red uniforms with those of the British and opened fire.[66] More confusion would result from the withdrawal of the Légion as they were again mistaken for advancing British troops. Losses amongst this unit were considerable, having been fired on by both sides. This was an unnecessary loss; the commander of the regiment had asked permission for his soldiers to wear their greatcoats to hide their red jackets, but had been denied by Loison.[67]

The reinforcements fed into the village by Ferey allowed the French to push the Allied infantry back as far as the buildings at the outskirts of the village towards the top of the ridge. The Allied troops rallied amongst the last few houses and the church, and also took up positions on the slopes above the village. The centre of the position above Fuentes de Oñoro was now threatened by the French advance.

In response to the French success, Wellington reinforced his troops. The wording of the dispatch is very clear: 'I reinforced the village successively with the 71st regt. under Lieut. Col. the Hon. H. Cadogan, and the 79th under Lieut. Col. Cameron, and the 24th under Major Chamberlain.'[68] A soldier of the 71st wrote, 'We were soon roused, by the coming up of General Spenser [sic] with orders for us to advance to the scene of action. "Come, my lads," said Colonel Cadogan, "you are to get biscuit and rum served out in that village …"'[69] Led by Cadogan, the 71st advanced at the run, encountering the Allied light infantry retreating before the French attack. Brunton reported that the fighting in Fuentes de Oñoro was fierce, and he was grateful for the respite that the reinforcements gave his men when they entered the

63   NAM: Brunton, 'Narrative of the Service of Lt Col Richard Brunton'.
64   Arvers, *Historique du 82e Régiment d'infanterie de Ligne et du 7e Régiment d'infanterie Légère, 1684-1876*, p.117.
65   Donaldson, *Recollections of the Eventful Life of a Soldier*, p.126.
66   Marbot, *The Memoirs of the Baron de Marbot*, vol.2, pp.161–162.
67   Henri Jeanpierre, 'Comte Louis-Henri Loison: General Divisionnaire 1771-1816', *The Napoleon Series*, <https://www.napoleon-series.org/research/biographies/c_loison.html>.
68   Wellington to Liverpool, Villar Formoso, 8 May, 1811, Gurwood, *Dispatches*, vol.4, p.795.
69   Anonymous, *Vicissitudes*, p.152.

struggle, as, '… we were completely exhausted'.[70] Around this time, Williams was severely wounded. This, '… compelled him to quit the field, and things were in some disorder'.[71] The 71st pushed into the village, forcing the French infantry back in brutal, close-quarters, hand-to-hand fighting: '… Cadogan called out, "No loading ; an inch of steel is worth a dozen of rounds." Our customary salute of three cheers was now given, the bagpipes struck up a warlike pibroch, and suddenly we rushed down the village street …'[72]

The 71st pushed through the village and over the river. Charles Stewart, an observer of the action, described how the 71st attempted to take an artillery piece on the right bank of the Dos Casas. On reaching their objective, they discovered not a cannon, but an ammunition wagon. This was dragged back to the village.[73] In counter-attacking, the 71st pushed too far: 'We pursued them about a mile out of the town, trampling over the dead and wounded; but their cavalry bore down upon us, and forced us back into the town'.[74] The French cavalry was stopped by artillery fire, possibly from Arentschildt's Portuguese guns that had taken up position on the edge of the plateau overlooking the northern end of the village of Fuentes de Oñoro. There is a pronounced knoll here which would provide an admirable spot to place guns for, '… annoying the enemy in his advance …'[75] Major Karl von Arentschildt's Portuguese brigade of 9-pounders was attached to Picton's 3rd Division, and placed as the division was, this would make sense.[76] The fire was not only from the Allied side, however. Simmons recalled that, 'A brisk cannonade was kept up by the French during the whole of the day'.[77]

Four regiments of Marchand's division now reinforced the attack on Fuentes de Oñoro, establishing a firm hold on the right bank, with none of the buildings on the left bank occupied.[78] Soldiers from the German states were fighting on both sides in and around the village on the first day of the battle: 'It was rather remarkable that the cavalry on both sides happened to be Germans. When this was understood, volleys of insulting language, as well as shot, were exchanged between them.'[79] The King's German Legion infantry, commanded by Major Aly of the 5th KGL Line, were engaged on the right side of the village. This force comprised some 190 men of the Line battalions' light companies, and probably the 86 men detached from the 1st and 2nd KGL Light Battalions. On the first day, the KGL lost 25 men.[80]

70   Brunton, 'Narrative of the Service of Lt Col Richard Brunton'.
71   Vane, *Narrative of the Peninsular War from 1808 to 1813*, p.508.
72   Anonymous, *Vicissitudes*, pp.154–155.
73   Vane, *Narrative of the Peninsular War from 1808 to 1813*, p.509.
74   Anonymous, *Vicissitudes*, pp.154–155.
75   Heights near Fuentes d'Onoro, 3rd May, 10 A.M., Murray, *Memoir Annexed to an Atlas*, pp.66–67.
76   Heights near Fuentes d'Onoro, 3rd May, 10 A.M. Murray, *Memoir Annexed to an Atlas*, p.66; Sarramon, 'Campagne de Fuentes de Oñoro, 15 Avril – 11 Mai 1811', p.41.
77   Simmons, *A British Rifle Man*, p.168.
78   Sarramon, 'Campagne de Fuentes de Oñoro, 15 Avril – 11 Mai 1811', p.41.
79   Donaldson, *Recollections of the Eventful Life of a Soldier*, p.124.
80   Bernhard Schwertfeger, *Geschichte Der Königlich Deutschen Legion 1803-1816* (Hannover: Hahnsche Buchhandlung, 1907), vol.2, p.294.

The viciousness of the fighting in Fuentes de Oñoro is remarked upon by many of the commentators. A soldier of the 71st recalled, '... as might be expected, all this honour could not be purchased without blood; two of our officers were mortally wounded, another received a severe thrust from a bayonet, and several of the privates were killed and wounded.'[81] Donaldson of the 94th wrote, 'In particular places of the village, where a stand had been made, or the shot brought to bear, the slaughter had been immense, which was the case near the river, and at the small chapel on our side of the town'.[82]

The casualties were heavy amongst the officers as well as the rank-and-file. Wellington reported that Lieutenant Colonel Williams, '... was unfortunately wounded, but I hope not dangerously; and the command devolved upon Lieut. Col. Cameron of the 79th.'[83] Cameron would be mortally wounded on the 5th. According to Private Robert Eadie of the 79th Highlanders, 'In the undisputed possession of this village we remained that night.'[84] However, others suggest the French occupied at least a small part of the village.[85] Picton, in a letter to his uncle, described the last action after Williams had been wounded: '... the enemy's efforts were attended with some success; but he was repulsed by the Seventy-first regiment, which made a spirited charge and drove the enemy from the village for the night.'[86] The attack would end the fighting on the 3rd. In his dispatch to Liverpool, Wellington wrote, 'The contest continued till night, when our troops remained in possession of the whole. I then withdrew the light infantry battalions, and the 83d regt., leaving the 71st and 79th regts. only in the village, and the 2d batt. 24th regt. to support them.'[87] The soldiers in the village found an unexpected bounty, but were suffering from the effects of the fighting: '... two-days had already elapsed since the smallest morsel had passed our lips ... We now felt the pangs of hunger to an indescribable degree ... The place being completely deserted by the inhabitants, in rummaging through the houses we procured some flour ; a stray pig was also discovered ...'[88]

On the right of the Allied position, the cavalry picquet had withdrawn before the French advance, with Slade's cavalry brigade retiring behind Nave de Haver and then closing up to the right of the main position. Anson's brigade (commanded by Lieutenant Colonel Friedrich von Arentschildt in Anson's absence) was posted to the right of the 6th Division, accompanied by six squadrons of Slade's brigade. The remaining two squadrons of Slade's brigade were posted to the left of the line, near Fuerte de la Concepción and covering the Almeida road.[89] The 1st Dragoons received a reinforcement of 50 men and horses in the morning, brought to the battlefield from Lisbon by Cornet Trafford.[90]

81   Anonymous, *Vicissitudes*, p.155.
82   Donaldson, *Recollections of the Eventful Life of a Soldier*, p.126.
83   Wellington to Liverpool. Villar Formoso, 8th May, 1811, Gurwood, *Dispatches*, vol.4, p.795.
84   Robert Eadie, *Recollections of the Life of Robert Eadie, Private of His Majesty's 79th. Regiment of Infantry* ... (Falkirk: Thomas Gibson, 1830), p.97.
85   Donaldson, *Recollections of the Eventful Life of a Soldier*, p.127.
86   Nava d'Aver, May 12th, 1811. Robinson, *Picton*, vol.2, p.19.
87   Wellington to Liverpool. Villar Formoso, 8 May, 1811, Gurwood, *Dispatches*, vol.4, p.795.
88   Anonymous, *Vicissitudes*, p.156.
89   Cocks, *Intelligence Officer in the Peninsula*, p.102.
90   Charles Philip De Ainslie, *Historical Record of the First or the Royal Regiment of Dragoons* (London: Chapman and Hall, 1887), p.117.

Although the fighting had been bitter, the result was a stalemate. The French advance had been brought to an abrupt halt, and the VI corps given a bloody nose. *Général de brigade* Thiébault wrote, 'The French had the advantage at first, and flushed out the enemy from part of the village; but the English general having his troops supported by strong reserves, they recaptured the part of the village which they had lost, which put the two armies back at the same point as before the battle.'[91]

Delagrave complained that by the end of 3 May, '… despite the greatest efforts, our men could never hold the upper part [of Fuentes de Oñoro] …'[92] Villargennes wrote, 'I was, during the greater part of the day, engaged *en tirailleurs*, and at night was placed with forty men at an out-post.'[93] Instructed by Loison to lead a reconnaissance patrol to establish the location of the Allied picquet, after a short but vicious hand-to-hand skirmish, Villargennes was captured and eventually sent to England.

Many of the French writers and commentators of the battle refer to the difficult terrain. Jomini states that the Fuentes position was on an, '… escarpment of difficult access …'[94] Sprünglin remarks, '… the English army was separated from ours by a deep and rocky ravine, which defended the front of the line from end to end …'[95] Jomini, famous for writing *The Art of War*, commented that on the first day, 'As at Busaco, [sic] the assailants fought in close column against the bulk of the English forces well posted and they suffered the fire of the entire enemy line without obtaining the slightest result.'[96]

The conclusion that the fighting was without result overlooks a significant achievement for Massena. While the French did not capture the village, the intense fighting successfully drew the Allied commanders' focus to it, creating an opportunity for Massena to reposition his army more advantageously. Although he did not act on this opportunity until the evening of 4 May, a reflection of his command style, it is important to recognise that similar situations, such as Buçaco, also saw delays in seizing the moment. But at Buçaco Massena successfully outflanked the Allied position and forced Wellington to retreat. This time, however, the delay in exploiting weaknesses in the Allied deployment was to prove disastrous for Massena's overall plan.

91   Anon. (ed.), *Apercu Nouveau Sur Les Campagnes de Francais En Portugal, En 1807, 1808, 1809, 1810 et 1811: Contenant Des Observations Sur Les Ecrits de MM. Le Baron Thiebaut, Nayleis [et] Gingret* (Paris: Delaunay, 1818), p.189.
92   Delagrave, *Campagne*, p.207.
93   Doisy de Villargennes, *Reminiscences*, p.62.
94   Jomini, *Guerre d'Espagne : Extrait Des Souvenirs Inédits du Général Jomini*, p.172.
95   Sprünglin, 'Souvenirs', p.479.
96   Jomini, *Guerre d'Espagne : Extrait Des Souvenirs Inédits du Général Jomini*, p.172.

9

The 4th of May

Invariably, within histories of the Battle of Fuentes de Oñoro, 4 May is passed over with a brief mention of Massena's reconnaissance of the right of the Allied line, and the formulation of the plans for the attack on the 5th. Thoumas, writing at the end of the nineteenth century, described the days of the battle in the following way: 'The Battle of Fuentes de Oñoro, fought by Masséna, [sic] lasted two days with a day of respite in between, on May 3 and 5, 1811.'[1]

Administratively, the 4th was like any other. The Loyal Lusitanian Legion battalions were officially converted to Caçadores by an *Ordem do dia* of 4 May 1811 issued by *Marechal* Beresford.[2] They would become the 7°, 8° and 9° Caçadores, although because of supply problems, their uniforms would take many months to change from green (or grey) to brown. However, the troops of both sides had to prepare as if an attack might occur that day, and to perform other duties. Charles Stewart wrote, 'As may readily be imagined, the dawn of the 4th had not yet appeared, when the whole of our line got under arms, and waited in anxious expectation for a renewal of the combat.'[3] The 71st were called to stand to, and, '… the French commenced firing at us : we were ordered not to return it, but to go down to the edge of the river and lie under cover.'[4] The right of the Allied line was formed by the 1st Division, with the 3rd to its left and the 7th behind. The Light Division was positioned behind the 6th Division, which covered the road from Alameda to San Pedro. The 5th Division was placed along the road leading from Alameda to Vale de la Mula.

Most of the French commentators and witnesses to the battle comment on the firing between the two sides in the village on the morning of the 4th, although Oman states this amounted to nothing more than 'bickering' between the opposing forces.[5] Fririon's recollection of the 4th indicates that there was heavy fighting in the village: 'The enemy, concerned to see Fuentes-de-Oñoro still partly occupied by our troops, made great efforts to dislodge them; but they were repulsed in all their attempts.

---

1   Charles Antoine Thoumas, *Les Grands Cavaliers du Premier Empire*, (Paris: Berger-Levrault, 1892), vol.2, p.272.
2   William Carr Beresford, *Compilação Das Ordens Do Dia Do Quartel General Do Exercito Portuguez Concernentes á Organização, Disciplina e Economia Militares Na Campanha de 1811* (Lisboa: Impressão Regia, 1815), vol.2, p.56.
3   Vane, *Narrative of the Peninsular War from 1808 to 1813*, p.509.
4   Anonymous, *Vicissitudes*, p.157.
5   Oman, *A History of the Peninsular War*, vol.4, p.315.

They occupied the walls and rocks which flanked this village with infantry, and succeeded in preventing us from occupying the upper extremity.'[6]

Massena's instructions to Ferey were simply to keep the Allies occupied, perhaps to attempt a distraction from the reconnaissance happening to the French left. The British regiments still held most of the village, with only the brook separating the two sides.

French authorities record that the lower parts of Fuentes de Oñoro were still in their hands.[7] Simmons recorded that there was, 'Smart fighting in Fuentes de Oñoro.'[8] A soldier of the 71st wrote, 'A flag of truce came from the enemy, for permission to bury their dead and carry off their wounded. The request being granted, we took the opportunity of doing the same services to our own fallen comrades; in consequence of this, the remainder of the day continued quiet.'[9] Both sides recovered their dead and wounded, and some fraternisation took place between the troops. Ensign John Mills of the Coldstream Guards recorded that there was firing in the village until approximately 10:00 a.m., then, 'About two, I went into the village of Fuentes, close to the French sentries. The town was much destroyed and I saw but few dead ...'[10] Lieutenant Ingilby of the artillery noted, '... the shallow stream which separated the advance posts was only a few paces across, and the troops of both Armies, by silent consent drank and filled their water canteens at opposite sides, but with their muskets loaded'.[11]

During this time, many of the soldiers on the Allied side were employed in improving the defences in and around the occupied villages, and along the ridge above Fuentes de Oñoro. Grattan of the 88th recalled, '... the avenues leading to Pozobello [sic] and Fuentes were barricaded in the best manner the moment would allow; temporary defences were constructed at the heads of the different streets, and trenches dug here and there as a protection'.[12] The 71st, '... took the precaution of slightly barricading the streets with loose stones.'[13]

Other defensive measures were taken, including the digging of trou de loups (wolf holes), or pits intended chiefly to trip and disable horses, and hinder them from moving over particular pieces of ground. Trenches were begun on the heights overlooking Fuentes de Oñoro. This activity was observed by the French. Delagrave related, '... [the enemy] applied himself to entrenching even more strongly on the heights which dominated this village, to provide the position with artillery and new troops'.[14]

In the afternoon, the French brought musicians down to a piece of flat ground between the armies, where they played music until sunset. Soldiers on the French

---

6   Fririon, *Journal Historique*, p.203.
7   Arvers, *Historique du 82e Régiment d'infanterie de Ligne et du 7e Régiment d'infanterie Légère, 1684-1876*, p.118.
8   Simmons, *A British Rifle Man*, p.168.
9   Anonymous, *Vicissitudes*, p.159.
10   John Mills, Ian Fletcher (ed.) *For King and Country: The Letters and Diaries of John Mills, Coldstream Guards, 1811-14*, (Staplehurst: Spellmount, 1995), p.31.
11   Lieutenant Ingilby, quoted in Lipscombe, *Wellington's Guns*, p.169.
12   Grattan, *Adventures with the Connaught Rangers, 1809-1814*, p.64.
13   Anonymous, *Vicissitudes*, p.159.
14   Delagrave, *Campagne*, p.208.

side occupied themselves dancing or playing football. On the Allied side, the troops in Fuentes de Oñoro cooked their remaining supplies of food. Ensign John Cowell-Stepney, also of the Coldstreams, part of the 1st Division, remembered:

> Thus the early morning passed; the heat of the day approached, with all its Spanish intensity; we lay on a dusty, sandy plain, unshaded and unshaved; the summer furnace of a southern temperature was, as the sun declined, succeeded by a beautiful calm evening … In the cool of the evening a parade took place of the cavalry and infantry of the Imperial Guard [sic]. In their rear and on their left flank were considerable woods of cork-trees and of the ilex or southern oak; in front of these our enemy stood out in strong relief and martial array, their bands playing as they passed in review before Marshals Massena and Bessieres [sic] … The moon rose, the bivouac fires were trimmed, the cigar smoked, and our soldiers sank to rest.[15]

Cocks recorded the day being spent, '… in trifling skirmishing between the cavalry, which wearied our horses and answered no other end than ascertaining the enemy's force, but I should have thought we had known this already.'[16] Massena seems to have had a lucky escape, although he was unaware of it. Cocks wrote that Brigadier General Hay had stopped Captain Bull of the Royal Horse Artillery from firing case-shot at the French commander as it would have been considered impolite.[17] On the French side, Parquin had been mirroring Cocks' activities, reconnoitring towards Almeida with a detachment of 50 chasseurs, although it is not clear which village Parquin reports on in his *Souvenirs*.[18]

To prepare for the *coup de grâce* against Wellington, Massena ordered Montbrun to carry out a cavalry reconnaissance in force that would investigate Wellington's right flank around Poço Velho and Nave de Haver. The results would dictate the next stage of the fighting. The extreme left flank of the *armée de Portugal* was formed by the cavalry brigade of VI corps, comprising the 15e chasseurs à cheval and 3e hussards. This brigade was complemented by the 13e chasseurs à cheval, who accompanied Montbrun.[19] This cavalry advanced toward Nave de Haver, and were met by the fire of the Spanish forces. Montbrun and a few officers continued forward on their reconnaissance, almost reaching the top of the ridge. *Lieutenant* Fromentin, of the 25e dragons and on Montbrun's staff, recalled:

> M. le Comte de Montbrun, before making his arrangements, proceeded at once to the enemy position which he was to seize. He had only a few officers with him and I was one of them. We circumvented Nave de Avel [sic] and approached as near as possible to the points which we had orders to attack and capture, and

15   Cowell-Stepney, *Leaves from the Diary of an Officer of the Guards*, pp.83–84.
16   Cocks, *Intelligence Officer in the Peninsula*, p.103.
17   Cocks, *Intelligence Officer in the Peninsula*, p.103.
18   Denis Charles Parquin, *Souvenirs de Gloire et d'amour* (Paris: Tallandier, 1911), p.207.
19   SHD: Rapport de quinzaine du 15 mai *Correspondance*, 7C12; Sarramon, 'Campagne de Fuentes de Oñoro, 15 Avril – 11 Mai 1811', p.45.

we established that the English cavalry, protected by folds in the ground, well-placed artillery, and doubtless more infantry than we could discover, was in a fairly good position: the enemy having his left at San Pedro and covering the high road to Almeida, and his right supported at La Coa, occupying Fuentes de Oñoro; the artillery was on a plateau dominating the position and near Atalaya [sic]. Finally, we pushed our reconnaissance to the brook called Elbodom [Tourões], however the enemy sent some cavalry in pursuit, but they could not catch us, M. le Comte de Montbrun having finished his observations resumed the road to his headquarters, we returned without incident.[20]

Pelet comments that as he accompanied Montbrun's cavalry:

> … I inspected the line and confirmed the feasibility of positioning our army on the enemy's right flank. This area was highly accessible, situated in the middle of a wide, unobstructed plateau, making an attack straightforward. According to tactical principles, we would exert pressure on the left with our best troops while holding the enemy with a slightly withdrawn right flank. The prince came to see the terrain, and based on his directives, I drew up the battle plan.[21]

The *armée de Portugal* was busy throughout the day with this reconnaissance and subsequent preparation for Massena's planned attack. Orders were issued for the various corps to make the necessary arrangements: 'Use the day for reconnaissance of the line. The Prince is preparing to give battle tomorrow; he will have bread and brandy distributed.'[22] The position of the *armée de Portugal* was similar to that of the previous afternoon. On the left were VI corps, Montbrun's cavalry and Fournier's chasseurs; in the centre, VIII corps and Watier's cavalry; on the right, at Alameda and to the north, II corps; at Gallegos were IX corps, the cavalry of the Guard, the supply convoy for Almeida and its escort.

The activities of the French were not unnoticed by the Allies. Charles Stewart observed, '… clouds of mounted and staff officers might be seen, riding, from time to time, along the opposite ridge, and examining, with apparent care and minuteness, into our dispositions.'[23] Montbrun reported to Massena that the terrain to the Allied right around these villages was suitable for manoeuvring bodies of cavalry as well as infantry. It was unoccupied except for cavalry picquet and the Spanish irregular force under Sánchez. The French reconnaissance temporarily dislodged Sánchez's force from Nave de Haver, indicating potential problems for the Allies on the following day if nothing was done to rectify the situation.[24] Following the reconnaissance, Massena laid out his orders for 5 May.

20   J.B. Morleix, 'Relation de la bataille de Fuentes de Oñoro (5 mai 1811)', *Bulletin Hispanique*, 5.3 (1903), p.305.
21   *Victoires*, vol.21, p.339.
22   SHD: Au bivouacq près de Fuentes D'Onoro le 4 mai. *Correspondance*, 7C12.
23   Vane, *Narrative of the Peninsular War from 1808 to 1813*, p.509.
24   Murray, *Memoir Annexed to an Atlas*, p.68.

Massena planned a left-hook with two divisions of VI corps supported by VIII corps while IX corps plus Ferey's division of VI corps fixed the Allied left-centre. The dispositions for the attack required the relocation of several units, which was to take place overnight. Marchand's and Mermet's divisions of VI corps were to move in front of Poço Velho. These divisions would advance in column of divisions and occupy the village. They were to be, '… ready to march perpendicularly on the enemy line.'[25] Montbrun's cavalry, the reserve *dragons*, and Fournier's and Watier's brigade were to deploy to the left of VI corps and be the main thrust in the turning action against Wellington's right flank. This was, effectively, the entire cavalry strength of the *armée de Portugal*, with only a small, detached force of cavalry being retained by the individual corps for reconnaissance. The aim appears to be for Marchand and Mermet to fix the Allied line in and to the south of Fuentes de Oñoro once Poço Velho had been occupied, allowing Montbrun to outflank Wellington's line through and around Nave de Haver, reaching to and over the Tourões, aiming ultimately at the Côa. The attack was meant to be carried out before dawn on the 5th.

To support this movement, sappers and labourers would accompany the troops to improve the paths through the marshy wooded ground between Nave de Haver and Poço Velho that the cavalry would need to negotiate.[26] Fascines, bundles of tightly tied tree branches, were constructed overnight to be ready for the advance. The fascines would be placed into the soft ground allowing a firmer footing for the cavalry and artillery.[27] VIII corps, effectively Solignac's single division, was to follow Mermet's division in its advance to the heights of Fuentes de Oñoro. This would also be Massena's location during the attack. Orders given to Junot on the 4th are more specific than the *dispositions générales* and perhaps add some confusion to the French deployment. Orders signed by Fririon, and clearly written in haste, instructed Junot to move, '… this evening at nightfall with your Army Corps to the right of the 6th Corps placed near Fuentes de Oñoro, and that you will be followed by your artillery and the Cavalry brigade of the General Watier; It is important to screen the movement from the enemy.'[28] In the *dispositions générales*, Watier's Brigade is under the orders of Montbrun and placed with the rest of the cavalry on the extreme left of the French line, so this order seems to be contradictory.

Ferey's division of VI corps would remain in its current position in front of Fuentes de Oñoro and retain the parts of the village that it already occupied. Ferey was to engage the Allied troops in Fuentes de Oñoro but, '… without taking any risks.'[29] Given the ferocity of the fighting in the village on the 3rd, this is a strange instruction. II corps was ordered to observe the road to Alameda and to make a general demonstration in front of the Allied line. If Wellington moved the troops on his left to support the centre and right, II corps was to attack as part of a wider

25   SHD: Dispositions Générales pour la journeé du 5 mai.Dispositions Générales pour la journeé du 5 mai. Au camp de Fuente D'ónôro, le 4 mai 1811. *Correspondance*, 7C12, para. 1.
26   Oman, *A History of the Peninsular War*, vol.4, p.317.
27   Marbot, *Marbot*, vol.2, p.464.
28   SHD: Au bivouacq près de Fuentes D'Onoro le 4 mai, *Correspondance*, 7C12.
29   SHD: Dispositions Générales pour la journeé du 5 mai. Au camp de Fuente D'ónôro, le 4 mai 1811. *Correspondance*, 7C12, para. 1.

pincer movement to catch the Allied army between it and the two Divisions of VI corps. If Reynier saw the opportunity, cavalry was to reconnoitre towards Fuerte de la Concepción. Massena also included orders that, in the event of a reverse, II corps was to retire on Gallegos. In orders sent to Drouet on the 4th, IX corps was to:

> ... move today and upon receipt of this letter, to Fuente de Onoro, [sic] where the 6th Corps is located, and where the 8th Corps is also to proceed. The intention is that this movement should not be noticed by the enemy; [Massena] recommends, therefore, that you halt the head of your column as soon as the reconnaissance you have pushed forward observes the enemy's line, which is in the vicinity of Fuente de Onoro, [sic] on the crest of the mountains.[30]

More specific orders were received as part of the *dispositions générales*. IX corps was to deploy in two lines with exaggerated space between each regiment, '... to give the enemy the impression that VI Corps still occupies the same position.'[31] The Corps would be followed by Bessières' cavalry and the corps' artillery. For the convoy of supplies for Almeida Drouet was directed to provide an, '... intelligent Colonel to command this escort, to whom you will give specific instructions, so that the Convoy is always ready to leave at the first order and to guard itself'.[32] The Imperial Guard troops recently brought by Bessières would, '... cooperate tomorrow with all the movements of the army.'[33] This last directive was to prove the weakest link of the entire attack.

Scovell recorded in his notebook, 'All quiet. The enemy keeping moving Cavalry along to their left, we can only account for two Corps the 2nd and 6th. The 8th no tidings are heard of. Their Cavalry exceed 3000. We have not more than they.'[34] The implications for Wellington were serious. If he could not place a significant part of Massena's army, and there is no mention of IX corps, then regardless of the apparent intentions of the French, he needed to be prepared for a range of possibilities.

Wellington faced a dilemma. He intended to maintain the blockade of Almeida whilst at the same time securing an open route for withdrawal via Nave de Haver to Sabugal. He had a choice, deeming it imprudent to pursue two objectives that were hardly compatible, and arrived at a decision on the evening of the 4th. In the event of the enemy initiating a broad movement against his right, he resolved to abandon the latter goal and reposition the right flank of the Allied army towards Freineda and the banks of the river Côa. This would maintain the blockade of Almeida, but threaten a withdrawal if the Allied army was forced into retreat.[35]

30   SHD: Ordre au Comte D'Erlon. Ou Camp prês Fuente-D'onoro, le 4 mai 1811. *Correspondance*, 7C12.
31   SHD: Dispositions Générales pour la journeé du 5 mai. Au camp de Fuente D'ónôro, le 4 mai 1811. *Correspondance,* 7C12, para. 5.
32   SHD: Ou Camp prês Fuente-D'onoro, le 4 mai 1811. *Correspondance*, 7C12.
33   SHD: Dispositions Générales pour la journeé du 5 mai. Au camp de Fuente D'ónôro, le 4 mai 1811. *Correspondance*, 7C12, para. 8.
34   TNA: WO 37/7a, Scovell, *Diary*, p.40.
35   Wellington to Liverpool. Villar Formoso, 8 May, 1811, Gurwood, *Dispatches*, vol.4, p.796.

With this in mind, there existed the possibility that the French reconnaissance, carried out with little attempt at concealment, was to divert the Allies' attention towards their probable route of retreat. However, Massena's intention to execute a manoeuvre against the right flank of the position seemed clear to Wellington, who had also sent his own cavalry on reconnaissance. With far fewer troopers than the French, the focus was on assessing the situation on the Allied right. He had seen the French cavalry reconnoitring, and he knew the weaknesses of his position to the south of Fuentes de Oñoro. Wellington wrote, 'I had imagined that the enemy would endeavor [sic] to obtain possession of Fuentes de Onoro, and of the ground occupied by the troops behind that village, by crossing the Dos Casas at Pozo Velho [sic]'.[36] Houston's 7th Division was to move to the Allied right and occupy Poço Velho to strengthen that end of the Allied line. This movement extended the Allied forces across a front spanning some 12 miles, including a two-mile gap between Fuentes de Oñoro and Poço Velho.

Houston was to, '… push forward strong piquets into the wood between Fuentes d'Onoro and Pozo Velho, which latter place he will occupy in considerable strength.'[37] The choice of this division may not have been the best if Wellington really considered his right flank to be under serious threat. The units that made up the 7th had only recently arrived in Portugal and were unaccustomed to battle and the climate. The Chasseurs Britanniques and Brunswick Oëls Jäger were known for their ill-discipline and a tendency to desert. Thus, Wellington's right flank, which was to take the brunt of the coming attack, was defended by a new and untried division of British, German, French and Portuguese troops, and Spanish *guerrilleros* of dubious value if faced with regular, experienced troops.

Poço Velho was occupied by the 2° Caçadores and 85th, with Cotton's cavalry picquet extending out to Nave de Haver. The latter village was occupied by Sánchez's small force. Captain Brotherton of the 14th Light Dragoons described this arrangement: 'I had been sent [on the night of the 4-5th of May] to the village of Nave d'Aver, [sic] which was occupied by that humbug, Don Julian Sánchez, with his Corps of infantry and cavalry. It was a strong post, on an eminence, surrounded by stone wall enclosures, similar to those in Ireland'.[38]

The absence of a strong force in this part of the field exposed the space between Poço Velho and Nave de Haver into which the French could manoeuvre and exploit their superiority in cavalry.

Wellington received disquieting news from French deserters regarding the arrival of a body of troops from the Imperial Guard. Stewart wrote, '… as evening approached, we observed no inconsiderable addition to the enemy's cavalry, particularly to their hussars and lancers, arrive.'[39] Given the inferiority of cavalry suffered by the Allies, and the open ground on parts of the battlefield and its surroundings, their arrival can only have caused concern.

---

36   Wellington to Liverpool. Villar Formoso, 8th May, 1811, Gurwood, *Dispatches*, vol.4, p.795.
37   Heights above Fuentes d'Onoro, 3 May, 6:00 p.m. Murray, *Memoir Annexed to an Atlas*, p.67.
38   Hamilton, *Historical Record of the 14th (King's) Hussars*, p.86.
39   Vane, *Narrative of the Peninsular War from 1808 to 1813*, p.509.

Wellington concluded that the main weight of Massena's force would be aimed at Fuentes de Oñoro and the right of his position. The left wing of his position being considered secure, at around sunset, the Light Division was ordered to move from the left to the centre of the Allied position, in reserve behind the 3rd Division, the position it had occupied on the previous day.[40] During the night of the 4th and 5th, Brigadier General Craufurd returned to take up command of the Light Division, much to the relief of everyone in the army. Wellington trusted Craufurd's ability as a rearguard commander as well as a fine field commander. Despite some rash actions, such as the withdrawal of the Light Division across the Côa in July 1810, which nearly lost the entire division, Wellington had employed him in the most arduous of tasks during the pursuit of the *armée de Portugal*. Of Craufurd's actions in July 1810, Wellington wrote:

> Although I shall be hanged for them, you may be very certain that not only I have had nothing to do with, but had positively forbidden, the foolish affairs in which Craufurd involved his out posts. ... You will say, if this be the case, why not accuse Craufurd? I answer, because, if I am to be hanged for it, I cannot accuse a man who I believe has meant well, and whose error is one of judgment, and not of intention ...[41]

The soldiers welcomed his return. Costello recalled, 'General Craufurd made his re-appearance amongst us from England, and was welcomed with much enthusiasm by the Division; although a strict disciplinarian, the men knew his value in the field too well'.[42] George Napier described Craufurd in the following terms: 'As a general commanding a division of light troops of all arms, Craufurd certainly excelled. His knowledge of outpost duty was never exceeded by any British general, and I much doubt if there are many in any other service who know more of that particular branch of the profession than he did.'[43] However, he had a foul temper: 'I believe the first impulse of General Craufurd's heart was kindness, but as he never made any attempt to control his passions the least opposition made that kindness vanish, and in its stead violence, harshness, and hatred ruled his feelings in spite of himself.'[44] Harry Smith wrote, 'The soldiers received him with every demonstration of joy. The officers at the time execrated him. I did not; he had appointed me his A.D.C. ... and he was always most kind and hospitable to me.'[45] The Light Division's discipline meant that Wellington relied on it in times of crisis, and for a reliable rear and advanced guard. The division, along with the 3rd under Picton, had fought hard during the pursuit of the French and had suffered accordingly. But they were now ready for the fight.

---

40   Leach, *Rough Sketches of the Life of an Old Soldier*, p.212.
41   Wellington to William Wellesley-Pole, Celorico, 31 July 1810, *Supplementary Despatches*, vol.6, pp.561–564.
42   Costello, *Memoirs*, p.119.
43   Napier, *Passages*, p.225.
44   Napier, *Passages*, p.227.
45   Smith, *Autobiography*, p.49.

Overnight, Wellington ordered that the 83rd and light companies were to withdraw from Fuentes de Oñoro. The village was to be occupied by the 71st and 79th. The 24th was in support on the hill directly behind the village. Many of the troops would not get a settled night. Cornet Francis Hall of the 14th Light Dragoons recalled, '… on the afternoon of the 4th May, we were in the woods of Duas Casas, [sic] our horses just turned to graze, and ourselves looking out for the thickest trees under which to pass the night.'[46] His troop was then instructed, or, as Wellington expressed it, were, 'prevailed upon' to move to support Sánchez at Nave de Haver.[47] His unit reached that location around midnight. The troop moved to the rear of the position, grazing the horses in the low ground of the Tourões, and took up their final position at Nave de Haver at daybreak.

Capitaine Marcel of the 69e Ligne recorded the apparent enthusiasm for the coming fight on the French side:

> During the night of the 4th to the 5th, fearing that the enemy might retreat, several men from my battalion got up to ask the advanced sentries if they could hear any signs of a retreat. One of them, whom I questioned, said to me, 'We've got the "Goddems" this time, and we should start the dance early in the morning to make the most of the day.'[48]

The last line in Scovell's diary for 4 May reads, 'They appear preparing for an attack.'[49]

---

46   Francis Hall, 'Recollections in Portugal and Spain During 1811 and 1812', *Royal United Services Institution Journal*, 56 (1912), p.1539.

47   Hall, 'Recollections in Portugal and Spain During 1811 and 1812', p.1539.

48   Marcel, *Campagnes du Captaine Marcel du 69e de ligne en Espagne et en Portugal (1808-1814)*, p.134.

49   TNA: WO 37/7a, Scovell, *Diary*, p.40.

10

The 5th of May – If Boney Had Been There

The Armies' Dispositions

The French
The initial deployment of the French units is subject to some controversy and, indeed, contradiction. The following description is based on the most reliable sources available.

On the left flank of the army was Montbrun's cavalry with Fournier's Brigade (7e, 13e, 20e chasseurs à cheval) on the left and Watier's Brigade (11e, 12e, 24e chasseurs à cheval, 5e Hussards) to its right. Behind and to the right were the *dragons* of the reserve cavalry (3e, 10e, 15e, 6e, 11e, 25e dragons) under *généraux de brigade* Lorcet and Ornano.[1] To the right was VI corps with its light cavalry brigade (3e hussards, 15e chasseurs à cheval). This brigade was possibly under the command of *colonel* Mourier of the 15e, having replaced Lamotte after his disgrace at Foz d'Arouce. It was deployed to the left of the infantry divisions of Mermet and Marchand. In front of Poço Velho was Solignac's division of VIII corps.

Généraux de division Claparède and Conroux had their divisions of IX corps deployed in extended order on the heights to the east of Fuentes de Oñoro. The cavalry of the *garde impériale* was behind IX corps. In and before the village was Ferey's division of VI corps. The extreme right was made up of II corps deployed with the 1e division in Alameda, and the 2e placed between Alameda and Fuentes de Oñoro. The corps cavalry was at Aldea del Obispo.

Despite Koch's assertion that the, '… various movements were executed in the evening and night silently and precisely', Pelet recorded the final deployment was delayed as troops became lost on their overnight move into their allocated positions.[2] In his orders for the attack, Massena had instructed Loison that, 'VI Corps will start moving tomorrow at 2 a.m.'[3] Marchand's and Mermet's divisions of VI corps had needed to make a wide detour to place themselves opposite Poço Velho, but as daylight dawned at approximately 4:30 a.m., the commanders realised they were well beyond the planned location. The two divisions were now forced to move northwards to take up their correct positions. Similarly, Montbrun's cavalry on the left flank of VI corps, assigned to launch the attack, experienced significant delays

---

1   Sarramon, 'Campagne de Fuentes de Oñoro, 15 Avril – 11 Mai 1811', p.52.
2   Koch, *Mémoires de Massena*, vol.7, p.532; SHD: *Correspondance*, 7C12.
3   SHD: Dispositions Générales pour la journeé du 5 mai. *Correspondance*, 7C12.

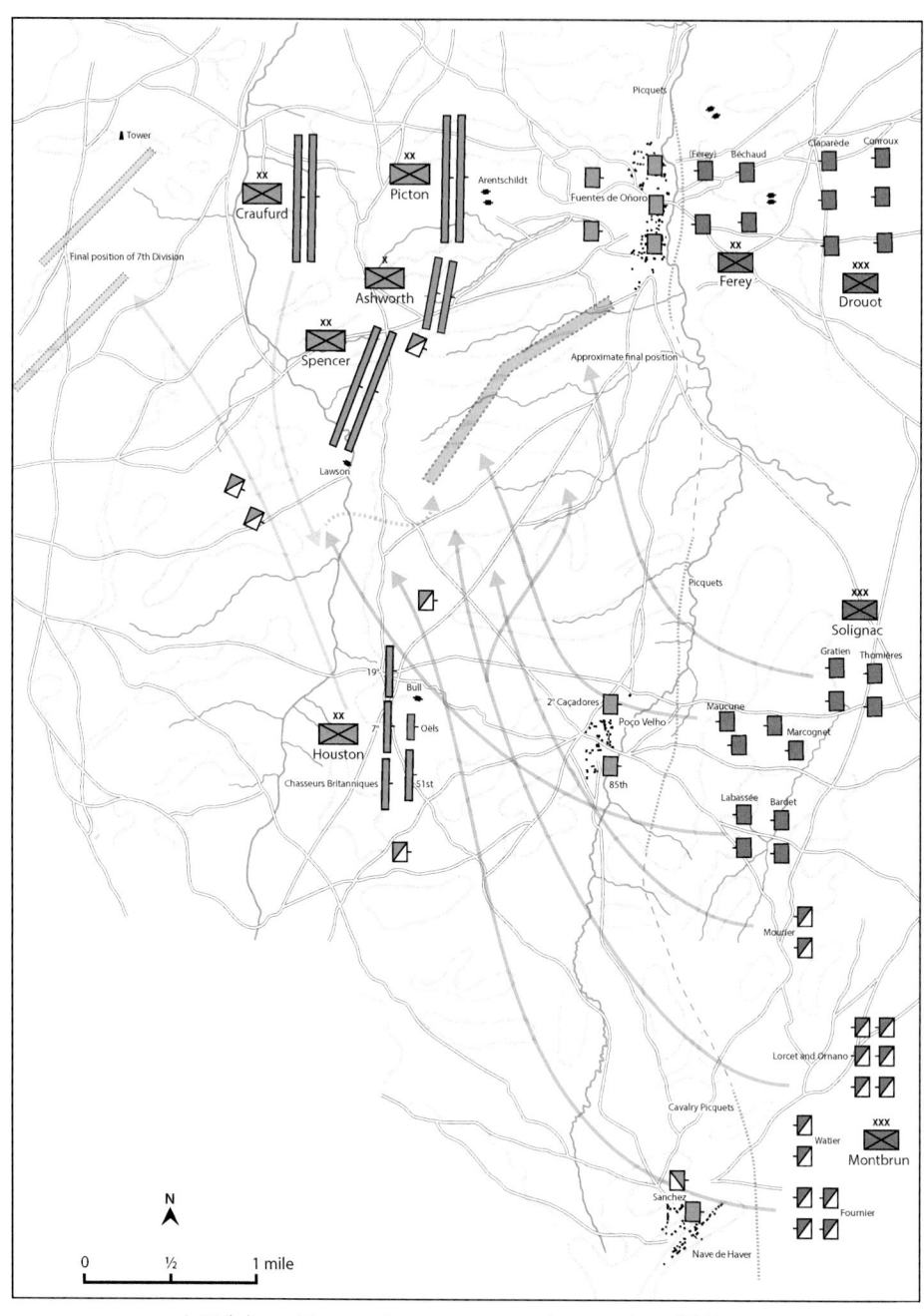

Initial dispositions and movements on the morning of 5 May.

as it moved past the wood to the south of Fuentes de Oñoro, into which the infantry of Solignac's division had moved to allow them passage. Consequently, an attack before daybreak was no longer feasible. Additionally, the Allied picquet had heard and seen much of the French movement, and this had been reported to Wellington.

The Allies

The Allied army stretched from its positions at Nave de Haver to Fuerte de la Concepción, a distance of approximately 12 miles as the crow flies.

On the left of the Allied position, to the south of Fuerte de la Concepción, Wellington placed the 5th Division under Erskine. To Erskine's right was Campbell's 6th Division and then a substantial gap before reaching the heights above Fuentes de Oñoro. Wellington had concentrated the bulk of his forces to the west of the village, with Spencer's 1st Division to the right of Picton's 3rd directly behind the village. Houston's 7th Division at Poço Velho was the far right of the main line, although Don Julian's forces occupied Nave de Haver. During the night of 4/5 May, the Light Division was brought into reserve behind the 3rd and 1st Divisions. Perceiving the weight of attack from the French was going to hit the right of his line, Wellington moved the cavalry under Stapleton Cotton with Bull's troop Royal Horse Artillery, along with the Light Division, to support Houston. Captain Lawson's foot battery of 9-pounders was posted on the right flank of the 1st Division.[4]

As a precaution against an adverse outcome, Wellington ordered two companies of the Royal Staff Corps under the command of Captain Todd to build two temporary bridges across the Côa. 'The point selected for this purpose was near the broken bridge of Pinhel; and by extraordinary exertion that able officer constructed two rough but ingenious bridges with such materials as could be collected in the adjacent villages, which were ready by mid-day on the 6th.'[5] Ensign Scott recorded the location for the bridges, '… were where the river narrowed, forming rapids so deep and strong that no hold could be got of the bottom.'[6]

In Fuentes de Oñoro Wellington kept the 24th, 71st and 79th regiments, supported by some of the light companies of the 1st and 3rd Divisions, the 6° Caçadores, and companies from the Portuguese regiments of Champalimaud's and Ashworth's Brigades.[7] Houston's 7th Division had been moved south on the evening of the 4th to strengthen the right flank of the army and to occupy Poço Velho. Part of Major General Sontag's Brigade of Houston's Division, Private William Wheeler wrote that his regiment, the 51st, '… soon took up our position – it was on the right of the line and at some distance from the main body.'[8] The extreme right at Nave de Haver was occupied by Don Julian Sánchez's force, which comprised approximately 1,000 infantry and 600 cavalry. Sánchez was described by Kincaid as a, '… middling-sized

---

4   Stothert, *A Narrative of the Principal Events of the Campaigns of 1809, 1810, & 1811, in Spain and Portugal*, p.244.

5   F S Garwood, 'The Royal Staff Corps, 1800-1837', *The Royal Engineers Journal*, 57 (1943), pp.81–96.

6   Garwood, 'The Royal Staff Corps, 1800-1837', p.89.

7   Wellington to Liverpool, Villar Formoso, 8 May, 1811, Gurwood, *Dispatches*, vol.4, p.797.

8   William Wheeler and Basil Henry Liddell Hart, *The Letters of Private Wheeler 1809-1828* (London: Michael Joseph Limited, 1951), p.54.

thick-set fellow, with a Spanish complexion, well whiskered and mustached, [sic] with glossy black hair, and dressed in a hussar uniform.'[9]

The Allied army stood to before dawn on 5 May. On the French side, the army was in motion before sunrise, and the first clashes occurred between the advanced guard of the French and the Allied picquet. This day's battle resolved into two distinct but overlapping combats: the French left hook; and the fight for the village of Fuentes de Oñoro.

The French Left Hook

In order to try and deceive Wellington as to the main thrust of the French attack, Reynier had been instructed to simulate an attack opposite Alameda by making, '… a general demonstration on the line.'[10] According to Wellington, 'The enemy manifested an intention to Erskine's post at Aldea del Obispo … with a part of the 2d corps; but the Major General sent the 2d batt. Lusitanian Legion across the ford of the Dos Casas, which obliged them to retire.'[11]

The 31e légère with two guns were brought up to the outposts with instructions to act once firing was heard from the left.[12] Staff officer Captain William Gomm wrote, '… they cannonaded us for a short time where the 5th Division was posted. We occupied the left of the line, from Fort Conception to the point where the great road from Rodrigo to Almeida crosses the ridge. This was done merely to engage our attention in this quarter, while the main attack was carrying on against our right.'[13] The feint was unsuccessful; Wellington was not drawn into sending any additional forces to the left during the day.

Before daybreak a company of voltigeurs crossed the marshy ground around Nave de Haver. Their role was to protect the sappers and labourers laying fascines to improve the ground for the advance. While this happened, Thomas Brotherton explained:

> … having requested [Don Julian] to show me where his picquets were posted, he pointed out to me what he said was one of them, but I observed to him that it appeared to me in the dusk of the morning too large to be one of his picquets. However, the sun rising rapidly … dispelled the fog and the illusion the same moment, for what Don Julian had pointed out to me as his picquet, proved to be a whole regiment of French cavalry dismounted. They mounted immediately and advanced.[14]

---

9   Kincaid, *Random Shots from a Rifleman*, p.187.
10 SHD: Dispositions Générales pour la journeé du 5 mai. *Correspondance*, 7C12.
11 Wellington to Liverpool, Villar Formoso, 8 May, 1811, Gurwood, *Dispatches*, vol.4, p.797.
12 Fririon, *Journal Historique*, p.204.
13 Camp on the Heights before Alameda, May 8, 1811. Gomm, *Letters and Journals of Field Marshal Sir William Maynard Gomm*, p.214.
14 Thomas Brotherton, *A Hawk at War: The Peninsular War Reminiscences of General Sir Thomas Brotherton, CB* (Chippenham: Picton, 1986), pp.39–40.

He continued, 'I commenced the battle by running away with two squadrons, for about two miles, pursued by a brigade of French cavalry.'[15] Cocks recorded that some of Don Julian's cavalry were manoeuvring in front of the advancing French, giving the impression to the British cavalry that the whole advancing force was Spanish. Slade's cavalry, the 1st Dragoons and 14th Light Dragoons, reassured that the cavalry were allies, halted but were soon disabused of the error and were charged by the French.[16] Brotherton continued:

> Captain Badcock, commanding a squadron of the 14th Light Dragoons, was sitting on his horse at the head of his squadron, when he took for Spaniards running away (a very usual occurrence) some cavalry rapidly approaching him in line, and remained perfectly steady, intending to charge those who appeared to be following the supposed Spaniards, the moment the latter had passed him. He was, however, not very agreeably surprised by being undeceived by a cut across the face from the French officer (for the supposed Spaniards were French). Badcock, however, who was an excellent officer, contrived, notwithstanding his surprise, to drive the enemy back in gallant style, with the loss, however, of two of his teeth; but he never thought of his wound till he had completed his duty, and then even never left the field for one moment.[17]

Cornet Francis Hall recalls his squadron moving across the open ground between Nave de Haver and Poço Velho, closely pursued by the French cavalry, with skirmishers of both sides between the two.[18] As Brotherton retired with the two squadrons of the 14th Light Dragoons, he warned the soldiers of the 85th Foot in Poço Velho of the enemy's advance, having to insist to one officer of that regiment that the approaching cavalry were, indeed, French. Confusion over the nationality of some troops was to be significant in the battle, as it had been for the French on the 3rd in Fuentes de Oñoro. A Spanish officer of Don Julian's cavalry had been shot by a British sentry early in the day. The mistake may have been because some of the Spaniards were wearing parts of French uniforms taken from a convoy some days earlier.[19]

Pelet indicates that Montbrun was meant to advance directly toward the heights of Freineda, but changed direction to his right, a more direct line towards the Allied heights.[20] This would have exposed his left flank to the Allied troops in Poço Velho and Nave de Haver, and tends to run counter to Massena's orders of the morning. A picquet of the 85th and skirmishers from the 2° Caçadores in Poço Velho slowed the chasseurs à cheval sufficiently for the two squadrons of the 14th Light Dragoons to

15   Brotherton, *A Hawk at War*, p.39.
16   Cocks, *Intelligence Officer in the Peninsula*, p.104.
17   Hamilton, *Historical Record of the 14th (King's) Hussars*, p.85.
18   Hall, 'Recollections in Portugal and Spain During 1811 and 1812', p.1540.
19   Cowell-Stepney, *Leaves from the Diary of an Officer of the Guards*, pp.85–86.
20   Jean Jacques Germain Pelet-Clozeau, *Mémoire sur ma campagne du Portugal: 1810-1811*, Collection du bicentenaire de l'épopée impériale (Paris: Teissèdre, 2003), p.586.

Poco Velho looking towards the French route of approach. (Author's photo)

retire successfully towards the main line of the Allied army. Hall's squadron of the 14th and a troop of the 1st Royal Dragoons again advanced, but this time were met by French infantry, suffering some casualties from their musket fire. Retiring on the main line once again, Hall was sent to carry a message, but to whom it is not clear. Upon his return, he saw both sides engaged in a mêlée with little order or control over the troopers. The general chaos had, '… subdivided into partial combats.'[21]

Brigadier General Charles Stewart, who had poor eyesight, ordered Brotherton to help Sánchez's guerrillas, who were under attack by French cavalry. Brotherton later recalled, 'I had not proceeded one hundred yards when Lord Wellington, who had just arrived on this part of the field, rode up to me and asked me where I was going. I told him the orders I had received from General Stewart. He made no further observation than 'Go back!'[22]

Soon after the battle, Wellington wrote to the Duke of York regarding the careful management of the cavalry in the Peninsula, commenting that:

> General Stewart is a very gallant and a very able officer of cavalry; and I have witnessed the effects of his exertions in the command of small bodies; and I have no doubt that his abilities would enable him to command large bodies. He labours, however, under two bodily defects, the want of sight and of hearing, which must ever prevent him from forming an immediate judgment of what is going on in the field, and from acting on that judgment with the promptitude which is necessary in an officer in the command of a large body of cavalry; and the defect in his sight having been occasioned by a wound, it cannot be remedied by the assistance of glasses. Under these circumstances I acknowledge that I should hesitate in putting General Stewart at the head of a large body of cavalry whose movements were to be directed by him … The defects of General Stewart's sight would entirely preclude him even from forming an opinion on these points; and I should be apprehensive that his gallantry would lead him into difficulties from

---

21   Hall, 'Recollections in Portugal and Spain During 1811 and 1812', p.1540.
22   Brotherton, *A Hawk at War*, p.41.

which even the superiority of our men and horses would not be able to extricate our cavalry.[23]

More eventful, and rather less successful, was the action by the Allied cavalry outposts near Poço Velho. These consisted of a squadron each from the 16th Light Dragoons and 1st KGL Hussars, commanded by Major Meyer.[24] These two squadrons, attempting to check the French advance, moved further forward than had been ordered, or indeed was advisable. Crossing some marshland, Meyer ordered the charge, but they were beaten back by the superior numbers of French cavalry with the loss of seven men killed, including Lieutenant Blake, and 30 to 40 as prisoners, including the newly arrived Captain Belli of the 16th.[25] Major Meyer, Captain von Gruben and Krauchenberg of the KGL Hussars were wounded. Cornet Hall recalled, 'We were near enough to hear the clink and clash of their swords, but were prevented by a small marsh from seconding their attack.'[26] Later in the battle, the KGL Hussars were confronted with their equivalents in the *armée de Portugal*, the cavalry of the Légion Hanovrienne, near Fuentes de Oñoro. Schaumann described how the Légion troopers, having jumped a wall to engage the KGL with the shout 'Hanoverian rascals', were pushed back with losses. He noted that, 'Almost the whole of this Legion ultimately deserted to our side.'[27]

Mention is made of a squadron of grenadiers à cheval attacking near Poço Velho, but these troops of the *garde impériale* were not engaged during the battle. It may be that the elite companies of the *dragons*, wearing similar headdress to a bearskin, were mistaken for the *garde impériale*. The elite companies of the 6e, 11e, 15e and 25e French dragons, led by *colonel* Ornano (Koch mentions one *capitaine* Brunel leading the elite company of the 6e), were engaged with the Allied cavalry outposts, and this may have led to the incorrect identification.[28]

The imbalance of cavalry was significant. The French had more than 2,500 involved in the turning move on their left flank. Against them the Allied cavalry numbered between 800 and 900. Of note is Schaumann's comment that Wellington had ordered the Allied cavalry to fight only in single squadrons.[29] How Schaumann came to know Wellington's mind is uncertain, but this is certainly substantiated by observers and participants alike. The French witnesses and subsequent historians have inflated the numbers of cavalry on the Allied side. Pelet noted, 'I witnessed the enemy cavalry forming in an impressive display of 24 squadrons'.[30]

---

23   Wellington to York. Quinta de S. João, 25 June 1811. Wellington, *Supplementary Despatches*, vol.7, pp.165–166.

24   Schwertfeger, *Geschichte Der Königlich Deutschen Legion 1803-1816*, vol.2, p.296.

25   Tomkinson, *Diary*, p.101; Cocks, *Intelligence Officer in the Peninsula*, p.103.

26   Hall, 'Recollections in Portugal and Spain During 1811 and 1812', p.1540.

27   Schaumann, *On the Road with Wellington*, p.304.

28   Parquin, *Souvenirs de Gloire et d'amour*, pp.210–211; Sarramon, 'Campagne de Fuentes de Oñoro, 15 Avril – 11 Mai 1811', p.53; Koch, *Mémoires de Massena*, vol.7, p.534.

29   Schaumann, *On the Road with Wellington*, p.302.

30   Pelet-Clozeau, *Mémoire sur ma campagne du Portugal*, p.587.

Several observers noticed that the French squadrons were without order or method, supposing them to be drunk.[31] This is a distinct possibility given Massena's order to issue brandy to the troops the night before.[32] Captain Lovell Badcock of the 14th Light Dragoons confirms, '… many of the French cavalry, when captured, were found to be intoxicated, officers and men.'[33] This may also explain why some commentators report the French cavalry as being somewhat delayed in their deployments earlier in the day.

Hall describes the brutality of the fighting:

> It was literally 'auferre, trucidare, rapere.'[34] Horses whose riders had been killed or overthrown ran wildly across the field, or lay panting in their blood … Two heavy Dragoons were in the act of felling a Chasseur with their broad swords; his chaco [sic] resisted several blows, but he at length dropped. Another was hanging in the stirrup, while his horse was hurried off by a German Hussar, eager to plunder his valise. Some were driving two or three slashed prisoners to the rear: one wretch was dragged on foot between two Dragoons, but as he was unable to keep pace with their horses, and the enemy were now forming for a second charge, he was cut down.[35]

Hall also described how ineffective the curved sabres of the Light Dragoons were against the tightly rolled cloaks, worn over the shoulder, of the chasseurs, making inflicting a telling wound difficult. Whether this was because of the sword's design or lack of a sharp edge, blunted by the metal scabbards, is a thorny problem that is still argued over. Conversely, the French sabre seemed to inflict a more serious wound more easily. Cornet Hall had a close escape during the withdrawal after Captain Brotherton warned him of the proximity of a *dragon* set with murderous intent. A quick parry of the enemy sword and Hall was clear, but conscious of his near miss.[36]

The Retreat of the 7th Division

The 7th Division was in the direct line of advance of the French. Picquet of the 85th and 2° Caçadores were posted in Poço Velho and the surrounding woods and broken ground. On the evening of the 3rd, Wellington had instructed Houston

---

31   Private journal of Colonel Elley, Adjutant-General of Cavalry, quoted in Viscountess Combermere and Knollys, *Memoirs and Correspondence of Field-Marshal Viscount Combermere*, vol.1, p.197; Cocks, *Intelligence Officer in the Peninsula*, p.104; W.H. Maxwell (ed.), *Peninsular Sketches; by Actors on the Scene*, (London: Colburn, 1845), vol.1, p.190.

32   SHD: Au le duc d'Abrantes, au bivouacq près de Fuentes D'Onoro le 4 mai, *Correspondance*, 7C12.

33   C.T. Atkinson, 'A Light Dragoon in the Peninsula: Extracts from the Letters of Captain Lovell Badcock, 14th Light Dragoons, 1809-1814', *Journal of the Society for Army Historical Research*, 34.138 (1956), p.74.

34   This is a quotation from Tacitus, and roughly translated means 'to destroy, to slaughter, to pillage'.

35   Hall, 'Recollections in Portugal and Spain During 1811 and 1812', p.1540.

36   Hall, 'Recollections in Portugal and Spain During 1811 and 1812', p.1541.

to, '... push forward strong piquets into the wood between Fuentes de Oñoro and Pozo Velho, [sic] which latter place he will occupy in considerable strength.'[37] The remaining units of the division, Doyle's Brigade of the 7° and 19° Infantaria, plus the 51st, Chasseurs Britanniques and Brunswick Oëls of Sontag's Brigade, were posted on a low ridge some distance to the rear of the village. On the morning of the 5th, Private Wheeler recalled seeing, '... the enemy in columns waiting for the words to attack us'.[38] Marchand's division headed the attack on the village: Maucune's brigade, in column of divisions *en echelon*, led the advance. The 6e légère was placed on the right, the 69e ligne to the left and slightly behind.[39] Marcognet's brigade, comprising the 39e ligne and 76e ligne, were in support *en echelon*. Mermet's division followed in the same formation. Pelet describes the formation in the following way, 'Mermet's division advanced in massed formations with two lines per brigade, while the Marchand's division deployed similarly from Pozzobello, [sic] positioning itself between the wood of Oñoro and Mermet's division. Solignac's division followed in reserve.'[40]

The Allied outposts of the 2° Caçadores and 85th were aware that French infantry was approaching, but were uncertain of their strength because of the cover offered by the terrain and trees. The infantry of Marchand's division got into Poço Velho, and, fighting at bayonet point through the village and wood, gained the upper hand. The 2° Caçadores and 85th were eventually forced from Poço Velho by sheer weight of numbers. Costello wrote, '... the 85th regiment were very roughly handled by the enemy.'[41] He credited them with being new to battle but handling the veteran French tirailleurs well despite their inexperience. Guingret described the withdrawal of the 85th as disordered and, '... was such, for a moment, that the soldiers of this regiment, instead of thinking of defending themselves, were all fleeing, stumbling over each other like a large flock of sheep'.[42] Pelet alludes to the local French plan; 'The light cavalry of the 6th Corps was supposed to circle around, allowing us to capture the infantry defending the village'.[43] The 1st Division moved in column to its right in order to mirror the movements of the French columns visible to the east, and also to provide support to the 7th. Ensign Mills of the Coldstream Guards recorded the 1st Division being moved, '... about half a mile to our right ...', at about the same time as the 7th Division was making its withdrawal.[44]

Général de brigade Maucune was wounded by a bullet in the heel, and *colonel* Fririon of the 69e was also wounded but remained with his regiment.[45] Marcel of the 69e recorded, 'Around half past six, the order was given to advance, and I can still

37   Extracts from the instructions communicated by the Q.M.G., Heights above Fuentes de Onoro, 3 May. 1811, 6:00 p.m. Gurwood, *Dispatches*, vol.4, p.781.
38   Wheeler, *The Letters of Private Wheeler 1809-1828*, p.54.
39   Marcel, *Campagnes du Capitaine Marcel*, p.134.
40   Pelet-Clozeau, *Mémoire sur ma campagne du Portugal*, p.588.
41   Costello, *Memoirs*, p.121.
42   Guingret, *Relation Historique*, p.204.
43   Pelet-Clozeau, *Mémoire sur ma campagne du Portugal*, p.586.
44   Cowell-Stepney, *Leaves from the Diary of an Officer of the Guards*, p.86; Mills, *For King and Country*, p.31.
45   Fririon, *Journal Historique*, n.209.

hear the joyful shouts of our soldiers, who were yelling so loudly that, at times, the sound of the cannons could no longer be heard. The village was taken in the blink of an eye, and we briskly pushed on towards Fuentes de Oñoro.[46]

The Allied cavalry fought several squadron-sized and smaller clashes but, being considerably outnumbered, were unable to hold back the advancing French. Montbrun's cavalry were able to push forward and threaten to turn the 7th Division's right. This caused the right wing of the 51st to be drawn back to protect the vulnerable flank.[47] As the French cavalry advanced, the picquet of the division in advance of the main position were driven in and reformed on the rest of the division. Two Portuguese guns were with the 7th Division, but these soon withdrew after one gun had been dismounted by French artillery. *Capitaine* de Montangons, an artillery officer from Bessières' force, had been directed by Massena to combine his guns with those of the *armée de Portugal*, providing up to 12 pieces to support the cavalry.[48]

The 51st were posted just in front of the crest of a small ridge with the Chasseurs Britanniques and Doyle's brigade of the 7° and 19° Infantaria and 2° Caçadores behind a stout stone wall on higher ground behind them. The Caçadores had regained the Allied line and reformed along with the 85th following their retreat from Poço Velho.

Wheeler remembered a French hussar officer appearing on the crest of the ridge to the front of the 51st. This officer beckoned to his troops: 'In an instant the brow was covered with cavalry.' As their trumpeter began to sound the charge a volley was delivered from the brigades of Sontag and Doyle, with the Portuguese, Oëls and Chasseurs Britanniques firing over the heads of the 51st, '… a dangerous but necessary expedient …'[49] The discomfiture of the French caused by this volley was increased as a squadron of the 1st Royal Dragoons and one of the 14th Light Dragoons from Slade's Brigade entered the fray. Major Samuel Rice of the 51st wrote on the day of the battle, 'We have suffered little, though the first attack was made on our regiment by a body of cavalry, who came up to the charge, but were soon convinced that we were not to be trifled with.'[50] However, numbers soon began to tell to the advantage of the French. The Allied troops, cavalry, infantry and artillery, were forced backwards. An event now occurred which reflected poorly on the commanding officer of the 51st. Lieutenant Colonel John Mainwaring, already known for some eccentricities, was concerned that his regiment would be surrounded. He ordered the colours to be burned to prevent their being lost to the enemy.[51] As a result of this disgrace, Mainwaring was soon dismissed from

---

46   Marcel, *Campagnes du Capitaine Marcel*, p.134.
47   Wheeler, *The Letters of Private Wheeler 1809-1828*, p.54.
48   Pelet-Clozeau, *Mémoire sur ma campagne du Portugal*, p.587.
49   Wheeler, *The Letters of Private Wheeler 1809-1828*, pp.54–55; Cowell-Stepney places this event after the withdrawal of the Light Division. Cowell-Stepney, *Leaves from the Diary of an Officer of the Guards*, p.88.
50   *The Life of a Regimental Officer During the Great War, 1793-1815*, pp.155–156.
51   G.C. Moore Smith (ed.), *The Life of John Colborne, Field Marshal Lord Seaton : Compiled from His Letters, Records of His Conversations, and Other Sources* (London: Murray, 1903), p.164; Mockler-Ferryman, *The Life of a Regimental Officer During the Great War, 1793-1815*, pp.164–170.

his command and sent home. Rice was put in temporary command until he was replaced in turn by Lieutenant Colonel Mitchell.

Houston ordered the 7th Division to withdraw independently by regiment to a stronger and less exposed position on the high ground on the right bank of the Tourões. Their withdrawal was to be covered by the Light Division, which had been ordered forward to their support. The 7th suffered from the effects of the French artillery as it retired into its new position. Rice described a near-miss: 'I had an "all-but," having my cap whisked off by a three-pounder, but received no other injury than a temporary stunning from the concussion.'[52] Stothert of the 3rd Foot Guards recalled:

> … the 7th division, which had been considerably advanced upon the plain, was directed to fall back and form on the brigade of guards posted on the right of the 1st division, and flanked by Captain Lawson's brigade of 9 pounders, and some squadrons of cavalry … Major General Houston was enabled to execute this retrograde movement in the face of an infinitely superior force, principally by the steadiness and gallant conduct of the 2 foreign corps: in his division, the Duke of Brunswick Oel's [sic] infantry, and the Chasseurs Britanniques, under Lieutenant-Colonel Eustace, who checked the advance of the French cavalry, by several well directed vollies [sic]. The enemy had previous to this opened a tremendous fire upon the first line of infantry; every shot that went over doing execution in the second line.[53]

Montbrun's cavalry continued to harass the 7th as it withdrew. Doyle's Brigade, comprising the 7° and 19°, made their retreat in square along the road to Villa Formosa.[54] For a moment, Houston was cut off from his Division but was rescued by his orderly, a trooper from the 1st Dragoons.[55] The troops crossed the Tourões, which Wheeler recollected as being, '… a narrow rapid stream, this we waded up to our armpits and from the steepness of the opposite bank we found much difficulty in getting out.'[56] Charles Stewart described the location of the right flank of the division as resting upon a hill, atop which was an old watch tower.[57] This is marked on Freeth's map as 'Houston's Tower'.[58] This location seems to correspond with a location marked on some modern maps as the Vértice Geodésico de Vilar Formoso. The tower's location is some two and a half miles (3.8 kilometres) west-north-west of the Iglesia de la Asunción de María in Fuentes de Oñoro. Stewart's description

---

52   Mockler-Ferryman, *The Life of a Regimental Officer During the Great War, 1793-1815*, pp.155–156.

53   Almadilla, 12th May, 1811. Stothert, *A Narrative of the Principal Events of the Campaigns of 1809, 1810, & 1811, in Spain and Portugal*, pp.244–245.

54   Soriano, *Historia Da Guerra Civil*, vol.3, p.413.

55   Wheeler, *The Letters of Private Wheeler 1809-1828*, p.56.

56   Wheeler, *The Letters of Private Wheeler 1809-1828*, p.55.

57   Vane, *Narrative of the Peninsular War from 1808 to 1813*, p.512.

58   TNA: WO 78/5937, James Freeth, *Route Fuentes de Onoro; Drawn by James Freeth, Royal Staff Corps*, 1811, 4 inches to the mile.

ties in with several other observers who describe the 7th Division taking position on the left bank of the Tourões along the ridgetop connecting with the right flank of the 1st Division. Nightingall describes the 7th's final position as securing the ridge behind that initially occupied by the Allied army.[59] Most observers agree that the 7th crossed the Tourões but occupied the top of the ridge rather than being perpendicular to the original position. There are some variations, such as Simmons describing the 7th's left as being on the Tourões and the right towards the Côa.[60] If the map from Murray's papers is accurate, and there is no reason to believe otherwise, the division was drawn up almost along the Tourões, between the watchtower and Freineda, placing them along the ridge rather than across it.[61] The left flank of the division was in contact with the right of the Guards Brigade, which formed the right of the 1st Division. The Guards had moved to the right from their original early morning position.[62] The strength of this position deterred the French from making anything more than demonstrations in this area.

After the battle, Wellington was fulsome in his praise of many units involved in the different combats of the battle. He wrote, 'I particularly observed the Chasseurs Britanniques, under Lieut. Col. Eustace, as behaving in the most steady manner; and Major Gen. Houstoun [sic] mentions in high terms the conduct of a detachment of the Duke of Brunswick's light infantry.'[63] The role of the Oëls in this action has been largely ignored, probably as a result of their woeful record subsequently. However, as Houston and other soldiers involved commented on their behaviour, they must have taken some active part in the action around Poço Velho. The Portuguese losses were slight for the line infantry: the 7° Infantaria suffered three killed, four wounded and one missing, whilst the 19° Infantaria lost two men wounded. The losses of the 2° Caçadores indicated they had been more heavily involved, losing 18 killed, 13 wounded, and 19 missing.[64] These losses are comparable to the rest of Houston's division on the 5th. The 51st, despite being heavily engaged, suffered six casualties; the 85th some 95; the Chasseurs Britanniques 58; and the Oëls 18. It seems, therefore, that the laurels for the 7th Division were equally spread. The 85th and 2° Caçadores had disputed the village of Poço Velho and the woods to the north and suffered accordingly. That the Oëls suffered more heavily than the 51st indicates they were perhaps more heavily engaged in the early skirmishing.

Marchand's division, having occupied the village and woods, now reformed. Adopting a line of columns, the division advanced towards the Allied position, preceded by skirmishers. Pelet described the advance: 'The second brigade of Marchand's division moved up to support the first, while Mermet's division advanced on their left. However, the 9th Corps, which had initially lagged on its

59   Glover, 'The Nightingall Letters', p.148.
60   Simmons, A British Rifle Man, p.170.
61   National Library of Scotland (NLS): Adv.MS.46.10.1(61), J.R. Colleton, 'Sketch of Part of the Ground about Fuentes and Villa Formosa Occupied by the Allied Army on the 5th and 6th May 1811. Signed J.R. Colleton, Royal Staff Corps', 1811.
62   Cowell-Stepney, Leaves from the Diary of an Officer of the Guards, p.86.
63   Wellington to Liverpool. Villar Formoso, 8 May, 1811, Gurwood, Dispatches, vol.4, p.796.
64   Soriano, Historia Da Guerra Civil, vol.3, pp.416–419.

left flank, had not aligned well with the 6th Corps.'[65] He explained that this now caused a significant vulnerability. Had the infantry extended to the left, this would have limited coordination with the attack into Fuentes de Oñoro and opened a gap between them. However, the attack by Marchand and Mermet needed to maintain links with Montbrun's cavalry to the left.

Supporting the withdrawal of the 7th was the Light Division and the Allied cavalry under Cotton, along with the attached foot and horse artillery. The Light Division had been moved towards the 7th once Wellington had recognised the vulnerability of the position around Poço Velho, and it formed to the left of the 7th.[66] It was moved southwards along the ridge, and riflemen were sent out as the Division advanced. Costello recalls passing the Guards Brigade, '... entrenched behind the town of Fuentes ...',[67] and taking up position in advance of the main Allied line, using the stone enclosure walls for cover. Ensign Cowell-Stepney of the Coldstream Guards recorded:

> About nine o'clock a.m. of this sultry morning they commenced a heavy cannonade on us from their left and centre. On reaching the gently-rising ground, eventually destined for our part of the position we witnessed a brilliant and animating sight. Looking toward our right flank, across a plain terminated by the thick cork wood, we beheld dense masses of men engaged in strife, and enveloped in dust and smoke. At first, little was clearly discernible; by degrees however, coming out from this confusion, were developed forms and shapes—horsemen charging—artillery, with their horses at full speed, thundering forward with an *impetus* that forced a way through the enemy — and the Light and Seventh Divisions coming forth from the chaos, and coolly retiring *en échelon* of squares, exposed alternately to the fire of the enemy's guns and the menaces of their cavalry, which were met and checked by our numerically weak squadrons.[68]

Mills, an ensign in the same regiment, had only just joined the battalion and was engaged in his first battle. He recalled, 'It was an extremely hot day and between the firing, lemonade was sold.'[69] Joseph Donaldson, of the 94th, part of Colville's Brigade of the 3rd Division, described the scene:

> The morning was uncommonly beautiful, the sun shone bright and warm, the various odoriferous shrubs, which were scattered profusely around, perfumed the air, and the woods rang with the songs of birds. The light division and cavalry falling back, followed by the columns of the French, the various divisions of the army assembling on the plain from different

65   Pelet-Clozeau, *Mémoire sur ma campagne du Portugal*, p.587.
66   Stothert, *A Narrative of the Principal Events of the Campaigns of 1809, 1810, & 1811, in Spain and Portugal*, p.245.
67   Costello, *Memoirs*, p.120.
68   Cowell-Stepney, *Leaves from the Diary of an Officer of the Guards*, pp.86–87.
69   Mills, *For King and Country*, p.33.

quarters, their arms glittering in the sun, bugles blowing, drums beating, the various staff officers galloping about to different parts of the line giving orders, formed a scene which realized to my mind all that I had ever read of feats of arms, or the pomp of war; a scene which no one could behold unmoved …[70]

The riflemen and other skirmishers were sent to occupy a large wood to oppose their French counterparts. The Light Division was now in position as the 7th withdrew towards the ridge, but was threatened by the large number of French cavalry in the open ground to the west of Nave de Haver and Poço Velho. Stewart wrote that on the right flank, the Allied cavalry, accompanied by, '… two or three pieces of horse-artillery …',[71] descended into low ground to protect the withdrawal of Sontag's Brigade. The Light Division, thus exposed, formed battalion squares, ready to receive the French cavalry, and Bull's guns were moved into the intervals between them. A square is a hollow formation without exposed flanks, as the name implies, although most tended to be oblong rather than square. They are formed to protect the infantry against cavalry attacks, but are vulnerable to artillery fire and attacks by other infantry. The squares were formed so that the faces had clear fields of fire and were mutually supporting. The small number of Allied cavalry was already mixed in with the French, but would offer support to the Light Division as it withdrew.

The withdrawal was undertaken in the face of attacks by the large numbers of French cavalry, available to the French commanders on the extreme left flank of their advance, and some batteries of horse artillery, notably the artillerie à cheval de la garde impériale, which had been brought forward by Bessières. Initially, the Light Division formed in square. Although not the most mobile of formations, it could move slowly if the troops were well-disciplined and kept their dressings. Craufurd then chose to change the formation of the division into columns of companies. Simmons mentions that the 95th '… formed column at quarter-distance ready to form square at any moment …',[72] although Cope wrote that the formation was close columns.[73] Close columns, as the name implies, are closed up tightly, more compact than a square, allowing the soldiers on the outside of the column to turn outwards, presenting a hedge of bayonets to approaching cavalry. Quarter-distance columns are slightly more open but allow for quicker deployment into other formations than do close columns. Regardless of exactly how they were arranged, the column was far more mobile than a square and would allow the units to withdraw from their vulnerable position much more quickly. They may also look very much like a square when viewed through dust and smoke.

From the French perspective, the attack by Montbrun's cavalry seemed a success. The withdrawal of the 7th and Light Divisions has been interpreted as a rout, and

---

70   Donaldson, *Recollections of the Eventful Life of a Soldier*, p.123.
71   Vane, *Narrative of the Peninsular War from 1808 to 1813*, p.511.
72   Simmons, *A British Rifle Man*, p.169.
73   Leach, *Rough Sketches of the Life of an Old Soldier*, p.213; William Henry Cope, *The History of the Rifle Brigade (the Prince Consort's Own) Formerly the 95th* (London: Chatto and Windus, 1877), p.85.

squares being broken are described in several French descriptions. Koch reported that Craufurd was captured and gave his sword to *adjudant-major* Dulimbert of the 13e chasseurs à cheval.[74] Stewart observed that the Allied cavalry was inter-mixed with the Light Division, and made several small counter-attacks on the French, causing problems not only for the enemy but also for the Light Division: '... a few squadrons charged from time to time through the intervals of the squares, with greater or less benefit, according as opportunities offered. In the end, however, this species of manoeuvre threatened to be productive of more harm than good. Our troopers, in retiring, got among our own squares, and threw them into confusion ...'[75] As the Light Division reached the main Allied line, companies of the Guards were wheeled back to provide openings for the battalions to pass through.[76]

The company of the 95th to which Kincaid belonged retreated along with the rest of the Light Division to join the main body of the army. He records that his unit took up its position on a low, rocky ridge with its left flank on the, '... then right of the British line ...' with the right on the Tourões.[77] This position is supported by Cope's description that places the 95th, '... near the Turones, [sic] and the French infantry which threatened them kept out of rifle range.'[78]

Harry Smith wrote, '... the enemy from Poza Velha [sic] turned our right flank and licked our cavalry (14th Light Dragoons and Royals) awfully.'[79] Despite Smith's pessimistic remarks, neither the Royals nor the 14th were out of the fight. Cocks wrote of three squadrons of Slade's brigade attacking some enemy artillery during the pause in the movement of the French infantry.[80] This was almost certainly the time that Captain Robert Knipe of the 14th Light Dragoons undertook a frontal attack on a French battery, although Hall wrote that it was two guns. The Captain had been discussing the best approach to take when assaulting artillery: 'He maintained, contrary to us all, that they ought to be charged in front, instead of the usual way in gaining their flanks, and thereby avoiding their fire.'[81] In testing his hypothesis, Knipe received a fatal wound of a piece of shot through his lungs, and several of his troopers were killed by a close-range discharge of canister.[82] As well as carnage there was chivalry on the battlefield. An officer of the 14th Light Dragoons, one-armed since having lost his right arm at Oporto, was ridden at by an officer of the 13e chasseurs à cheval, who, upon seeing that his opponent had only one arm, saluted him rather than striking him.[83] Lieutenant William Freer of the 43rd recalled, 'We had not been long in this position before we observed the enemy forming columns in the wood opposite to that occupied by the sharpshooters'.[84]

74   Koch, *Mémoires de Massena*, vol.7, p.537.
75   Vane, *Narrative of the Peninsular War from 1808 to 1813*, pp.511–512.
76   Simmons, *A British Rifle Man*, p.169.
77   Kincaid, *Adventures*, p.76.
78   Cope, *The History of the Rifle Brigade (the Prince Consort's Own) Formerly the 95th*, p.85.
79   Smith, *Autobiography*, p.49.
80   Cocks, *Intelligence Officer in the Peninsula*, p.104.
81   Brotherton, *A Hawk at War*, p.41.
82   Hall, 'Recollections in Portugal and Spain During 1811 and 1812', p.1542.
83   Cowell-Stepney, *Leaves from the Diary of an Officer of the Guards*, p.87.
84   Leicester and Rutland Record Office (LRRO): 16D521/21, 'Freer Family Papers'.

The Attack on the 1st Division

As the 7th and Light Divisions withdrew through and around the 1st Division, the French continued their advance. The Light Division, on gaining the main Allied position, were still pursued by French cavalry and infantry, but after exchanging small arms fire, these troops withdrew, and their artillery took over the fight. A battery of French guns was brought up and began to fire on the 1st Division, causing some casualties. Wellington ordered the men to lie down to reduce the effect. Allied guns under the command of Captain Lawson, attached to the division, was posted to the front and returned fire. Lawson's guns, '… opened their fire with effect on the enemy, which, together with our Light Infantry and Rifles, covering our right flank (for we were en potence), and our piquets skirmishing in advance, guarded our front against any sudden predatory attack.'[85] Lieutenant Colonel George Hill of the 3rd Guards commanded the picquet. The oddities of the British rank system meant officers of the Guards had a rank superior to their equivalent in the line regiments. Thus, Hill's regimental rank was Captain, but his army rank was lieutenant colonel. This arrangement demonstrates the 1st Division complying with the general order issued on 4 May 1809, instructing that the light companies of units, and the rifle companies attached to each brigade, were to be formed into a temporary 'light battalion' commanded by a field officer or captain of light infantry.[86] Cowell-Stepney states the number in the picquet line as being 100 rank-and-file, but this is likely an understatement. The two Guards battalions show 1,685 rank and file in the return of 1 May, which would give approximately 168 men in two light companies.[87] The picquet would consist of the light companies of the Guards' Brigade, plus the attached rifle company of the 5/60th, another 44 men. Thus, we can expect that there were approximately 200 men in the picquet line in front of the 1st Division. The Guard's light companies had not previously been sent into Fuentes de Oñoro, and thus are unlikely to have suffered significant casualties on the 3rd or 4th.

The first assault of the French cavalry on the 1st Division position was driven off by the picquet of the Guards and the fire of Lawson's guns. Following this attack, the picquet were withdrawing onto the 42nd, which was drawn up in column on some broken ground acting as support. As they withdrew, they were caught in open order, from the flank and rear, by another attack from French cavalry which had approached unseen from behind a small rise. Hall described the French cavalry making, '… a dart at the pickets … with the expectation of sweeping off the line before our cavalry could support them.'[88] In this action, the French troopers guessed correctly, and the skirmishers were cut down before they could gain the shelter of the 42nd's column. With no time to form square, Cornet Hall described the guardsmen clustering into small knots, or 'hiving', to protect themselves against cavalry.[89] Despite this, losses in the light companies were severe. Hill was taken prisoner by

85   Cowell-Stepney, *Leaves from the Diary of an Officer of the Guards*, p.89.
86   General Order, Coimbra, 4 May 1809. Gurwood, *General Orders*, p.188.
87   TNA: WO 17/2467, 'Monthly Returns to the Adjutant General, January to June'.
88   Hall, 'Recollections in Portugal and Spain During 1811 and 1812', p.1542.
89   Hall, 'Recollections in Portugal and Spain During 1811 and 1812', p.1542.

sous-lieutenant Mognot (spelled Monnot in Martinien and Monniot in Pelet[90]) of the 13e chasseurs à cheval, along with many of his officers and men who had been in the skirmish line: only 30 escaped unhurt.[91] French sources have exaggerated the losses inflicted on the guards in this attack. Fririon described how, 'Montbrun engaged and defeated two infantry squares that were charged by our chasseurs. These squares would have remained in our control if it weren't for heavy gunfire and a hail of grapeshot that overwhelmed our cavalry. Nevertheless, they managed to bring back 300 royal English guard hussars, including a lieutenant colonel and four officers.'[92] According to Pelet: 'General Fournier, at the head of the seventh and thirteenth chasseurs à cheval, sabred three battalions of English guards … these battalions laid down their arms'.[93]

Fournier's horse was killed, and the commanders of the two chasseur regiments, *colonel* Alexandre Montbrun of the 7e and *colonel* Joachim Lepic of the 13e, were wounded. Fournier was given a horse by *maréchal des logis* Fleurot of the 13e chasseurs à cheval.[94] According to Pelet, these events caused confusion and disorder in the ranks of the *chasseurs*.[95] *Chef de Bataillon* Marie Baudus, ADC to *maréchal* Bessières, records that, 'We captured twelve hundred prisoners, and the enemy retreated in extraordinary disorder and confusion.'[96] Despite these claims, the Allied casualty returns show far fewer men missing than French participants or historians maintain. The likelihood is that the fighting was confused, and perhaps the whole picquet line appeared, at least temporarily, to be in the hands of the French. Most accounts attribute the recovery of the prisoners from French hands to the cavalry counter-attack by the Allies. A squadron each of the Royals and 14th moved forward to cover the retreat of what was left of the light infantry. Before they could be hurried to the rear by the French troopers, the muddle of battle meant many could find their way back to the Allied lines. The mayhem was increased as Lane's two guns, part of Lawson's battery, began firing canister into the French cavalry, '… and mowed them down …', but this also had the unfortunate effect of hitting Allied soldiers.[97] Canister is an indiscriminate weapon and turns a cannon into an enormous shotgun. Simmons suggests that the French cavalry, '… menaced a charge upon our guns and came up in the boldest manner, receiving repeated discharges of grape-shot, that literally made lanes through them. Finding it of no use, the cavalry moved off.'[98] Grattan, on the ridge above Fuentes de Oñoro had a clear view of proceedings and expressed his frustration:

90   Martinien, *Tableaux Des Officiers*, p.597; Pelet-Clozeau, *Mémoire sur ma campagne du Portugal*, p.590.
91   Cowell-Stepney, *Leaves from the Diary of an Officer of the Guards*, p.90; Pelet-Clozeau, *Mémoire sur ma campagne du Portugal*, p.590.
92   Fririon, *Journal Historique*, p.206.
93   *Victoires*, vol.21, p.339.
94   Pelet-Clozeau, *Mémoire sur ma campagne du Portugal*, p.591.
95   Pelet-Clozeau, *Mémoire sur ma campagne du Portugal*, p.590.
96   Marie Élie Guillaume de Baudus, *Études Sur Napoléon* (Paris: Debécourt, 1841), vol.2, p.318.
97   Cowell-Stepney, *Leaves from the Diary of an Officer of the Guards*, p.90.
98   Simmons, *A British Rifle Man*, p.171.

... a small rugged ravine separated us from our comrades; but although the distance between us was short, we were, in effect, as far from them as if we were placed upon the Rock of Lisbon. We felt much for their situation, but could not afford them the least assistance, and we saw them rode down and cut to pieces without being able to rescue them, or even discharge one musket in their defence.[99]

The 42nd was also attacked by cavalry, but were able to fend it off. The battalion had formed line and was able to dissuade the enemy cavalry by volleys of musketry. Cowell-Stepney described the effects as giving, '... the enemy no encouragement to make a second attempt on them.'[100] Low's Brigade of King's German Legion infantry and Howard's Brigade were positioned in reserve behind the main line of the 1st Division, placed in, '... the hollow in our rear, sinking toward the Turones [sic] river'.[101] Despite this sheltered position, artillery rounds which overshot the first line or ricocheted over found targets here. Nightingall mentioned the difficulty of his brigade's position: 'We lost ... more men by cannon shot than I expected from the circumstance of the line being enfiladed. The second line, consisting of Howard's Brigade lost more than the first.'[102] Cowell-Stepney goes on to describe the effects of one roundshot which reached the second line:

... after striking close to our people, plumped amidst a group of staff and field officers assembled together in the bottom, taking off the head of General Howard's horse, traversing the carcase of that of his aide-de-camp Captain Battersby, carrying off the leg of Major Stewart of the 92nd, and, knocking down two rank and file of that regiment, went hopping on like a cricket-ball, as if it had done nothing ...[103]

A note in Schneider's collection of Pelet's *Mémoire* records the 4° Caçadores, under *Tenente-coronel* Luis do Rego, fending off an attack by the French cavalry. However, this battalion was part of Pack's Brigade, deployed around Almeida to keep the siege.[104]

The Myth of Ramsay's 'Charge'
Since its first publication in 1828, Napier's *History* has influenced most accounts of the Battle of Fuentes de Oñoro.[105] His work also courted controversy, most notably around his views regarding the actions of some other veterans of the Peninsula War. The targets for his attacks included *Marechal* Beresford for his handling of the army at the Battle of Albuera, and John Gurwood, who had served in the 52nd and later compiled *The Dispatches of the Field Marshal the Duke of Wellington*.

---

99   Grattan, *Adventures with the Connaught Rangers, 1809-1814*, p.65.
100 Cowell-Stepney, *Leaves from the Diary of an Officer of the Guards*, p.91.
101 Cowell-Stepney, *Leaves from the Diary of an Officer of the Guards*, p.94.
102 Glover, 'The Nightingall Letters', p.149.
103 Cowell-Stepney, *Leaves from the Diary of an Officer of the Guards*, p.93.
104 Pelet-Clozeau, *Mémoire sur ma campagne du Portugal*, n.591.
105 Napier, *History of the War in the Peninsula*, vol.3, p.151.

One part of Napier's work which stands out in its overemphasis is his description of the withdrawal of two guns, under the commander of Captain Norman Ramsay, of Captain Bull's troop of the Royal Horse Artillery. The loss of guns was a shameful event, second only to losing a regiment's colours. The fight over a single howitzer at Sabugal and the subsequent argument over its ownership show how valuable artillery pieces could be to a unit's prestige. This also demonstrates how much blood might be spilled attempting to capture them. Napier wrote:

> … a great commotion was observed amongst the French squadrons; men and officers closed in confusion towards one point where a thick dust was rising, and where loud cries and the sparkling of blades and flashing of pistols, indicated some extraordinary occurrence. Suddenly the multitude was violently agitated, an English shout arose, the mass was rent asunder, and Norman Ramsay burst forth at the head of his battery, his horses breathing fire and stretching like greyhounds along the plain, his guns bounding like things of no weight, and the mounted gunners in close and compact order protecting the rear.[106]

We can dismiss much of Napier's hyperbole. He describes Ramsay's artillery 'battery' escaping from being surrounded by French cavalry. Ramsay commanded a 'division', comprising two guns, of Bull's troop of six guns. The French cavalry certainly surrounded the guns commanded by Ramsay, and his gunners and himself were lucky not to be captured, but the purple prose of Napier's description obscures the true events. Lawson's brigade of guns was attached to the 1st Division, with Bull's troop attached to the cavalry. Arentschildt's Portuguese artillery was attached to various divisions (see above), but his name is identified on the map of the battlefield, occupying a prominence, and marked as 'Arenchild's B[atter]y'.[107] That the artillery was heavily engaged is not in doubt, although some seem to have suffered more than others.

Posted near the 7th Division, the Allied cavalry and accompanying horse artillery commanded by Ramsay descended from a strong position on high ground to protect the withdrawal of Sontag's Brigade.[108] The French cavalry advanced into the opening caused by Sontag's retreat, threatening the 7th Division as described above by Wheeler. This also brought them close to the Light Division as that infantry came up to support the right of the Allied line. Ramsay's two guns were now exposed: artillery would be extremely vulnerable to enemy cavalry if caught unsupported or from the flank or rear. Worse could be expected if the guns were being limbered. We should expect that removing the guns would be necessary to keep them from being captured or spiked by the French.

A comparison with an eyewitness presents an entirely different perspective on the events. Tomkinson, writing at the time, noted that, '… the enemy's advance charged up the rising ground on which our horse artillery was posted, and passed two guns

---

106 Napier, *History of the War in the Peninsula*, vol.3, p.151.
107 TNA: WO 78/5937, Freeth's map.
108 Vane, *Narrative of the Peninsular War from 1808 to 1813*, p.511.

of Captain Bull's troop. Their advance was not well supported. Our cavalry came on …' in an attempt to push back the French.[109] Scovell observed the following in his notebook: 'The enemy came on with great impetuosity and almost unexpectedly, so that two of the light Guns were nearly in their possession. They were gallantly met by our dragoons, and many of them killed or taken.'[110] Scovell was a direct observer of events, writing in his diary immediately after the battle.

A squadron of the 14th Light Dragoons and one of the 1st Royal Dragoons intervened to provide sufficient distraction that Ramsay's guns could be retrieved. 'A party of [French] cavalry made a splendid attack, and captured two guns of Captain Bull's troop of horse artillery, when a squadron of the Royal Dragoons, dashing forward, re-took the guns and brought them into the British lines, together with several prisoners.'[111] Lieutenant Freer of the 43rd also had a clear view of events, observing:

> … their cavalry collected in great force although played upon by some guns of Bull, Horse Artillery. The object [of the French] was to take the guns, which they attempted by moving rapidly forward … and had passed the guns and continued the charge against our horse … The Guns when passed by, by the enemy, succeeded in escaping by charging through them and joining the cavalry.[112]

Once the two guns had been limbered, they were driven back to the main Allied line, '… followed by the French chasseurs, and the number of chasseurs and hussars of the French appeared to be much greater than that of anything opposing them.'[113] Wheeler recounts the wonders performed by a squadron of the 14th Light Dragoons and 1st Royal Dragoons, '… but they were soon obliged to fall back – for the enemy outnumbered them twenty to one or more; we now sorely felt the want of artillery and cavalry.'[114] Ross of the Royal Horse Artillery, in a letter of 9 May, mentions that the French cavalry, '… charged through Bull's guns, who mounted his detachments and sabred a good many of them, and brought his guns off.'[115] He also indicated that the French cavalry were, '… all drunk …'. However, in his own words, he wrote, 'I had nothing to say to the affair, being on the left of the whole position.'[116] We can thus discount his version of events as being, at best, second-hand. Hall recalled the French cavalry, '… surrounded two of our 9-pounders, but Lieutenant [sic] Ramsay and his artillerymen drew their swords and gallantly repulsed them.'[117] Fromentin recalled a similar situation but from the opposite side: 'Our skirmishers moved

109 Tomkinson, *Diary*, p.100.
110 TNA: WO 37/7a, Scovell, *Diary*, p.40.
111 De Ainslie, *Historical Record of the First or the Royal Regiment of Dragoons*, p.118.
112 LRRO: 1/21, 'Freer Family Papers'.
113 Maxwell, *Peninsular Sketches; by Actors on the Scene*, vol.1, p.191.
114 Wheeler, *The Letters of Private Wheeler 1809-1828*, p.55.
115 Ross, *Hew Ross of the Chestnut Troop*, p.33.
116 Ross, *Hew Ross of the Chestnut Troop*, p.32.
117 Hall, 'Recollections in Portugal and Spain During 1811 and 1812', p.1541. The guns would have been 6 pounders.

forward, well supported; the English squadrons moved towards us, supported by their artillery which did us great harm.'[118]

Although the exact course of events is impossible to discern, Ramsay's guns were exposed and surrounded by French cavalry. The gunners bravely stayed with their pieces and got them limbered up. Now troopers of the 14th Light Dragoons and Royals came to their aid. A combination of determined action by the artillerymen and cavalry allowed the guns to be pushed through the melee and into the protection of the main Allied line.

Captain Brotherton at the head of a squadron of the 14th Light Dragoons covering the retreat of the Light Division and attached artillery, charged into the melee, accompanied by Charles Stewart, the adjutant general, who captured an officer of chasseurs called La Motte or Lamotte by dragging him bodily from his horse. According to the history of the 1st Dragoons, a *colonel* Latour was knocked off his horse and surrendered to Lieutenant Gubbins.[119] It is unclear whether they are the same French officer. The Allied reports indicated that a *colonel* of the 13e chasseurs à cheval had been taken prisoner. However, one French source gives his name as *chef d'escadron* De Lamotte, commanding the 2eme Régiment provisoire de cavalerie légère.[120] Schaumann recounts meeting a *colonel* of chasseurs at Castello Bom, describing him as, '... a fine big fellow, whose enormous bearskin cap, fiery blue eyes, and huge fair moustache, lent him a splendid and martial air.'[121] He had been captured and brought to the rear, and may lend weight to the story of Lamotte being a *colonel* of chasseurs rather than a *chef d'escadron*. It is unlikely that it was *général de brigade* Auguste Lamotte. He had been sent back to France in disgrace by *maréchal* Ney after his negligent behaviour at Foz de Arouce. He subsequently appears in the 1813 campaign commanding a brigade in the 6e division of V cavalry corps.

The Light Division was moved into reserve behind the main fighting line. Cowell-Stepney indicates that the Light and 7th Divisions were placed in reserve and supporting the 1st Division on their right-rear. In a dispatch to Liverpool, Wellington described the position of the Allied divisions after the withdrawal of the Light and 7th Divisions:

> Our position thus extended on the high ground from the Turones [sic] to the Dos Casas. The 7th division, on the left of the Turones, covered the rear of the right; the 1st division, in 2 lines, were on the right; Col. Ashworth's brigade, in 2 lines, in the centre; and the 3d division, in 2 lines, on the left; the Light division and British artillery in reserve; and the village of Fuentes in front of the left. Don Julian's infantry joined the 7th division in Freineda; and I sent him with his cavalry to endeavor to intercept the enemy's communication with Ciudad Rodrigo.[122]

---

118 Morleix, 'Relation de la bataille de Fuentes de Oñoro (5 mai 1811)', p.305.
119 De Ainslie, *Historical Record of the First or the Royal Regiment of Dragoons*, p.118.
120 Sarramon, 'Campagne de Fuentes de Oñoro, 15 Avril – 11 Mai 1811', p.53. This provisional regiment was made up of the 4th squadron of the 12e Chasseurs and the 5e Hussars.
121 Schaumann, *On the Road with Wellington*, p.302.
122 Wellington to Liverpool. Villar Formoso, 8 May, 1811, Gurwood, *Dispatches*, vol.4, p.796.

A Missed Opportunity

According to Judge-Advocate General Larpent, Wellington described a situation during the battle when he was close to being taken by French *dragons*:

> The whole of head-quarters, general and all ... English dragoons and French dragoons, were all galloping away together across the plain, and he more than once saw a French dragoon in a green coat within twenty yards of him. One Frenchman got quite past them all, and they could not knock him off his horse. At last they caught his bridle and stopped him.[123]

The Allied right flank was in some disarray, and the cavalry were significantly outnumbered. Napier claimed that, '... there was not during the whole war a more perilous hour.'[124] He described a scene of confusion in the Allied lines, '... the vast plain was covered with commissariat animals and camp-followers, with servants, led horses, baggage, and country people, mixed with broken detachments and piquets returning from the woods ...'[125] However, he is the only observer to have described the impedimenta in the immediate rear of the Allied position but many subsequent writers have taken Napier's view. There was certainly some confusion in the fighting taking place amidst dust and smoke, and even a penetration of the Allied line which reached as far as the Tourões.

The confusion, however serious, provided Massena with an opportunity to take advantage of the situation and push through to the Côa. There does seem to have been some coordination between the cavalry advance and Mermet's division. The voltigeurs of the 27e ligne reached the Tourões by manoeuvring around the right flank of the 1st Division, between that division and the 7th.[126] This happened at approximately the same time as the 1st Division was under attack by Fournier's troopers. The 27e's position indicates the leading elements had continued their advance following the occupation of Poço Velho. The penetration probably took place in the low ground which separated the 1st and the 7th Divisions, and had they been successful, would have provided the advancing French troops with access to the rear of the Allied position. The French advance shown on Freeth's map indicates troops very close to the Tourões west of Poço Velho, and this position reflects both the observed French troop movements and the supposed thrust of attack.[127]

The voltigeurs were opposed by five companies from the 95th under the command of Major O'Hare. Fighting took place in the rocky, steep valley of the Tourões and in the nearby walled enclosures.[128] Simmons wrote, 'Five companies of Rifle Men occupied some rugged ground through which the Turon [sic] pursued its course, on

---

123 Sir George Larpent, *The Private Journal of Judge-Advocate Larpent* ... (London: Bentley, 1854), p.93.

124 Napier, *History of the War in the Peninsula*, vol.3, p.152.

125 Napier, *History of the War in the Peninsula*, vol.3, p.152.

126 SHD: Rapport au 15 mai, 361. *Armée d'Espagne: Correspondance*; Also cited in Sarramon, 'Campagne de Fuentes de Oñoro, 15 Avril – 11 Mai 1811', p.71.

127 TNA: WO 78/5937, Freeth's map.

128 Leach, *Rough Sketches of the Life of an Old Soldier*, p.214.

the right of the 1st Division, and between it and the 7th.'[129] First Lieutenant John Cox wrote that the Rifles were deployed, '… into a broken valley through which flows the river Teuron, [sic] and assisted by the light companies of the Guards repulsed the French voltigeurs in an attempt to push through it.'[130] Stothert and Cox mention that the light companies of the Guards under Lieutenant Colonel John Guise took part in the fighting and that this occurred at approximately the same time as the picquet of the brigade were attacked by French cavalry. It is possible that the picquet of the Guards to the right were untouched by the cavalry attack and were able to take part in repulsing the French skirmishers.[131] The French troops were eventually forced back from this most dangerous of positions.

The orders given to Loison indicated that VI corps was supposed to move level with the right of Montbrun's troopers, advancing between the cavalry and the woods to the south of Fuentes de Oñoro. They were to advance perpendicularly to the Allied line, so this would imply the line of advance would be generally westwards. This also fits with the instructions given in the orders from Massena intended to deny Wellington the bridge at Castelo Bom. Pelet, in his narrative of the battle, provided a description of the plan was for the attack:

> General Loison should have emerged from the woods as quickly as possible, deploying his two excellent divisions in two lines. The first brigade was to position itself behind, along the edge of the woods, deployed to support the other divisions with its fire. Then, they would advance quickly from one ravine to the next: the cavalry would follow along the ridge, where it could quickly regroup. General Ferey, supported by this movement and aided by the 9e Corps, which turned as far as possible and protected its flanks, would take the village and form a mass reserve near the last houses. At the same time, the 9e Corps would break through. Then, these six divisions, organised in two lines, would occupy the entire width of the plateau with the cavalry, pushing back the English army.[132]

However, at this point, the infantry of Marchand and Mermet, having advanced from the wood in front of the Allied-held ridge, paused. Some had veered too far to the right into the woods and were now facing the spur of land on which the higher parts of Fuentes de Oñoro stand, rather than the ridge of land between the Dos Casas and the Tourões. Many of the French commentators remark on the absence, or inactivity, of infantry to exploit the advantages gained by Montbrun.[133] However, given the exploits of the 27e, we cannot assume that other units from the two divisions were completely static, nor do we have enough evidence to suggest they were not. Despite this, a large proportion of the VI corps involved in the turning manoeuvre

129 Simmons, *A British Rifle Man*, p.170.
130 Glover and Burnham, *Riflemen of Wellington's Light Division*, p.109.
131 Stothert, *A Narrative of the Principal Events of the Campaigns of 1809, 1810, & 1811, in Spain and Portugal*, p.246.
132 Pelet-Clozeau, *Mémoire sur ma campagne du Portugal*, p.594.
133 For example, see Morleix, 'Relation de la bataille de Fuentes de Oñoro (5 mai 1811)'.

remained below the Allied position or possibly even became involved on the edges of the fight for the village of Fuentes de Oñoro itself.

There may be several explanations for the pause, but the most obvious one is a failure of initiative and capability by the commander of VI corps. According to Guingret, Loison hesitated for an hour awaiting orders from Massena.[134] Jomini was explicit and explained the delay was because of Ney's absence.[135] *Chef de bataillon du génie* Belmas reinforces this view of Loison's hesitancy, stating he did not have the bold and aggressive nature of Ney, and thus missed the opportunity of establishing the infantry of VI corps on the ridge.[136] De Baudus wrote, 'Unfortunately ... the troops of the Sixth Corps, deprived of their former general, the fiery Marshal Ney, who had just left them, commanded at that time by the leader imposed on them by the caprice of seniority, set the first example of disastrous inaction'.[137]

Sprünglin expressed the situation more robustly: '... victory slipped away at that moment from the triumphant troops. There was only one cry in the army: Where is Marshal Ney? — A fearless and vigilant soldier, a skilled captain, he could have gathered the laurels that Massena, worn out, let slip from his hands.'[138]

Undoubtedly, *général de division* Loison was no substitute for *maréchal* Ney. He had been bested by Wellington at Vimiero and Buçaco. Loison also knew by now that he was to be replaced by Marmont, who was currently on his way to the army. He had been a discontented commander throughout the campaign, beginning by criticising Ney.[139] Subsequent relations between Ney and Loison had not been the best, with Ney condemning Loison's deployment at Fonte Coberta on 13 March. He was not held in high regard by the senior officers, and Pelet described Loison as self-seeking.[140] Loison's conduct during the campaign, and leadership on the 5th, left a lot to be desired. The situation was summed up by Béchet: 'That confidence between the leader and the soldiers, which inspires extraordinary feats, no longer existed.'[141]

Despite Loison's lacklustre performance, both Guingret and Sprünglin apportioned some blame to Massena for failing to provide clear orders and for not being on the spot when direction was needed. A reason offered to explain Massena's lethargy on 5 May is that he was suffering from what his physician, Dr Brisset, described as '... inflammation of the stomach.'[142] This may be from an ulcer, or perhaps what is now described as irritable bowel syndrome. He had suffered several injuries in his career, not least in the campaign in Austria in 1809. However, Pelet recorded that Massena was there, and actively looking for a breakthrough: '... the Prince threw himself into the middle of the skirmishers; he was forced to dismount and, alone with me, he walked the line several times, looking for the point where he could

134 Guingret, *Relation Historique*, p.208.
135 Jomini, *Guerre d'Espagne : Extrait Des Souvenirs Inédits du Général Jomini*, p.173.
136 Belmas, *Journaux Des Siéges*, vol.1, p.179.
137 de Baudus, *Études Sur Napoléon*, vol.2, p.319.
138 Sprünglin, 'Souvenirs', p.481.
139 Pelet, *The French Campaign in Portugal*, p.115.
140 Pelet, *The French Campaign in Portugal*, p.484.
141 Béchet, *Souvenirs*, p.375.
142 Béchet, *Souvenirs*, p.378; Marshall-Cornwall, *Marshal Massena*, p.251.

still penetrate [the Allied position].'[143] The suggestion that Massena was there is supported by the presence of a volunteer aide de camp, *capitaine* Achille Septeuil, who, in the battle, had one of his legs shattered and whose horse was killed under him.[144] Septeuil had been ADC to Berthier in the 1809 campaign and had volunteered to go with the *armée de Portugal* after being sent to Valladolid.[145] In an unforgiving tone, Béchet wrote:

> I will always remember that fateful breakfast Massena ordered on the battlefield, and the feeling of despair we felt upon witnessing his incomprehensible apathy. The soldiers were bristling with indignation, eager to march against the enemy, but nothing could move the impassive commander-in-chief. When I later asked General Pelet the reasons for such conduct, he assured me he was completely unaware of them and, despairing at the turn of events, had gone to the front lines hoping to get himself killed.[146]

Added to this lack of activity and coordination was the absence at the front line of the cavalry of the *garde impériale*, an impressive brigade-sized formation of veteran troopers. Montbrun wanted to take advantage of the apparent disorganisation in the enemy ranks by bringing these elite cavalry units into action as quickly as possible. His cavalry was tiring, and fresh horses could give the French advance the edge. *Lieutenant* Oudinot, one of Massena's ADCs, was sent with an order to move this cavalry forward from behind Solignac's division. The order was refused. Guingret explains that the arrogance of the commanders of the *garde impériale* often led them to ignore, 'generals of the line'.[147] Oudinot, covered in sweat, returned to Massena, who asked him 'Where is the cavalry of the Guard?' Oudinot replied, 'Prince, I was unable to bring it.' *Général de brigade* Lepic had declared to Oudinot that he answered only to the Duke of Istria, *maréchal* Bessières, and that he would not draw his sword without his order.[148] However, this is contradicted by both Guingret and Marbot, who record the officers' impatience at not being engaged in the battle. The Polish Lancers were demanding the right to attack the Allied squares. According to Marbot, 'Lepic, biting his sword blade in desperation, replied, with much regret, that his immediate chief, Marshal Bessières, had forbidden him to take the Guard into action without his order.'[149] This seems a likely explanation. Problematically, Bessières was nowhere to be found. Several ADCs were hastened off to find the errant *maréchal*, eventually discovering him investigating the marshland over which Montbrun's cavalry had earlier passed. Regardless of the reason, the cavalry of the *garde impériale* remained unengaged at the crucial moment. There is always the possibility that the élan of these veteran troops might have carried the day. Despite

143 *Victoires*, vol.21, p.341.
144 Pelet-Clozeau, *Mémoire sur ma campagne du Portugal*, p.595.
145 de Baudus, *Études Sur Napoléon*, vol.2, pp.319–320.
146 Béchet, *Souvenirs*, p.378.
147 Guingret, *Relation Historique*, p.263.
148 Oudinot, 'Souvenirs intimes', p.40.
149 Marbot, *The Memoirs of the Baron de Marbot*, vol.2, p.166.

hurrying back to his command, the decisive moment had gone, and Bessières earned the ire of both Massena and, eventually, Napoleon.

The success, or otherwise, of the flanking movement depended to a large extent on fixing Wellington's focus on the village of Fuentes de Oñoro and attempting to draw in as many troops as possible in order to weaken the Allied flanks. What is certain is that there was little or no practical coordination between Montbrun's cavalry on the left and the mass of Loison's infantry to their right. Had there been, it is conceivable that Wellington's position might have been successfully turned. A bold thrust of combined infantry and cavalry, commanded by an enterprising leader such as Ney, might very well have unhinged the position. Whilst the Light and 7th Divisions were redeploying, and others were being realigned, Wellington's left flank was vulnerable.

11

The Action in Fuentes de Oñoro

On the morning of 5 May, the 71st and 79th Foot were placed into Fuentes de Oñoro, and the 24th positioned above the village to provide direct support. The light and rifle companies of the 1st and 3rd Divisions, the 6° Caçadores and companies from the Portuguese regiments of Champalimaud's and Ashworth's Brigades also occupied Fuentes de Oñoro.[1] Behind the village, hidden along the crest of the ridge, were the rest of the 1st and 3rd Divisions. The 1st Division was on the Allied right, Ashworth's Brigade in the centre, with the 3rd Division to the left and positioned directly above the village. Each division had its brigades formed in two lines, and if the orders for the 3rd are any guide, we may assume that the second line at least was formed in column. In Wellington's dispatch, he mentioned that the, '... light infantry battalions of the 1st Division, commanded by Major Dick [42nd], Major M'Donnell [92nd], and Major Aly [5th KGL]' were present in Fuentes de Oñoro, but at least part of those units were acting as picquet to the right of the village, and would be caught up in the cavalry action against the 1st Division. The assumption made here is that the light companies of the Guards' Brigade were not involved in the fighting in the village.

At approximately 10:00 a.m., following a heavy cannonade, Ferey's infantry attacked the village. Ferey's division was instructed to, '... make preparations as if it were going to attack the enemy at this point, without, however, risking anything.'[2] Despite this instruction to make a demonstration in front of Fuentes de Oñoro, Ferey launched a ferocious attack once Montbrun's outflanking manoeuvre appeared to be making headway. This attack was supported by three battalions of Conroux's division led by *général de brigade* Gérard. These were three *demi-brigades*, one *légère* and two *ligne*, comprised of three 4e battalions each from a variety of regiments (see Appendix 2). Harry Smith recalled, 'There never was a more heavy fight than for several hours in the village of Fuentes. Here I saw the 79th Regiment, in an attack on the head of a French column coming up the road, bayonet eight or nine French officers and upwards of 100 men, the only real bayonet conflict I ever witnessed.'[3]

Private Eadie was bayoneted in the chin but, managing to extract himself, slew his attacker: 'Though our charge was again successful, yet the battle continued to rage

---

1   Wellington to Liverpool. Villar Formoso, 8 May, 1811, Gurwood, *Dispatches*, vol.4, p.797.
2   SHD: Dispositions pour la journée du 5. *Correspondance*, 7C12; See also Oman, *A History of the Peninsular War*, vol.4, p.629.
3   Smith, *Autobiography*, p.49.

in this place, as hot, and sanguinary as ever, from the heavy columns of infantry that kept pouring in upon as we had not received any orders to retire'.[4]

The French units in Fuentes de Oñoro were disorganised with, at times, parts of several different brigades pressed into the village. The same disorganisation obtained for the Allies. The streets were blocked, and the French infantry presented densely packed targets to the Allied muskets. Command and control of the French units had broken down, and even if there was an opportunity for a counterattack, it could not be properly coordinated. Despite this, the Allied troops were pushed further back by weight of numbers. According to one participant, 'We foiled them in every attempt to take the town, until about eleven o'clock, when we were overpowered and forced through the streets, contesting every inch.'[5] A large group of the 79th was trapped by the voltigeurs of the 32e led by *lieutenant* Budo and forced to surrender.[6] Oman shows the 79th regiment as losing 153 men killed and wounded, but also 94 missing, which may very well account for the troops lost at this point.[7] The usual story is that a company of the 79th was surrounded in the village, but Wellington complained later of, 'The frequent instances which have occurred lately of severe loss, and, in some instances, of important failure, by officers leading the troops beyond the point to which they are ordered and beyond all bounds, such as the loss of the prisoners taken in front of the village of Fuentes, on the 3d and 5th inst.'[8] This would suggest that some troops had been pushed too far forward and had been captured during a French counterattack. Grattan described the French attacking the village with their usual impetuosity. They broke down the barricades that the Allied troops had constructed across the streets and alleyways. The fighting ebbed and flowed through the village, eventually seeing the Allies pressed to the very edge around the church toward the top of the slope. Men from both sides were fighting in the graveyard, even across individual tombstones.[9] Donaldson recalled that the French, having pushed through the village, formed close columns between it and the Allied line. What were probably Arentschildt's guns, posted on a rise in front of the Allied line, opened fire upon the columns, forcing them to move to a safer position.[10] This is partly corroborated by the observations of a soldier of the 71st who wrote, 'No sooner had we formed our pêle-mêle ranks into good array, than the French emerged from the village, and drew up opposite to us, within musket shot … We still continued giving and receiving a constant fire.'[11]

The statements by Allied witnesses are further verified by at least one French commentator. Three battalions of IX corps moved around the village to the south and advanced toward the Allied line, but were brought to a halt by the 21° Infantaria, commanded by *Tenente-coronel* João Maria de Araújo Bacellar, from Picton's

4   Eadie, *Recollections of the Life of Robert Eadie*, p.99.
5   *Journal of a Soldier of the Seventy-First*, p.136.
6   Natalia Griffon de Pleineville, 'Le Second Jour de la Bataille : 5 Mai', *Gloire & Empire*, 42 (2012), p.52.
7   Appendix XI, Oman, *A History of the Peninsular War*, vol.4, p.623.
8   *Dispatches*, vol.5, p.15.
9   Grattan, *Adventures with the Connaught Rangers, 1809-1814*, p.67.
10 Donaldson, *Recollections of the Eventful Life of a Soldier*, p.128.
11 Anonymous, *Vicissitudes*, p.162.

Division. The 21° lost eight soldiers killed, 41 wounded, and four missing over the course of the battle.[12]

Drouet now threw three elite battalions into the combat, made up of the 18 grenadier companies from the divisions of the IX corps. The 71st was certainly faced with these elite troops, as one soldier reported that in the exchange of fire, '... the loss was the more important to the enemy, as those killed were chiefly grenadiers.'[13] These pushed the Allied troops back up the slope towards the church. Delagrave recorded that 'General Claparède's division charged forward with brilliant valour to outflank the village; they even briefly captured some of the heights that overlooked it. However, overwhelmed by grapeshot and musket fire striking them from all sides, they were unable to hold the positions they had taken.'[14] More reinforcements from IX corps were fed into the village and were met by the 24th Foot moving down from its supporting position above the village.

The presence of French infantry between the village and the main Allied line, coupled with the turning movement to the right flank of the Allied army, indicated how dangerous the situation had become. At the point of most threat to the centre of the Allied position, Colonel Henry Mackinnon was given orders by Sir Edward Pakenham, Deputy Adjutant General, to move into the village. Grattan records a conversation with Lieutenant Colonel Wallace of the 88th in a somewhat Shakespearean style:

> Sir Edward Pakenham galloped up ... and said, 'Do you see that, Wallace?'—'I do,' replied the Colonel, 'and I would rather drive the French out of the town than cover a retreat across the Coa.'—'Perhaps,' said Sir Edward, 'his lordship don't think it tenable.' Wallace answering said, 'I shall take it with my regiment, and keep it too.'—'Will you?' was the reply; 'I'll go and tell Lord Wellington so; see, here he comes.' In a moment or two Pakenham returned at a gallop, and, waving his hat, called out, 'He says you may go—come along, Wallace.'[15]

Mackinnon led two battalions, the 74th and the 88th of his Brigade, into the attack, leaving the third, the 45th, as a reserve. This brigade had taken the brunt of fighting at the pass above San Antonio do Cantaro at Buçaco the year before and was an experienced formation. According to Grattan, the 88th, advancing in column of sections at the trot, did not stop to fire at the French but forced a path into the village at bayonet point. However, Eadie mentions that, '... the 88th, or Connaught Rangers, was sent to our assistance. As they were just descending from a rising ground immediately behind us, they fired a volley over our heads.'[16] This is corroborated by a soldier from the 71st. Regardless of the details, the 74th and 88th, supported by the remnants of the garrison of the village, pushed into Fuentes de Oñoro under fire

12   Soriano, *Historia Da Guerra Civil*, vol.3, p.419.
13   Anonymous, *Vicissitudes*, p.161.
14   Griffon de Pleineville, 'Gloire & Empire 42', p.52.
15   Grattan, *Adventures with the Connaught Rangers, 1809-1814*, p.67.
16   Eadie, *Recollections of the Life of Robert Eadie*, p.100.

from the French infantry and artillery. Grattan recalled, 'A battery of eight-pounders advanced at a gallop to an olive-grove on the opposite bank of the river ...', but the fire from the French artillery had little effect on the Allied advance.[17] The 88th was opposed by the 4e bataillon of the 9e légère of Conroux's division of IX corps, which had advanced the furthest into but also beyond the village. Fririon commented that Conroux's division, '... of the 9th corps received the order to march on its left to link up with the 1st division of the 6th corps ...', but before this could happen, the units had become disorganised by their movement through the village.[18] The Allied troops now pushed into the village, using their bayonets. Occasionally, a group of French soldiers would be cut off in a blind alley or on the wrong side of a barricade, and the fight would then be to the bitter end, such as the assault commanded by Lieutenant George Johnston of the 88th that trapped a group of French grenadiers and killed them to a man.[19] This successful Allied counterattack gave time for the remnants of the 71st and 79th to rally and re-enter the fight. As the 71st, '... passed over the ground where [the French] had stood, it lay two and three deep of dead and wounded. While we drove them before us through the town, in turn, they were reinforced, which only served to increase the slaughter.'[20]

Pelet claimed he arrived in Fuentes de Oñoro and found:

> The 1st Division ... at the top of the village; I entered further inside and found it clogged with troops. I encountered Generals Drouet, Claparède, Conroux, Ferey, and Marchand. Four divisions were massed there, blocking all the streets and avenues, and presenting large targets to the enemy's mobile forces. Although there was some order among a few reserves, which were poorly positioned, there was no unity in the directions and movements; there could hardly be any among these divisions from different corps. A terrible and pointless skirmishing raged everywhere, causing us to lose many men needlessly.[21]

It is of note here that Pelet, Massena's chief aide-de-camp and claimant to much of the planning and arrangements for the battle, bemoans the lack of organisation in the choice of higher formations sent in to attack the village. This must surely be the responsibility of Massena himself, but also of the divisional commanders given the task of organising the attack. The higher formation commanders would at least be familiar with one another and possibly more able to coordinate their actions. Marchand's presence is also surprising, as his division was meant to be involved in the left hook. The seemingly arbitrary splitting of higher formations for the left hook and the attack on Fuentes de Oñoro may, to some extent, indicate the reason for the confusion and subsequent failure of both attacks. However, the eye-witness

17   Grattan, *Adventures with the Connaught Rangers, 1809-1814*, p.68.
18   Fririon, *Journal Historique*, p.206.
19   Grattan, *Adventures with the Connaught Rangers, 1809-1814*, p.69.
20   Anon., *Journal of a Soldier of the Seventy-First*, p.138.
21   Pelet-Clozeau, *Mémoire sur ma campagne du Portugal*, p.595; Also quoted in Griffon de Pleineville, 'Gloire & Empire 42', 2012, p.55.

from the 71st mentioned that, '... we were suddenly surprised by the entrance of the French on the right ...' indicating that at least some of Loison's men had made it into the village.[22]

The counterattack by the Allies was the final straw. The French retreated over the Dos Casas, and some of the Allied soldiers pursued them too far, coming under fire from those enemy posted on the right bank. Soon, the village was largely under the control of the Allies, and the French reorganised themselves on the right bank as best they could.

Lieutenant Colonel Philip Cameron of the 79th was severely wounded, and Captain Christopher Irwine of the 88th was killed as the Allied troops took up positions behind walls and in the buildings in the village. Private Eadie of the 79th recalled, 'As we advanced to the charge, the enemy commenced a discharge of musketry; at this instant I saw the reins drop from [Cameron's] hands, and in the next, he tumbled to the ground. By the faithful zeal of those that ran to afford him assistance, he was speedily borne from the field.'[23]

Major Alexander Petrie, seeing some hesitation in the soldiers of the 79th, seized a colour and called out, 'There are your colours, lads, follow me!'[24] Colonel Mackinnon and Lieutenant Colonel Wallace attracted artillery fire as they gave directions for the defence of the village. Edward Pakenham escaped being hit despite remaining on horseback and, '... riding through the streets with that daring bravery for which he was remarkable; if he stood still for a moment, the ground about him was ploughed up with round shot.'[25]

Marchand's and Mermet's divisions of VI corps advanced from their position at Poço Velho, but rather than moving westwards to coordinate with Montbrun's sweep around the right flank of the Allied army's position, they advanced in a more northwesterly direction, seemingly to cut Fuentes de Oñoro off from the main Allied line. However, the divisions never came into direct contact with the main Allied line, nor did they join up with those units which had forced their way through the village and near the Allied line. Oman states that this is because they were awaiting the success of Montbrun before attacking the 1st and 3rd Divisions.[26] The French attacks were summed up by Major General Nightingall, wounded in the battle, who wrote, 'The enemy made his principal effort (and indeed his only one with infantry worth mentioning) on the village of Fuentes d'Honoré [sic] where we had the 24th, 71st and 79th regt's, the light battalion, K.G. Legion and the Light companies of the two divisions, supported by the 74th and 88th regts.'[27]

Although some witnesses and historians have written that grenadiers of the *garde impériale* were present on the 5th and involved in the fighting in and around Fuentes, this is incorrect.[28] Grattan of the 88th noticed, 'French Grenadiers, with

22   Anon., *Vicissitudes*, p.160.
23   Eadie, *Recollections of the Life of Robert Eadie*, p.98.
24   Herbert R. Clinton, *The War in the Peninsula, and Wellington's Campaigns in France and Belgium* (London: Warne, 1878), p.177.
25   Grattan, *Adventures with the Connaught Rangers, 1809-1814*, p.70.
26   Oman, *A History of the Peninsular War*, vol.4, pp.336–337.
27   Castello Bom, 9th May, 1811. Glover, 'The Nightingall Letters', p.149.
28   Buttery, *Wellington against Massena*, pp.160 & 164; Ross, *Hew Ross of the Chestnut Troop*, p.33.

their immense caps and gaudy plumes ...'[29] lying dead in the village. He described them later as, '... grenadiers of the Guard ...',[30] but this is clearly mistaken. The *Vieille Garde* (Old Guard) of Napoleon's *garde impériale* wore the bearskin as part of their regular uniform, but there was no infantry of the *garde impériale* regiments with the *armée de Portugal*, nor had Bessières brought any *garde* infantry with him. Grenadiers of the *infanterie de ligne* wore bearskin caps as part of their dress uniform, and these would sometimes be worn in battle. Drouet's formation of elite battalions for the attack into Fuentes de Oñoro on the 5th may also have led to their incorrect identification.

The Rearranged Dispositions

Various written sources indicate that the Allied forces were deployed in a right angle, with the apex at Fuentes de Oñoro, in response to the French attack on the right flank of the line.[31] The description of the Allied army throwing its right flank back may have been misinterpreted by later historians. Some have taken this to mean that the army was now placed at right angles, with the village of Fuentes de Oñoro at the angle. However, the descriptions given by observers indicate that the right flank was withdrawn, but the main line remained almost parallel to the Dos Casas, rather than wheeling back.

Two contemporary maps cast doubt on those supposed deployments. One map in the Murray Papers in the National Library of Scotland and one in the National Archives in Kew support the idea that the Allied troops were not drawn up along the high ground westwards from Fuentes, but rather almost parallel to the Dos Casas and Tourões.[32] Both are surveyed directly from the topography of the battlefield; indeed, the survey lines can be seen clearly on the map by Freeth. The original maps also show the extensive earthworks thrown up by the Allied army along the ridges. A copy of Murray's map appears in Charles Stewart's *Narrative of the Peninsular War*, although some units' locations and orientation have been altered slightly from the original.[33] The map also appears to be the basis for those used in Wyld's publication, which are also almost identical to those published by the War Office.[34] Again, some units' locations have been slightly changed from the original. It appears that the original is a more accurate representation of the later deployment of the Allied army and the location of the attacking French units, although the individual

---

29   Grattan, *Adventures with the Connaught Rangers, 1809-1814*, p.66.
30   Grattan, *Adventures with the Connaught Rangers, 1809-1814*, p.69.
31   Oman, *A History of the Peninsular War*, vol.4, pp.339–340.
32   NLS: Adv.MS.46.10.1(61), 'Sketch of Part of the Ground about Fuentes and Villa Formosa...'; TNA: WO 78/5937, Freeth's map.
33   Vane, *Narrative of the Peninsular War from 1808 to 1813*.
34   TNA: WO 78/5642, 'Lithograph from the Original Drawing in the Quarter Master General's Office at the Topographical Department of the War Office', 1869; *Maps and Plans, Showing the Principal Movements, Battles & Sieges in Which the British Army Was Engaged during the War from 1808 to 1814, in the Spanish Peninsular and the South of France* (London: James Wyld, 1840).

identities of those are anonymous on this map. The deployment along the ridge, north to south, was also confirmed by Stewart, the adjutant general:

> Fuentes de Honoro [sic] was not, strictly speaking, embraced in our posi-tion, and though occupied by the light troops of the 1st and 3rd divisions supported by the 7th regiment [sic], it was held merely as an advanced post. Yet, in spite of its advanced situation, it possessed so many defen-sible features, as to form, in point of fact, one of the main bulwarks of our ground …[35]

Wellington, in his report to Liverpool on 8 May, wrote that the 1st and 3rd Divisions were moved '… to their right, along the ridge between the Turoes [sic] and Dos Casas rivers …'.[36] The final positions, as recorded by Wellington in the same dispatch, also coincide with Murray's map. The 7th Division was on the left bank of the Tourões with the 1st Division, formed in two lines, on the right bank of that river. Stothert mentions that the 7th Division was placed on the left bank of the Tourões, '… formed upon the hill in rear of the present line, on which, should Lord Wellington think proper to refuse his right, a new position was intended to be taken up.'[37] Ashworth's brigade was in the centre with the 3rd Division on the left. The Light Division and the British artillery were in reserve. This placed Fuentes de Oñoro in front of the centre of the main Allied position.

If we are to take the entrenchments shown on Murray's map as being along the final position of the Allied forces on the 5th, this also indicates that the line was not formed at right angles to the initial dispositions, but only as far as the crest of the ridge overlooking Fuentes de Oñoro.

Almost every account of the fighting in the village of Fuentes de Oñoro mentions the piles of dead and wounded. The casualties returned for those units involved on the 5th reflect the gravity of the fighting. On the Allied side, the 71st, for example, took 137 casualties from a strength of 483, or some 35 percent. The 79th lost, including captured, 256 from a strength of 922, or some 27 percent. The fighting in the village was not the only serious combat, however. The 85th suffered signifi-cantly, beginning with only 387 men, losing in total 95, or 24 percent. The returns for the cavalry reflect smaller levels of casualties. The 1st Dragoons, having only 364 horses to mount their troopers, suffered 41 casualties, or 11 percent, which is typical. The cavalry shows significantly more wounded than killed, demonstrating perhaps the frenetic action and lack of killing power of the swords of both sides. One must also remember that if a trooper's mount is killed, he is effectively out of the battle unless he can gather a remount: the loss of horses would weaken any cavalry unit quite quickly. Following the battle, the role of the Allied cavalry was recognised by Wellington in a dispatch recommending several officers for promotion, including, '… Lieuts. Weyland and Tomkinson of the 16th Light Dragoons; Lieuts. Townshend

35   Vane, *Narrative of the Peninsular War from 1808 to 1813*, p.501.
36   Wellington to Liverpool. Villar Formoso, 8 May, 1811, Gurwood, *Dispatches*, vol.4, p.795.
37   Stothert, *A Narrative of the Principal Events of the Campaigns of 1809, 1810, & 1811, in Spain and Portugal*, p.247.

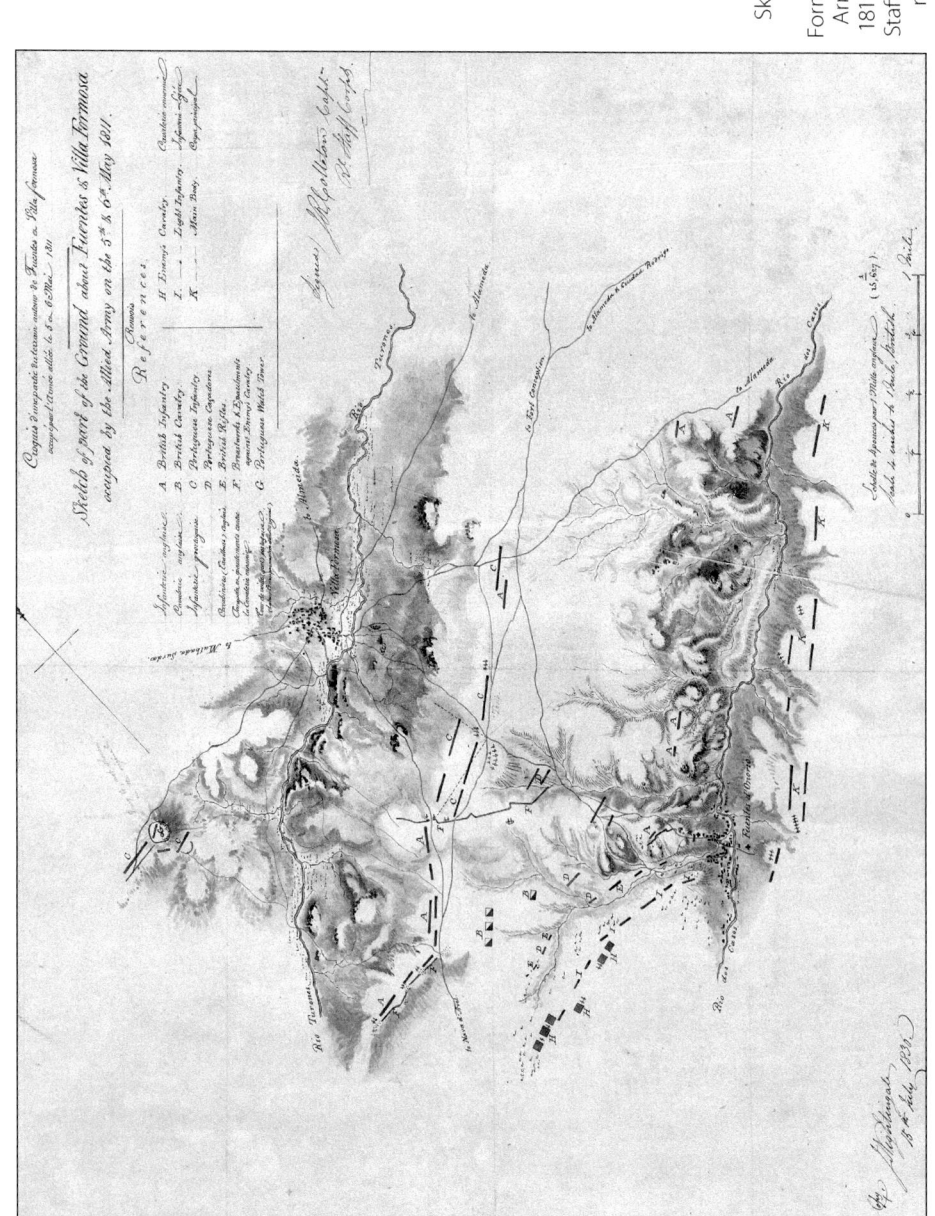

Sketch of Part of the Ground about Fuentes and Villa Formosa Occupied by the Allied Army on the 5th and 6th May 1811. Signed J R Colleton, Royal Staff Corps, 1811, 4 inches to the mile. (Author's collection)

and Badcock of the 14th Light Dragoons; Lieuts. Krauchenberg, Cordemann, and Wish of the 1st Hussars; Lieut. Eckersley of the Royal dragoons'.[38] Napier minimises the number of casualties from the battle. He wrote that the loss, '... of the enemy was estimated at five thousand, upon the erroneous supposition that four hundred dead were lying about Fuentes Oñoro [sic]. All armies make rash estimates on such occasions. Having had charge to bury the carcases immediately about the village, I found only one hundred and thirty bodies, one-third being British'.[39]

Despite extensive planning, Éblé informed Massena that there were only four cartridges per man left in reserve, which, when added to those remaining in the men's cartridge pouches, would give about 30 per man. This would be insufficient to engage with a determined enemy.[40] Oudinot states that the blame for the lack of ammunition and the delay in obtaining more lay squarely with Bessières. Massena ordered the immediate dispatch of the wagons to Ciudad-Rodrigo to procure new provisions. However, Bessières informed him that he refused to let the wagons leave until the men had rested for a night, as they had been exhausted during the battle. 'Massena ... vehemently opposed the Guard's claims. Bessières remained inflexible, standing firm on his independence within the Army of Portugal'.[41] Noël confirms this situation and lays the blame squarely on those who, '... responsible for supplying the army, allowed [the ammunition] to arrive in half-empty caissons'.[42] Pelet suggests that Massena called a halt to the action in order to reorganise and prepare an attack for the following morning, but the attack was called off due to the lack of ammunition.[43]

The fighting faded early in the afternoon of the 5th, and by around 2:00 p.m. the battle was over. Delagrave recalled, '... around two o'clock in the afternoon, the firing ceased on both sides. Such was the outcome of that day, the glory of which undoubtedly belonged to us'.[44] Grattan wrote, 'By two o'clock the town was comparatively tranquil. The cannonading on the right of the line had ceased, but the enemy continued to fire on the town; this proceeding was attended with little loss to us, and was fatal to many of their wounded ... Towards evening the firing ceased altogether'.[45]

As the battle drew to an end, French cavalry covered the withdrawal of their artillery and voltigeurs. Cowell-Stepney wrote of the effect of Shrapnel's spherical case-shot:

> Lane opened three guns on them with spherical case-shot: the practice was excellent, the shells bursting within a hundred to a hundred and fifty yards from the head of their columns, creating chasms in their ranks, destroying and rolling over horses and riders, and drilling openings in their masses as

38   Wellington to the C-in-C, Villar Formoso, 14 May 1811, Gurwood, *Dispatches*, vol.5, p.13.
39   Napier, *History of the War in the Peninsula*, vol.3, p.153.
40   Maurice Girod de l'Ain, *Le Général Éblé (1758-1812)* (Paris: Berger-Levrault, 1893), p.81.
41   Oudinot, 'Souvenirs intimes', p.40.
42   Noël, *With Napoleon's Guns*, p.123.
43   *Victoires*, vol.21, p.341.
44   Delagrave, *Campagne*, p.212.
45   Grattan, *Adventures with the Connaught Rangers, 1809-1814*, p.71.

if cut down with scythes. The fourth shot sent them to the right about; and galloping off, they escaped the storm of lead and iron from our guns.[46]

Baron Jomini was to write that the French had fought at Fuentes de Oñoro as they had at Buçaco; in tight columns against a well-positioned enemy force.[47]

After the battle, Eadie walked through the village and, '… surveyed for a while this scene of desolation, I returned amidst serious reflections, to the place where our regiment lay, and spent the remainder of the day in such a manner as became as child of transitory existence.'[48] The battle was summed up by Major General Picton:

> During these operations the light division, under General Crawfurd, was rather roughly handled by the enemy's cavalry; and had this arm of the French army been as daring and active upon this occasion as they were when following us to the lines of Torres Vedras, they would doubtless have cut off the light division to a man, and probably have destroyed our cavalry; but they let the golden moment pass, and I hope they will never have another. Our loss has been very severe, more especially in the third division.[49]

At the end of each day, the dead and wounded had been removed from the village of Fuentes de Oñoro by both sides, to the best of their abilities. This perhaps accounts for the reduced numbers that Napier saw after the battle was over. At the southern end of the position, Deputy Assistant Commissary George Head mentions that he, '… walked over the bed of the slain, though the dead were for the most part removed … French cavalry horses lay dead on the ground in considerable numbers'.[50]

Some units that came under fire suffered relatively few casualties, as was recorded by Lieutenant John Carss of the 2/53rd:

> About four o'clock p.m. the enemy tried to force our centre. They commenced with a very heavy cannonading and sharpshooting. The 53rd was in the centre, we were ordered forward to support our sharpshooters, who appeared to have the worst of it at that moment. We had about half a mile to advance. During the whole time the enemy were playing upon our regiment with seven pieces of cannon with ball and shell, and to the astonishment of every person looking on we had not one man killed, only one captain, one drummer and myself slightly wounded – so slightly that we would not allow ourselves to be returned Lord Wellington's despatches. When our regiment got to the ground pointed out, the enemy's sharpshooters gave

46   Cowell-Stepney, *Leaves from the Diary of an Officer of the Guards*, pp.95–96.
47   Jomini, *Guerre d'Espagne : Extrait Des Souvenirs Inédits du Général Jomini*, p.172.
48   Eadie, *Recollections of the Life of Robert Eadie*, p.103.
49   Robinson, *Picton*, vol.2, p.21.
50   George Head, *A Home Tour through Various Parts of the United Kingdom, a Continuation of the 'Home Tour through the Manufacturing Districts'. Also, Memoirs of an Assistant Commissary-General* (John Murray, 1837), p.260.

way, also their cannon. It was now about dusk, when the firing ceased on every part on both sides.[51]

The fact that these wounded were not included in the returns is reflected in Oman, who noted, 'No losses whatever' for the 6th Division.[52] The official return of dead, wounded and missing for the Allied army is recorded in Wellington's *Dispatches* as 235 killed, 1,234 wounded, and 317 missing.[53]

Casualties on the French side are more difficult to attribute to specific events. What is clear is that VI corps took a severe beating, with some 652 men lost on the 3rd and 944 on the 5th, as did IX corps with losses of 835 on the 5th.[54] However, some details are available: the 4e and 6e bataillons of the 82e ligne counted 37 officers and 570 men on 1 May.[55] By the end of the 5th, 10 officers had been killed or wounded, some 27 percent.[56] The 9e légère, having been heavily engaged in the attack on Fuentes de Oñoro on the 5th, lost five officers wounded and one killed.[57]

The depleted and exhausted Allied troops in Fuentes de Oñoro were withdrawn and fresh troops moved in. Grattan described the 88th moving out of the village one company at a time in order to deceive the French as to their intentions. His company being the first to move, he was intercepted by an apparently wounded Pakenham, who queried his movement. Grattan informed Pakenham that Colonel Mackinnon had arranged the withdrawal, but he would remain if ordered to:

'Oh no,' said he, 'the 88th have done enough for this day; but the regiment that replaces you would do well to bring a keg of ammunition, each man, in addition to his sixty rounds, for, while I have life, the town shall not be taken.' He was in a violent perspiration and covered with dust, his left hand bound round with his pocket-handkerchief.[58]

The Light Division was given the task of occupying the village and relieving the existing garrison.

On the 6th and 7th the armies remained in the positions reached at the end of the 5th. The Allied troops had begun to dig in along the ridgeline on the 5th, '... strengthening our right every hour by trenches, *trous de loup*, etc.'[59] The trenches

---

51 John Carrs, 'The 2nd/53rd in the Peninsular War: Contemporary Letters from an Officer of the Regiment', *Journal of the Society for Army Historical Research*, 26.105 (1948), p.12.

52 Oman, *A History of the Peninsular War*, vol.4, p.624.

53 Return of the killed, wounded, and missing in the battle at Fuentes de Oñoro, on the 3d and 5th May, 1811, Gurwood, *Dispatches*, vol.4, p.798 The Portuguese killed, wounded, and missing, are included in the above numbers.

54 Oman, *A History of the Peninsular War*, vol.4, p.630.

55 SHD : *Armée de Portugal: Situation 1er Mai 1811*.

56 Martinien, *Tableaux Des Officiers*, p.292; Arvers, *Historique du 82e Régiment d'infanterie de Ligne et du 7e Régiment d'infanterie Légère, 1684-1876*, p.118.

57 *Sous-Lieutenant* François killed, *Chef de Bataillon* Pianchet, *Capitaine* Pouthier, *Lieutenant* Migeon, *Sous-Lieutenant* Barberis, *Sous-Lieutenant* Soffréon wounded. Martinien, *Tableaux Des Officiers*, p.410.

58 Grattan, *Adventures with the Connaught Rangers, 1809-1814*, p.73.

59 Gomm, *Letters and Journals of Field Marshal Sir William Maynard Gomm*, p.218.

were extensive and made the Allied position on the high ground almost impenetrable. Cornet Hall wrote,

> The business of the day concluded … We bivouacked, as we had the night before, among the enclosures in the rear … The infantry passed the night on the ground they had occupied during the day, sheltering themselves as they could, or not at all: the poor Portuguese, having no great coats, huddled together, and looked miserable enough in the morning. The Guards built themselves neat huts of boughs and earth. The weather was luckily dry, and so warm that, as a French officer observed, there was no need of a battle to make it hotter.
>
> On the morning of the 6th we were on our former ground: some field works had been thrown up on our right … Massena kept his position, making an ostentatious display of his force, but showed no disposition to renew his attack.[60]

Massena's troops occupied the ground they had taken on the 5th, and a line of pickets was established between the two armies, each carefully observing the other. Ferey's, Conroux's and Claparède's divisions were encamped on the heights facing Fuentes de Oñoro, with Marchand, Mermet, and Solignac on the edge of the wood south of the village. Montbrun's forces were further south around Poço Velho. Kincaid observed the French establishing a six-gun battery opposite his position in the village, and this prompted much activity to strengthen the defences against artillery. He also recorded the parade of prisoners by the French, '… chiefly guardsmen and highlanders, whom they marched past the front of our position, in the most ostentatious way … and the day following, a number of their regiments were paraded in the most imposing manner, for review.'[61]

In his dispatch of 6 May, Massena reported his reason for withdrawing following the battle:

> During this day, when all the honour of arms remained with the army, it captured a thousand men, including a lieutenant colonel and many officers, and killed or wounded over 2,000 of the enemy. The army completely overran the enemy's right wing and gained more than a league of ground.
>
> The night following the battle, the enemy spent fortifying the summit of the plateau it occupies, constructing five large defensive works, positioning a significant amount of artillery, and digging trenches for skirmishers. Additionally, the enemy established barricades in the ravines and behind the rocks, as well as at the summits of the villages of Fuentes de Oñoro and Villar Formoso. In doing so, they called upon all the resources of fortification to guard against a direct and forceful assault.
>
> In order to capitalise on the advantages of this day and to feed the army, which, due to a lack of provisions, would have been forced to retreat, I had

---

60   Hall, 'Recollections in Portugal and Spain During 1811 and 1812', p.1543.
61   Kincaid, Adventures, p.81.

the convoy intended to resupply Almeida brought to the camp. My intention is to move closer to the fortress, withdraw its garrison, and destroy it, in accordance with the authorisation of His Majesty.[62]

The aim of delivering supplies to Almeida was abandoned. Consequently, Massena ordered that these provisions, currently gathered at Gallegos, be distributed among the army. *Maréchal* Marmont, duc de Raguse, arrived at the *armée de Portugal* on the 7th May and took command of VI corps. Marcel recalled, '… the duc de Raguse reviewed us, and we hoped that the battle would resume'.[63] Despite this enthusiasm, orders were issued around 11:00 p.m. to withdraw the army to Ciudad Rodrigo.[64] Wellington wrote to Liverpool on the 8th, 'In the course of last night the enemy commenced retiring from their position on the Dos Casas; and this morning, at daylight, the whole was in motion.' II corps started its move at 11:00 a.m. The 1e division crossed the Agueda at the Aldea de Partenobis ford, located near Castillejo de Martin Viejo, while the 2e division crossed the Agueda via the bridge at Puerto Seguro to proceed to San Felices, where it was to prepare to receive Almeida's garrison once it had been evacuated. VI corps moved towards Ciudad Rodrigo, pausing briefly around the heights of Carpio.[65] In his official dispatch to Liverpool, Wellington added detail to his previous commentary on the French withdrawal:

> The enemy retired on the 8th to the woods between Espeja, Gallegos, and Fuentes, in which position the whole army were collected on that day and yesterday, with the exception of that part of the 2d corps which continued opposite Almeida. Last night the whole broke up, and retired across the Azava, [sic] covering their retreat by their numerous cavalry; and this day the whole have retired across the Agueda, leaving Almeida to its fate. The 2d corps retired by the bridge of Barba de Puerco, and the ford of Val de Espino on the Agueda.
>
> Our advanced posts are upon the Azava and on the Lower Agueda, and the army will be tomorrow in the cantonments on the Dos Casas.[66]

Harry Smith reflected the thoughts of many on the Allied side, 'After the battle of Fuentes d'Onoro, [sic] the French retired unmolested, for we were glad to get rid of them. As they had such a formidable body of cavalry, on that open country we literally could not molest them.'[67]

The withdrawal of the *armée de Portugal* thus left Almeida exposed to the full force of the Allied army, and a formal siege was expected.

---

62 Le Maréchal Massena, Prince d'Essling, à S. A. le Prince de Wagram et de Neufchâtel, Major Général, Torres Novas, le 6 Mars, 1811, Gurwood, *Dispatches*, vol.4, p.828.

63 Marcel, *Campagnes du Captaine Marcel du 69e de ligne en Espagne et en Portugal (1808-1814)*, p.137.

64 SHD: *Correspondance*, 7C12.

65 Fririon, *Journal Historique*, p.213.

66 Wellington to Liverpool, Villar Formoso, 10 May, 1811, Gurwood, *Dispatches*, vol.5, p.3.

67 Smith, *Autobiography*, p.49.

12

You Are No Longer Massena

At about 10:00 a.m. on 11 May, Lieutenant Cuyler of the Royal Dragoons arrived at Allied Headquarters in Villar Formoso.[1] He had the unenviable task of delivering a verbal report directly to Wellington of the escape of the French garrison from Almeida. Major General Alexander Campbell, via Cuyler, provided Wellington with very little information regarding the current situation and requested orders. Wellington replied, in writing, 'It is not easy to forward orders upon so indistinct a representation of the situation in which you find yourself, and I had hoped that I should receive some report from you in writing.'[2] The reaction to the escape of the garrison would have lasting repercussions in the army.

With the advance of the French on 2 May, Wellington concentrated his forces in preparation to shield the fortress, but this meant the blockade itself was reduced to a minimum force. Campbell's 6th Division was withdrawn from the blockade and moved into the battle line, and Pack's Brigade and Barbacena's cavalry were left to observe Almeida. The blockading troops consisted of three regiments of Portuguese infantry (the 4° Caçadores, 1° and 16° Infantaria) with the 2nd (Queen's) Foot attached from Burne's Brigade of the 6th Division. Barbacena's cavalry brigade consisted of the 4° and 10° Cavallaria, the combined total of which amounted to approximately 300 men.[3] Two Portuguese artillery pieces were attached.

Pack, an experienced brigade commander who had worked closely with Craufurd and the Light Division, seemed to be feeling under some pressure as he wrote, 'A more distressingly anxious command I never had.'[4] His brigade and Barbacena's cavalry had been selected for this role since the general exhaustion and poor condition of the men meant they were considered unfit for battle.

Once the *armée de Portugal* had been repulsed at Fuentes de Oñoro, Wellington ordered the resumption of the full blockade of the fortress. Instructions were issued on 10 May for the 6th Division and Pack's Brigade to reestablish the positions around Almeida at Cinco-Vilas, Malpartida, Vale de la Mula and Junça. 'The 6th

---

1   When editing Wellington's *Dispatches*, Gurwood must have mistranscribed the name as there's no Cuyler in the 1st Dragoons in the army list, Conyers or Keilly are the only similar names.
2   Wellington to Major General Alex Campbell, Villar Formoso, 11 May, 1811, 10½ A.M, Gurwood, *Dispatches*, vol.5, p.4.
3   Soriano, *Historia Da Guerra Civil*, vol.3, p.417.
4   Quoted in S. G. P. Ward, 'Brenier's Escape from Almeida, 1811', *Journal of the Society for Army Historical Research*, 35.141 (1957), p.27.

division resumed the duty of the blockade of Almeida on that evening, and Major Gen. Sir W. Erskine was ordered to send a battalion to Barba de Puerco [sic] to guard the bridge there'.[5] Campbell resumed command of the blockade and moved Pack's troops back to Cinco-Vilas.[6] Campbell's reasons for wanting command of the blockade were explained by Charles Stewart:

> General Campbell, a zealous and enterprising officer, was exceedingly desirous that the arrangement of the blockade should be intrusted entirely to himself; and being ambitious, as it was but natural that he should, of the honour of reducing this important place through his own skill, he requested and obtained permission to conduct all details without any interference.[7]

Pack reported that, 'The picquets were placed in 3 divisions, denominated those of right, centre and left … each division under a Field officer in the fullest manner empowered to act for himself without waiting for my orders.'[8] The orders to Erskine were sent by Murray:

> Lord Wellington desires that you will be so good as to push one Battalion of infantry to your left to the distance of two or three miles beyond Fort Conception. This battalion should place pickets at the passes over the Dos Casas riverlet which lead from the side of Villar de Ciervo and Barba del Puerco towards Malpartida, and should communicate to the rear with Br.Gen. Pack at Malpartida. It had better be moved to its station at dusk and should take care to conceal its post and its force as much as possible from the enemy.[9]

Wellington was later to write, 'Major Gen. Sir W. Erskine was ordered to send a battalion to Barba de Puerco to guard the bridge there, which had been previously ordered, and had been posted to observe the passages of the Dos Casas between Aldea del Obispo and Barba de Puerco.[10] The order was clear in that it identified the bridge at Barba del Puerco as a vulnerable point, and posting a battalion there would rectify the problem. The 4th (King's Own) Foot should have been moved the previous day into this position by Erskine.[11] However, on the night of the escape, they were near a bridge over the Dos Casas, which S.G.P. Ward identifies as the bridge between Villar de Ciervo and Aldea del Obispo, directly east of Almeida at a distance of more than five miles from the fortress and seven from the bridge at Barba del Puerco.[12]

---

5   Wellington to Liverpool. Villar Formoso, 15 May 1811, Gurwood, *Dispatches*, vol.5, p.20.
6   Major Gen. Alex. Campbell to Wellington. Malpartida, 12 May, 1811, Gurwood, *Dispatches*, vol.5, n.14.
7   Vane, *Narrative of the Peninsular War from 1808 to 1813*, pp.517–518.
8   Pack to Campbell, Cinco Villas, 12 May, 1811, Gurwood, *Dispatches*, vol.5, n.15.
9   NLS: Adv.MSS.46-4-16-126, 'The Murray Papers'; also quoted in Hunter, *Wellington's Scapegoat*, pp.141–142.
10   Wellington to Liverpool. Villar Formoso, 15 May, 1811, Gurwood, *Dispatches*, vol.5, p.18.
11   Wellington to Liverpool. Villar Formoso, 15 May 1811, Gurwood, *Dispatches*, vol.5, p.19.
12   Ward, 'Brenier's Escape from Almeida, 1811', p.30.

Brenier Escapes

Having failed to get the convoy of supplies into Almeida, Massena appealed for volunteers to take a message to Brenier, offering a reward of 6,000 francs if successful. Several soldiers came forward, and a staff officer conducted a draw.[13] Copies of the message were made on small pieces of paper, which the soldiers were instructed to eat if they were caught. *Chasseur* André Tillet of the 6e légère departed armed with two loaded pistols given to him by his *colonel*.[14] He was able to make the journey safely into Almeida, reaching it on the 7th. The message instructed Brenier to destroy the fortress and all matériel, and evacuate the garrison by withdrawing to Barba del Puerco.[15] Brenier was to inform Massena of the receipt of the order by firing salvos from the fortress guns, fired five minutes apart, beginning at 10:00 p.m.[16]

Brenier planned to escape in two columns: the left, led by Brenier himself, was composed of the 5e bataillon of the 82e Ligne. It would be preceded by the grenadier company under *capitaine* Foucault, and the voltigeur company under *capitaine* Berthier. These elite troops would clear the way for the rest of the column. The right column was led by two companies of gunners under *capitaine* Lechêne; this column, made up of various detachments from the VI and VIII corps, was commanded by *chef de bataillon* Thruiller, commander of the engineers of IX corps. *Chef de bataillon* Morlet was left in command of the rearguard which comprised two companies of sappers and the miners who were ordered to set the explosives and to prevent the inhabitants from disturbing the operation whilst the troops withdrew.[17] The baggage was the last to leave with the intention of delaying any pursuit by offering an easy chance of loot. All the soldiers were under strict orders to maintain silence and not respond to enemy fire. Reynier established a force at San Felices prepared to receive the garrison.[18]

Around midnight on the night of 10/11 May, an explosion was heard emanating from Almeida. However, there had been similar noises over previous evenings, as well as almost constant skirmishing, and this seems to have lulled the Allied commanders and many soldiers into a false sense of security. Following the explosion in the early morning of 11 May, Wellington noted:

> ... the Queen's regt. in particular, and the other troops employed in the blockade, were induced to believe that the explosion which they heard on the morning of the 11th was of the same description with those which they

---

13   Delagrave, *Campagne*, p.215.
14   Marcel, *Campagnes du Captaine Marcel du 69e de Ligne En Espagne et En Portugal (1808-1814)*, p.137.
15   Known today as Puerto Seguro. The bridge there is called Puente de los Franceses, or the French Bridge.
16   Koch, *Mémoires de Massena*, vol.7, p.547.
17   Le général Brenier au Maréchal Marmont, Duc de Raguse, Commandant en Chef l'Armée de Portugal. Salamanque, le 17 Mai, 1811, Gurwood, *Dispatches*, vol.5, appendix 1.
18   Le général de division Regnier au Maréchal Massena, Prince d'Essling, Duc de Rivoli. Au pont de S. Felices el Grande, ce 11 Mai, 1811, Gurwood, *Dispatches*, vol.5, appendix 1.

had heard on the preceding nights; and the Queen's regt. did not move at all, nor the other troops, till the cause of the explosion had been ascertained.[19]

The French columns advanced from the São João de Deus bastion and came initially against the outposts of the 1° Infantaria under *Major* Dursbach. Hearing the explosion and subsequent firing, Pack advanced with 80 men of the outpost, but, realising the strength of the enemy column, soon sent for the rest of the regiment. Pack reported that, 'The killed and wounded on the ground … shows that picquet did its duty.'[20] He remarked:

> So precious, indeed, did the moments appear, I was myself going to the Queen's [2nd]; but reflecting that the fire which I could and did constantly keep up all the way, together with stragglers and prisoners, would sufficiently mark our track and bring support, and that I might probably lose myself and fail in both objects, I therefore determined to remain in sight of the enemy. His march was rapid and compact, and made in perfect silence. He was admirably guided through a very intricate country by paths but little frequented. No insult to his column could induce him to act on the offensive or fire a single shot before daylight.[21]

Other observers remarked that the French columns moved quickly and without noise, and also without responding to the musketry aimed at them.[22] Their movements were marked by the dead and wounded, but no resistance was offered. Major General Campbell took eight companies of the 36th Foot in pursuit, the light company becoming lost, and the grenadier company detached to the right.[23] A local peasant indicated to Captain Auchmuty the route taken by the French. The French column was delayed briefly between Villar de Ciervo and Barba del Puerco when a detachment of the Royal Dragoons commanded by Captain Purvis was found in Villar de Ciervo and mustered by Captain Beresford, DAQMG of the 6th Division. This cavalry skirmished with the column and slowed it sufficiently for the pursuing Allied troops to make up the ground between them, as the pursuing Portuguese had now been reduced to *Major* Dursbach, one sergeant and 10 men. Brenier reported:

> At dawn, I found myself between Villar de Ciervo and Barba de Puerco, heading toward the Agueda. Between these villages, before reaching the ridge, enemy cavalry caught up on my right, skirmishing as they advanced parallel to us, either to delay us or signal our route to pursuing troops. I saw troops occupying ridges to my left, manoeuvred to avoid them, and finally reached a path leading to the bridge at San Felices.[24]

19   Wellington to Liverpool. Villar Formoso, 15 May, 1811, Gurwood, *Dispatches*, vol.5, p.19.
20   Pack to Campbell, Cinco Villas, 12 May, 1811, Gurwood, *Dispatches*, vol.5, nn.15–16.
21   Pack to Campbell, Cinco Villas, 12 May, 1811, Gurwood, *Dispatches*, vol.5, nn.15–16.
22   Vane, *Narrative of the Peninsular War from 1808 to 1813*, p.519.
23   Campbell to Wellington, Malpartida, 12 May, 1811, Gurwood, *Dispatches*, vol.5, n. 14.
24   Le général Brenier au Maréchal Marmont, Duc de Raguse, Commandant en Chef l'Armée de Portugal. Salamanque, le 17 Mai, Gurwood, *Dispatches*, vol.5, p.769.

The 8° Infantaria were positioned at Junça to the South-East of Almeida. On hearing the explosion, they were quickly gathered and were led to the Barba del Puerco bridge by *Tenente-coronel* Douglas, a march of more than 12 miles. Reaching the bridge before the first French soldiers, all was peaceful except for a small cavalry picquet. Douglas thought the French had gone a different way and decided to search for them. Consequently, a significant opportunity to prevent the French escape was lost. To add to the missed opportunities that night, Erskine had sent an officer from Aldea del Obispo to Almeida, a round trip of some 10 miles, to ascertain the cause of the noise at the fortress before he sent the light companies of the 5th Division in pursuit of the French column.[25]

The rearguard of the garrison had closed up on the left column as it approached the river. Harassed by the Allied troops, Brenier recognised that forces on the other side of the river were French. A detachment from II corps at San Felices, consisting of the 31e légère and the *voltigeurs* of the 4e ligne, had been moved to the bridge at Barba del Puerco to cover the retreat of the garrison as they crossed. Had Erskine effected the orders received from Murray on the 9th and Wellington on the 10th, a full battalion of British infantry would have been present at the bridge. This force might have been capable of holding off the French column until reinforcements had arrived. However, the route was clear for Brenier and his men.

The column came under attack from the eight companies of the 36th Foot in pursuit, commanded by Lieutenant Colonel Cochrane, and a detachment of nine companies of the 4th commanded by Lieutenant Colonel Bevan. Wellington observed that, '... the flank battalions of the 5th division which Sir W. Erskine had detached from Aldea del Obispo (so long after he had heard the explosion, that he had sent an officer to Almeida, between 5 and 6 miles, to ascertain what it was, and this officer had returned), arrived nearly at the same time.'[26]

Some of the British infantry, carried away by the pursuit, crossed the bridge but were quickly overwhelmed by the French, losing some 17 men as prisoners. Wellington blamed Cochrane for the losses, and wrote to the divisional commander, Campbell, stating, 'This advance ... and his passage of the bridge, was an imprudence to which all the losses of the day must be attributed.'[27] Brenier reported that 1,000 men had made it back, but many had been lost, including approximately 150 killed and 200 prisoners.[28]

The many missed opportunities would trigger questions about the failure to send orders on promptly after they had been received. Wellington complained:

> ... I have to reproach myself for not having been on the spot ... I did not think it probable that the attempt to escape would be made; and having employed 2 divisions and a brigade, to prevent the escape of 1400 men ... the necessity of my attending personally to this operation, after I had been

25   Wellington to Liverpool. Villar Formoso, 15 May, 1811, Gurwood, *Dispatches*, vol.5, p.21.
26   Wellington to Liverpool, Villar Formoso, 15 May, 1811, Gurwood, *Dispatches*, vol.5, p.21.
27   Wellington to Campbell, Villar Formoso, 15 May, 1811, Gurwood, *Dispatches*, vol.5, p.15.
28   Le général Brenier au Maréchal Marmont, Duc de Raguse, Commandant en Chef l'Armée de Portugal. Salamanque, le 17 Mai, 1811, Gurwood, *Dispatches*, vol.5, appendix. 1.

the whole day on the Azava, did not occur to me. However, it is that alone in the whole operation in which I have to reproach myself, as every thing [sic] was done that could be done in the way of order and instruction.[29]

On 12 May Wellington wrote to Beresford, 'I think the escape of the garrison of Almeida (although we have taken and destroyed a good lot of them) is the most disgraceful military event that has yet occurred to us. Excepting a few cavalry, which I believe crossed this morning, the whole French army have crossed the Agueda, and quitted Ciudad Rodrigo.'[30] Wellington wrote to his brother on 15 May, furious at the escape of the garrison, but naming no individual as blameworthy: 'I begin to be of opinion, with you, that there is nothing on earth so stupid as a gallant officer. They had about 13,000 men to watch 1400 ... There they were all sleeping in their spurs even; but the French got off.'[31]

The 'gallant' officer in question seems to be Lieutenant Colonel Cochrane of the 36th who crossed the bridge at Barba del Puerco in the face of opposition by units of Reynier's II corps. Campbell reported to Wellington that the '... ill timed gallantry of [Cochrane], untempered by prudence ...' resulted in the capture of one officer and 15 men of the 36th and 4th, with 19 men killed or wounded.[32] Harry Smith wrote, 'My long friend Ironmonger, [sic] then of the Queen's ... was grievously to blame.'[33] Lieutenant Colonel William Iremonger, 2nd Foot, was known as a strict disciplinarian but an unsatisfactory leader and commander. Complaints had been made against him regarding his conduct. Overall, the battalion was not in a fit state for campaigning and was still suffering from the effects of Walcheren fever when it sailed for the Peninsula.[34] Iremonger had already arranged to sell his commission, so he may have been complacent in his actions, anticipating his departure from the Peninsula.

Following the publication of Wellington's dispatch of 15 May, a controversy arose around responsibility for the escape of Brenier's men. Some saw the dispatch as blaming Lieutenant Colonel Charles Bevan for not reaching the bridge in time. Many names were put forward for the blame to be attached, from Erskine and Campbell to Wellington himself.[35] Some blamed Erskine for not transmitting the order from Murray until late that night. When Bevan received the order, it was early morning, and he did not begin his movement until approximately 3:00 a.m., reaching the bridge at Barba del Puerco at around 6:00 a.m. Bevan wrote to Dunlop on the 11th:

29   Wellington to Liverpool, Villar Formoso, 15 May, 1811, Gurwood, *Dispatches*, vol.5, p.21.
30   Wellington to Beresford, Villar Formoso, 12 May, 1811, Gurwood, *Dispatches*, vol.5, p.6.
31   Wellington to William Wellesley Pole, Villar Formoso, 15 May, 1811. Wellington, *Supplementary Despatches*, vol.7, p.123.
32   Campbell to Wellington. Malpartida, 12 May, 1811, Gurwood, *Dispatches*, vol.5, pp.14–15.
33   Smith, *Autobiography*, p.48.
34   Andrew Bamford, *Sickness, Suffering, and the Sword: The British Regiment on Campaign, 1808-1815* (Norman: University of Oklahoma Press, 2013), pp.74–76.
35   Natalia Griffon de Pleineville, 'L'evasion de La Garnison d'Almeida', *Gloire & Empire*, 42 (2012), pp.81–99; John Timewell, Willoughby Verner, 'The Diary of a Private Soldier in the Peninsular War', *Macmillan's Magazine*, 77 (1897), p.5; Ward, 'Brenier's Escape from Almeida, 1811'.

… I arrived here with the 4th Regiment about 6 this morning. And further, as a reason for my not having marched last night, that, although I had ascertained that one party of the enemy's troops had crossed the river, I was by no means certain that others were not moving in the same direction. I therefore thought it might be more essential to retain my position at the bridge and march in the morning, which I accordingly did, having sent a patrol from the Portuguese to reconnoitre Barba de Puerco.[36]

Bevan was so hurt by what he saw as a blemish on his honour that he committed suicide on 8 July 1811. Brenier, on the other hand, was commended for his bravery in bringing out the garrison and destroying the fortress.

Both Massena and Wellington had some extraordinarily capable commanders, but they were also subject to the incompetence or inability of some of their subordinates. Massena had been given an impossible task, and while trying to achieve it, had to handle unruly and vainglorious generals. Wellington had similar problems, as he stated in his own words: 'I certainly feel, every day, more and more the difficulty of the situation in which I am placed. I am obliged to be everywhere, and if absent from any operation, something goes wrong.'[37]

Massena

Foy returned to the *armée de Portugal* on 10 May carrying several dispatches from Paris. He handed over a letter to Massena who noted that the envelope had been partially torn. Observing that the letter could have been read, Massena asked if it contained his recall to France. Foy remained silent and then left to deliver other dispatches to the Bessières. The letter contained several documents, one of which informed him that *maréchal* Marmont, duc de Raguse, had been appointed commander of VI corps, and Foy had been promoted to *général de division* and been given command of the 1e division of VI corps.[38] In a letter dated 17 April, Massena was criticised by Napoleon, via Berthier, for almost every aspect of the campaign he had undertaken, from the loss of Coimbra to the final evacuation of Portugal:

> The Emperor, prince, has charged me to say that he expects more from your energy and from the opinion which the glorious events to which you have so often taken part have given him of you. The Emperor has repeated to you what his intentions were. At the distance he is, he cannot add anything to them; but his Majesty is saddened, and we are all sorry to see the army withdraw before the English, who are so inferior in number.[39]

---

36   NLS: Adv.MSS.46-2-12-220Murray, 'The Murray Papers'.
37   Wellington to Liverpool, Villar Formoso, 15 May, 1811, Gurwood, *Dispatches*, vol.5, p.21.
38   Girod de l'Ain, *Vie Militaire du Général Foy*, p.361. Paris, 15 Avril 1811. Pièces Justificatives No 48.
39   Koch, *Mémoires de Massena*, vol.7, p.604, 17th April 1811, Pièces Justificatives No XVI.

That evening, Foy dined with Massena. During dinner, Bessières arrived carrying the letter of recall which Berthier had sent via him, written on 20 April. It read:

> The Emperor, Marshal prince d'Essling, having judged it advisable to give the command of his army of Portugal to the Marshal duc de Raguse, His Majesty's intention is that immediately after you have handed over your command, you will return to Paris. The Emperor expressly orders that you bring with you only your son and one other of your aides-de-camp. Colonel Pelé, [sic] all your other aides-de-camp, and all staff officers must remain with the Duke of Ragusa.[40]

Massena then erupted in violent reproaches against Foy, accusing him of ingratitude and admonishing him for supposedly opening the letter. Foy was also accused of colouring Napoleon's view of Massena's behaviour. Foy firmly rejected the accusation of impropriety, but was stung by the allegation. He would write a long letter to Massena, explaining the situation, 'Whatever happens, Monseigneur, and whatever your opinion of me, I will constantly do justice to your campaign in Portugal … If fortune brings me back under your orders again, my faculties and my life will be devoted, Monseigneur, to erasing in the mind of Your Highness the unfavourable impressions which I have the misfortune to have caused him.'[41]

Massena handed over command to Marmont and began his ignominious journey back to Paris. Noël wrote:

> … if there were some who were gratified by this disgraceful incident, this was not true of most of the officers and soldiers, who gave full credit to the strength of character displayed by our commander-in-chief throughout this difficult war. They did not blame him either for our failure or our sufferings. His departure did nothing to appease an unhappiness that verged on anger. If, by striking at him, Napoleon had wished to turn him into a scapegoat, then he was mistaken for it was he himself whom the army blamed for its troubles.[42]

Noël might be overstating somewhat the general feeling of the army, but there was still a significant number of men loyal to their old *maréchal*.

Once Massena returned to France, he was subject to more demeaning behaviour from his Emperor. Napoleon at first refused to receive him, but finally agreed to meet him, exclaiming, 'Well! Prince d'Essling, you are no longer Massena?'[43] This expression mirrored those of the senior commanders when Massena was appointed to the command of the *armée de Portugal* in 1810, 'Foy observed that he was, "… no longer the Massena with the sparkling eye …" Bonnal commented, "… Massena, at

---

40   Koch, *Mémoires de Massena*, vol.7, p.558.
41   Le général Foy au maréchal Massena, Salamanque, 14 Mai 1811. Pièces Justificatives No 49, Girod de l'Ain, *Vie Militaire du Général Foy*, pp.361–364.
42   Noël, *With Napoleon's Guns*, p.123.
43   Koch, *Mémoires de Massena*, vol.1, p.LVI.

the moment when he received the command of the army of Portugal, was no more than the shadow of Massena of Zurich and Genoa".[44]

On being interviewed by Napoleon, de Baudus reported:

> I will never forget the effect that the tone of disparagement had on me when he spoke to me in Cherbourg in 1811 about Marshal Massena's conduct during the Battle of Fuentes de Onoro; [sic] the just discontent caused by the lack of success in this matter, which I had come to report on behalf of Marshal Bessières, cannot excuse the inappropriate expressions he used.[45]

Wellington was later to rate Massena as the ablest opponent he faced.[46] But Massena was from a different mould than Wellington. The son of a Niçois merchant, he had served on board a ship before joining the army and rising to the rank of *adjudant-chef* in the Régiment Royal-Italien. Because of his lowly origins, he could rise no further and left the army in 1789. He joined the revolutionary army in 1791, where origins and humble birth were no bar to promotion. By the next year had risen to *colonel*, reaching *général de division* in 1793. He was made *maréchal* in 1804. He had a reputation as an aggressive and tactically astute commander, almost the equivalent of Napoleon, certainly during the early part of their respective careers. On St Helena, in 1815, Napoleon said, 'Massena was endowed with extraordinary courage and firmness, which seemed to increase in excess of danger. When conquered, he was always as ready to fight the battle again as though he had been the conqueror.'[47] In contrast, he commented that Ney was a, '... common place kind of [General], having no recommendation save personal courage.'[48]

Massena's level of activity during the 1810–1811 campaign had ebbed and flowed. From a sluggish start, he had occasionally displayed the behaviour for which he was best known: courage and action. At other times, he was slow to act, reluctant to make decisions and, if some of the more scurrilous stories are to be believed, happier relaxing than commanding. Probably the gravest moment for Massena was his dismissal of Ney following their confrontation during the final stages of the retreat from Santarém. Junot and Reynier, amongst others, had written to Massena during the abortive advance, complaining of the lack of food as had Ney. Massena needed to retain discipline, but also needed to listen to reason. Napoleon's words were indicative of the temper of Massena, that he could be indomitable, but he needed to lead as well as to command. The use of the two verbs is not mutually exclusive, but neither are they synonymous. Command of the situation, recognising the state of his army, might have been better demonstrated by continuing the withdrawal, but his relations with Ney had become untenable. Both *maréchaux* needed to demonstrate true

44   White, *The Key to Lisbon*, p.74.
45   de Baudus, *Études Sur Napoléon*, vol.2, p.295.
46   Stanhope, *Notes of Conversations with the Duke of Wellington, 1831-1851*, p.46.
47   Emmanuel-Auguste-Dieudonné Las Cases, *Memorial de Sainte Hélène: Journal of the Private Life and Conversations of the Emperor Napoleon at Saint Helena* (London: Colburn, 1823), vol.1, pt.1, p.295.
48   Emmanuel-Auguste-Dieudonné Las Cases, *Memorial de Sainte Hélène*, vol.2, pt.1, p.231.

leadership, one by compromise and the other with consideration. Neither did, and the results for the common soldiery were next to calamitous.

After Napoleon's abdication following Waterloo, Wellington met Massena at a dinner held by Marshal Soult, then Minister of War:

> I knew Massena, afterwards, well at Paris; and met him first at a dinner at Marshal Soult's, who was then Minister of War. In the course of our talk I reminded him of his former discussion with D'Alorna and Pamplona, to which he replied, *Ce sont deux mauvais coquins* (These are two bad scoundrels).
>
> Massena was much excited at first seeing me, made a great noise, and greeted me very cordially. *Ah, Monsieur le Maréchal, que vous m'avez fait passer des mauvais momens!* (Ah, Marshal, you've given me some difficult times!) And he declared to me that I had not left him one black hair on his body; he had turned grey, he said, all over. I answered that I thought we had been pretty even – things nearly balanced between us. No, he said, how near you were taking me two or three times – which I was.[49]

Despite Napoleon's previous glowing comments regarding Massena's military capabilities, he also criticised him for his avarice and proclivity for involving himself too much with female company whilst on campaign. Regardless of his detractors, he maintained his principles even under pressure to do otherwise. Massena had been part of the court martial that put Ney on trial, but had refused to judge him. He retired following the Second Restoration and died in 1817.

Wellington

Many historians seem to consider Wellington some type of superhuman general, capable of performing without error. Nevertheless, in this campaign, he made numerous errors. Where he may differ from other generals is in accepting and working to correct those errors once they were identified. Making fewer mistakes than one's enemy is of great importance in war.

Wellington has been accused by some French writers of lacking ability and being timid. Pelet remarked he found Wellington, '… in this campaign and even elsewhere, to be quite unfamiliar with both strategy and tactics.'[50] Fririon wrote about Redinha, 'It can be stated that if Lord Wellington had been a less cautious commander, Mermet's division would have faced a considerable threat of being completely overwhelmed, as its position was challenging, with a defile at its rear serving as the sole avenue for retreat.'[51]

---

49   Stanhope, *Notes of Conversations with the Duke of Wellington, 1831-1851*, pp.162–163.
50   *Victoires*, vol.21, p.340.
51   Fririon, *Journal Historique*, p.149.

Pelet mentions the '... slowness and even the timidity with which the English army followed our retrograde movement.'[52] This misinterprets Wellington's intention. Rather than attempting to destroy the French in battle during their retreat, he was content to shepherd them out of Portugal and to inflict a defeat upon them if the opportunity arose. He knew that sickness and hunger had worn the *armée de Portugal* down while it waited outside Lisbon. The attrition that had begun there would inflict more casualties on the French without Wellington needing to risk a battle. He wrote, 'I'll fight them only where I am pretty sure of success.'[53] Wellington commanded the main British field army and were he to suffer a reverse, the opposition, both military and political, in Britain would demand his return, and probably that of the entire army.

Not all French commanders were as dismissive of Wellington's ability. *Général de division* Foy, writing of the Battle of Salamanca, might have been writing with Fuentes de Oñoro in mind: 'Until now we had had the opportunity to know [Wellington's] prudence, his choice of positions, his art in taking advantage of them; ... he waited for our movement before making his own'.[54] Picton, not known for his diplomacy or subtlety, summed up Wellington's overall approach in a letter to his uncle:

> Lord Wellington's plans throughout the pursuit appear to have been to avoid as much as possible a general engagement; for, although retreating, the enemy is still too strong for us to meet him on open ground. He is, in fact, more frightened than hurt, and more alarmed by what might have happened if he had stayed any longer in Portugal than by any real injury. In consequence, our movements have all been to keep up this alarm, by giving him no time for reflection, and, by constantly outflanking his position, compelling him either to continue his retreat, or give us battle at a disadvantage. Fortunately he has preferred the former; for the result of the latter would have depended a good deal upon the behaviour of our allies. Hitherto they have behaved very well, and will perhaps stand when it comes to a matter of importance ...[55]

Wellington wished to minimise his casualties. Thus, his 'cautious system' continued.[56] Napoleon's viewpoint, which very much supported Wellington's approach, was summed up when Foy reported, 'According to the Emperor, where things stand, Lisbon is Portugal. From Santarém we blockade the capital and force England into excessive expense, for an uncertain future. It is less strength than patience that will decide victory; it belongs to the army that can exist the longest.'[57]

---

52   Pelet, *The French Campaign in Portugal*, p.297.
53   Wellington to C. Arbuthnot, Alcobaça, 5 October 1810, Wellington, *Supplementary Despatches*, vol.6, p.612.
54   Girod de l'Ain, *Vie Militaire du Général Foy*, p.178.
55   Nava d'Aver, [sic] May 12th, 1811, Robinson, *Picton*, vol.2, pp.17–18.
56   White, *The Key to Lisbon* , ch.5.
57   Koch, *Mémoires de Massena*, vol.7, p.315.

Napoleon's idea of occupying the countryside around Lisbon failed to account for the lack of food available to the army and its complete isolation from communications with other French armies in Spain. As much as the French denuded the countryside around Santarem, so the British were shipping in food, supplies, and most importantly, fresh troops.

Wellington displayed the sort of activity of mind and body lacking from Massena's conduct during the campaign. In addition to his custom of riding to hounds when possible, he was also often in the saddle inspecting troops and locations. Paradoxically, however, it was as an administrator, working at his desk, where Wellington excelled. One just needs to read his dispatches to see not only his regard for his men's well-being, but his adept handling of the political situation both at home and in Portugal. It is true that his concern for his men's welfare was mostly in order to field the strongest force possible, but we can also discern some human concerns in the pages.

He was both a commander and a leader. He commanded his army, ensuring as far as possible that it had food, equipment, ammunition, and clothing suitable for its role in the field. He manoeuvred the army, mostly within its limits of endurance and capability. He also expected it to perform on the battlefield with discipline and determination. Despite many historians decrying his apparent lack of recognition of subordinates, one only needs to read a few dispatches to see that Wellington was free in his praise of units and individuals. Like most commanders, he was subject to his own bias, and also to the limits of what he could see when recording those he chose to praise. He was also willing to acknowledge genuine errors, such as Craufurd's near disaster with the Light Division near Almeida in July 1810.[58]

As a leader of men, he was not afraid to risk his safety riding along the front line in battle. He did not shirk the dangers, and he seemed to expect the same disregard for personal safety from his aides and subordinate commanders. He is usually thought of as a skilled tactician, but is regarded by some historians as a 'defensive' general. Many of Wellington's campaigns can be thought of as operationally aggressive and offensive, but perhaps tactically defensive, making the most of the characteristics of the army under his command. Wellington himself described his approach to a subordinate in India in the following terms, 'By defensive I do not mean that you should wait in any particular place till you should be attacked, but that you should attack any party that may come within ... your reach.'[59]

However, opinion is divided about Wellington's choice of position at Fuentes de Oñoro, or his conduct of the battle, and indeed the entire campaign. This is one area where historians should, in this author's opinion, be careful about criticising the actions of those who were there. Napier, an eyewitness, criticises the position as having only one avenue open for retreat: the bridge at Castello Bom.[60] Wellington was facing difficult circumstances against an enemy capable of quick recovery and manoeuvre. There was more than one enemy army to consider, but only one Allied army in the field capable of offering serious opposition to the French. Wellington

---

58   White, *The Key to Lisbon*, pp.113–118.
59   Michael Howard (ed.), *Wellingtonian Studies* (Aldershot: privately printed, 1959), ch.2.
60   Napier, *History of the War in the Peninsula*, vol.3, p.149.

was brutally honest concerning how close to disaster the Allied army under his command had come. He wrote, 'If Boney had been there, we should have been beaten.'[61] Cocks recalls that immediately after the battle, '... at his table [Wellington] thought he had never been in a worse scrape.'[62] Scovell recorded that Wellington did, '... confess that ... from the moment it began that he had committed an error in endeavouring to cover two ... roads to Lisbon – namely that by Almeida and the road by Sabugal – the latter he immediately abandoned & ... threw back his Right resting it on the Côa.'[63] Later, Wellington was more specific. In discussion with Baron Wimpfen and Francis Larpent, he explained that he had extended the Allied right flank too far but had rectified the situation without the French taking advantage of it.[64]

Fririon goes so far as to call the Allied deployment at Fuentes de Onoro, 'unmilitary'.[65] The position had the river Côa at its back, limiting Wellington's route of retreat in case of a reverse. According to French sources, the only real option, should the route to Almeida be blocked, was the bridge at Castelo Bom. Wellington had issued orders for the routes to be taken in the event of a French victory.[66] These orders moved the army south-westwards, but this route may have been compromised had Massena's attack on the 5th been successful. However, there was more than one bridge over the Côa. Additionally, Wellington's orders allowed for a retreat which, although it would unmask Almeida, would preserve the army. Presumably, he expected Massena to resupply Almeida and then withdraw to Spain.

Probably the most damning, and wholly inaccurate, description of Wellington's efforts in the Peninsula comes from A.G. Macdonell:

> Probably no general in history has ever had such an easy task as Wellington had. Working on interior lines, with a mercenary army, in a country where every peasant and priest was at once an ally, a source of information, and an active assassin, with a constant flow of supplies from England and with the complete command of the sea, the Duke of Wellington had the game in his hands, and yet it took him nearly six years to advance from Lisbon to the Pyrenees.[67]

This description echoes to some extent the comments of French writers. This particular quotation demonstrates in the most explicit fashion a wilful misunderstanding of strategy, operations and tactics. It also takes no account of that most important component of strategy, the enemy.

---

61   Wellington to the Right Hon. W. W. Pole, Quinta de S. João, 2nd July, 1811. *Supplementary Despatches*, vol.7, p.177.
62   Cocks, *Intelligence Officer in the Peninsula*, p.104.
63   TNA: WO 37/7a, Scovell, *Diary*, p.42.
64   Larpent, *The Private Journal of Judge-Advocate Larpent*, p.65.
65   Fririon, *Journal Historique*, p.201.
66   Villar Formoso, 3 May, 1811, 8 A.M., Gurwood, *Dispatches*, vol.4, p.784.
67   Archibald Gordon Macdonell, *Napoleon and His Marshals* (London: Macmillan & Co, 1934), p.130.

I hope that this account has shown that Wellington did not have such an easy task as Macdonell suggests. Massena, the terrain, the weather, and it must be said some of his allies and generals, made it amongst the most dangerous and complicated campaigns ever undertaken by Wellington, which gave him some bad times indeed.

Appendix 1

Fortnightly State of the Forces in Portugal, Villa Formosa, 1 May 1811[1]

Division	Brigade	Unit	Effective Strength					Guns
			Officers	Sgts	Drms	R&F	Total	
1st Division								
Lt Gen. Brent Spencer	1st Brigade	1/Coldstream Guards	31	60	18	831	940	
Maj. Gen. Miles Nightingall	Col. Edward Stopford	1/3rd Guards	24	65	16	854	959	
		Coy, 5/60th Rifles	2	3	1	38	44	
	2nd Brigade	2/24th Foot	20	26	14	309	369	
	Maj. Gen. Miles Nightingall	2/42nd Foot	28	26	17	376	447	
	Lt Col. Lord Blantyre	1/79th Foot	39	39	15	829	922	
		Coy, 5/60th Rifles	1	3	1	31	36	
	3rd Brigade	1/50th Foot	45	35	16	501	597	
	Maj. Gen. Kenneth Howard	1/71st Foot	42	27	10	404	483	
		1/92nd Foot	41	39	16	668	764	
		Coy, 5/60th Rifles	3	5	2	68	78	
	4th Brigade	1st KGL Line	37	30	13	442	522	
	Maj. Gen. Baron Löw	2nd KGL Line	30	28	10	416	484	
		5th KGL Line	29	29	12	352	422	
		7th KGL Line	21	25	14	350	410	
		Detachment 1 & 2 Light Battalion	5	4	1	76	86	
	Artillery	8th Battalion, RA						6 x 9-pdrs

1   TNA: WO 1/249. Artillery from Dickson, *The Dickson Manuscripts*, vol.3, for the year 1811, p.535.

Division	Brigade	Unit	Officers	Sgts	Drms	R&F	Total	Guns
				Effective Strength				
3rd Division								
Maj. Gen. Thomas Picton	1st Brigade	1/45th Foot	24	34	19	431	508	
	Col. Henry MacKinnon	1/74th Foot	24	24	16	421	485	
		1/88th Foot	32	38	19	600	689	
		3 Coys, 5/60th Rifles	6	13	2	162	183	
	2nd Brigade	2/5th Foot	28	36	20	420	504	
	Maj. Gen. Charles Colville	2/83rd Foot	33	24	17	386	460	
		2/88th Foot	28	25	19	395	467	
		94th Foot	31	39	15	457	542	
	Portuguese Brigade	9th Portuguese Line (2 bns)				910	910	
	Brig. Manley Power	21st Portuguese Line (2 bns)				740	740	
	Artillery	1st Regt, Portuguese Foot Artillery						6 x 9-pdrs
		2nd Reg, Portuguese Foot Artillery						6 x 6-pdrs
5th Division								
Maj Gen. Sir William Erskine	1st Brigade	3/1st Foot	34	37	20	576	667	
	Col. Andrew Hay	1/9th Foot	29	37	15	547	628	
		2/38th Foot	21	26	19	336	402	
		Coy, Brunswick Oels	3	4	1	61	69	
	2nd Brigade	1/4th Foot	30	45	14	519	608	
	Maj. Gen. James Dunlop	2/30th Foot	23	35	17	432	507	
		2/44th Foot	27	25	19	366	437	
		Coy, Brunswick Oels	2	3	2	60	77	
	Portuguese Brigade	3rd Portuguese Line (2 bns)				724	724	
	Brig. William Spry	15th Portuguese Line (2 bns)				556	556	
		8th Caçadores				484	484	

Division	Brigade	Unit	Effective Strength					Guns
			Officers	Sgts	Drms	R&F	Total	
	Artillery	7th Battalion, Royal Foot Artillery						6 x 6-pdrs
		1st Regiment, Portuguese Foot Artillery						6 x 6-pdrs
6th Division								
Maj. Gen. Alexander Campbell	1st Brigade	1/11th Foot	49	40	18	730	837	
	Col. Richard Hulse	2/53rd Foot	21	27	11	400	459	
		1/61st Foot	31	30	16	620	697	
		Coy, 5/60th Rifles	2	5	1	40	48	
	2nd Brigade	1/36th Foot	32	29	14	439	514	
	Col. Robert Burne	2nd Foot (at Almeida)	30	32	10	486	558	
	Portuguese Brigade	8th Portuguese Line (2 bns)				915	915	
	Brig. Baron Eben	12th Portuguese Line (2 bns)				1,222	1,222	
	Artillery	8th Battalion, Royal Foot Artillery						6 x 6-pdrs
		2nd Regiment, Portuguese Foot Artillery						6 x 6-pdrs
7th Division								
Maj Gen William Houston	1st Brigade	51st Foot	39	33	16	502	590	
	Maj Gen John Sontag	5 coys 85th Foot	22	24	9	332	387	
		Chasseurs Britanniques	31	43	15	750	839	
	Major General Alten	1st Light Battalion KGL	At Talavera do Real					
		2nd Light Battalion KGL	At Talavera do Real					
		9 coys Brunswick Oels	32	37	13	511	593	
	Portuguese Brigade	7th Portuguese Line (2 bns)					713	
	Brig. John Doyle	19th Portuguese Line (2 bns)					1,026	
		2nd Caçadores				442	442	
Light Division								
Brig. Gen. Robert Craufurd	1st Brigade	1/43rd Foot	27	44	18	655	744	

Division	Brigade	Unit	Officers	Sgts	Drms	R&F	Total	Guns
					Effective Strength			
	Lt Col. Thomas Beckwith	1/95th Rifles (4 Coys)	13	22	5	314	354	
		2/95th Rifles (1 Coy)	4	3	1	68	76	
		3rd Caçadores				447	447	
	2nd Brigade	1/52nd Foot	32	44	20	739	835	
	Col. George Drummond	2/52nd Foot	32	44	16	459	551	
		1/95th Rifles (4 Coys)	14	18	7	318	357	
		1st Caçadores				450	450	
	Portuguese Brigade	6th Portuguese Line (2 bns)				986	986	
	Brig. Charles Ashworth	18th Portuguese Line (2 bns)				1,130	1,130	
		6th Caçadores				423	423	
	Artillery	A Troop, Royal Horse Artillery						6 x 6-pdrs
Cavalry								
Maj Gen Stapleton Cotton	Cavalry Brigade	1st Dragoons	21	27	5	400	453	
	Maj. Gen. John Slade	14th Light Dragoons	21	30	4	388	443	
	Colonel Head	13th Light Dragoons	20	30	3	359	412	
	Cavalry Brigade	16th Light Dragoons	25	26	4	367	422	
	Lt Col. Frederick von Arentschildt	1st Hussars KGL	27	26	6	371	430	
	Cavalry Brigade	3rd Dragoons Guards	21	33	7	377	438	
	Col. De Grey	4th Dragoons	29	31	6	379	445	
	Portuguese Cavalry Brigade	4th Portuguese Dragoons				104	104	
	Brig. Count Barbacena	10th Portuguese Dragoons				208	208	
	Artillery	I Troop, Royal Horse Artillery						6 x 6-pdrs

Appendix 2

Situation des Troupes Composant l'Armée de Portugal, 1 May 1811[1]

Le maréchal Massena, commandant en chef
Le général de division Éblé, commandant en chef l'artillerie
Le général de division Lazowski, commandant en chef le genie
Le général de division Fririon, chef de l'état-major général
L'inspecteur aux revues Lambert, intendant général de l'armée

Grand quartier général

Etat-Major	58
Gendarmerie	132
Artillerie	209
Equipages Militaires	186
Genié	88
Marins	692

Army of the North (cavalry)		Bataillons/ Escadrons	Total
Maréchal Jean-Baptiste Bessières			
Imperial Guard Cavalry Brigade	Chevau-légers Lanciers de la Garde	2	340
Général de Brigade Louis Lepic	Chasseurs à Cheval de la Garde	2	222
	Grenadiers à Cheval de la Garde	2	185
	Mamluks de la Garde	1	69
Light Cavalry Brigade	1re Régiment provisoire de cavalerie légère		
Général de Brigade Pierre Watier	4e escadron 11e Chasseurs à Cheval	1	220
	4e escadron 24e Chasseurs à Cheval	1	193
	2e Régiment provisoire de cavalerie légère		
	4e escadron 12e Chasseurs à Cheval	1	172
	4e escadron 5e Hussards	1	165
			1,566

---

1   Main numbers from SHD: Situation des Troupes Composant l'Armée de Portugal for 1 May 1811, Carton C7/28. Situation of 1st May 1811, Koch, p.596. IX Corps from SHD: C7 28, 20 avril 1811. Armee du Nord from Oman.

II Corps	Bataillons/ Escadrons/ Cannon		noms des Officiers		Total	Chevaux presens
Général de Division Jean Reynier						
1e Division	Etat-major de la division					14
Général de Division Pierre Hugues Victoire Merle						
1e Brigade	2e légère		Colonel	Rameaux		15
Général de Brigade Jacques Thomas Sarrut		1e	cdb[2]	Puison	439	
		2e	cdb	Godiu	273	
		3e	cdb	Laporte	249	
					961	
	36e ligne		Colonel	Berlier		28
		1e	cdb	Maréchal	500	
		2e	cdb	Guidon	349	
		3e	Capitaine	Lagabe	350	
					1,199	
2e Brigade	4e légère		Colonel	Desgraviers		29
(Not listed, but probably commanded by colonel Desgraviers-Berthelot, 4e légère)		1e	cdb	Chapuzet	503	
		2e	Capitaine	Bertrand	376	
		3e	Capitaine	Flandin	392	
					1,271	
2e Division	Etat-major de la division					30
Général de Division Étienne Heudelet de Bierre						
1e Brigade	17e légère		Colonel	Beuret		18
Colonel Pinoteau		1e	cdb	Cordeilhac	302	
		2e	cdb	Fourlet	289	
		3e	cdb	Boulon	277	
					868	
	70e ligne		Colonel	Desmarix		26
		1e	cdb	Besson	448	
		2e	cdb	Lavigne	329	
		3e	cdb	Prévost	323	
					1,100	
2e Brigade	31e légère		Colonel	Gavotti		
Général de Brigade Jean Arnaud		1e	cdb	Aubers	644	
		2e	cdb	Gay	454	
		3e	cdb	Piovani	485	
					1,583	
	47e ligne		Colonel	*None listed*		
		1e	cdb	Cornebise	643	
		2e	cdb	Deleau	481	
		3e	cdb	Meyon	482	

---

2   cdb = *chef de bataillon*. cde = *chef d'escadron*.

II Corps		Bataillons/ Escadrons/ Cannon		noms des Officiers	Total	Chevaux presens
					1,606	
Cavalry Brigade	1e Hussards		Colonel	Merlin		
		1e	cde	Dagoreau	88	90
		2e	cde	Turot	66	63
		3e	cde	*None listed*	63	56
					217	**209**
	22e Chasseurs à Cheval		Colonel	Desfossis		
		1e	cde	André	123	100
		2e	cde	*None listed*	117	97
					240	**197**
	8e Dragons		Colonel	*None listed*		
		1e	cde	Devaux	111	110
		2e	cde	Legentil	148	150
					259	**260**
Artillerie et train						
1e Division						
	3e rég. à pied				69	6
	3e rég. à cheval				41	49
	2e batallion du train				87	75
					197	**130**
2e Division						
	3e rég. à pied	15e			49	7
	3e rég. à cheval	6e			65	45
	5e bataillon bis du train	3e			110	98
	6e bataillon bis du train	3e			41	55
					216	**205**
Parc de reserve						
	3e rég. à pied				171	21
	2e rég. à cheval				59	56
	ouvriers d'artillerie				44	5
	armouriers d'artillerie				8	
	2e bataillon bis du train				102	48
	5e bataillon bis du train				9	16
	6e bataillon bis du train				125	101
	10e bataillon bis du train				74	64

II Corps		Bataillons/ Escadrons/ Cannon	noms des Officiers	Total	Chevaux presens
	11e bataillon du princ du train			117	118
				709	**429**
	1e bataillon du sapeurs	6e		101	9
	1e bataillon du equipage	2e		72	77
	Mulets de bât			47	73
	Gendarmes impériaux			18	12
Materiel de l'artillerie					
	Bouches à feu	de 8		4	
		de 4		6	
		de 3		4	
		d'obusier		2	
	Assutre de rechange	de 8		1	
		de 4		1	
		d'obusier		1	
	Caisson	de 8		7	
		de 4		6	
		d'obusier		5	
		d'Infanterie		35	
	Chariots à Munitions			6	
	Forger			3	
Cartouches					
	Boulets	de 8		583	
		de 4		666	
		de 3		312	
		d'obusier		246	
	Balles	de 8		153	
		de 4		223	
		de 3		57	
		d'obusier		22	
		d'infanterie		596,174	
	Pierres à feu			52,604	

VI Corps	Bataillons/ Escadrons/ Cannon		noms des Officiers	Total	Chevaux presens
Général de Division Louis Henri Loison					
(Maréchal Ney is still listed as the *commandant en chef*)					
1e Division	Etat-major de la division				90
Général de Division Jean Gabriel Marchand					
1e Brigade	6e légère		Colonel	Molard	21
Général de Brigade Antoine de Maucune	1e	cdb	Tascher	448	
	2e	cdb	Delom	434	
	4e	cdb	Frossard	452	
				1,334	**0**
	69e ligne		Colonel	Fririon	40
	1e	cdb	Giraud	413	
	2e	cdb	Rolland	419	
	3e	cdb	Duthoya	421	
	4e	cdb	Descolignier	457	
				1,710	**0**
2e Brigade	39e ligne		Colonel	Chevenet	18
Général de Brigade Marcognet	1e	cdb	Lippe	424	
	2e	cdb	Maurice	378	
	3e	cdb	Herrenberger	388	
	4e	cdb	Poncoze	349	
				1,539	**0**
	76e ligne		Colonel	Chemineau	24
	1e	cdb	Genevay	383	
	2e	cdb	Portement	401	
	3e	cdb	Gleize	398	
	4e	cdb	Castillon	520	
				1,702	**0**
2e Division	Etat-major de la division				85
Général de Division Julien Augustin Joseph Mermet					
1e Brigade	25e légère		Colonel	de Conchy	
Général de Brigade Labassée	1e	cdb	Dupraz	602	
	2e	cdb	Preux	479	
	4e	cdb	*Not listed*	424	
				1,505	**0**
	27e ligne		Colonel	Menne	
	1e	cdb	Martin	453	
	2e	cdb	Colette	342	
	3e	cdb	Barral	421	
	4e	cdb	*Not listed*	335	
				1,551	**0**

VI Corps		Bataillons/ Escadrons/ Cannon		noms des Officiers	Total	Chevaux presens
2e Brigade	50e ligne		Colonel	Frappart		22
Général de Brigade Bardet		1e	cdb	Jacquinot	467	
		2e	cdb	Commant	556	
		4c	cdb	Boluz	304	
					1,327	**0**
	59e ligne		Colonel	Coste		23
		1e	cdb	Maulmont	479	
		2e	cdb	Ducheiron	457	
		3e	cdb	Darièr	469	
		4e	cdb	*Not listed*	333	
					1,738	**0**
3e Division	Etat-major de la division					64
Général de Division Claude François Ferey						
(Loison is still listed in the *1e mai situation*)						
1e Brigade	32e légère		Colonel	*None listed*		
(Ferey is still listed in the *1e mai situation*)		2e	cdb	Martinel	280	12
	Légion du Midi		Colonel	*None listed*		
		1e	cdb	Spring	385	7
	Légion Hanovrienne		Colonel	Herman		
		1e			608	19
	82e ligne		Major	Morel		
		4e	cdb	Lefizelier	300	10
		6e	cdb	Rocheron	307	6
					607	**16**
2e Brigade						
Colonel Béchaud	26e ligne		Colonel	*None listed*		
		4e	cdb	Guillemin	335	10
		5e	cdb	Cordier	315	6
		6e	cdb	*None listed*	299	6
					949	**22**
	66e ligne		Colonel	Béchaud		
		4e	cdb	Duchemin	450	10
		5e	cdb	Izambort	355	4
		6e	cdb	Vivarès	430	4
					1,235	**18**
Etat-major de la cavalerie						25
Cavalry Brigade	3e hussards		Colonel	*None listed*		
Colonel Pierre Mourier, 15e Chasseurs		1e	cde	Devienne	46	53
		2e	cde	*None listed*	38	33
		3e	cde	*None listed*	46	44

VI Corps		Bataillons/ Escadrons/ Cannon		noms des Officiers	Total	Chevaux presens
					130	**130**
	15e chasseurs		Colonel	Mouries		
		1e	cde		64	71
		2e	cde		42	47
		3e	cde	Gerbault	74	65
					180	**183**
Artillerie et train	Etat-major					80
1e Division	1e rég. à pied	14e comp	Capitaine	Michon	67	9
	Ouvriers	4e comp		*None listed*	4	
	5 bataillon princ. du train	1e comp	Lieutenant	Delamotte	75	83
		6e comp	Lieutenant	Perillur	79	89
					225	**172**
2e Division	1e rég. à pied	13e comp	Capitaine	Coger	80	9
	Ouvriers	4e comp			4	
	5 bataillon princ. du train	2e comp	Lieutenant	Champlan	72	43
		5e comp	Lieutenant	Girinon	84	90
		6e comp				2
					240	**144**
3e Division	3e rég. à pied	8e comp	Capitaine	Lichtniker	47	7
	Ouvriers	4e comp			2	
		9e comp			3	
	6 bataillon bis	4e comp	Lieutenant	Pommier	101	151
	10 bataillon princ. du train	2e comp	Lieutenant	Schmitt	36	33
					189	**191**
Cavalerie	2e rég. à cheval	5e comp	Capitaine	Binner	63	50
	10 bataillon princ. du train	4e comp	Lieutenant	Lafoureade	62	67
		5e comp			11	16
					136	**133**
Reserve	1e rég. à pied	5e comp	Capitaine	Audry	70	9
	5e rég. à pied	21e comp	Capitaine	Augé	80	9
	Ouvriers	4e comp	Capitaine	Moyeux	22	5
		9e comp			5	
		16e comp			6	
	5 bataillon princ. du train	Etat Major	Capitaine	Boileau	7	5
	10 bataillon princ. du train	Etat Major			5	1
		1e comp	Lieutenant	Morel	49	12
		2e comp			15	17
		3e comp	Lieutenant	Garnier	25	5

VI Corps		Bataillons/ Escadrons/ Cannon		noms des Officiers	Total	Chevaux presens
		4e comp			0	3
		5e comp	Lieutenant	Präun	49	43
		6e comp	Lieutenant	Gauthier	57	69
	12 bataillon princ. du train	2e comp			65	37
		4e comp			54	17
					509	**232**
	4 bataillon du sapeurs	2e comp		Dussard	104	8
	Gendarmerie			Pousignon	19	26
	Equipage Militaires	4e comp		Reboulin	50	27
	Mulets de bat			Banal	35	62

Materiel de l'artillerie

	Bouches à feu	
	de 8	6
	de 4	5
	d'obusier	6
	Assutre de rechange	
	de 8	3
	de 4	1
	d'obusier	2
	Caisson	
	de 8	26
	de 4	6
	d'obusier	24
	d'Infanterie	28
	Chariots à Munitions	7
	Forger	4

Cartouches

	Boulets	
	de 8	1,701
	de 4	595
	d'obusier	1,191
	Balles	
	de 8	554
	de 4	249
	d'obusier	107
	d'infanterie	333,995
	Pierres à feu	56,423

VIII Corps		Bataillons/ Escadrons/ Cannon		noms des Officiers	Total	Chevaux presens
Général de Division Jean-Andoche Junot						
Etat-major du 8e Corps						
1e Division						
Général de Division Clausel						
1e Brigade	19e ligne	4e	cdb	Dupont	249	12
Général de Brigade Ménard						
	25e ligne	4e	cdb	Aberjoux	293	12
	28e ligne	4e	cdb	Bragairat	239	9
	34e ligne	4e	cdb	Gruet	258	
					1,039	**33**
2e Brigade	36e ligne	4e	cdb	Dornier	534	11
Général de Brigade Taupin						
	46e ligne	4e	cdb	Vigier	317	5
	75e ligne	4e	cdb	Servant	266	
					1,117	**16**
3e Brigade	22e ligne			L'ereix		
Général de Brigade Godard		1e			509	
		2e			466	
		3e			420	
		4e			413	
					1,808	
2e Division	Etat-major de la division				14	72
Général de Division Jean-Baptiste Solignac						
1e Brigade	15e ligne					
Général de Brigade Gratien		1e			286	16
		2e			287	9
		3e		Dein	295	13
		4e			0	0
					868	**38**
	65e ligne		Colonel	Coutard		
		1e			519	
		2e			522	
		3e			490	
		4e			363	
					1,894	
2e Brigade	86e ligne					
Général de Brigade Thomières		1e			339	
		2e			288	
		3e		Lacroix	383	
		4e			282	
					1,292	
	Régiment Irlandais	2e		Malley	400	
	Infanterie de Prusse	1e		Dubier		

VIII Corps		Bataillons/ Escadrons/ Cannon		noms des Officiers	Total	Chevaux presens
	Gendarmerie Imperiale				11	11
	10e batallion des equipage	6e		Dubourguet	43	32
	8e Brigade de mulets de bat			Bénomont	13	15
Artillerie et train						
1e Division	8e rég. à pied	11e	Capitaine	Lambert	96	9
	Ouvriers	12e			2	
	5 bataillon princ. du train				8	11
	11e bat	4e	Lieutenant	Baudry	37	
	15e bat	6e	Lieutenant	Labarre	59	15
					202	**35**
2e Division	2e à cheval	6e	Capitaine	Bauzel	70	61
	ouvriers	6e et 12e			2	
	2e bataillon bis	3e	Lieutenant	Lafeuille	41	11
	4e bataillon de détachement				35	59
	3e bataillon bis détachement					4
	11e bataillon de détachement				55	19
					203	**154**
Parc	7 à Pied	20e	Capitaine	Mazoy	35	9
	ouvrier détachement	6e			5	
	12e bataillon détachement				9	
	1e bataillon détachement				17	2
	4e bataillon détachement		Capitaine	Cory	309	85
	5e bataillon détachement				2	2
	19e bataillon	3e	Lieutenant	Massot	23	2
	19e bataillon bis	détachement			11	
		2e	Lieutenant	Brasseur	35	3
	11e bataillon bis	détachement			10	8
	12e bataillon bis	5e	Lieutenant	Boiel	62	12
	Berg		Lieutenant	Klapmann	28	3
	Wurtzbourg				8	
	6e regt à cheval		Capitaine	Coquart	70	62
	12e bataillon bis	détachement			34	24
					202	**101**
Materiel de l'artillerie						
	Bouches à feu de 4				10	

VIII Corps		Bataillons/ Escadrons/ Cannon	noms des Officiers	Total	Chevaux presens
	obusier de 6 pouces			2	
	Caisson				
	à canon de 4			10	
	à obusier de 6 pouces			6	
	d'Infanterie			11	
	Forger			3	
Cartouches	Boulets				
	de 4			1,066	
	à obusier de 6 pouces			376	
	Balles				
	de 4			285	
	à obusier de 6 pouces			27	
	d'infanterie			163,245	
	Pierres à feu			16,180	
Roues et rechange	d'affute à canon de 4			5	
de Derriere	de caisson, forger, etc			8	
d'avant train	d'affute à canon de 4			2	
	de caisson, forger, etc			7	
Outils a pionniers	pelle quarrée			11	
	pic hoyaux			2	

IX Corps	Bataillons/ Escadrons/ Cannon		noms des Officiers	Total	Chevaux presens
Général de Division Jean-Baptiste Drouet, Comte d'Erlon					
1e Division					
Général de Division Claparède					
Général de Brigade Vichery					
2e demi-brigade légère					
54e ligne	4e	cdb	Brusza	364	
21e légère	4e	cdb	Payrar	387	
28e légère	4e	cdb	Desperasnon	349	
				1,100	
7e demi-brigade de ligne		Colonel	Bonnaire		
40e ligne	4e	cdb	Guillos	341	
63e ligne	4e	cdb	Michel	365	
88e ligne	4e	cdb	Barbos	407	
				1,113	
8e demi-brigade de ligne		Colonel	Poulon		
64e ligne	4e	cdb	Guer	566	
100e ligne	4e	cdb	D'Auger	425	
103e ligne	4e	cdb	Baudin	502	
				2,606	
2e Division					
Général de Division Conroux					
Général de Brigade Gérard					
3e demi-brigade légère					
9e légère	4e	cdb	Planchet	511	
16e légère	4e	cdb	Assigbet	358	
27e légère	4e	cdb	Legros	375	
				1,244	
1re demi-brigade de ligne		Colonel	Chabert		
8e ligne	4e	cdb	Brugnoir	397	
24e ligne	4e	cdb	Rijse	361	
45e ligne	4e	cdb	Gregoire	284	
				1,042	
2e demi-brigade de ligne		Colonel	Aulart		
94e ligne	4e	cdb	Snauf	441	
95e ligne	4e	cdb	Muller	358	
96e ligne	4e	cdb	Touin	454	
				1,253	

IX Corps		Bataillons/ Escadrons/ Cannon		noms des Officiers	Total	Chevaux presens
Cavalry Brigade	7e Chasseurs à Cheval	3e, 4e	Major	Poizier	499	434
Général de Brigade François Fournier	13e Chasseurs à Cheval	3e, 4e			463	418
	20e Chasseurs à Cheval	3e, 4e	Major	Baibè	445	429
					2,660	**0**
Cavalry Brigade	1e provisoire de dragons					
Général de Brigade Soult	2e provisoire de dragons					
	3e provisoire de dragons					
Artillerie et train	7e rég. artillerie à pied	13e			71	5
	6e regt train d'artillerie (Bis)	5e			90	143
	13e regt train d'artillerie (Bis)	1e			49	121
	6e rég. artillerie à pied	3e			73	9
	10e regt train d'artillerie (?)	3e			58	74
	Ouvriers d'artillerie	6e			5	
		16e			0	
					143	**352**

Reserve Cavalry Division		Bataillons/ Escadrons/ Cannon		noms des Officiers	Total	Chevaux presens
Général de Division Louis-Pierre Montbrun						
1e Brigade	3e Dragons	Etat Major		Berruyeu	10	24
Général de Brigade Lorcet		1e		Labarbée	34	31
		2c			70	60
		3e		Barbui	59	45
		4e			78	61
					251	**197**
	6e Dragons	Etat Major		Picque	10	19
		1e			155	158
		2e		Lecomte	108	108
		3e			112	108
		4e			115	105
					500	**498**
2e Brigade	10e Dragons	Etat Major		Domange	6	14
Colonel Cavrois		1e		Pillay	114	105
		2e			94	96
		3e		Guerin	54	55
		4e			54	55
					322	**325**
	11e Dragons	Etat Major		Dejean	10	19
		1e		Leblond	137	104
		2e			89	86
		3e		Robineau	73	93
		4e			73	74
					382	**376**
3e Brigade	15e Dragons	Etat Major		Bondinhon	10	19
Colonel (Général de Brigade) Ornano		1e			174	169
		2e		Marsanges	118	151
		3e			103	83
		4e			104	92
					509	**514**
	25e Dragons	Etat Major		Ornano	10	21
		1e		Cazeneu	158	132
		2e			138	104
		3e		Chappuis	140	100
		4e			135	95
					581	**452**
					2,545	**2,362**
Artillerie						
	5e régiment à pied	5e	Capitaine	Grailla	97	104
	Ouvriers	12e	Lieutenant	Admiraul	4	
	2e batt. du train	2e	Lieutenant	Souhain	61	86
	4e batt. du train	5e	Lieutenant	Lefranc	4	4

Reserve Cavalry Division		Bataillons/ Escadrons/ Cannon	noms des Officiers	Total	Chevaux presens
	12e batt. du train	5e		6	7
				172	**201**

Materiel de l'artillerie

	Bouches à feu				
	de 4			4	
	obusier de 6 pouces			2	

Bibliography

Archival Sources

Service historique de la Défense (SHD)
7C10, *Armée de Portugal. Correspondance du Même Au Même (Octobre-Décembre 1810)*
7C11, *Armée de Portugal. Correspondance du Maréchal Prince d'Essling, Adressée aux Généraux Éblé et Reynier Ainsi Qu'au duc d'Elchingen (1er Janvier-15 Mars 1811)*
7C12, *Armée de Portugal: Correspondance*, (1811)
7C20, *Armée de Portugal: Correspondance*, (1811)
7C28, *Armée de Portugal: Situation Des Troupes Composant Armée de Portugal à l'époque du 1er Mai 1811*
C8, *Armée d'Espagne: Correspondance*, (1811)
C8-251, *Correspondance du Général Reynier*, (1814)
918/2, *Papiers Pelet*

The National Army Museum (NAM)
NAM 1968-07-461, Brunton, Richard, 'Narrative of the Service of Lt Col Richard Brunton'

National Library of Scotland
Adv.MS.46.10.1(61), Colleton, J.R., *Sketch of Part of the Ground about Fuentes and Villa Formosa Occupied by the Allied Army on the 5th and 6th May 1811. Signed J R Colleton, Royal Staff Corps*, 1811, 4 inches to the mile
Adv.MSS.46.1.1-46.10.2, Murray, General Sir George, 'The Murray Papers'

Biblioteca Virtual de Defensa
Ar.E-T.7-C.3-399, *Croquis de Fuentes de Oñoro*, (1800)

Leicester and Rutland Record Office
16D52, 'Freer Family Papers'

The National Archives (TNA)
MR 1/183/12, Mitchell, T., *Plan of the Field of Battle of Fuentes de Oñoro 3 & 5 May 1811*, 1811, 1:21120
PRO 30/43/52, 'Sir Galbraith Lowry Cole: Papers', 1810
PRO 30/43/53, 'Sir Galbraith Lowry Cole: Papers', 1810

WO 17/2467, 'Monthly Returns to the Adjutant General, January to June', 1811

WO 37/7a, Scovell, George, *Diary of the Campaigns of 1810-1812. War Office Papers, General Sir George Scovell, Intelligence Branch of Quartermaster General in Spain.* (1812)

WO 37/11/24, 'Arrangements for the Attack on the Enemy near Pombal', 11 March 1811

WO 37/11/25, 'Original Orders (in Pencil) by Sir George Murray for the Attack at Redinha.', 12 March 1811

WO 78/5642, *Lithograph from the Original Drawing in the Quarter Master General's Office at the Topographical Department of the War Office*, Battle of Fuentes D'Onoro, Fought on 3rd and 5th May 1811, Plate 2, 1869

WO 78/5937, Freeth, James, *Route Fuentes de Onoro; Drawn by James Freeth, Royal Staff Corps*, 1811, 4 inches to the mile

WO 78/5974, Mitchell, T., *Sketch of the Action at Sabugal, 3 April 1811*, 1811

Biblioteca Nacional de Portugal
cota CC-1226-R, Homem da Cunha de Eça, Lourenço, *Carta Militar Das Principaes Estradas de Portugal*, Lisbon: Romão Eloy, 1808, 1:470000

Arquivo Histórico Militar (AHM)
PT/AHM/DIV/1/14/270/09, Mosinho, Ajutante-General do Exercito Portuguez, Manoel de Brito, 'Ordem Do Duque Wellington Para Serem Recompensadas as Pessoas Que Entregaram Desertores e Castigados Os Que Trataram Mal', Headquarters at Lagioza, 17 August 1810

University of Southampton, (UoS)
1/312, 'The Wellington Papers', General correspondence and memoranda, 1790-1832
1/315, General correspondence and memoranda, 1790-1832

Books and Journals

Anon., *The Confidential Correspondence of Napoleon Bonaparte with His Brother Joseph, Sometime King of Spain. Selected and Translated, with Explanatory Notes, from the 'Memoires du Roi Joseph.'* (New York: D. Appleton and Company, 1856)

Anon., *Vicissitudes in the Life of a Scottish Soldier* (London: Colburn, 1827)

Arvers, Paul, *Historique du 82e Régiment d'infanterie de ligne et du 7e Régiment d'infanterie légère, 1684-1876* (Paris: Lahure, 1876)

Atkinson, C.T., 'A Light Dragoon in the Peninsula: Extracts from the Letters of Captain Lovell Badcock, 14th Light Dragoons, 1809-1814', *Journal of the Society for Army Historical Research*, 34.138 (1956), pp.70–79

Bamford, Andrew, *Sickness, Suffering, and the Sword: The British Regiment on Campaign, 1808-1815* (Norman: University of Oklahoma Press, 2013)

Baudus, Marie Élie Guillaume de, *Études sur Napoléon* (Paris: Debécourt, 1841)

Béchet, Louis Samuel, *Souvenirs (Écrits en 1838-1839): Publiés et Annotés par Christian Schneider* (Paris: Editions Historiques Teissèdre, 2000)

Belmas, Jacques Vital, *Journaux Des Siéges faits ou soutenus par les Français dans la Peninsule, de 1807 à 1814*, (Paris: Didot, 1837)

Beresford, Marcus de la Poer, *Marshal William Carr Beresford: The Ablest Man I Have yet Seen with the Army* (Dublin: Irish Academic Press, 2019)

Beresford, William Carr, *Compilação Das Ordens Do Dia Do Quartel General Do Exercito Portuguez Concernentes á Organização, Disciplina e Economia Militares Na Campanha de 1811*, (Lisboa: Impressão Regia, 1815)

Beresford, William Carr, *Instrucções Para a Formatura, Exercicio e Movimentos Dos Regimentos de Infanteria* (Lisboa: Impressão Regia, 1809)

Beresford, William Carr, *Strictures on Certain Passages of Lieut.- Col. Napier's History of the Peninsular War.* (London: Longman, Rees, Orme, Brown and Green, 1831)

Blond, Georges, Marshall May (trans) *La Grande Armée* (London: Arms and Armour Press, 1995)

Bonnal, Henri, *La Vie Militaire du Maréchal Ney, duc d'Elchingen, Prince de La Moskowa* (Paris: Chapelot, 1914)

Braquehay, Auguste, *Le Général Baron Merle, 1766-1830* (Montreuil-sur-Mer: A. Becquart, 1892)

Brett-James, Antony (ed.), *Wellington at War 1794-1815 : A Selection of His Wartime Letters* (London: Macmillan & Co, 1961)

Brocardo, Estevão (ed.), *Observador Portuguez, Histórico, e Político de Lisboa* (Lisbon: Impressão Regia, 1809)

Brotherton, Thomas, Bryan Perrett (ed.), *A Hawk at War: The Peninsular War Reminiscences of General Sir Thomas Brotherton, CB* (Chippenham: Picton, 1986)

Buttery, David, *Wellington Against Massena: The Third Invasion of Portugal, 1810-1811* (Barnsley: Pen & Sword Military, 2007)

Campos, João, *Almeida: Três Pontas Notáveis Numa Estrela Singular* (Almeida: Câmara Municipal, 2010)

Carrs, John, 'The 2nd/53rd in the Peninsular War: Contemporary Letters from an Officer of the Regiment', *Journal of the Society for Army Historical Research*, 26.105 (1948), pp.2–17

Charles-Lavauzelle, Henri (ed.), *Historique du 69e Régiment d'infanterie* (Paris: Imprimerie Librairie Militaire, 1887)

Clausewitz, Carl von, Michael Howard and Peter Paret (trans), *On War* (London: Campbell, 1993)

Clinton, Herbert R., *The War in the Peninsula, and Wellington's Campaigns in France and Belgium* (London: Warne, 1878)

Cocks, Edward Charles, Julia V. Page (ed.), *Intelligence Officer in the Peninsula: Letters and Diaries of Major the Hon. Edward Charles Cocks, 1786-1812* (Tunbridge Wells: Spellmount, 1986)

Colecção Das Ordens Do Dia Do Illustrissimo e Excellentissimo Senhor Guilherme Carr Beresford, Anno 1809 (Lisboa: António Nunes dos Santos)

Cooper, John Spencer, *Rough Notes of Seven Campaigns in Portugal, Spain, France, and America, During the Years 1809-15* (London: Smith, 1869)

Cope, William Henry, *The History of the Rifle Brigade (the Prince Consort's Own) Formerly the 95th* (London: Chatto and Windus, 1877)

Corrêa, Monteiro Miguel, and others, *The Lines of Torres Vedras: A Defence System to the North of Lisbon* (Torres Vedras: PILT, 2011)

Costello, Edward, *The Adventures of a Soldier; or, Memoirs of Edward Costello* (London: Henry Coulburn, 1841)

Cowell-Stepney, Lieut. Col. Sir John, *Leaves from the Diary of an Officer of the Guards* (London: Chapman and Hall, 1854)

Croker, John Wilson, Louis J. Jennings (ed.), *The Croker Papers: The Correspondence and Diaries of the Late Right Honourable John Wilson Croker, LL.D, F.R.S, Secretary to the Admiralty, 1809 to 1830*, Second Edition, Revised (London: John Murray, 1885)

De Ainslie, Charles Philip, *Historical Record of the First or the Royal Regiment of Dragoons* (London: Chapman and Hall, 1887)

Delagrave, Andre, *Campagne de l'Armée Française en Portugal, Dans Les Années 1810 et 1811, Avec Un Précis de Celles Qui l'ont Précédée.* (Paris: Dentu, 1815)

Dickson, Alexander, *The Dickson Manuscripts: Being Diaries, Letters, Maps, Account Books, with Various Other Papers, for the Year 1811* (Cambridge: Trotman, 1986-1988)

Doisy de Villargennes, Adelbert, *Reminiscences of Army Life Under Napoleon Bonaparte* (Cincinnati: Robert Clarke & Co, 1884)

Donaldson, Joseph, *Recollections of the Eventful Life of a Soldier* (Edinburgh: Robert Martin, 1847)

Drouet, Jean Baptiste, *Le Maréchal Drouet, Comte d'Erlon. Vie Militaire Écrit Par Lui Même* (Paris: G. Barba, 1844)

Dupont, Marcel, *Fournier Sarlovèze: Le plus Mauvais Sujet de l'armée* (Paris: Librairie Hachette, 1936)

Eadie, Robert, *Recollections of the Life of Robert Eadie, Private of His Majesty's 79th. Regiment of Infantry; Giving a Concise Account of His Campaigns in Ireland, Denmark, Walcheren & the Peninsula.*, 2nd edn (Falkirk: Gibson, 1830)

Espírito Santo, Gabriel, and Pedro de Brito, *A Logística Do Exército Anglo-Luso Na Guerra Peninsular: Uma Introdução* (Lisboa: Tribuna da História, 2012)

Franklin, Carl E., *British Napoleonic Field Artillery: The First Complete Illustrated Guide to Equipment and Uniforms* (Stroud: Spellmount, 2012)

Fresnel, Henri du, *Un Régiment à Travers l'histoire Le 76e* (Paris: E. Flammarion, 1894)

Fririon, François Nicolas, *Journal Historique de la Campagne de Portugal, entreprise par les Français, sous les ordres du Maréchal Masséna, prince d'Essling, (du 15. Sept. 1810 Au 12. Mai 1811)* (Paris: Leneuve, 1841)

Garrety, Thomas, *Memoirs of a Sergeant, Late in the Forty-Third Light Infantry Regiment during the Peninsular War* (London: Mason, 1835)

Garwood, F.S., 'The Royal Staff Corps, 1800-1837', *The Royal Engineers Journal*, 57 (1943), pp.81–96

General Orders. Spain and Portugal. January 1st to December 31st, 1811 (London: Egerton, 1812)

General Orders. Spain and Portugal. January 2nd to December 29th, 1810 (London: Egerton, 1811)

Girod de l'Ain, Maurice, *Le Général Éblé (1758-1812)* (Paris: Berger-Levrault, 1893)

Girod de l'Ain, Maurice, *Vie Militaire du Général Foy* (Paris: E Plon, 1900)

Glover, Gareth, and Robert Burnham, *Riflemen of Wellington's Light Division in the Peninsular War; Unpublished and Rare Memoirs of the 95th Rifles 1808-14* (Barnsley: Frontline Books, 2023)

Glover, Gareth, and Robert Burnham, *The Men of Wellington's Light Division: Unpublished Memoirs From the 43rd Light Infantry in the Peninsular War* (Barnsley: Frontline Books, 2022)

Glover, Michael, 'The Nightingall Letters: Letters from Major General Miles Nightingall in Portugal February to June 1811', *Journal of the Society for Army Historical Research*, 51.207 (1973), pp.129–154

Godart, Roch, J-B Antoine (ed.), *Mémoires du Général Baron Roch Godart (1792-1815)*, (Paris: E. Flammarion, 1895)

Gomm, Sir William, Francis Carr-Gomm (ed.), *Letters and Journals of Field Marshal Sir William Maynard Gomm, G.C.B. &c, &c, from 1799 to Waterloo, 1815* (London: John Murray, 1881)

Grattan, William, Charles Oman (ed.), *Adventures with the Connaught Rangers, 1809-1814*, (London: E. Arnold, 1902)

Griffon de Pleineville, Natalia, 'Le Second Jour de La Bataille : 5 Mai', *Gloire & Empire*, 42 (2012), pp.39–80

Griffon de Pleineville, Natalia, 'Les Derniers Combats d'arrière-Garde', *Gloire & Empire*, 70 (2017), pp.31–50

Griffon de Pleineville, Natalia, 'L'évacuation du Portugal', *Gloire & Empire*, 70 (2017), pp.61–98

Griffon de Pleineville, Natalia, 'L'evasion de La Garnison d'Almeida', *Gloire & Empire*, 42 (2012), pp.81–99

Guingret, Pierre François, *Relation Historique et Militaire de la Campagne de Portugal, sous le maréchal Massena, Prince d'Essling* (Limoges: Chez Bargeas, 1817)

Gurwood, John (ed.), *The Dispatches of the Field Marshal The Duke of Wellington. An Enlarged Edition in Eight Volumes* (London: John Murray, 1844-1852)

Gurwood, John (ed.), *The General Orders of the Field Marshal, the Duke of Wellington, K. G., &c., &c., &c., in Portugal, Spain, and France, from 1809 to 1814, and the Low Countries* (London: Forgotten Books, 2016)

Hall, Francis, 'Peninsular Recollections, 1811–12', *Royal United Services Institution Journal*, 56.416 (1912), pp.1389–1408

Hall, Francis, 'Recollections in Portugal and Spain During 1811 and 1812', *Royal United Services Institution Journal*, 56 (1912), pp.1535–1546

Hamilton, Colonel Henry, *Historical Record of the 14th (King's) Hussars* (London: Longmans, Green and Co, 1901)

Head, George, *A Home Tour through Various Parts of the United Kingdom, a Continuation of the 'Home Tour through the Manufacturing Districts'. Also, Memoirs of an Assistant Commissary-General* (London: Murray, 1837)

Howard, Michael (ed.), *Wellingtonian Studies* (Aldershot: privately printed, 1959)

Hulot, Jacques-Louis, *Souvenirs Militaires du Baron Hulot (Jacques-Louis), Général d'artillerie, 1773-1843* (Paris: Spectateur militaire, 1886)

Hunter, Archie, *Wellington's Scapegoat: The Tragedy of Lieutenant-Colonel Charles Bevan* (Barnsley: Cooper, 2003)

Jeanpierre, Henri, 'Comte Louis-Henri Loison: General Divisionnaire 1771-1816', *The Napoleon Series*, <https://www.napoleon-series.org/research/biographies/c_loison.html>

Jomini, Antoine Henri de, Ferdinand Lecomte (ed.), *Guerre d'Espagne : Extrait Des Souvenirs Inédits du Général Jomini* (Paris: Baudouin, 1892)

Jones, John T., and Harry Jones, *Journals of Sieges Carried on by the Army Under the Duke of Wellington, in Spain, During the Years 1811 to 1814: With Notes and Additions ; Also Memoranda Relative to the Lines Thrown up to Cover Lisbon in 1810* (London: John Weale, 1846)

Kincaid, John, *Adventures in the Rifle Brigade, in the Peninsula, France and the Netherlands from 1809 to 1815* (London: Boone, 1847)

Kincaid, John, *Random Shots from a Rifleman* (London: Boone, 1847)

Koch, Jean Baptiste, *Mémoires de Massena Rédiges d'apres les Documents Qu'il a laissés et sur ceux du Dépôt de la Guerre et du Dépôt de Fortifications* (Paris: Paulin and Lechavelier, 1848)

Larpent, Sir George, *The Private Journal of Judge-Advocate Larpent, Attached to the Head-Quarters of Lord Wellington During the Peninsular War, from 1812 to Its Close* (London: Bentley, 1854)

Las Cases, Emmanuel-Auguste-Dieudonné, *Memorial de Sainte Hélène: Journal of the Private Life and Conversations of the Emperor Napoleon at Saint Helena* (London: Colburn, 1823)

Leach, Jonathan, *Rough Sketches of the Life of an Old Soldier: During a Service in the West Indies, at the Siege of Copenhagen in 1807, in the Peninsula and the South of France in the Campaigns from 1808 to 1814, with the Light Division, in the Netherlands in 1815, Including the Battles of Quatre Bras and Waterloo* (London: Longman, Rees, Orme, Brown and Green, 1831)

Lemonnier-Delafosse, Marie Jean Baptiste, *Campagnes de 1810 à 1815. Souvenirs militaires.* (Havre: Lemale, 1850)

Lipscombe, Nick, *Wellington's Guns: The Untold Story of Wellington and His Artillery in the Peninsula and at Waterloo* (Oxford: Osprey, 2013)

Lynch, John, 'The Lessons of Walcheren Fever, 1809', *Military Medicine*, 174.3 (2009), pp.315–319

Macdonell, Archibald Gordon, *Napoleon and His Marshals* (London: Macmillan, 1934)

Marbot, Jean-Baptiste-Antoine-Marcelin, Arthur Butler (trans), *The Memoirs of Baron De Marbot: Late Lieutenant-General in the French Army* (London: Longmans, 1913)

Marcel, *Campagnes du Capitaine Marcel, du 69e de ligne, en Espagne et en Portugal (1808-1814), Mises en Ordre, Annotées et Publiées par le Commandant Var* (Paris: Libraire Plon, 1913)

Marcel, Nicolas, with Louis Var, *Campagnes du Capitaine Marcel du 69e de ligne en Espagne et en Portugal (1808-1814)* (Paris: Plon-Nourrit et Cie, 1913)

Marshall-Cornwall, James, *Marshal Massena* (London: OUP, 1965)

Martinien, Aristide, *Tableaux, Par Corps et Par Batailles, des Officiers Tués et Blessés Pendant les Guerres de l'Empire (1805-1815)* (Paris: Charles-Lavauzelle, 1899)

Maurice, Major-General Sir J.F. (ed.), *The Diary of Sir John Moore* (London: Edward Arnold, 1904)

Maxwell, W.H. (ed.), *Peninsular Sketches; by Actors on the Scene* (London: Coulburn, 1845)

Mills, John, Ian Fletcher (ed.), *For King and Country: The Letters and Diaries of John Mills, Coldstream Guards, 1811-14* (Staplehurst: Spellmount, 1995)

Mockler-Ferryman, Lieutenant Colonel A.F. (ed.), *The Life of a Regimental Officer During the Great War, 1793-1815* (London: Blackwood, 1913)

Molières, Michel, *Les Expéditions Françaises en Portugal de 1807 à 1811* (Paris: Publibook, 2007)

Moore, Gene, 'History and Legend in "The Duel"', *The Conradian*, 41.2 (2016), pp.28–46

Moore Smith, G.C. (ed.), *The Life of John Colborne, Field Marshal Lord Seaton : Compiled from His Letters, Records of His Conversations, and Other Sources* (London: Murray, 1903)

Moorsom, William, *Historical Record of the Fifty-Second Regiment (Oxfordshire Light Infantry)*, 2nd edn (London: Bentley, 1860)

Morleix, J.B., 'Relation de la bataille de Fuentes de Oñoro (5 mai 1811)', *Bulletin Hispanique*, 5.3 (1903), pp.304–306

Murray, George, *Memoir Annexed to an Atlas Containing Plans of the Principal Battles, Sieges and Affairs in Which the British Troops Were Engaged During the War in the Spanish Peninsula and the South of France from 1808 to 1814* (London: J Wyld, 1841)

Murray, George, and Thomas Mitchell, *Maps and Plans, Showing the Principal Movements, Battles & Sieges in Which the British Army Was Engaged during the War from 1808 to 1814, in the Spanish Peninsular and the South of France* (London: Wyld, 1840)

Napier, George, William Napier (ed.) *Passages in the Early Military Life of General Sir George T. Napier, K. C. B* (London: John Murray, 1884)

Napier, William, *History of the War in the Peninsula and in the South of France, from the Year 1807 to the Year 1814* (London: Warne, n.d)

Napier, William, *The Life and Opinions of General Sir Charles James Napier, G. C. B.*, (London: Murray, 1857)

Noël, Jean-Nicolas-Auguste, Rosemary Brindle (trans), *With Napoleon's Guns: The Military Memoirs of an Officer of the First Empire* (London: Greenhill, 2005)

Oman, Charles, *A History of the Peninsular War* (London: Greenhill Books, 2004)

Oman, Charles, *Studies in the Napoleonic Wars* (London: Methuen, 1929)

Oudinot, Marc, 'Souvenirs intimes et militaires du général Victor Oudinot, duc de Reggio Campagnes de Portugal : 1810 et 1811', *Napoleonica La Revue*, 5.2 (2009)

Parquin, Denis Charles, *Souvenirs de Gloire et d'amour* (Paris: Tallandier, 1911)

Pelet, Jean Jacques, Donald D. Horward (ed.), *The French Campaign in Portugal, 1810-1811*, (Minneapolis: University of Minnesota Press, 1973)

Pelet-Clozeau, Jean Jacques Germain, *Mémoire sur ma campagne du Portugal: 1810-1811*, Collection du bicentenaire de l'épopée impériale (Paris: Teissèdre, 2003)

Picard, Ernest, and Louis Tuetey (eds), Louise Seymour Houghton (trans), *Unpublished Correspondence of Napoleon I Preserved in the War Archives* (New York: Duffield and Company, 1913)

Pivka, Otto von, *The Black Brunswickers* (Reading: Osprey Publishing, 1973)

Plon, Henri, and J Dumaine (eds), *Correspondence de Napoléon I* (Paris: Imprimerie Impériale: 1865-1867)

Robinson, Heaton Bowstead, *Memoirs of Lieutenant-General Sir Thomas Picton, Including His Correspondence, from Originals in Possession of His Family* (London: R. Bentley, 1836)

Rodrigues, Manuel A. Ribeiro, Manuel A. Ribeiro Rodrigues and Carlos Alberto Santos (eds.), *Infantaria: 1806-1815* (Lisboa: Ed. Destarte, 2001)

Ross, Sir Hew Dalrymple, with Francis Duncan, *Hew Ross of the Chestnut Troop: With the Royal Horse Artillery During the Peninsular War and ... at Waterloo* (n.p: Leonaur, 2020)

Rules and Regulations for the Formations, Field Exercise and Movements of His Majesty's Forces (London: Adjutant General's Office, 1812)

Sarramon, Jean, 'Campagne de Fuentes de Oñoro, 15 Avril – 11 Mai 1811', *Carnet de La Sabretache*, 425 (1962)

Schaumann, August, *On the Road with Wellington* (London: Heinemann, 1924)

Schwertfeger, Bernhard, *Geschichte Der Königlich Deutschen Legion 1803-1816* (Hannover und Leipzig: Hahnsche Buchhandlung, 1907)

Simmons, George, Willoughby Verner (ed.), *A British Rifle Man* (London: A. & C. Black, 1899)

Smith, Digby, *Napoleon's Regiments: Battle Histories of the Regiments of the French Army, 1792-1815* (London: Greenhill, 2000)

Smith, Harry, G.C. Moore Smith (ed.), *The Autobiography of Lieutenant-General Sir Harry Smith Baronet of Aliwal on the Sutlej G.C.B.* (London: Murray, 1903)

Soriano, Simão José Da Luz, *Historia Da Guerra Civil E Do Estabelecimento Do Governo Parlamentar Em Portugal*, Segunda Epocha (Lisboa: Imprensa Nacional, 1874)

Sprünglin, Emmanuel Frédéric, 'Souvenirs d'Emmanuel-Frédéric Sprünglin, Publiés Par G. Desdevises du Dezert', *Revue Hispanique*, 1904, pp.299–537

Stanhope, Charles, *Notes of Conversations with the Duke of Wellington, 1831-1851* (New York: Longmans, 1888)

Stothert, William, *A Narrative of the Principal Events of the Campaigns of 1809, 1810, & 1811, in Spain and Portugal* (London: Martin, 1812)

The 2nd Duke of Wellington (ed.), *Supplementary Despatches, Correspondence, and Memoranda Of Field Marshal Arthur Duke of Wellington, K.G.* (London: Murray, 1860-1871)

Thiébault, Paul Charles, *Memoires du general baron Thiébault* (Paris: E Plon, Nourrit, 1894-1896)

Thiébault, Paul Charles, *Apercu Nouveau sur les Campagnes de Francais en Portugal, en 1807, 1808, 1809, 1810 et 1811: Contenant des observations sur les Ecrits de MM. le baron Thiebault, Nayleis [et] Gingret* (Paris: Delaunay, 1818)

Thoumas, Charles Antoine, *Les Grands Cavaliers du Premier Empire* (Paris: Berger-Levrault et cie, 1892)

Timewell, John, 'The Diary of a Private Soldier in the Peninsular War', *Macmillan's Magazine*, 77 (1897)

Tomkinson, William, *The Diary of a Cavalry Officer*, 2nd edn (London: Swan Sonnenschein & Co, 1895)

d'Urban, Benjamin, I.J. Rousseau (ed.), *The Peninsular Journal, 1808-1817* (London: Greenhill, 1988)

Vane, Lord Londonderry, Charles William, *Narrative of the Peninsular War from 1808 to 1813* (London: Coulburn, 1828)

Vassais, Jules, *Historique du 69e Régiment d'infanterie (1672-1912)* (Paris: M. Imhaus, 1913)

Verner, Willoughby, *History & Campaigns of the Rifle Brigade* (London: Bale, 1919)

Victoires, Conquêtes, Désastres, Revers et Guerres Civiles des Français, de 1792 À 1815, (Paris: C.-L.-F. Panckoucke, 1820)

Viscountess Combermere, Mary, and Captain W. W. Knollys, *Memoirs and Correspondence of Field-Marshal Viscount Combermere* (London: Hurst and Blackett, 1866)

Ward, S.G.P., 'Brenier's Escape from Almeida, 1811', *Journal of the Society for Army Historical Research*, 35.141 (1957), pp.23–35

Ward, S.G.P., *Wellington's Headquarters* (Barnsley: Pen & Sword Military, 2017)

Wheeler, William, Basil Henry Liddell Hart (ed.), *The Letters of Private Wheeler 1809-1828* (London: Michael Joseph, 1951)

White, Kenton, *The Key to Lisbon: The Third French Invasion of Portugal, 1810-11* (Warwick: Helion, 2019)

Zamoyski, Adam, *1812: Napoleon's Fatal March on Moscow* (London: HarperCollins, 2004)

From Reason to Revolution – Warfare 1721-1815

http://www.helion.co.uk/series/from-reason-to-revolution-1721-1815.php

The 'From Reason to Revolution' series covers the period of military history 1721–1815, an era in which fortress-based strategy and linear battles gave way to the nation-in-arms and the beginnings of total war.

This era saw the evolution and growth of light troops of all arms, and of increasingly flexible command systems to cope with the growing armies fielded by nations able to mobilise far greater proportions of their manpower than ever before. Many of these developments were fired by the great political upheavals of the era, with revolutions in America and France bringing about social change which in turn fed back into the military sphere as whole nations readied themselves for war. Only in the closing years of the period, as the reactionary powers began to regain the upper hand, did a military synthesis of the best of the old and the new become possible.

The series examines the military and naval history of the period in a greater degree of detail than has hitherto been attempted, and has a very wide brief, with the intention of covering all aspects from the battles, campaigns, logistics, and tactics, to the personalities, armies, uniforms, and equipment.

Submissions

The publishers would be pleased to receive submissions for this series. Please email reasontorevolution@helion.co.uk, or write to Helion & Company Limited, Unit 8 Amherst Business Centre, Budbrooke Road, Warwick, CV34 5WE

You may also be interested in:

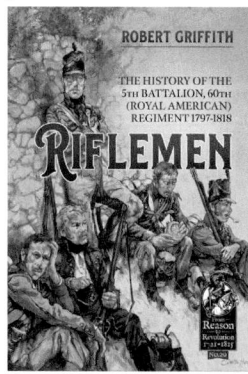

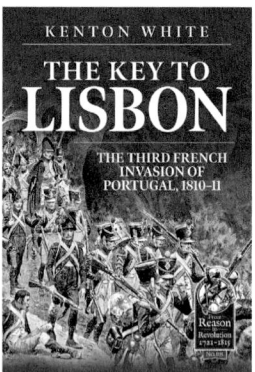

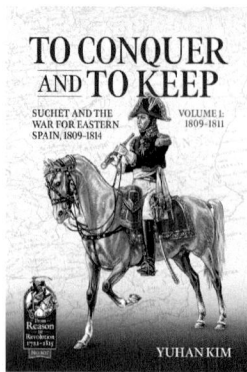

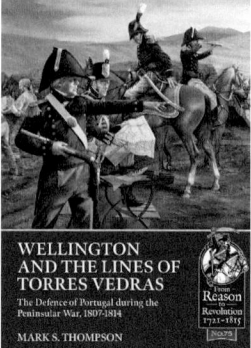

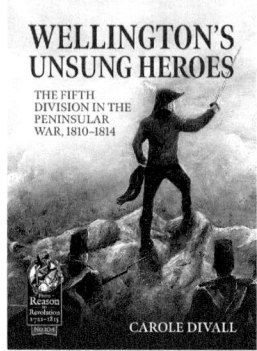